HEGEL AND ITALIAN POLITICAL THOUGHT

Across Italy in the nineteenth century, a generation of intellectuals engaged with Hegel's philosophy while actively participating in Italian political life. *Hegel and Italian Political Thought* traces the reception and transformation of these ideas, exploring how Hegelian concepts were reworked into political practices by Italians who had participated in the 1848 revolution, who then led the new Italian government after unification, and who continued to play a central role in Italian politics until the end of the century. Fernanda Gallo investigates the features of Italian Hegelianism demonstrating how intellectuals insisted on the historical and political dimension of Hegel's idealism. These thinkers presented a critical Hegelianism closer to practice than ideas, to history than metaphysics. This study challenges conventional hierarchies in the study of Italian political thought exploring how the ideas of Hegel acquired new-found political power when brought into connection with their specific historical context.

FERNANDA GALLO is Associate Professor in History and Politics at Homerton College, University of Cambridge. She specialises in Italy and the Mediterranean in the long nineteenth century, German Idealism, and the history of ideas of Europe. Previous publications include *Dalla Patria allo Stato: Bertrando Spaventa, una biografia intellettuale* (2013).

IDEAS IN CONTEXT

Edited by DAVID ARMITAGE, RICHARD BOURKE
and JENNIFER PITTS

The books in this series will discuss the emergence of intellectual traditions and of related new disciplines. The procedures, aims and vocabularies that were generated will be set in the context of the alternatives available within the contemporary frameworks of ideas and institutions. Through detailed studies of the evolution of such traditions, and their modification by different audiences, it is hoped that a new picture will form of the development of ideas in their concrete contexts. By this means, artificial distinctions between the history of philosophy, of the various sciences, of society and politics, and of literature may be seen to dissolve.

A full list of titles in the series can be found at:
www.cambridge.org/IdeasContext

HEGEL AND ITALIAN POLITICAL THOUGHT

The Practice of Ideas, 1832–1900

FERNANDA GALLO

Homerton College, University of Cambridge

CAMBRIDGE
UNIVERSITY PRESS

Shaftesbury Road, Cambridge CB2 8EA, United Kingdom

One Liberty Plaza, 20th Floor, New York, NY 10006, USA

477 Williamstown Road, Port Melbourne, VIC 3207, Australia

314–321, 3rd Floor, Plot 3, Splendor Forum, Jasola District Centre, New Delhi – 110025, India

103 Penang Road, #05-06/07, Visioncrest Commercial, Singapore 238467

Cambridge University Press is part of Cambridge University Press & Assessment, a department of the University of Cambridge.

We share the University's mission to contribute to society through the pursuit of education, learning and research at the highest international levels of excellence.

www.cambridge.org
Information on this title: www.cambridge.org/9781009494120

DOI: 10.1017/9781009494137

First published 2024

A catalogue record for this publication is available from the British Library.

A Cataloging-in-Publication data record for this book is available from the Library of Congress

ISBN 978-1-009-49412-0 Hardback

To Armando,
who walks through life by my side,
facing it with courage,
filling it with kindness,
warming it with love.

Contents

Figures

Acknowledgements

This book is the result of a long intellectual journey begun ten years ago, shortly after the publication of my first monograph in 2013. This has been also a journey through the precariousness of academic life: while writing this book I have moved with my family across three different countries and worked at four different institutions before securing an established post. This has also been the journey from the life of a young woman to that of a not-so-young mother of two beautiful children. Along the way there have been multiple challenges and bumps on the road, and it is only thanks to an amazing community that I was able to move forward. My path has been studded with very generous people who have supported me through the hard times and have shared my joy in the good times. Many are the colleagues and friends who have shared their ideas, discussed, and commented on my work down the years, and it would be difficult to find space for them all here. There are some, though, who have been my lighthouse along this path.

Eugenio Biagini has unconditionally supported my work and my career for more than a decade, believing in me and in my ideas more than I ever did, always offering a word of encouragement with his kindness and gentle manners. Richard Bourke has been one of the most supportive colleagues I could ever hope to have encountered; our Hegelian chats and discussions attempting to make sense of Hegel as historians have been an inspiration and run through the whole book. I will always treasure the conversations with Christopher Clark beside the River Cam, during the darkest times of the pandemic, discussing the 1848 revolutions. He has been the most generous mentor and one of the finest scholars I have ever had the pleasure to work with. Axel Körner has been the kindest scholar I could possibly have met on arrival in the United Kingdom; our intellectual exchanges have been the bread that has fed this work for many years, and his support has given me the strength to continue on a path that I once thought impossible. Douglas Moggach and his impressive scholarship on German political thought have inspired this work since the beginning, first with his writings and then with his friendship.

This journey began while I was working at the University of Italian Switzerland in Lugano, when completing my PhD dissertation under the supervision of Maurizio Viroli. I could not have endured the difficulties of those early years in the career of a scholar without my sisterhood, and for this I wish to thank in particular Gloria Dagnino, Francesca Galli, Maria Rikitianskaia, and Sara Sermini. The very same sisterhood helped me through my first appointment in the United Kingdom at the Faculty of POLIS at the University of Bath, where Anna Cento Bull, Adalgisa Giorgio, Galadriel Revelli, and Milena Romano in different ways guided me through the maze of British academia. When I first arrived in London, the generosity and support of my dear friend and colleague Matthew D'Auria were immensely valuable to me, and I greatly enjoyed the conversations with Alessandro De Arcangelis during the many lunches and coffee breaks at the British Library.

At the University of Cambridge, I have encountered the best intellectual context I could ask for to develop my research. I owe a huge debt of gratitude for all the conversations with my amazing colleagues at the Modern European History Seminar and the Political Thought and Intellectual History Seminar, with whom I have spent countless Monday and Tuesday evenings debating and reflecting on our discipline, coming back to my writing always inspired by what I had heard. Some colleagues have been so kind as to read and comment on parts of this book, and I wish to thank in particular Eugenio Biagini, Christopher Brooke, Charlotte Johann, Jean-Michel Johnston, Jessica Patterson, Lucia Rubinelli, Rocco Rubini, and Felix Waldemann. I wish to also thank Marcus Colla, Celia Donert, Shruti Kapila, Niamh Gallagher, Simone Maghenzani, Gareth Stedman Jones, and Pedro Ramos Pinto, who have endured conversations about Hegel and nineteenth-century Italy and solicited more reflections on my research. All the discussions around our works in progress with the crew of the Mediterranean History Research Cluster have been invaluable. My work has benefited immensely from the feedback offered by John Arnold, Andrew Arsan, Arthur Asseraf, Melissa Calaresu, Sara Caputo, Caroline Goodson, Mary Laven, Dror Weil, and Madeline Woker.

Beyond the intellectual stimulation, the leadership of the Faculty of History at the University of Cambridge has been impressive during one of the most difficult periods we have experienced as a community, providing extra support to those with childcare duties during lockdowns, going above and beyond to make sure I could complete this book. For this I wish particularly to thank Alex Walsham, Lucy Delap, and Mary Laven. In a similar way, my Homerton College family made sure that I was alright, that I could have the time to work on my research, and that I could be the best teacher I could possibly be. Homerton College has been a place I could call home since the first day I joined the Fellowship, and I am so very grateful for the hugely supportive and caring work environment it provides. In this regard I wish to thank Penny Barton, Robin Bunce, Bill Foster, Georgie Horrell, Louise Joy, Melanie Keene, and Alison Wood. I wish to also thank in particular the Med Club members Roberto Sileo, Sofia Singler, and our inspiring Principal Lord Simon Woolley of Woodford.

I wish to express my deepest gratitude to those institutions that have provided the intellectual and financial support enabling me to carry on with my research. The Istituto Italiano per gli Studi Filosofici in Naples has been a beacon of hope for many Italian early-career scholars, and the work of its late President Gerardo Marotta for over forty years has kept the tradition of Italian Hegelianism alive and strong in the Peninsula. The Swiss National Science Foundation has likewise supported this research, first awarding me the Early Post Doc Mobility Fellowship and then the SINERGIA grant, offering the indispensable resources needed to develop this monograph. The Career Support Fund awarded by the University of Cambridge has also played a crucial role in boosting my research after the difficulties caused by the pandemic. Some of the outcomes of this research have appeared in the *Journal of Modern Italian Studies* (especially parts of the Introduction and Chapter 4) and in *History: The Journal of the Historical Association* (especially parts of Chapters 2 and 3).

I wish also to thank the anonymous reviewers for taking the time and effort to review the manuscript and for their insightful comments and precious suggestions that greatly improved this work. This book would not have its present form without the irreplaceable proofreading work of Martin Thom, who not only helped me with the English language and with the translations from Italian to English but whose insightful comments and recommendations have enhanced the formal and intellectual content of this book.

Special thanks go to my lifelong friends Iacopo Di Girolamo, Eliana Di Stefano, Marianna Valle, and their families, who could not care less about Hegel and Italian political thought but tolerated my conversations anyway and rooted for me since my childhood. It is the love of my family that kept me going along this journey: my dear Vovo Fernanda, who unfortunately will not see this book completed but who has always been very proud of her niece's intellectual achievements and made sure the whole of Portugal knew about them; my mum Teresa, who has loved me unconditionally and is my greatest fan; my late beloved father Donato, who runs through each and every word of this book as an example of the sort of scholar I wish I could one day be; my kids Vincenzo and Eleonora, who bear the names of two Neapolitan Jacobin revolutionaries and often act like them. They have reminded me every day of the things in our life that are more important than finishing books and encouraged me to take time off to enjoy their company. This book is dedicated to my husband Armando, who has been taking care of me each and every day for the last twenty years, who has embarked on many adventures with me to make sure I could keep doing the job that I love, who has tolerated many conversations on Hegel and Italian political thought, even attempting to show some interest, who is the best father my kids could ask for, and who fills with love and kindness every day of our lives.

Introduction
Hegel from the Margins

Italian revolutionaries were still licking their wounds in prison or exile after the armed repression of the 1848/49 revolutions, when, in October 1850, one of their number, Bertrando Spaventa (1817–1883), then in exile in Turin, received a letter from his fellow revolutionary Pasquale Villari (1826–1917). The latter, himself then in exile in Florence, urged his friend to keep teaching and studying the philosophy of Hegel. Although it was difficult to promote foreign philosophies in Turin, especially those expressed in the German language and therefore tainted by association with the Austrian 'invader', Hegel's was the philosophical system best able to sustain a nation intent on developing its self-consciousness. Villari thus believed the promotion of the Hegelian philosophy to be the most urgent task facing Italy at that time:

> If we could only get Italians to understand Hegel, Italy would be regenerated .... Without philosophy we cannot become a nation .... Italy needs to find a system representing the whole of its nationality, one that gathers together whatever elements of life there are in the whole peninsula; but, first of all, it needs to recover its self-consciousness, and no system is more capable of this than the Hegelian.[1]

Both Spaventa and Villari were hounded by the Bourbon police on account of their active participation in the 1848 Neapolitan revolution. They were therefore obliged to flee the Kingdom of Two Sicilies and seek refuge in another Italian state. The Kingdom of Piedmont-Sardinia, in particular when under the guidance of Camillo Benso Count of Cavour (1810–1861), had become one of the most appealing destinations for Italian revolutionaries, the only Italian State to have retained its 1848 Constitution, the Statuto Albertino (Albertine Statute). The Savoyard state had undergone what Christopher Clark has termed a 'European revolution

---

[1] Silvio Spaventa, *Dal 1848 al 1861. Lettere, scritti, documenti*, ed. Benedetto Croce (Bari: Laterza, 1923), p. 78.

in government', exemplified by the promulgation of the Sicardi Law, which had eliminated privileges of clergy and alienated the former aristocratic rights.[2]

The regeneration of the nation to which Villari refers was indeed a widespread preoccupation in nineteenth-century nationalisms. Italian patriots thus frequently employed the words 'Regeneration' and 'Resurgence' (*Risorgimento*) to indicate their common endeavour. What is crucial, though, is that the philosophy to be understood and 'popularised' was Hegel's, a philosophy entirely oriented towards the understanding of the State rather than of the nation. In order to regenerate the nation, Hegel needed to be 'translated' for the Italian public: 'Hegel is the Aristotle of the new civilization ... but Hegel cannot be translated like Aristotle, one needs to understand him, render him intelligible without superficiality, render him *popular*, not *vulgar*.'[3] This is because Hegel's philosophy argues that liberty is the unfolding in history of a process of self-consciousness and that the political liberty of a community is possible only through the development of the self-consciousness of the people about their past and their national character. This was the path delineated by the philosophy of Hegel, and Italians now had to creatively adapt this path to suit their own intellectual past and local philosophical tradition.

Hegel and Italian Political Thought uncovers a forgotten meaning of philosophical ideas by investigating readings of Hegel's thought in Italy during the nineteenth century: ideas have political power when they are elaborated in connection with the historical context. By looking at the nineteenth-century Italian reception of Hegel, a practical dimension of ideas emerges, and this with a twofold meaning. First of all, Hegel's ideas are turned into political practices by those Italians who had participated in the 1848 revolution, who then would lead the new Italian government after unification, between 1861 and 1876, and who finally would continue to play a central role in Italian political life until the end of the century. Secondly, the practical dimension of ideas refers to the peculiarities of Italian Hegelianism, which serve to distinguish it from the broader European reception of Hegel: it insisted on the historical and political dimension of Hegel's idealism, merging Giambattista Vico's understanding of history with Hegel's philosophy of history; it reformed Hegel's

---

[2] Christopher Clark, 'After 1848: The European Revolution in Government', *Transactions of the Royal Historical Society*, vol. 22 (2012), pp. 171–197. For a wider understanding of the 1848 revolutions in Europe, see Christopher Clark, *Revolutionary Spring: Fighting for a New World 1848–49* (London: Penguin, 2023).

[3] B. Spaventa, *Scritti inediti e rari (1840–1880)*, ed. G. D'Orsi (Padua: CEDAM 1966), p. 506.

dialectic by providing a phenomenological reading of the categories of the *Science of Logic*; it engaged with the outcomes of positivism and the natural sciences by presenting a *critical Hegelianism* closer to realism than to idealism, to reality than to metaphysics, to history than to logic, to life than to science, to practice than to ideas. Italian Hegelianism presents itself as a continuous attempt to elaborate a reading of Hegel that highlights the union between philosophy and history, and the synthesis of idea and fact, centring Hegelianism on the historical reality of life, without however losing sight of the metaphysical and logical dimension of the German philosopher's thought.

This book rethinks Italian political thought by taking into consideration the specific location of Italy in the imaginary map delineated by nineteenth-century Italian Hegelians in their conversation with their northern European critics and counterparts. It therefore criticises the conventional hierarchies in the study of Italian political thought, interrogating intellectual relationships within Italy as well as between Italy and the wider world. Challenging notions of centre and periphery, this book investigates the long process of transition whereby Italy ceased to be a cluster of dominated and isolated states and became a single nation-state. It does so by exploring the influence of Hegelian thought in shaping a new political vocabulary, in large part through the contribution of the Italian Hegelians. It is the story of a generation of intellectuals born at the start of the century, the majority of them from Southern Italy, who experienced the collapse of the Kingdom of Two Sicilies and the dissolution of the common cultural and political space of Southern Italy, and who helped to forge modern Italian political thought.

By uncovering this neglected intellectual inheritance, the book recovers a world characterised by multiple cultural, intellectual, and political affiliations that have since been obscured by the conventional narrative of the formation of nation-states. It thus rethinks the origins of Italian nationalism and of the Italian state, highlighting the intellectual connections between Germany, the Habsburg Empire, Switzerland, and France, and re-establishing the lost link between the changing geopolitical contexts of western and northern Europe and the Mediterranean. It shows how nations emerged from an intermingling, rather than a clash, of ideas concerning the State and liberalism, modernity and religion, history and civilization, revolution, and conservatism, South and North. Through the story of this generation of Hegelians, who began to engage with Hegel's philosophy shortly after his death, in 1832, and continued to grapple with it until the end of the century, this work contributes to the most recent

scholarly debates on Hegel and Italian Hegelianism, to the broader field of
the history of political thought, as well as to the research on nineteenth-
century Italian political thought.

I.1   Hegel and Italian Hegelianism

Following the classical works of the 1970s, recent years have witnessed a
return to Hegel studies, and from a survey of the latest publications it
seems clear that the phenomenon is currently at its peak.[4] This so-called
third wave of Anglophone scholarship on Hegel has largely developed as a
result of readings divided over the question of whether Hegel's idealism
should be considered as metaphysical or non-metaphysical,[5] reopening a
dialogue between different fields and tendencies in philosophy while
paying a particular attention to the German nineteenth-century context,[6]
Hegel's mature thought and his enduring influence[7] as well as its relationship with German Idealism.[8] The insights contained in the various fairly
recent reconstructions of Hegel's philosophy, mostly brought about by
German and American philosophers, have barely been taken up by historians or political theorists.[9] Consequently, research since the 1970s on
Hegel's moral and political ideas has tended to isolate this subject matter
from his speculative concerns. In this vein, scholars have opted to examine

---

[4] Among the key classical works in the 1970s see Shlomo Avineri, *Hegel's Theory of the Modern State*
(Cambridge: Cambridge University Press, 1972); G. D. O'Brian, *Hegel on Reason and History* (Chicago:
University of Chicago Press, 1975); Bernard Cullen, *Hegel's Social and Political Thought* (Dublin: Gill &
Macmillan, 1979); Charles Taylor, *Hegel* (Cambridge: Cambridge University Press, 1975); Charles
Taylor, *Hegel and Modern Society* (Cambridge: Cambridge University Press, 1979).

[5] See D. Moyar (ed.), *The Oxford Handbook of Hegel* (Oxford: Oxford University Press, 2017); F. C.
Beiser, 'Hegel and Hegelianism', in *The Cambridge History of Nineteenth-Century Political Thought*, ed.
G. Stedman Jones and G. Claeys (Cambridge: Cambridge University Press, 2011), pp. 110–146.

[6] For a general overview, see M. N. Forster and K. Gjesdal (eds.), *The Oxford Handbook of German
Philosophy in the Nineteenth Century* (Oxford: Oxford University Press, 2015); A. De Laurentiis and
L. J. Edwards (eds.), *The Bloomsbury Companion to Hegel* (London: Bloomsbury, 2012). See also
Terry Pinkard, *Hegel: A Biography* (Cambridge: Cambridge University Press, 2001).

[7] M. Bauer and S. Houlgate (eds.), *A Companion to Hegel* (Hoboken, NJ: Wiley-Blackwell, 2011);
Robert Pippin, *Hegel's Practical Philosophy: Rational Agency as Ethical Life* (Cambridge: Cambridge
University Press: 2008); Robert B. Pippin and Otfried Höffe (eds.), *Hegel on Ethics and Politics*
(Cambridge: Cambridge University Press, 2004).

[8] F. C. Beiser (ed.), *The Cambridge Companion to Hegel* (Cambridge: Cambridge University Press,
2008); Ludwig Siep, *Aktualität und Grenzen der praktischen Philosophie Hegels* (Leiden: Brill, 2010).

[9] See, for example, Klaus Hartmann, 'Hegel: A Non-Metaphysical View', in *Hegel*, ed. A. MacIntyre
(New York: Doubleday, 1972), pp. 101–124; Robert Pippin, *Hegel's Idealism: The Satisfactions of
Self-Consciousness* (Cambridge: Cambridge University Press, 1989); Robert Brandom, *Tales of the
Mighty Dead* (Cambridge, MA: Harvard University Press, 2002); Dieter Henrich, *Konstellationen:
Probleme und Debatten am Ursprung der idealistischen Philosophie (1789–1795)* (Stuttgart: Klett-
Cotta, 1991).

Hegel's ethics and politics without reference to his metaphysics.[10] This approach was initiated by Benedetto Croce (1866–1952) when attempting to distinguish what was 'living' from what was 'dead' in Hegel's philosophy, yet the problem with this viewpoint is that it makes it difficult to integrate the disparate elements of his project.[11] Not only does it render the *Logic* irrelevant to his social thought, but it also makes it hard to explain the role of both the *Phenomenology of Spirit* (1807) and the *Lectures on the Philosophy of History* (1822, 1828, 1830). In addition, this strategy presupposes that ethics and metaphysics have a distinct and determinate status in speculative philosophy, and it implicitly disregards the encyclopedic ambition of the Hegelian system. At the same time, despite their major advances in scholarship, philosophers have for the most part opted not to analyse Hegel's social, economic, and constitutional ideas. In fact, few political theorists today, and scarcely any historians, devote themselves to the study of Hegel's thought. Admittedly, there have been a number of exceptions, such as Duncan Forbes, Douglas Moggach, and Warren Breckman, or indeed Frederick Beiser, who has combined a commitment to the history of philosophy with an interest in Hegel. Only very recently have historians of political thought, such as Richard Bourke and Elias Buchetmann, engaged with Hegel's philosophy, insisting on a historical and contextual understanding of Hegel's political thought and stimulating a renewal of Hegel scholarship within the field of political thought, which has in turn prompted a reconsideration of the Hegelian tradition of political philosophy.[12]

Notwithstanding the intellectual significance of this revival, these works have shown little interest in important aspects of Hegel's reception, which in their own right are crucial for recent developments in intellectual history

---

[10] See Z. A. Pelczynski in 'An Introductory Essay' to his edition of *Hegel's Political Writings*, trans. by T. M. Knox (Oxford: Clarendon Press, 1964); Steven Smith, *Hegel's Critique of Liberalism* (Chicago: University of Chicago Press, 1989), p. xi; Allen Wood, *Hegel's Ethical Thought* (Cambridge: Cambridge University Press, 1990), pp. 4–6; Mark Tunick, *Hegel's Political Phiosophy* (Princeton: Princeton University Press, 1992), pp. 14, 17, 86, 99; Michael Hardimon, *Hegel's Social Philosophy* (Cambridge: Cambridge University Press, 1994), p. 8; and Alan Patten, *Hegel's Idea of Freedom* (Oxford: Oxford University Press, 1999), pp. 16–27; Paul Franco, *Hegel's Philosophy of Freedom* (New Haven, CT: Yale University Press, 1999), pp. 83–84, 126, 135–136, 140, 151–152, 360–361; John Rawls, *Lectures on the History of Moral Philosophy* (Cambridge, MA: Harvard University Press, 2000), p. 330.

[11] Benedetto Croce, *Ciò che è vivo e ciò che è morto della filosofia di Hegel* (Bari: Laterza, 1906), now in Benedetto Croce, *Saggio sullo Hegel* (Naples: Bibliopolis, 2006).

[12] Richard Bourke, *Hegel's World Revolutions* (Princeton: Princeton University Press, 2023); Elias Buchetmann, *Hegel and the Representative Constitution* (Cambridge: Cambridge University Press, 2023).

and the history of political thought. While participants in the recent debate pay due attention to the study of the Young Hegelians and British Idealism, as well as to the American, German, and French receptions of Hegel, the Italian reception has been almost wholly neglected.[13] This is despite the relevance of Hegel both for Italian political developments and for the broader transnational landscape of Italian idealism, associated mainly with Benedetto Croce (1866–1952) and Giovanni Gentile (1875–1944), figures who greatly enriched the European understanding of Hegel's philosophy and played a central role in the dissemination of Hegelian thought. There are a few exceptions to this general trend, such as Bruce Haddock and James Wakefield's volume, which endeavours to rethink Gentile's thought beyond the classical readings of his work as 'Fascist philosophy'.[14] With the focus on differences between Croce and Gentile's philosophies, David Roberts's work for its part addresses wider problems surrounding politics and liberalism.[15] He also denounces the marginalisation of modern Italian political thought, relegated from the wider European canon to the field of Italian Studies, where Italy is accorded the status of a periphery that passively received the discoveries and novelties of German, French, and British political thought. Relatively few works have resisted this general trend towards marginalisation, emphasising instead the originality and the relevance of Hegel's Italian reception within a broader range of European political thinkers and highlighting the transnational dimension of Italian political thought and its peculiarities.[16]

---

[13] For the different national receptions, see respectively Gareth Stedman Jones, *Karl Marx: Greatness and Illusion* (Cambridge, MA: Harvard University Press, 2016); W. J. Mander, *British Idealism. A History* (Oxford: Oxford University Press, 2011); T. Rockmore, *Hegel, Idealism, and Analytic Philosophy* (New Haven, CT: Yale University Press, 2005); T. Rockmore, *Hegel, Idealism, and Analytic Philosophy* (New Haven, CT: Yale University Press, 2005); Douglas Moggach, *The New Hegelians: Politics and Philosophy in the Hegelian School* (Cambridge: Cambridge University Press, 2006); Douglas Moggach, *Politics, Religion and Art: Hegelian Debates* (Evanston, IL: Northwestern University Press, 2011); Lisa Herzog (ed.), *Hegel's Thought in Europe: Currents, Crosscurrents and Undercurrents* (Basingstoke: Palgrave Macmillan, 2013), pp. 239–261.

[14] Bruce Haddock and James Wakefield (eds.), *Thought Thinking: The Philosophy of Giovanni Gentile* (Cardiff: Imprint Academic, 2015).

[15] David Roberts, *Historicism and Fascism in Modern Italy* (Toronto: University of Toronto Press, 2007).

[16] See, in particular, the works by Richard Bellamy, *Modern Italian Social Theory: Ideology and Politics from Pareto to the Present* (Stanford, CA: Stanford University Press, 1987); Richard Bellamy, *Croce, Gramsci, Bobbio, and the Italian Political Tradition* (Colchester: ECPR Press, 2014). See also Brian P. Copenhaver and Rebecca Copenhaver, *From Kant to Croce. Modern Philosophy in Italy 1800–1950* (Toronto: University of Toronto Press, 2012); Rocco Rubini, *The Other Renaissance* (Chicago: Chicago University Press, 2014); Rocco Rubini, *Posterity: Inventing Tradition from Petrarch to Gramsci* (Chicago: Chicago University Press, 2022). For a general overview, see the special issue

Considering the intellectual prominence of Giovanni Gentile and Benedetto Croce in Italy and their central role in bringing to light the majority of books, letters, and manuscripts by the nineteenth-century Italian Hegelians, it does not come as a surprise that, within Italian scholarship, the understanding of the phenomenon of Hegel's reception in nineteenth-century Italy has been dominated by their two different interpretations, left unchallenged for almost fifty years. While Gentile had traced a direct line between nineteenth-century Italian Hegelianism and his own *Actualism*, Croce tried to trace the thread of the Italian liberal tradition from the Neapolitan Revolution of 1799 to the Italian Risorgimento. The historiographical debate was reopened in the 1950s and the 1960s by a group of Marxist scholars who criticised both approaches. Thanks to the publication of the correspondence between Bertrando Spaventa and his pupil, the Marxist Antonio Labriola, intellectuals such as Palmiro Togliatti and Giuseppe Berti, as well as Giuseppe Vacca and Domenico Losurdo later on, tried to identify a line of development of Italian historicism from Spaventa and Labriola to the work of Antonio Gramsci.[17]

The very diverse attempts to reconstruct a unitary vision of the development of Hegelianism in Italian political thought were contested by a number of different scholars in the 1980s. In this period, the focus on the historical context of nineteenth-century Italy and the political experience of the Risorgimento was enhanced by the availability of new archival sources that were published in the course of the following decades (correspondence, lectures, manuscripts, etc.), offering a fruitful ground for those seeking to avoid ideological approaches and univocal interpretations.[18]

---

edited by Fernanda Gallo and Axel Körner, 'Hegel in Italy: Risorgimento Political Thought in Transnational Perspective', *Journal of Modern Italian Studies*, 24, no. 2, 2019.

[17] For an overview of the different approaches, see Giovanni Gentile, *Bertrando Spaventa e la riforma dello hegelismo*, in *Opere*, vol. XXIX, ed. G. Gentile (Florence: Le Lettere 2001). Gentile's approach in the aftermath of World War II was contested only by Felice Alderisio, *Esame della riforma attualistica dell'idealismo in rapporto a Spaventa e a Hegel* (Naples, 1959). Gentile's interpretation was later reiterated by Italo Cubeddu, 'Bertrando Spaventa pubblicista (giugno – dicembre 1851)', in *Giornale critico di filosofia italiana*, 42, 1963: 46–93; and Italo Cubeddu, *Bertrando Spaventa* (Florence: Sansoni, 1964). Among the studies with a marxist approach, see Giuseppe Berti, 'Bertrando Spaventa, Antonio Labriola e l'hegelismo napoletano', *Società*, X, 1954: 406–430; XI, 583–607; XII, 764–791; Palmiro Togliatti, 'Per una giusta comprensione del pensiero di A. Labriola', *Rinascita*, XI, 1954: 254–256, 336–339, 387–393, 483–491; Sergio Landucci, 'Il giovane Spaventa fra hegelismo e socialismo', *Annali dell'Istituto Giangiacomo Feltrinelli*, VI, 1963: 647–707; Gaetano Arfé, 'L'hegelismo napoletano e Bertrando Spaventa', *Società*, VIII, 1952: 45–62.

[18] For an overview of the catalogues of manuscripts and unpublished works of the Neapolitan Hegelians, see *Gli hegeliani di Napoli e la costruzione dello Stato unitario. Mostra bibliografica e documentaria* (Rome: Istituto Poligrafico e Zecca dello Stato, 1989); Alessandro Savorelli, *Le Carte*

Some critics have concentrated on the ethical and political aspects of Italian Hegelianism[19], while others have highlighted the contribution made to the theoretical and philosophical debate or to the understanding of the general historical context.[20]

In very recent years, German and Italian scholarship has witnessed a revival of interest in Hegel's reception in Italy in the nineteenth century, partly on account of the bicentenary of the birth of both its most prominent figures, Bertrando Spaventa (1817–1883) and Francesco De Sanctis (1817–1883).[21] Although this revival has fostered a renewed engagement with the recent debate in the history of philosophy and the history of literature, it remains within the categories of interpretation developed during the 1980s and very closely related therefore to internal German and Italian academic debates and by the same token at odds with the most recent – and, indeed, highly fruitful – tendency in intellectual history, which considers Italy in the broader transnational and global context.[22]

Spaventa della Biblioteca Nazionale di Napoli (Naples: Bibliopolis, 1980); Bertrando Spaventa, *Epistolario*, vol. I (1847–1860), ed. M. Rascaglia (Rome: Istituto Poligrafico e Zecca dello Stato, 1995); Rosa Franzese and Emma Giammattei (eds.), *Studi su Vittorio Imbriani* (Naples: Guida, 1990); Nicola Capone (ed.), *Silvio Spaventa e i moti del Quarantotto. Articoli dal 'Nazionale' e scritti dall'ergastolo di Santo Stefano* (Naples: La scuola di Pitagora, 2006); Francesco Fiorentino, *Manuale di storia della filosofia ad uso dei licei*, 4 vols. (Naples: La scuola di Pitagora, 2007); Antonio Labriola, *Carteggio (1861–1904)*, vols. I–V, ed. Stefano Miccolis (Naples: Bibliopolis, 2000–2006); Theodor Sträter, *Lettere sulla filosofia italiana* (Bomba: Troilo, 1999); Alessandro Savorelli, *Biblioteche di hegeliani e positivisti (maestri, convertiti, apostati)* in *Biblioteche filosofiche private in età moderna e contemporanea*, ed. F. M. Crasta (Florence: Le Lettere, 2010), pp. 237–249.

[19] See, for example, Eugenio Garin, *Filosofia e politica in Bertrando Spaventa* (Naples: Bibliopolis, 2007); Luigi Gentile, *Coscienza nazionale e pensiero europeo in Bertrando Spaventa* (Chieti: Noubs, 2000).

[20] See, for example, P. Piovani, *Indagini di storia della filosofia* (Naples: Liguori, 2006); Fulvio Tessitore, *La cultura filosofica tra due rivoluzioni (1799–1860)*, in *Storia di Napoli*, vol. IX (Naples: ESI, 1972), pp. 225–293; Guido Oldrini, *La cultura filosofica napoletana dell'Ottocento* (Bari: Laterza, 1973).

[21] Enza Biagini, Paolo Orvieto, Sandro Piazzesi (eds.), 'Francesco De Sanctis, 1817–2017', special issue of *Rivista di Letteratura italiana*, 35, no. I, 2017. For a very recent overview of the secondary literature on Bertrando Spaventa, see Marcello Mustè, Stefano Trinchese and Giuseppe Vacca, *Bertrando Spaventa. Tra coscienza nazionale e filosofia europea* (Rome: Viella, 2018); see also Bertrando Spaventa, *Epistolario*, ed. M. Diamanti, M. Mustè, and M. Rascaglia (Rome: Viella, 2020). On Hegel's reception in Italy, see F. Iannelli, F. Vercellone, K. Vieweg, *Hegel und Italien, Italien und Hegel: Geistige Synergien von Gestern und Heute* (Milan: Mimesis, 2019); Marco Diamanti (ed.), *La fortuna di Hegel in Italia nell'Ottocento* (Naples: Bibliopolis, 2020).

[22] The exception within this debate is the very recent special issue edited by Fernanda Gallo and Axel Körner, 'Hegel in Italy: Risorgimento Political Thought in Transnational Perspective', *Journal of Modern Italian Studies*, 24, no. 2, 2019.

This book on the contrary engages with the most recent debates in intellectual history and with the international scholarship on Italian political thought, combining it with new archival sources that offer fresh perspectives on the topic. Fredrick Beiser has summarised the dilemma facing scholars of Hegel and of Hegel's reception in terms of a choice between a metaphysical or non-metaphysical understanding of the German philosopher, insisting that accurate historical research has to confront Hegel with his metaphysical concerns, which are 'alien to the spirit of contemporary philosophical culture, which mistrusts metaphysics'.[23] However, a non-metaphysical understanding of Hegel would be less historically accurate, as it would appear more as 'a construction of our contemporary interests than the real historical school'.[24] It is at this juncture that historians, concerned with past issues for their own sake, move away from political theorists and political philosophers, preoccupied as they are with contemporary controversies. There is indeed at this point an opportunity for historians of political thought to close the gap, the study of nineteenth-century Italian Hegelianism offering a fresh perspective on this problem.

Italian Hegelians investigated and discussed both the metaphysical and the non-metaphysical Hegel, moving confidently from the most difficult pages of the *Science of Logic* to the *Phenomenology of Spirit*, which Silvio Spaventa called 'the book with the seven seals' (Il libro dai sette sigilli): as intellectual historians, they explored Hegel's texts and analysed his ideas in depth, while reconstructing his context and German intellectual debates; as philosophers, they selected and reshaped those ideas within Hegel's philosophy that answered to their contemporary political concerns; as politicians, they tried to enhance their political practice, deriving inspiration from their reformulation of Hegelian ideas. While accurately reconstructing the Italian context and this network of intellectuals, the present book reflects on the prominent place that philosophy assumed in nineteenth-century political debates and the key role that ideas played in the political arena.

I.2 The History of Political Thought

Rather than reading political statements as facts, as was customary in most of the idealist accounts of Italy's national resurgence, which established a

---

[23] Frederick Beiser, 'Introduction: The Puzzling Hegel Renaissance', in *Hegel and Nineteenth-century Philosophy*, ed. F. Beiser (Cambridge: Cambridge University Press, 2008), pp. 1–14, 5.

[24] Beiser, 'Introduction', p. 6.

teleological straitjacket of idealised standard accounts of national history, more recent, critical approaches tend to read them as speech acts within a complex framework of contextual references, where the representation of social and political realities had aimed to achieve specific political outcomes.[25] Many of these contextual references are embedded in international and sometimes global debates, which themselves require careful analysis, such as a comparison of the relationship between the history of political thought and the political cultures of the different countries within which it has been practised.[26] Despite a long and erudite tradition in Italy of studying these ideas as 'storia delle dottrine politiche' (history of political thought), a more analytical and theoretically informed approach based on methodological engagement with, for instance, Anglo-American studies of political theory, the so-called Cambridge school, or a Koselleckian history of concepts has emerged only relatively recently.[27] Since then, the history of Italian political thought has rapidly developed into a vibrant field of research.[28]

[25] Quentin Skinner, *Visions of Politics, Vol. 1: Regarding Method* (Cambridge: Cambridge University Press, 2002), p. 107.

[26] Stefan Collini, 'Postscript. Disciplines, Canons, and Publics: The History of "the History of Political Thought" in Comparative Perspective", in *The History of Political Thought in National Context*, ed. D. Castiglione and I. Hampsher-Monk (Cambridge: Cambridge University Press, 2001), pp. 280–302.

[27] On the field of history of political thought in Italy, see Angelo D'Orsi, 'One Hundred Years of the History of Political Thought in Italy', in *The History of Political Thought in National Context*, ed. D. Castiglione and I. Hampsher-Monk (Cambridge: Cambridge University Press, 2001), pp. 80–106; on Anglo-American studies of political theory, see John G. A. Pocock, *Political Thought and History. Essays on Theory and Method* (Cambridge: Cambridge University Press, 2009), pp. 3–19; on the German school, see Jahn-Werner Müller, 'On Conceptual History', in *Rethinking Modern European Intellectual History*, ed. D. M. McMahon and S. Moyn (Oxford: Oxford University Press, 2014), pp. 74–93, 77.

[28] See Richard Bellamy, *Modern Italian Social Theory: Ideology and Politics from Pareto to the Present* (Stanford, CA: Stanford University Press, 1987); Richard Bellamy, *Croce, Gramsci, Bobbio, and the Italian Political Tradition* (Colchester: ECPR Press, 2014); Maurizio Isabella, 'Nationality Before Liberty? Risorgimento Political Thought in Transnational Context', *Journal of Modern Italian Studies*, 17, no. 5, 2012: 507–515; David Ragazzoni, 'Giuseppe Mazzini's Democratic Theory of Nations', in *Nazione e nazionalismi. Teorie, interpretazioni, sfide attuali*, ed. A. Campi, S. De Luca and F. Tuccari (Rome: Historica, 2018), pp. 279–305; Sandro Recchia and Nadia Urbinati (eds.), *Giuseppe Mazzini, A Cosmopolitanism of Nations. Giuseppe Mazzini's Writings on Democracy, Nation Building, and International Relations* (Princeton, NJ; Oxford: Princeton University Press, 2009); Roberto Romani, 'Reluctant Revolutionaries: Moderate Liberalism in the Kingdom of Sardinia, 1849–1859', *The Historical Journal*, 55, no. 1, 2012: 45–73; Fabio Sabetti, *Civilization and Self-Government. The Political Thought of Carlo Cattaneo* (Lanham, MD: Lexington Books, 2010); Martin Thom, 'City, Region and Nation: Carlo Cattaneo and the Making of Italy', *Citizenship Studies*, 3, no. 2, 1999: 187–201; Nadia Urbinati, *Le civili libertà: Positivismo e liberalismo nell'Italia unita* (Venice: Marsilio, 1990).

This book's approach to Italian political thought actively engages with recent broader debates in the history of political thought, while also entering into a dialogue with the scholarship on the intellectual history of the Mediterranean. It does so by enlarging the range of sources usually deployed by intellectual historians, following the invitation that histories of ideas should encompass a broader understanding of context by reconstructing 'the complete range of the inherited symbols and representations that constitute the subjectivity of an age', both through immersion in the archives and by grappling with philosophical, legal, and political texts.[29] This research relates to the trends in the field that integrate the analysis of philosophical and political texts with biographical information;[30] explore the circulation of books and translation of classical texts;[31] and reconstruct national and international networks of intellectuals by focussing on correspondence, exile, as well as on relevant periodicals and journals.[32] Combining these different approaches to the field, this book reveals unexpected paths to the identification of one of the bodies of political thought, in which ideas are closely connected to the practical experiences of authors, the circulation of intellectual flows, and the access variously granted to texts.

If, as Pocock affirmed, a body of political thought can only be said to exist when a context 'lasts long enough to give discourse some command over itself', and if conversations within and between cultures must be stable and durable in order to produce significant bodies of political thought, then the Italian Hegelians had indeed represented a body of political thought in modern Italy.[33] But how is it that this body of

---

[29] Quentin Skinner, 'Motives, Intention, and Interpretation', in *Visions of Politics*, p. 102.

[30] See Maurizio Viroli, *Niccolo's Smile: A Biography of Machiavelli* (Princeton: Princeton University Press, 1999); Gareth Stedman Jones, *Karl Marx: Greatness and Illusion* (Cambridge, MA: Harvard University Press, 2016); Andrew Fitzmaurice, *King Leopold's Ghostwriter: The Creation of Persons and States in the Nineteenth Century*, (Princeton: Princeton University Press, 2021).

[31] See Edward Jones Corredera, *The Diplomatic Enlightenment: Spain, Europe, and the Age of Speculation* (Leiden: Brill, 2021); Axel Körner, *America in Italy: The United States in the Political Thought and Imagination of the Risorgimento, 1763–1865* (Princeton: Princeton University Press, 2017); see also the very recent project on translations in the Age of Revolutions: Rachel Hammersley 'Experiencing Political Texts', https://gtr.ukri.org/projects?ref=AH%2FVo13378%2F1.

[32] See Ann Thomson, *Bodies of Thought: Science, Religion, and the Soul in Early Enlightenment* (Oxford: Oxford University Press, 2008), Maurizio Isabella, *Risorgimento in Exile: Italian Émigrés and the Liberal International in the Post-Napoleonic Era* (Oxford: Oxford University Press, 2009); Konstantina Zanou, *Transnational Patriotism in the Mediterranean, 1800–1850: Stammering the Nation* (Oxford: Oxford University Press, 2018).

[33] J. G. A. Pocock, 'On the Unglobality of Contexts: Cambridge Methods and the History of Political Thought', *Global Intellectual History*, 4, no. 1, 2019: 77; see also J. G. A. Pocock, *Virtue, Commerce, and History* (Cambridge: Cambridge University Press, 1985).

nineteenth-century political thought did not enter the main surveys in the field when by contrast Niccolo Machiavelli or Antonio Gramsci loom so large? There are hidden intellectual hierarchies that structure and constrain the field: very recent research in the history of political thought, in particular on the twentieth century, is indeed now presenting alternative bodies of political thought, very influential in their own contexts. These works explore the connections between theory and political practice by highlighting the 'power of political ideas', such as Shruti Kapila's recent monograph on modern Indian political thought, as well as collective efforts to reconstruct a 'democratic canon', such as the edited volume on African-American political thought by Melvin Rogers and Jack Turner.[34] The present book assumes the social and political influence of ideas 'since people's behaviour is deeply influenced by what they think, and especially by what they believe firmly'.[35]

These recent studies are the result of the efforts that have shaped the field in the last few decades in order to present a multiplicity of bodies of political thought, paying attention to a broader field of intellectual pro-duction.[36] The different sub-fields have contributed greatly to this approach. Those engaged in writing the history of international and legal political thought have thus attempted to highlight the contested, fruitful, and shifting nature of classical works. The reshaping of classical authors by a wide range of actors, who might have different intentions, is often the site of negotiation of ideas. This book is interested in the way Hegel had been reinvented by nineteenth-century Italian thinkers, 'emphasising the personal, institutional, social, and political dynamics that underpinned the posthumous trajectory' of Hegel's philosophy 'and what these dynamics tell us about their goals, priorities, and world views'.[37] This different context might also offer a reading of the author that is quite far from their original intentions. The sub-field of comparative political thought would appear to have been moving in a similar direction. Indeed, some of its

---

[34] See Shruti Kapila, *Violent Fraternity: Indian Political Thought in the Global Age* (Princeton, Princeton University Press, 2021); See also the book review by Emma Stone Mackinnon, 'Toward a Democratic Canon', *Contemporary Political Theory*, 2022: 1–13. The review analyses the edited volume by Melvin L. Rogers and Jack Turner (eds.), *African American Political Thought: A Collected History* (Chicago: University of Chicago Press, 2021).

[35] E. F. Biagini, *Liberty, Retrenchment and Reform: Popular Liberalism in the Age of Gladstone, 1860–1880* (Cambridge: Cambridge University Press, 1992), p. 2.

[36] Siep Stuurman, 'The Canon of the History of Political Thought: Its Critique and a Proposed Alternative', *History and Theory*, 39, no. 2, 2000: 147–166.

[37] Paolo Amorosa and Claire Vergerio, 'Canon-making in the History of International Legal and Political Thought', *Leiden Journal of International Law*, 35, 2022: 469–478, 470. See also Mira Siegelberg, *Statelessness: A Modern History* (Boston: Harvard University Press, 2020).

practitioners have gone so far as to highlight the potential theoretical (not historical) value of creative misreadings of thinkers from the past.[38]

A very interesting criticism of the established bodies of political thought has emerged in particular from the studies on women's intellectual production, an interest that has crossed the diverse sub-fields, proposing exciting studies in international political thought, in intellectual history, as well as in political theory.[39] These works uncover stories of female political thinkers and philosophers who have contributed to the development of political thought in traditional or less traditional ways, aiming at presenting alternative views of political thought. This book recovers the work of the female philosopher Marianna Bacinetti, better known by her married name of Marianna Florenzi Waddington, who greatly contributed to the history of Italian Hegelianism.

Exciting new works on Italian political thought highlight how asymmetries in relations of power, which often produced revolutions, diasporas, or exiles, have affected the identification of bodies of political thought and recast relationships between centre and peripheries.[40] Most of these works appeared within the wider field of the intellectual history of the modern Mediterranean.[41] Studies in modern intellectual history of the

---

[38] Adrian Blau, 'How (Not) to Use the History of Political Thought for Contemporary Purposes', *American Journal of Political Science*, 2020: 359–372; see also Navid Hassanzadeh, 'The Canon and Comparative Political Thought', *Journal of International Political Theory*, 11, no. 2, 2015: 184–202. For an overview on this debate, see Duncan Bell, 'International Relations and Intellectual History', in *The Oxford Handbook of History and International Relations*, ed. Mlada Bukovansky, Edward Keene, Christian Reus-Smit, and Maja Spanu (Oxford, Oxford University Press, 2023), pp. 94–110.

[39] For a wide-ranging effort to recover the international thought of women, see K. Hutchings and P. Owens, 'Women Thinkers and the Canon of International Thought: Recovery, Rejection, and Reconstitution', *American Political Science Review*, 115, no. 2, 2021: 347–359; see also P. Owens and K. Rietzler (eds.), *Women's International Thought: A New History* (Cambridge: Cambridge University Press, 2021); I. Tallgren (ed.), *Portraits of Women in International Law: New Names and Forgotten Faces* (Oxford: Oxford University Press, 2023). Regarding the developments in the field of intellectual history and political theory, see, for example, Hilda L. Smith, 'Women's History as Intellectual History: A Perspective on the Journal of Women's History', *Journal of Women's History*, 20, no. 1, 2008: 26–32; Ben Griffin, 'From Histories of Intellectual Women to Women's Intellectual History', *Journal of Victorian Culture*, 24, no. 1, 2019: 130–133; Lisa L. Moore, Joanna Brooks, and Caroline Wigginton (eds.), *Transatlantic Feminisms in the Age of Revolutions* (Oxford: Oxford University Press, 2012); Penny A. Weiss, *Canon Fodder: Historical Women Political Thinkers* (State College: Penn State University Press, 2009), pp. 3–29.

[40] See T. Hauswedell, A. Körner, and U. Tiedau (eds.), *Remapping Centre and Periphery: Asymmetrical Encounters in European and Global Context* (London: UCL Press, 2019).

[41] Peregrine Horden and Nicholas Purcell, *The Corrupting Sea: A Study of Mediterranean History* (Oxford: Blackwell, 2000); see also David Armitage and Alison Bashford, 'Introduction: The Pacific and its Histories', in *Pacific Histories: Ocean, Land, People*, ed. David Armitage and Alison Bashford (London; New York: Palgrave Macmillan, 2014), pp. 1–28. For a wider overview of the recent development in Mediterranean intellectual history, see F. Gallo and M. D'Auria (eds.),

Mediterranean have reconstructed the entanglement of interactions and shared experiences in the Mediterranean in the long nineteenth century, highlighting the capacity of local authors, scholars, and intellectuals to use foreign ideas for their own purposes and shedding new light on the creative amalgamation with local cultural and political traditions.[42] Moreover, they have investigated how the peoples of Southern Europe and the Ottoman Empire, which all experienced diverse forms of subordination to northern 'great powers', had to struggle with broader changes in ideas about states while striving to maintain their political and cultural autonomy.[43] Nineteenth-century Italian political thought is no exception.

The renewed interest in modern Italian political thought within the field of intellectual history of the Mediterranean has produced very interesting works as well as new challenges to the identification of alternative bodies of political thought. New research that investigates Italian political thought within the scholarship on Mediterranean history has also insisted on the 'connectivity', a dimension embodied in the biographies of intellectuals who travelled across the Mediterranean space, often following revolutionary moments, in the networks they created and in the ideas they exchanged.[44]

The reconstruction of network-based liberalism at a specific moment, such as the 1820s or 1848 revolutions, and the mapping of ramifying connections among liberals across Europe and the World (especially Latin America or the Indian Ocean) help little in identifying an alternative body of political thought. However, liberals from Southern Europe were in a particular predicament (compared, for example, to liberals in Britain): they endured various moments of political oppression that forced them into

Mediterranean Europe(s): Rethinking Europe from Its Southern Shores (London: Routledge, 2022), pp. 1–19.

[42] Maurizio Isabella and Konstantina Zanou, *Mediterranean Diasporas. Politics and Ideas in the Long Nineteenth Century* (London: Bloomsbury, 2015).

[43] Joanna Innes and Mark Philp (eds.), *Re-Imagining Democracy in the Mediterranean, 1780–1860* (Oxford: Oxford University Press, 2018); see also Peter Hill, *Utopia and Civilization in the Arab Nahda* (Cambridge: Cambridge University Press, 2020).

[44] See, for example, Peregrine Horden and Nicholas Purcell, 'The Mediterranean and "The New Thalassology"', *American Historical Review*, 111, 2006: 722–740; Peregrine Horden and Sharon Kinoshita (eds.), *A Companion to Mediterranean History* (Chichester: John Wiley & Sons, 2014); David Abulafia, *The Great Sea: A Human History of the Mediterranean* (Oxford: Oxford University Press, 2011); Alina Payne (ed.), *Dalmatia and the Mediterranean: Portable Archaeology and the Poetics of Influence* (Leiden: Brill, 2013); Michele Bacci et al., 'On the Mediterranean Space in the Middle Ages', *Perspective*, 2, 2014: 271–292; Elisabeth A. Fraser (ed.), *The Mobility of People and Things in the Early Modern Mediterranean: The Art of Travel* (New York: Routledge, 2020).

exile, and there was a constant flux of streams of exiles.[45] These moments of exile were certainly moments of reflection, writing, and exchange of ideas with the local contexts hosting them, but then these people returned to their own countries and most of them subsequently occupied key roles in governments and parliaments. The peculiarity of these moments of 'pause' (and sometimes fight) as well as moments of real politics becomes even more interesting if tracked across a longer timespan, which allows us to recognise the interactions between ideas and political practices, identifying then a particular body of political thought, one that was especially relevant in modern Italy.

Intellectual historian working on the Mediterranean invite us also to consider more seriously the role of space in the history of political thought. Intellectual history for a long time resisted a reflection on space. However, more recently, scholars have suggested that space be considered a key element in the understanding of intellectual history, even going so far as to define space as 'the final frontier for intellectual history'.[46] If we then consider space not as a mere context but as 'a mode of intellectual production deserving of interpretation in its own right', taking it seriously and, therefore, reading 'deliberately against the grain',[47] we have to agree with Antonio Gramsci when in his *Prison Notebooks* he notes that North, South, East, and West, although 'arbitrary and conventional [historical] constructions', more or less explicitly 'expressed (and still express) a value-judgement' with very real intellectual and political consequences.[48] Engaging with the history of political thought by including the specificities of spaces and entanglements that characterised the Mediterranean region in modern times means that we consider also these 'value-judgements' that provide a new understanding of Italian political thought. This book investigates the history of Italian political thought also by reflecting on the wider spatial and intellectual context of the Mediterranean in the nineteenth century and its place in the intellectual and political hierarchies at the time. It explores how engagement with a classical and influential thinker such as Hegel from the margins of its geo-philosophical borders

---

[45] Maurizio Isabella, *Southern Europe in the Age of Revolutions* (Princeton, Princeton University Press: 2023); Michalis Sotiropoulos, *Liberalism after the Revolution: The Intellectual Foundations of the Greek State, c. 1830–1880* (Cambridge, Cambridge University Press, 2023).
[46] Armitage, 'The International Turn in Intellectual History', p. 239.
[47] Randolph, 'The Space of Intellect and the Intellect of Space', 225; Brett, 'The Space of Politics and the Space of War', 34. On this debate, see also Daniel S. Allemann, Anton Jäger, and Valentina Mann, *Conceptions of Space in Intellectual History* (London: Routledge, 2019).
[48] Antonio Gramsci, *Quaderni del carcere* (Turin: Einaudi, 2014), II, 874.

(nineteenth-century Italy) has produced an alternative body of political thought, which was equally influential in its own context. Rather than a passive reception of ideas thought elsewhere, nineteenth-century Italian Hegelianism represents a creative amalgamation of different intellectual flows, local and international, offering an original and interesting reading of Hegel. Rethinking Italian political thought through the lens of Hegel's 'presence' in Italy means also to recenter the Peninsula in modern historical time. As Franco Cassano argued:

> For a long time the south has been seen like an error, a negation, or a delay. To reverse this picture, the first thing that is required is to give back to the south the ancient dignity of being a subject of thought, rather than being thought of from the standpoint of others. In a similar manner, the Mediterranean has long been regarded as a sea of the past. It is in fact a central place of contemporary history – a place in which the north and the west meet the east and the south of the world.[49]

Re-establishing the dignity of subjects of thought for the Italians and recovering the 'thread of their philosophical tradition' in order to develop the self-consciousness of the Italian nation were indeed the main aims of the Italian Hegelians, who in the first instance engaged with Hegel's philosophy of history as a history of liberation from intellectual and political oppression.

I.3   Italian Political Thought and the Risorgimento

Since the first translation of one of Hegel's works into Italian, the *Philosophy of History* (*Filosofia della storia*) published in 1840 and translated by Giambattista Passerini (1793–1864) during his exile in Switzerland, Hegel was presented to Italian readers almost as a historian, whose philosophy of history, due to the certainty of future political freedom, seemed directly relevant to the revolutionary tremors leading to 1848, at the height of which Antonio Turchiarulo translated Hegel's *Philosophy of Right* (*Filosofia del diritto*). In his introduction, Turchiarulo highlighted the relevance of Hegel's political thought for Italy's national emancipation, describing it as a path to political freedom and civilisation.

What the first Italian Hegelians found so attractive in Hegel's philosophy of history was both the notion of freedom as the liberation of humanity through the struggle of Spirit in its historical existence and the

---

[49] Franco Cassano, 'Southern Thought', *Thesis Eleven*, 67, no. 1, 2001: 1–10, 1.

ideas of progress and liberation addressed to all nations. At this early stage, Italian Hegelianism was open to receiving the revolutionary potential of Hegel's philosophy. Against Hegel's own express warning, the dialectical philosophy of history now helped those studying it to look into the future, confirming the promise of a new age to come. Responding to Hegel's call for liberation, Italy would once again be part of European culture – as it had been during the Renaissance.[50]

While the political implications of Hegel's thought seemed obvious, there were important differences in its reception between the North and the South of the peninsula. The diffusion of Hegel's thought in northern Italy before 1848 was not based on direct knowledge of Hegel's original texts in German but on their mediation through Victor Cousin's French school of Eclecticism, which itself had followers in the South of the peninsula, including Stanislao Gatti (1820–1870) and Stefano Cusani (1815–1846). This book begins in 1832, when the first work on Hegel appeared in Italian, written by Giandomenico Romagnosi (1761–1835) in the Florentine journal *Antologia*, with the title *Alcuni pensieri sopra un'ultra-metafisica filosofia della storia* (*Some Thoughts on an Ultra-Metaphysical Philosophy of History*), commenting very critically on Hegel's *Philosophy of History*, his account being based on Eugène Lerminier's (1803–1857) exposition of Hegel's philosophy in his *Introduction générale à l'histoire du droit* (*General Introduction to the History of Right*, 1829).[51] It was in the South, however, that Hegelianism assumed the role of a proper philosophical movement, commonly referred to as Neapolitan Hegelianism, which over the years also came to assume an important role on the national stage.

It was at the Neapolitan school of the Kantian Ottavio Colecchi (1773–1847), who had studied in Königsberg, that the group of liberals subsequently at the heart of Italian Hegelianism, gained access to German texts in the original language and became familiar with the language of German idealism and the scholarly debates in Germany. As a more systematic intellectual current, Neapolitan Hegelianism lasted for approximately forty years, from 1841, when Stanislao Gatti and Stefano Cusani founded the periodical *Il Museo*, up to the beginning of the 1880s, when its main exponents died. In the last two decades of the nineteenth century, that tradition was reshaped and reinterpreted by a number of different Italian intellectuals, and in particular it was adapted by Antonio Labriola (1843–1904) to the new intellectual challenges posed by the then current reflections on socialism. This book ends with Labriola's re-elaboration of

[50] See Nuzzo, 'An Outline of Italian Hegelianism (1832–1998)'.   [51] *Antologia*, vol. 96, p. 289.

this tradition in his 'philosophy of praxis', presented in a series of three Marxist essays appearing between 1895 and 1898 with the title *Saggi intorno alla concezione materialistica della storia* (*Essays on the Materialistic Conception of History*) and in his fourth and last essay *Da un secolo all'altro* (*From One century to the Next*), written between 1897 and 1903 and published posthumously by his young friend Benedetto Croce.

The protagonists of Neapolitan Hegelianism at the beginning of the movement were for the most part young scholars who, while fighting for the national cause, endeavoured to read, translate, and interpret Hegel's philosophy in direct relation to their political concerns. Before 1848, they had largely worked as a clandestine group, hiding from the Bourbon police. After the revolution of 1848 and its subsequent repression, its advocates continued their studies in prison or in exile, mostly in Piedmont, Switzerland, or France. It was only after Italy's political unification in 1861 – when De Sanctis became Minister of Public Education, Silvio Spaventa was appointed vice secretary of Internal Affairs, and Bertrando Spaventa was elected a deputy to the national Parliament – that Neapolitan Hegelianism became officially part of Italy's national canon of political thought. It was largely due to Labriola, who as a pupil of Bertrando Spaventa was closely connected to the Neapolitan Hegelians, and his vigorous resistance to materialism that towards the turn of the century a younger generation of thinkers developed a new interest in Hegel's philosophy. In the case of Benedetto Croce and Giovanni Gentile, Labriola's own anti-materialist Marxism came to form the basis for their engagement with Hegel's thought, in Croce's case assuming the guise of a new historicism and in Gentile's case that of a neo-idealism.

From the perspective of a Hegel scholar, much of the Italian reading of Hegel might seem a distortion of the German philosopher's thought. Most of the debates in which Italians placed their understanding of Hegel were fundamentally different from the German context of political thought at the beginning of the nineteenth century. The Neapolitan Hegelians' quests and needs were closely related to the political context of the Risorgimento, with the result that Hegel's philosophy of history was drawn closer to the anti-metaphysical overtones of Vichian historicism. Within this context, Hegel's understanding of the Protestant Reformation as the key event in the making of the modern world is deprived of its theological element and turned into the earthly and philosophical experience of the Renaissance. Hegel's ideas regarding civil society were reshaped beyond economic and corporative relations to become the embodiment of society's cultural dimension. Hegel's marginalisation of the role of the nation in favour of that of the State was overturned by adopting a new concept of 'nationality', which included a cultural (though not an ethnic) dimension as the basis of the rule of law. Hegel's 'Dialectic' and his Logic were reinterpreted from the perspective of the *Phenomenology of Spirit*. Italian Hegelians redefined Hegel's concept of parties in terms of electoral organisations affecting the relationship between the State and civil society. Therefore, understanding Italian Hegelianism implies a readiness to hear Hegel's philosophy in a different voice. This entails a willingness to consider the amalgamation of Hegelian thought with Italy's own fruitful intellectual ground, including the legacy of Vico's *Scienza Nuova* and the rediscovery of Giordano Bruno and Tommaso Campanella's philosophy.

Beyond the study of particular intellectual currents, the importance of Italy's political context is one of the present book's main concerns. As Eugenio Garin asserted, Hegel's Italian reception was never a matter of purely academic debate or of 'scientific neutrality'. Instead, Hegelianism has always constituted a central aspect of Italy's political culture, where Hegel's philosophy was constantly rethought and reshaped according to different moments of the nation's political development.[52] As Norberto Bobbio noted, in Italian political history 'all roads lead to Hegel, or, rather, all roads begin from Hegel'.[53] On a similar note, Sergio Landucci has argued that, in Italy, Hegelianism always represented an 'element of the nation's civil life', a 'civil force' in support of national unification.[54] Therefore, unlike certain strands of interpretation elsewhere in Europe, in Italy Hegel retained a revolutionary potential. Thus, by looking at Italian political thought through the lens of Hegel's 'presence' in Italy, this book not only fills a gap in philosophical scholarship but also sheds new light on Italian political thought.

The focus on Italian Hegelianism exemplifies an approach to the history of political thought that accentuates different modes of reception and the amalgamation of ideas into new intellectual contexts. It also helps to place the study of Italian Hegelianism within a wider context of recent historiographical approaches to Risorgimento political thought. Italian engagement with Hegel was a direct response to Italians' own experiences of a dramatic change in the semantics of historical time since the end of the Seven Years' War, followed shortly after by the American and French

---

[52] Eugenio Garin, 'La "fortuna" nella filosofia italiana', in *L'opera e l'eredità di Hegel*, ed. G. Calabrò (Bari: Laterza, 1972), pp. 123–138.

[53] Norberto Bobbio, *Da Hobbes a Marx. Saggi di storia della filosofia* (Naples: Morano, 1965), p. 237.

[54] Sergio Landucci, 'L'hegelismo in Italia nell'età del Risorgimento', *Studi Storici*, 4, 1965: 597–628.

Revolutions. Due to its transnational perspective, the interest in Italian Hegelianism shares important ground with other fields of modern Italian history that over the last few decades have examined, for instance, the impact of European romanticism on Italy's cultural and intellectual development[55] or the role of international experiences in shaping ideas in the Italian peninsula.[56]

A central purpose of this book is to understand this shift from the intellectual reconstruction of the Italian national narratives during the Risorgimento to the political movement leading to Italian unification. The 'nation', is a continuous process of historical and cultural reconstruction and political negotiation that was far from being a straightforward or self-evident entity. The prevailing understanding of the idea of nation during the Risorgimento is linked to the debate on 'national character', a term that, as highlighted by Georgios Varouxakis, was often used by nineteenth-century European historians as an 'explanatory category'.[57] Emphasising the Risorgimento's many different political voices means highlighting Italy's intellectual diversity during the eighteenth and nineteenth centuries but also its close connection with wider European thought and with multiple political experiences.

The term 'regeneration' had been most current during the 'revolutionary triennium' (1796–1799) in Italy, when the influence of French republicanism was at its height. As Lucien Jaume has recently pointed out, the discourse on the French Revolution continually refers to the principle of regeneration (*régénération*).[58] Scrutiny of French dictionaries suggests that during the Enlightenment and, indeed, up until the French Revolution,

---

[55] Alberto Mario Banti and Paul Ginsborg (eds.), *Storia d'Italia. Annali 22. Il Risorgimento* (Turin: Einaudi, 2007); Silvana Patriarca and Lucy Riall (eds.), *The Risorgimento Revisited. Nationalism and Culture in Nineteenth Century Italy* (New York: Palgrave Macmillan, 2014); Lucy Riall, 'The Politics of Italian Romanticism: Mazzini and the Making of a Nationalist Culture', in *Giuseppe Mazzini and the Globalisation of Democratic Nationalism 1830–1920*, ed. C. A. Bayly and E. F. Biagini (Oxford: Oxford University Press, 2008), pp. 167–186; Martin Thom, *Republics, Nations and Tribes* (London: Verso, 1995).

[56] Enrico Dal Lago, *The Age of Lincoln and Cavour. Comparative Perspectives on Nineteenth-Century American and Italian Nation-Building* (New York: Palgrave: 2015); Isabella, *Risorgimento in Exile*; Oliver Janz and Lucy Riall (eds.) 'The Italian Risorgimento: Transnational Perspectives', *Modern Italy*, 19, 1, 2014; D. Kirchner Reill, *Nationalists Who Feared the Nation. Adriatic Multi-Nationalism in Habsburg Dalmatia, Trieste, and Venice* (Stanford, CA: Stanford University Press, 2012); Axel Körner, 'Transnational History: Identities, Structures, States', in *International History in Theory and Praxis*, ed. B. Haider-Wilson, W. D. Godsey and W. Mueller (Vienna: Verlag der Österreichischen Akademie der Wissenschaften, 2017), pp. 265–290.

[57] Georgios Varouxakis, 'The Discreet Charm of 'Southernness', *Journal of Modern Italian Studies*, 17, no. 5, 2012: 547–550.

[58] Lucien Jaume, 'Réformer, Régénérer, Renaître: Un imaginaire de l'Occident? La clef Révolution française', *Transversalités*, 137, 2016: 23–35.

the term *'régénération'* was used only with a religious meaning and was not deployed in the political arena. After 1789, this term passed from the religious domain, to which it had previously been restricted, to the political, moral, and social domains.[59] The myth of the regeneration of the nation is indeed also connected with the widespread attempt among nineteenth-century historians to reconstruct the various 'national characters', related to the diverse narratives concerning the origins of the nation. The political culture of the national movement in the first half of the nineteenth century in Italy was far from uniform, and the different definitions offered of the Italian national character were connected to the diverse interpretations of the origins of the nation – such as the debate on the antiquity of the Italian nation, or the myth of the Catholic roots of Italian culture, as well as the narrative tracing the origins of the Italian nation back to the 'communal age of freedom' and the early medieval *comuni*.[60] The idea of the regeneration of the nation implies therefore the return to a human essence, forgotten or suppressed, and this is possible only through a revolution. Revolution, in short, offers the promise of emancipation, which has shifted from the religious to the political sphere, involving as it does what Jaume calls a *transfert de religiosité(s)*.[61] This definition highlights the inner, subjective tensions within the general aspiration towards regeneration, entailing something other than the merely external dimension of ceremonies and symbols related to the new cults.

[59] See Mona Ozouf, *L'homme régénéré: Essais sur la Révolution française* (Paris: Gallimard, 1989), pp. 116–157

[60] For a general overview regarding the debate on the different myths building Italian national narratives, see the recent work by Rosario Forlenza and Bjørn Thomassen, *Italian Modernities: Competing Narratives of Nationhood* (Basingstoke: Palgrave Macmillan, 2016). Regarding the myth of Roman and Etruscan origins, see in particular Antonino De Francesco, *The Antiquity of the Italian Nation: The Cultural Origins of a Political Myth in Modern Italy, 1796–1943* (Oxford: Oxford University Press, 2013); Paolo Casini, *L'antica sapienza italica. Cronistoria di un mito* (Bologna: Il Mulino, 1998); Axel Körner, *Politics of Culture in Liberal Italy: From Unification to Fascism* (London: Routledge, 2009). For a deeper understanding of the narrative of the Catholic roots of the Italian nation, see Guido Formigoni, *L'Italia dei cattolici. Dal Risorgimento ad oggi* (Bologna: Il Mulino, 2010), pp. 35–59; Francesco Traniello, *Religione cattolica e Stato nazionale. Dal Risorgimento al secondo dopoguerra* (Bologna. Il Mulino, 2007), pp. 7–57; Martin Papenheim, 'Roma o Morte: Culture Wars in Italy', in *Culture Wars: Secular-Catholic Conflict in Ninetenth-Century Europe*, ed. Christopher Clark and Wolfram Kaiser (Cambridge: Cambridge University Press, 2003), pp. 202–226. The republican myth has been explored by Forlenza and Thomassen, *Italian Modernities*, pp. 23–55; see also Norma Bouchard (ed.), *Risorgimento in Modern Italian Culture: Rethinking the Nineteenth-Century Past in History, Narrative, and Cinema* (Cranbury, NJ: Farleigh Dickinson University Press, 2005).

[61] Lucien Jaume, *Le Religieux et le politique dans la Révolution française. L'idée de régénération* (Paris: PUF, 2015), p. 7; on this debate, see also Josep R. Llobera, *The God of Modernity: The Development of Nationalism in Western Europe* (London: Bloomsbury, 1996); Anthony W. Marx, *Faith in Nation: Exclusionary Origins of Nationalism* (Oxford: Oxford University Press, 2003).

In Italian, the two terms 'regeneration' (*rigenerazione*) and 'resurgence' (*risorgimento*) coexisted during the first half of the nineteenth century, while in its latter half the word '*Risorgimento*' took precedence.[62]

During the nineteenth century, Italian political language underwent a radical transformation: while the term *Risorgimento* had generally indicated a specific period of modern history (approximately from the fourteenth to the sixteenth centuries), by the end of the century that term began to be identified with the Italian struggles for national emancipation.[63] At the same time, the word *Renaissance* began to be used to indicate the period of early modern history between the fourteenth and the sixteenth centuries, also identified with the birth of 'Modernity'. This change in the language represents a shift from an interpretation that highlights the religious and moral dimensions of the principle of Italian modernity to one that stresses its historical characteristics. Such a shift from an ethical-political meaning to a historiographical one consists of an interpretative transformation of the origins of modern national culture: initially the Renaissance was considered a political and moral model, to emulate or to condemn, but it then assumed the role of a historiographical category.

That transformation in the language represents a change of ideas or rather, in this case, of the way the intellectual and political leaders of the Risorgimento interpreted the failed religious and moral reformation in Italy of the early modern period. While recent scholarship has highlighted how the term *Risorgimento* came to mark a 'symbolic repositioning from the religious to the political' dimension of the term, it was still confused with the *Renaissance* as then understood.[64] Linguistic studies have traced a semantic history of the two terms, *Risorgimento* and *Rinascimento*, illustrating how political and ideological factors conditioned their use and the meanings they carried.[65] This book investigates this change in the political language, proving that it was also a consequence of a deeper study and understanding of the Renaissance as a historical period and its main

---

[62] See Erasmo Leso, *Lingua e rivoluzione: Ricerche sul vocabolario politico italiano nel triennio rivoluzionario 1796–1799* (Venice: Istituto Veneto di Scienze, Lettere e Arti, 1991), pp. 153–154. By 'language' here I refer mainly to the notion elaborated by J. G. A. Pocock, 'Introduction: the State of the Art', in *Virtue, Commerce and History: Essays on Political Thought and History, Chiefly in the Eighteenth Century* (Cambridge: Cambridge University Press, 1985), pp. 1–34.

[63] On the complex debate regarding the dating of the Renaissance, see Delio Cantimori, 'La periodizzazione dell'età del Rinascimento', (1955), in *Storici e storia* (Turin: Einaudi, 1971), pp. 553–557.

[64] Banti et al., *Atlante culturale del Risorgimento*, p33.

[65] Alessio Cotugno, 'Rinascimento e Risorgimento (sec. XVIII–XIX)', *Lingua e Stile*, 2, 2012: 265–310.

protagonists, such as Giordano Bruno, Tommaso Campanella, or Niccolo' Machiavelli, promoted by the Italian Hegelians.

The idea of the need for a regeneration (or resurgence) of the moral and intellectual life of Italians was connected to the widespread assumption among European and Italian intellectuals that the Italian character suffered from a backwardness, laziness, and indolence.[66] In order to assume a new role as a modern nation, the Italians needed first, or so it was supposed, a moral and intellectual revolution: the incessant references to the regeneration of the nation in Italian political discourse, from the republicans to the most conservative political groups, demonstrate a process of self-othering among the national elites. As Lucy Riall has emphasised: 'nationalism in Italy was born from a sense of weakness: of resistance to Napoleon's conquests; of inferiority towards Italy's neighbours, and of loss relative to a glorious past .... Even nationalism's appeal in Italy comes from a feeling of failure, offering as it does the dream of regeneration (*risorgimento*), against which the squalid state of the present-day nation is judged and found lacking'.[67] Historians, philosophers, and publicists played a fundamental role in readapting and reshaping collective memories, as well as in creating a national narrative.[68] This book contributes to the understanding of these narratives by engaging with the scholarly debates regarding the role of the Italian South in the Risorgimento.

The process of Italian unification has often been portrayed in the historiography as a process of royal conquest, whereby its principal architect, Cavour, together with the King Vittorio Emanuele, imposed Piedmontese rule on the rest of the Peninsula. Moreover, the representation of Southern Italy in many Northern Italian accounts as a backward and uncivilised land has led historians in recent years to portray the South

---

[66] For a more specific analysis of these stereotypes regarding the Italian national character, see Silvana Patriarca, 'Indolence and Regeneration: Tropes and Tensions of Risorgimento Patriotism', *The American Historical Review*, 110, no. 2, April 2005: 380–408.

[67] Lucy Riall, 'Which Italy? Italian Culture and the Problem of Politics', *Journal of Contemporary History*, 39, no. 3, 2004: 437–446, 438.

[68] For an overview of historical narratives, see Alun Munslow, *Narrative and History* (Basingstoke: Palgrave, 2007). Also see Hayden White, *The Content of the Form: Narrative Discourse and Historical Representation* (Baltimore: Johns Hopkins University Press, 1990). For national narrative, see Homi Bhabha (ed.), *Nation and Narration* (London: Routledge, 1990). Also see the essays in Stefan Berger, Linas Eriksonas, and Andrew Mycock (eds.), *Narrating the Nation: Representations in History, Media, and the Arts* (New York: Berghahn, 2008); and Joep Leerssen, 'Setting the Scene for National History', in *Nationalizing the Past: Historians as Nation Builders in Modern Europe*, ed. Stefan Berger and Chris Lorenz (Basingstoke: Palgrave Macmillan, 2010), pp. 71–85. For a discussion on this scholarship, see the recent work by Matthew D'Auria, *The Shaping of French National Identity: Narrating the Nation's Past, 1715–1830* (Cambridge: Cambridge University Press, 2020).

through the 'logic of coloniality'.[69] Studies by Jane Schneider, John Dickie, Nelson Moe, and Silvana Patriarca have thus explored the widespread proliferation of stereotypes representing Southern Italy in the aftermath of unification, in the process often going beyond the analysis of the so-called Southern Question – which investigates instead the economic and political differences between the North and the South of the Peninsula.[70]

Very recently, scholars such as Roberto Dainotto, Luigi Carmine Cazzato, and Claudio Fogu have considered the process of Italian nation-building through the lens of postcolonial critical studies, applying the logic of Edward Said's Orientalism to Southern Europe, and Southern Italy, and so proposing a discursive construction of the 'Souths' of Europe dubbed 'Meridionism'.[71] Although the key role of Piedmont in the unification process is beyond dispute, these approaches tend to overshadow local and popular participation, in particular within the Kingdom of Two Sicilies, as well as the work of Southern Italian political representatives in the new Parliament.

This book explores the contribution of the political thought and political practices of Italian Hegelians, most of whom were from the South, to the building of the new Italian State. Many of them had first served the Kingdom of Italy in the Southern provinces during the delicate transition period, then in the central government and parliament in the early years of state-building, between 1861 and the 1880s, serving as representatives in both of the main parties, the Historical Right (*Destra Storica*), and the Historical Left (*Sinistra Storica*). They reshaped the Hegelian theory of the State to serve the new Italian political context and contributed to the understanding and designing of the new Italian State. In the history of

---

[69] Claudio Fogu, *The Fishing Net and the Spider Web: Mediterranean Imaginaries and the Making of Italians* (London: Palgrave, 2020), p. 17.

[70] On this, see Silvana Patriarca, *Italian Vices: Nation and Character from the Risorgimento to the Republic* (Cambridge; New York: Cambridge University Press, 2010); Jane Schneider (ed.), *Italy's 'Southern Question': Orientalism in One Country* (London: Bloomsbury, 1998), parts 1 and 3; Nelson Moe, *The View from Vesuvius: Italian Culture and the Southern Question* (Berkeley: University of California Press, 2002), especially pp. 187–223; John Dickie, *Darkest Italy: The Nation and Stereotype of the Mezzogiorno, 1860–1900* (London: Macmillan, 1999).

[71] Roberto Dainotto, *Europe (in Theory)* (Durham NC: Duke University Press, 2007); Fogu, *The Fishing Net and the Spider* Web; Luigi Carmine Cazzato, 'Fractured Mediterranean and Imperial Difference: Mediterraneanism, Meridionism, and John Ruskin', *Journal of Mediterranean Studies*, 26, no. 1, 2017: 69–78. On this, see also Matthew D'Auria and Fernanda Gallo, 'Ideas of Europe and the (Modern) Mediterranean', in *Mediterranean Europe(s): Rethinking Europe from Its Southern Shores*, ed. Fernanda Gallo and Matthew D'Auria (London: Routledge, 2022), pp. 1–19.

Italian Hegelianism, Naples and the South played a particularly prominent role. This work will therefore present a critique of conventional hierarchies in the study of Risorgimento political thought.

Within the history of Italian Hegelianism, the pre-eminent role assumed by Naples and the South was never quite matched by North Italian interest in the German philosopher. This discrepancy constitutes the basis for a key argument in this book and addresses a central issue of historiographical debates on modern Italy, namely, the relationship between North and South and the South's role in Italy's relationship to the wider world. In this context, it is important to note that the stereotyping of the Italian South as backward and different from the North emerged early in the history of Risorgimento political thought. Since the late eighteenth century, various thinkers associated with the Neapolitan Enlightenment, Antonio Genovesi and Gaetano Filangieri among them, had identified a number of social and cultural problems that allegedly were specific to the Italian South and made it difficult to reform the Kingdom of Naples. Many of their arguments were then reiterated by the protagonists of the Neapolitan revolution of 1799, the men and women around Vincenzo Cuoco[72], and subsequently by the Napoleonic administration in Naples.[73] After 1815, political thinkers from the North used this debate on the South to define what it was that made their own realms allegedly more progressive. Writing in the 1840s, Carlo Cattaneo argued that the South lacked most of the features his native Lombardy shared with Central and Northern Europe, due to its arbitrary and oppressive system of government. He describes an entirely foreign country, one whose culture contrasts dramatically with the cosmopolitan spirit that characterises the middle classes of Northern Europe.[74] Whereas Cattaneo, relying upon this analysis, and as a matter of principle, would for a long time question the rationale of politically unifying the Italian peninsula into a single

---

[72] See Marta Petrusewicz, *Come il Meridione divenne una Questione. Rappresentazione del Sud prima e dopo il Quarantotto* (Soveria Mannelli: Rubbettino, 1998), pp. 17–20; Franco Venturi, *Riformatori napoletani* (Milan-Naples: Ricciardi, 1962).

[73] John Davis, *Naples and Napoleon. Southern Italy and the European Revolutions, 1780–1860* (Oxford: Oxford University Press, 2006).

[74] Nelson Moe, *The View from Vesuvius. Italian Culture and the Southern Question* (Berkeley: University of California Press: 2002), pp. 104–107; Fabio Sabetti, *Civilization and Self-Government. The Political Thought of Carlo Cattaneo* (Lanham, MD: Lexington Books: 2010); On Cattaneo's views on Southern Italy, see F. Gallo, 'The United States of Europe and the "East (s)": Giusppe Mazzini, Carlo Cattaneo, and Cristina Trivulzio di Belgiojoso', in *Europe and the East: Historical Ideas of Eastern and Southeast Europe, 1789–1989*, ed. Mark Hewitson and Jan Vermeiren (London: Routledge, 2023), pp. 133–162.

nation-state, other political thinkers concluded that the North was under an obligation to lead the South into political modernity.

The study of Italian Hegelianism presents us with a very different image of the South. Taking account of its flourishing tradition of philosophical debate, it becomes obvious that the Italian South in no way represented an intellectual periphery of Europe – an argument that can easily be extended to the South's role in the history of European art and music or in the history of science. There is a long tradition of Anglophone historiography from Patrick Chorley, *Oil, Silk and Enlightenment. Economic Problems in XVIIIth-Century Naples* to the works of John Robertson, such as *The Case for the Enlightenment. Scotland and Naples, 1680–1760* and John Davis' *Naples and Napoleon. Southern Italy and the European Revolutions, 1780–1860*, that has attempted to raise the profile of the Southern contribution to Italian intellectual history of the late eighteenth and the early nineteenth century.[75] The transnational orientation of its cultural and intellectual life bears witness to the centrality of its position within the Italian peninsula and within Europe. As a consequence, the South also assumes a particularly prominent role when the history of Italy's political emancipation is placed in the context of larger transnational debates and of Italy's multiple imperial connections.[76] Moreover, Italians were conscious of their own contribution to the ideas and the political institutions of the world's most progressive nations.

As recent studies on the representations of the 'margins' of Europe, from Ireland to the Balkans, have indicated, these lands have undergone a process of Othering since the eighteenth century in connection with Europe's attempts to define its identity and with the rise of nationalism.[77] This book aspires to rethink Italian political thought by focussing on how the creative amalgamation of Hegel's ideas with Italian culture led to a

---

[75] See Patrick Chorley, *Oil, Silk and Enlightenment. Economic Problems in XVIIIth-Century Naples* (Naples: Istituto Italiano per gli Studi Storici in Napoli, 1965); John Robertson, *The Case for the Enlightenment. Scotland and Naples, 1680–1760* (Cambridge: Cambridge University Press, 2005); John Davis, *Naples and Napoleon. Southern Italy and the European Revolutions, 1780–1860*.

[76] See the works of Maurizio Isabella, *Risorgimento in Exile*; and 'Nationality Before Liberty?'; Axel Körner, 'National Movements against Nation States. Bohemia and Lombardy between the Habsburg Empire, the German Confederation and Piedmont', in *The 1848 Revolutions and European Political Thought*, ed. D. Moggach and G. Stedman Jones (Cambridge: Cambridge University Press, 2018), pp. 345–382; Konstantina Zanou, *Transnational Patriotism in the Mediterranean, 1800–1850. Stammering the Nation*, (Oxford: Oxford University Press, 2018).

[77] See Marta Petrusewicz, 'Rethinking Centre and Periphery in Historical Analysis: Land-based Modernization as an Alternative Model from the Peripheries', in *Remapping Centre and Periphery: Asymmetrical Encounters in European and Global Context*, ed. T. Hauswedell, A. Körner and U. Tiedau (London: UCL Press, 2019), pp. 17–26; Maria Todorova, *Imagining the Balkans* (Oxford: Oxford University Press, 1997).

rethinking of historical and political concepts that greatly influenced the intellectual history of modern Italy and, indeed, of Europe as a whole.

The narrative offered by Italian Hegelians was intended to shape the idea of a modern Italian State regenerated by the encounter of their own fruitful intellectual traditions with the most advanced European philosophy, namely the Hegelian. As clearly described by Axel Körner in his recent work *America in Italy*, the process of amalgamation is never simply a matter of passive reception but is rather a translation into a new context, a complex process that leads to results that often bear little similarity to the original.[78] Analysing Italian Hegelianism allows us to reject the idea that engagement with foreign ideas describes a process of passive learning, in the sense of adopting supposedly more advanced ideas from abroad; and the same applies to intellectual flows within the Italian peninsula. As Marta Petrusewicz has explained, North and South exist in a relationship of otherness, where self-perceptions of the North depend on the image of an Other in the South, which in turn is then internalised by Italians from all over the peninsula.[79] Such processes of internalisation are foundational of hegemonic relationships and teleological distortions, whereby the South supposedly needs the North in order to leave its position of self-imposed inferiority. Rather than accepting such intellectual hierarchies, this book tries to identify original acts of creative amalgamation. Each of the five chapters of this book analyses one of these acts of amalgamation.

In Chapter 1, 'The Vico-Effect', this research explores how, in different parts of the Peninsula, Hegel's thought circulated in the guise of translations and commentaries from 1832 up to 1848. It then reconstructs the intellectual context of Naples and the Kingdom of Two Sicilies, paying particular attention to how the interpretation of the philosophy of Giambattista Vico (1668–1744), often viewed in relation to Victor Cousin's (1792–1867) reading of the Neapolitan philosopher, was combined with the study first of the philosophy of Immanuel Kant (1724–1804) and then of G. W. F. Hegel (1770–1831). Key figures in this process are Ottavio Colecchi, Stanislao Gatti, Stefano Cusani, and Francesco De Sanctis. Finally, it defines the context in which the school of

---

[78] Axel Körner, *America in Italy: The United States in the Political Thought and Imagination of the Risorgimento, 1763–1865* (Princeton: Princeton University Press, 2017).

[79] Marta Petrusewicz, *Come il Meridione divenne una Questione. Rappresentazione del Sud prima e dopo il Quarantotto* (Soveria Mannelli: Rubbettino, 1998); on this topic see also Silvana Patriarca, *Italian Vices. Nation and Character from the Risorgimento to the Republic* (Cambridge: Cambridge University Press, 2010).

Neapolitan Hegelianism arose, highlighting the novelty of the 'principle of nationality' as a product of this amalgamation. The elaboration in 1848 of the idea of 'nationality' characterising an organicist view of the law and the State, connected to the unitary aspirations and endeavours of the Risorgimento, would transform Neapolitan Hegelianism from a local tradition of thought into a national experience. By engaging with Hegel's ideas, the Neapolitan intellectuals developed their political revolutionary practice in 1848. After the revolution, while in prison or exile, Italian Hegelians further refine the reflection on Italian philosophy in order to enhance that process of self-consciousness of the nation.

Chapter 2, 'The Renaissance', illustrates how Italian Hegelians, and in particular Marianna Florenzi Waddington and Bertrando Spaventa, between 1848 and the 1860s, contributed to the understanding of the philosophical tradition of the Italian Renaissance by rediscovering the works of Giordano Bruno. They traced a line of continuity between the Italian Renaissance and German Idealism by arguing that 'the last disciple of Bruno was Hegel'. They challenged the myth of the Hegelian 'Protestant Supremacy', amalgamating the widespread criticism regarding Italian Catholicism, and presented an alternative path to 'Modernity' traced by the Italian philosophers of the Renaissance. Bruno insisted on the autonomy of conscience and the infinite value of human dignity by reformulating existing notions of moral and political liberty. They affirmed the peculiar bond between historiography, philosophy, and politics that characterised Italian culture during the nineteenth century.

This connection is also at the heart of Chapter 3, 'The Risorgimento', in which it is the key figure of Niccolo' Machiavelli that allows Italian Hegelians, and in particular Francesco De Sanctis, Francesco Fiorentino, and Pasquale Villari, to challenge the idea of an Italian 'missed Reformation', recasting the Renaissance as 'the Italian version of the Reformation'. The rediscovery of Machiavelli's work is connected to the radical change that nineteenth-century Italian political language underwent regarding the nexus of *Rinascimento–Risorgimento*. This chapter demonstrates that the change in the language represents a shift from an interpretation that highlights the religious and moral dimensions of the principle of Italian modernity to one that stresses its historical characteristics.

It is in Chapter 4, 'The Ethical State', that the context of the Risorgimento is explored more closely while scrutinising Hegel's political thought and comparing his texts with Italian Hegelians' commentaries and interpretations of Hegel's philosophy. It focuses in particular on Marianna

Florenzi Waddington, Bertrando Spaventa, and Silvio Spaventa. It then examines how nineteenth-century interpretations of Hegel were rehearsed and redeployed by the main Italian scholars of Idealism in the twentieth century, Benedetto Croce and Giovanni Gentile.

Chapter 5, 'Hegelians in Charge', extends further the key argument of the book, exploring the contribution of the political thought and political practices of Italian Hegelians, to the building of the new Italian State. This chapter focuses in particular on Silvio Spaventa and Francesco De Sanctis and how they reshaped the Hegelian theory of the State to serve the new Italian political context and to contribute to the understanding and designing of the nascent Italian State. It investigates the laws they proposed, the Parliamentary speeches they delivered, and the political pamphlets they wrote, discussing contemporary political issues often addressed by having recourse to Hegel's ideas reshaped to respond to the challenges presented by their own time. The chapter concludes by exploring the influence of Italian Hegelianism on Antonio Labriola's 'philosophy of praxis', which is an original reading of Marxism and one that preserves some of the key traits of the Italian Hegelian reading of Hegel. Italian Hegelianism was shaped by a 'practical' understanding of Hegel's philosophy, whereby it insisted on the historical, ethical, and political dimensions of Hegel's metaphysics and attempted to realise Hegelian political ideas in the practice of political life. This critical approach would be passed on to the Italian Hegelians' dearest pupil, Labriola, and would persist as a trait of Italian engagement with Marx's political thought.

The Epilogue focuses on the influence and legacy of nineteenth-century Italian Hegelianism by investigating how Benedetto Croce, Giovanni Gentile, and Antonio Gramsci re-elaborated this tradition at the turn of the new century in order to develop their own philosophical systems, their interpretation of Hegel, Marx, and the relationship between politics and ethics, as well as their understanding of Italian history and of the role of intellectuals in the formation of the Italian state.

By presenting the story of this generation of intellectuals who engaged with Hegel's philosophy while actively participating in Italian political life in the nineteenth century, this book contributes to the scholarly debates on Hegel and Italian Hegelianism, on the history of political thought and intellectual history, and on Italian political thought and the Risorgimento. It traces the development through the century of the political and philosophical ideas of a group of scholars and politicians who from the Southern periphery of Europe engaged with the philosophy of Hegel and raised them as subjects of thought. It offers a perspective on a time of radical political and intellectual transformation undergone by one of the most spectacular instances of nation- and state-building of nineteenth-century Europe by presenting one of the many bodies of political thought, certainly one of the most influential in modern Italy. It is in history that philosophy acquires its political relevance.

CHAPTER I

The 'Vico-Effect'

If modern philosophy is ever to have a future . . ., this will not unfold in Germany, France, or England, but in Italy, and in particular on these marvellous shores of Southern Italy [the Mezzogiorno].
—Theodor Sträter, *Briefe über die Italianische Philosophie*, 1864

While gazing at the River Neva in Saint Petersburg from the palace of the Russian Academy of Science, with its bright yellow plasterwork and dazzling white pillars – the work of the neoclassicist Venetian architect Giacomo Quarenghi (1744–1817) – Abbot Ottavio Colecchi (1773–1847) must surely have pondered how markedly the vista differed from that of his own home town, for he had been born in a place almost completely hidden by the mountains of the Apennines, the village of Pescocostanzo, in the Abruzzo, one of the most remote provinces of the Kingdom of Two Sicilies.[1] That morning of May 1818, after lecturing on 'Paraboloid', Colecchi received the honour of being elected correspondent member of the Academy for Mathematics.[2] This probably seemed to him the crowning moment of his career, after many years spent studying and teaching mathematics and philosophy, having originally entered the Dominican convent in Ortona del Mare (Abruzzo) in 1794. He was the firstborn of a family of humble origins, and, after the death of his father, an ecclesiastical career seemed the only plausible path to pursuing his studies further and supporting his family. During the French domination of Naples (1806–1815) under the rule first of Joseph Bonaparte (1768–1844) and then of Joachim Murat (1767–1815), religious orders

---

[1] S. D. Skazkin, *Russia and Italy: From the History of Russian-Italian Cultural and Societal Relations* (in Russian) (Moscow: Nauka, 1968), p. 22.

[2] The Archive of the Academy of Science holds the manuscript of the lecture by Abbot Ottavio Colecchi 'Paraboloid', presented on the 20th of May 1818. See also *List of Members of the Imperial Academy of Science, 1725–1907* (Saint Petersburg: The Imperial Academy of Sciences, 1908).

were suppressed, and Colecchi, a secular priest, moved to Naples, where he published his first mathematical works.[3]

After the Congress of Vienna and the change in the political regime, Colecchi was suspected by the ecclesiastical authorities of being of a liberal political orientation. He was then sent in 1816 to Russia to teach at the University of Saint Petersburg. During this time abroad he spent a period of study in Königsberg, where he came into contact with the philosophy of Kant and learnt German. When in the autumn of 1819 Colecchi returned to his own country to teach physics and mathematics at the gymnasium in L'Aquila (Abruzzo), very few would have imagined that the main interpreter and advocate of Kant in Italy was taking up his post in that remote Southern province.

Being one of the very few Italian scholars of Kant capable of reading the original German texts, he was by the same token an original interpreter of his philosophy, which he was the very first to present in its full complexity to Italian readers. When the 1820/21 revolution broke out in Naples, he did not hide his liberal sympathies, eventually losing his job after the suppression of the revolution in 1821, when, indeed, a very dark period began for liberals in the Kingdom of Two Sicilies. King Ferdinando I di Borbone (1751–1825) was very hostile to intellectuals, or 'scribblers' (*pennaruli*), as he used to call them, reckoning that they bore the chief responsibility for the opposition to the crown since the 1799 Neapolitan republic.

After the revolutionary triennium in Italy (1796–1799) and the revolutions of 1820/21 in Naples, Palermo, and Turin, Italian intellectuals were mainly concerned to make sense of those historical events and perhaps to reassess and even renegotiate the meaning of the revolutionary experiences. Colecchi shared these preoccupations. Discussions about the utility and conceptualisation of history, and therefore about the philosophy of history, were at the heart of the intellectual debate. There were three philosophies that seemed, to Italian intellectuals, able to support the understanding of these revolutionary processes and that, combined in different ways, determined the peculiar reading of Hegel developed in Italy: the philosophies of Giambattista Vico (see Figure 1.1), Immanuel Kant, and Victor Cousin. Colecchi was the first to merge these three approaches. The precise way in which these theories were discussed and combined with Hegel's philosophy differed markedly for the various authors this chapter investigates, both because of the diversity of political contexts across the Italian States in

---

[3] See 'Memoria sulle forze vive' and 'Riflessioni su alcuni opuscoli che trattano delle frazioni fratte', *Biblioteca analitica*, 1811.

Figure 1.1   Giambattista Vico, 1861, Naples, Villa Comunale

the first half of the nineteenth century and because of the greater or lesser access to original sources and texts these intellectuals enjoyed. Despite these differences, the main tendency in Italian political thought was to interpret Hegel's philosophy as being closer to realism than to idealism, to history than to philosophy, to reality than to theory, to practice than to ideas. To Italian intellectuals at that date it seemed evident that, as Richard Bourke has phrased it, 'philosophy, to be effective, needs to work with the grain of history'.[4]

This chapter will first explore how, in different parts of the Peninsula, Hegel's thought circulated in the guise of translations and commentaries from 1832 up to 1848. It will then reconstruct the intellectual context of Naples and the Kingdom of Two Sicilies, starting with Ottavio Colecchi's philosophy and moving on to his students Stanislao Gatti and Stefano Cusani, as well as Francesco De Sanctis. It pays particular attention to how the interpretation of the philosophy of Vico, often in those years associated with Cousin's reading of the Neapolitan philosopher, was combined with the study of the philosophy of Kant first and latterly of Hegel. Finally, it will define the context in which the school of Neapolitan Hegelianism arose and will highlight the novelty of the 'principle of nationality' as a product of this amalgamation. The elaboration in 1848 of the idea of 'nationality' characterising an organicist view of the law and the State, connected to the unitary aspirations and endeavours of the Risorgimento, would transform Neapolitan Hegelianism from a local tradition of thought to a national experience. By engaging with Hegel's ideas, the Neapolitan intellectuals would develop their political revolutionary practice in 1848.

1.1   Hegel in Italy

Hegel's philosophy had been debated and discussed in Italy even before it was really known. Very few intellectuals there were familiar with German, and most of them were influenced by French eclecticism and its interpretations or translations of Hegel, as well as by the philosophy of Giambattista Vico. Even at the outset, or the very first time one of Hegel's works was discussed in Italy, it was associated with Vico's philosophy and, in particular, with his *New Science*, although it was sometimes more an 'obligatory reference' than a real comparison. When in 1832 Giandomenico Romagnosi (1761–1835) had published in the Florentine *Antologia* – one of the most important and widely read journals in nineteenth-century Italy, directed by Giovan Pietro Vieusseux and Gino Capponi – a letter entitled 'Alcuni pensieri sopra un'ultra-metafisica filosofia della storia' (Some Thoughts on an Ultra-Metaphysical Philosophy of History), his comments on Hegel's *Philosophy of History*

---

[4] Richard Bourke, *Hegel's World Revolutions* (Princeton: Princeton University Press, 2023), p. 152.

were anticipated by the sentence: 'The science of human affairs and histories was begun in Italy by Vico.'[5] Vico was not at the heart of this essay, nor was the comparison further developed, but it sets the tone for the Italian approach to the reading of Hegel. The author also clarifies that his knowledge of Hegel was based on the comments made by Eugène Lerminier (1803–1857) in his *Introduction générale à l'histoire du droit* (*General Introduction to the History of Right*, 1829), from which he translated parts into Italian in order to prove that Hegel's notion of *Weltgeist* (World Spirit) is abstract and that his *Philosophy of History* presents a metaphysical understanding of history in which the Universal Spirit would seem to be completely separate from history as such.[6] Romagnosi's understanding of Vico was connected to his own cultivation of a 'civil philosophy' dedicated to the notion of human perfectibility (*incivilimento*) and concerned with 'the study of the concrete processes (economic, moral, and political) that attend to the making of civilisation'.[7] Romagnosi's civil philosophy was influenced by Vico's notion of the historical development of humanity wherby knowledge advances in association with the socio-historical context. At the heart of the Romagnosian perspective were the historical process and the natural order: law and rights, were not the product of a social contract but the result of a rational natural order and its historical development.[8] This was Vico's legacy.

In northern Italy, in the republican circles in Milan, comments on Hegel's *Philosophy of History* appeared in the works of one of Romagnosi's students, Giuseppe Ferrari (1811–1876), with a clear reference to Giambattista Vico. These contributions must be understood in the context of a general rediscovery of Vico across the Italian States in the 1830s, when plans to publish Vico's works were being mooted in different

---

[5] *Antologia*, vol. 96, p. 289.

[6] Giandomenico Romagnosi, 'Alcuni pensieri sopra un'ultrametafisica filosofia della storia', *Antologia. Giornale di Scienze, Lettere e Arti*, 46, no. 16, 1832: 23–36; then published in G. Romagnosi, *Dell'indole e dei fattori di incivilimento con esempio del suo Risorgimento in Italia* (Florence: Piatti, 1834), pp. 289–304. See also J. L. E. Lerminier, *Introduction générale à l'histoire du droit* (Brussels: Tarlier, 1829).

[7] Rocco Rubini, 'The Vichian "Renaissance" between Giuseppe Ferrari and Jules Michelet', *Intellectual History Review*, 26, no. 1, 2016: 9–15, 11.

[8] On this, see Giuseppe Grieco, 'A Legal Theory for the Nation State. Pasquale Stanislao Mancini, Hegelianism and Piedmontese Liberalism after 1848', *Journal of Modern Italian Studies*, 24, no. 2, 2019: 266–292; G. Cospito, 'Romagnosi e Cattaneo tra istanze illuministiche ed eredità vichiane', *Materiali per una storia della cultura giuridica*, 32, no. 2, 2002: 413–415; P. Costa, *Civitas. Storia della cittadinanza in Europa*, vol. 2: *L'età delle rivoluzioni (1789–1848)* (Rome-Bari: Laterza, 2000), pp. 497–511.

parts of the Peninsula.[9] Between 1835 and 1837 Ferrari published Vico's works in six volumes in the edition *Opere di Giambattista Vico ordinate e illustrate coll'analisi della mente di Vico in relazione alla scienza della civiltà*.[10] Ferrari's interpretation considers Vico's work a 'miniature of the 19th century... for his ideas on poetry, myths, religions, history ... and the course of history'.[11] The 1725 edition of the *New Science* loomed especially large since there, according to Ferrari, the Neapolitan philosopher had investigated the history of humanity through the history of ideas, without forcing the facts into an abstract system of ideas. Ferrari disagreed, however, with Vico's theory of historical courses and recourses and therefore with a circular vision of history that foresaw the inevitable return of barbarism, for this vision was at odds with the progressive conception of civilisation, influenced by the Milanese Enlightenment, and Ferrari's 'theory of mind'. This theory, reminiscent to some degree of Hegel's *Geist* (spirit), endorses the progress made in human history, as described by Vico, 'an ideal eternal history traversed in time by the histories of all nations'.[12] As Ferrari states, 'Philosophy seeks out the elements of human reason in the unfolding of history: for Hegel history is the thought of world history, [while] philosophy is the final scene in the drama of humanity.'[13] In Ferrari's case his reflection on the meanings and uses of history also draws attention to Vico and Hegel. When Ferrari moved to Paris in 1838, his essay on Vico was published in French with the title *Vico et l'Italie* (1839) and adapted to a French audience, contextualising Vico's contribution within his conception of the Italian tradition of thought since the sixteenth century. Years later, in his *Filosofia della rivoluzione* (1851) Ferrari affirmed that Hegel 'is the most powerful observer of the contradictions that have troubled the philosophers and the legislators. In this field he is no longer metaphysical but physical, historical'.[14] Hegel's

---

[9] On this, see the work by Marina Piperno, *Rebuilding Post-revolutionary Italy: Leopardi and Vico's 'New Science'* (Oxford: Voltaire Foundation, 2018).

[10] This edition was published by the Società Tipografica de' Classici Italiani. On this, see M. Martinaro, *Giuseppe Ferrari editore e interprete di Vico* (Naples: Guida, 2001), pp. 45–76. See also M. Martinaro, 'Giambattista Vico a Milano: le interpretazioni di Francesco Predari e Giuseppe Ferrari', *Il Pensiero Italiano. Rivista di Studi Filosofici*, 2, nos. 1–2, 2018: 19–42.

[11] Giuseppe Ferrari, 'Preface' to *La mente di Giambattista Vico* (Milan: Società tipografica dei classici italiani, 1837), p. 170.

[12] G. Vico, *Principi di Scienza Nuova* in *Giambattista Vico: Opere*, ed. A. Battistini (Milan: Mondadori, 1990) (original edition 1744), para. 7. (henceforward *Sn44*). This same phrase recurs, with very slight and inessential variations in paras 114, 145, 245, 393.

[13] Giuseppe Ferrari, 'Preface' to *La mente di Giambattista Vico* (Milan: Società tipografica dei classici italiani, 1837), p. 191.

[14] Giuseppe Ferrari, *Filosofia della rivoluzione* (Milan: Casa Editrice Sociale, 1921), p. 195.

philosophy of history was being interpreted as serving the historical facts, in the same way as Vico's thought was.

When reviewing Ferrari's French publication *Vico et l'Italie* in the periodical *Il Politecnico* in 1839, Carlo Cattaneo (1801–1869) likewise associated the Neapolitan and the German philosopher, recognising how they were the only two theorists to have focused on the history of ideas in the context of an *Ideology of Society*: 'Vico and Hegel embarked upon the history of the ideas of the peoples, they embarked upon the ideology of society.'[15] While Cattaneo greatly admired the work of Vico, who had pointed out important similarities in the historical development of the different nations, he too, like Ferrari, rejected Vico's theory of historical recurrence. In Cattaneo's judgement, the history of civilisation was a slow, constant progress rather than a perpetual cycle of progress and decay: 'The *perpetual cycle* is broken .... Our century has surpassed the humanistic thought of Vico with the two principles of progress and variety.'[16] Regarding his understanding of the philosophy of history, Cattaneo therefore seemed closer to Hegel than to Vico: 'A century later, Hegel recovered the ideology of man-as-people; dissolving Vico's circle, he substituted for it the modern idea of progress.'[17] However, Cattaneo strongly criticised Hegel's metaphysical system: 'All of these abstractions [e.g. Hegel's metaphysical stages] show a tendency to wrap simple principles in an impressive scientific apparatus.'[18] According to Cattaneo, individual and social needs should be met not on the basis of abstract metaphysical notions but rather on concrete data.[19] What was missing in Vico and in Hegel was the connection between the ideology of the individual and that of society, which would constitute Cattaneo's theory of the psychology of societies (*Psicologia delle menti associate*).[20]

---

[15] Carlo Cattaneo, *Scritti filosofici, letterari e vari di Cattaneo*, ed. Franco Alessio (Florence: Sansoni, 1963), p. 67.

[16] Carlo Cattaneo, *Vico et l'Italie*, in 'Il Politecnico', 1839, vol. II, fasc. 9, pp. 251–286; now Carlo Cattaneo, *Su la 'Scienza Nuova' di Vico*, in *Scritti filosofici, letterari e vari di Cattaneo*, ed. Franco Alessio (Florence: Sansoni, 1963), p. 64. On this, see also C. Laicata and F. Sabetti, 'Carlo Cattaneo and Varieties of Liberalism', in *Civilization and Democracy*, ed. C. G. Lacaita and F. Sabetti (Toronto: University of Toronto Press, 2006), pp. 3–52.

[17] Carlo Cattaneo, *Scritti filosofici* (Bari: Laterza, 1965), p. 158.

[18] Carlo Cattaneo, *Scritti filosofici, letterari e vari di Cattaneo*, ed. Franco Alessio (Florence: Sansoni, 1963), p. 66.

[19] See Clara Maria Lovett, *Carlo Cattaneo and the Politics of the Risorgimento, 1820–1860* (The Hague: Mārtiņus Nijhoff, 1972), pp. 10–16.

[20] On Cattaneo's thought, see Lovett, *Carlo Cattaneo and the Politics of the Risorgimento*; see also Filippo Sabetti, *Civilization and Self-Government: The Political Thought of Carlo Cattaneo* (Lanham, MD: Lexington Books, 2010). For a selection of Cattaneo's writings in English translation, see Carlo G. Lacaita and Filippo Sabetti, eds., *Civilization and Democracy: The Salvemini Anthology of*

It was within the context of the Milanese republican circle of Ferrari and Cattaneo that, a few years later, the Princess Cristina Trivulzio di Belgiojoso (1808–1871) published in 1844 the French translation of Vico's *New Science*. She was the host of an intellectual salon in Paris, where she spent long periods of time to avoid the persecution by the Austrian police. In her introductory essay, Belgiojoso acknowledges the beautiful translation of some of Vico's texts by Jules Michelet in his 1827 *Principes de la Philosophie de l'Histoire*, but 'she questions its accuracy, and identifies its eloquence as a domesticating act of cultural imperialism rather than a "proper" translation'.[21] Belgiojoso's translation was widely read in Europe, Karl Marx going so far as to recommend her edition to Ferdinand Lassalle should he wish to understand the 'philosophical view of the spirit of Roman law'.[22] The princess interpreted Vico's theory of 'historical courses and recourses' not as a cycle but as an ascendant movement to the divine source.[23] Like a good number of the other Milanese patriots, she embraces fully the philosophy of history outlined in Vico's *New Science*, and, like Ferrari, she presents the Neapolitan philosopher as a nineteenth-century intellectual *ante litteram*. Indeed Belgiojoso's works, despite the diverse topics on which she published, involved the manifestation of an immanent principle, subject to human action, which transcended the boundaries of individuals and societies.[24] Milanese republican circles thus echoed Jules Michelet's belief – expressed in his 1827 *Discourse on the System and the Life*

Cattaneo's Writings (Toronto: Toronto University Press, 2006). Cattaneo's philosophical texts on social ideology have recently been translated into English by David Gibbons. See Carlo Cattaneo, *Psychology of the Associated Minds*, ed. Barbara Boneschi (Milan: EGEA, 2019).

[21] Sharon Wood, 'Cristina di Belgiojoso: Scholar in Exile', *The Italianist*, 33, no. 1, 2013: 49–73, 56; See Jules Michelet, *Principes de la Philosophie de l'Histoire Traduits de la Scienza Nuova de J. B. Vico, et Précédés d'un Discours sur le Système et la vie de l'Auteur* (Paris: Renouard, 1827). A new and more comprehensive edition of Vico's writings (*Œuvres choisies de Vico*) was then published by Michelet in 1835. On this, see also Joseph Mali, *The Legacy of Vico in Modern Cultural History: From Jules Michelet to Isaiah Berlin* (Cambridge: Cambridge University Press, 2012), pp. 12–70.

[22] Karl Marx and Friedrich Engels, *Collected Works*, vol. 41 (London: Lawrence and Wishart, 1985), p. 355 (Letter, 28 April 1862). First published in *F. Lassalle. Nachgelassene Briefe und Schriften* (Stuttgart-Berlin, 1922).

[23] C. Belgiojoso, *Essai sur Vico* (Milan: Turati 1844), p. 90.

[24] For the most recent account of Belgiojoso's life, see Karoline Rörig, *Cristina Trivulzio di Belgiojoso (Milano 1808–Milano 1871): Storiografia e politica nel Risorgimento* (Milan: Scalpendi, 2021). See also L. Severgnini, *La principessa di Belgiojoso. Vita e opere* (Milan: Edizioni Virgilio, 1972); Beth Archer Brombert, *Cristina: Portraits of a Princess* (Chicago: University Chicago Press, 1977); Ludovico Incisa and Alberica Trivulzio, *Cristina di Belgiojoso. La principessa romantica* (Milan: Rusconi, 1984). Regarding Vico's influence on Belgiojoso, see Sharon Wood, 'Cristina di Belgiojoso: Scholar in Exile', *The Italianist*, 33, no. 1, 2013: 49–73, 51; see also Fernanda Gallo, 'The United States of Europe and the "East(s)": Giuseppe Mazzini, Carlo Cattaneo and Cristina Trivulzio di Belgiojoso', in *Europe and the East: Historical Ideas of Eastern and Southeast Europe, 1789–1989*, ed. Mark Hewitson and Jan Vermeiren (London: Routledge, 2023), pp. 133–162.

of Vico (with a second edition in 1835) – that Vico was the philosopher who had discovered what was perhaps the most fundamental of historical principles: 'That this world of nations has certainly been made by men, and its guise must therefore be found within the modifications of our own human mind. And history cannot be more certain than when he who creates the things also narrates them.'[25] History was a human creation and, as such, could be explored and understood.

It is not by chance that Ferrari, Cattaneo, and Belgiojoso all had close links with France and French culture. Ferrari and Belgiojoso in particular were on familiar terms with key figures in the French historiographical debate such as Augustin Thierry (1795–1856), Pierre Simon Ballanche (1776–1847), François Guizot (1787–1874), and especially Victor Cousin (1792–1867), Jules Michelet's master, who had connected Vico and Hegel in an attempt to forge a new understanding of history, clarified this in his 1828 *Cours de Philosophie. Introduction à l'Histoire de la Philosophie*. The French eclectic school, therefore, combined the Vichian and Hegelian philosophies of history and thereby influenced the rediscovery of this connection in northern Italy in the 1830s. However, Cousin's work was also extremely popular in the city of Naples, where the link between Vico and Hegel would be developed in greater depth thanks to a direct access to German philosophical texts and an informed knowledge of Kant's philosophy.

Here it seems important to note that the diffusion of Hegel's thought in northern Italy before 1848 was not based on direct knowledge of Hegel's works but was mediated by the French school of Eclecticism and by a wider knowledge of, and engagement with, Vico's philosophy. It would be from 1840 onwards, when the first translation of a work by Hegel appeared in Italian, being actually the first time that any text by Hegel had been translated into a foreign language, that a wider engagement with the German philosopher ensued.[26] In 1840, Giambattista Passerini

---

[25] Giambattista Vico, *The New Science*, trans. Thomas G. Bergin and Max H. Fisch (Ithaca, NY: Cornell University Press, 1968), p. 349.

[26] In actual fact, the very first Italian translation of Hegel's works was in 1837, when the Greek poet Dionysios Solomos commissioned his friend Nikolaos Lountzis to undertake a translation of Hegel's collected works into Italian, his language of study, but the translations were completed only in 1842. Lountzis translated many works of German philosophers for Solomos between 1834 and 1854. The twenty-five volumes of Lountzis' translations for Solomos (probably only a small part of a wider translation process) are held at the Solomos Museum in Corfu (Zakynthos). For Hegel's reception in Greece and especially the Ionian Islands, see Coutelle Louis, 'N. Lountzi's translations for Solomos' (Zakynthian codices) ('Οι μεταφράσεις του Ν. Λούντζη για τον Σολωμό (Οι κώδικες της Ζακύνθου)', in *Framing Solomos (1965–1989)* (*Πλαισιώνοντας τον Σολωμό [1965–1989]*) (Athens: Nefeli, 1990), pp. 23–48; Giorgos Veloudis, *Dionysios Solomos, Romantic Poetry and Poetics: The German Sources* (Διονύσιος Σολωμός. Ρομαντική ποίηση και ποιητική. Οι

(1793–1864) published his translation of the *Philosophy of History* (entitled *Filosofia della Storia*) with Elvetica Press in Capolago (Canton Tessin, Switzerland), whose publications have been considered by historians to be the 'preparatory laboratory' of nineteenth-century Italian political thought.[27] Passerini was a disciple of the French eclectic school, born in Brescia under Habsburg rule, and at the time of the translation was in exile in Zurich. He had lived in Berlin between 1825 and 1828 and thanks to his friendship with Eduard Gans (1797–1839) was able to attend Hegel's lectures in 1826–1828, mainly on the philosophy of history, religion, art, and the history of philosophy. He decided to translate the philosophy of history, reckoning that a public unaccustomed to the speculative tones of German idealism might, he judged, find it easier to understand. It was also the text that best served Passerini's liberal aspirations. Eduard Gans himself, in his Introduction to the 1837 edition of Hegel's *Vorlesungen über die Philosophie der Geschichte* (*Lectures on the Philosophy of History*), had in fact applauded Giambattista Vico's idea of history as ruled by absolute laws and Reason.[28]

In 1848, the *Filosofia del Diritto* (*Philosophy of Right*) was published in Naples by Vito Antonio Turchiarulo (1825–1898), a jurist from Apulia, who had studied in Naples and was interested in philosophy, history, and aesthetics. He participated in the 1848 revolution in Naples and helped to circulate Hegel's ideas. Hegel's positing of a profound connection between law and history led these nineteenth-century interpreters to present the philosopher from Stuttgart to Italian readers as almost a historian, whose philosophy of history, due to the certainty of future political freedom, seemed directly relevant to the revolutionary tremors culminating in 1848. In his *Preface* to the Italian translation, Passerini highlights the nexus between the notion of history and the notion of progress, one that helped to inaugurate a new vision of history as the science of progress, implying by the same token a militant and political commitment. In a similar way, Turchiarulo's *Preface* focused on Hegel's idea of history as tied to a determinate end, the realization of liberty, and its association with the

γερμανικές πηγές) (Athens: Gnosi, 1989); Giorgos Veloudis, 'The Ionian Hegelianism', in *Odd and Even: Ten Modern Greek Studies* ('Ο επτανησιακός εγελιανισμός', στο Μονά ζυγά. Δέκα νεοελληνικά μελετήματα) (Athens: Gnosi, 1992), pp. 79–96; in English, see Roxanne Argyropoulos, *Approaches in Modern Greek Philosophy* (Προσεγγίσεις της Νεοελληνικής Φιλοσοφίας) (Thessaloniki: Vanias, 2004).

[27] On the Elvetica press in Capolago, see Rinaldo Caddeo, *La tipografia Elvetica di Capolago: Uomini, vicende, tempi* (Milan: Bompiani, 1931); Caddeo, *Le edizioni di Capolago: Storia e critica* (Milan: Bompiani, 1934); Fiorenzo Bernasconi, *Per un catalogo delle edizioni di Capolago* (Bellinzona: Archivio Storico Ticinese, 1984); Emilio Motta, *Le tipografie del Canton Ticino dal 1800 al 1859* (Lugano: Topi, 1964).

[28] Eduard Gans, *Herausgegeben* to G. W. F. Hegel, *Vorlesungen über die Philosophie der Geschichte* (Berlin: Duncker & Humblot, 1837), p. ix.

notion of progress. Turchiarulo's engagement with Hegel's thought was mainly political and his philosophical understanding of the German philosopher quite limited, as some of the choices in his translation indicate (e.g., he does not distinguish linguistically between *Moralität* and *Sittlichkeit*, using in either case the term 'morality'; *vernünftig* is translated as 'reasonable' instead of 'rational'; *Selbstbewusstsein* as 'consciousness' instead of 'self-consciousness'). Conversely, there is evident in Passerini's work a critical and philosophical interest, reflected in particular in his correct understanding of the key notion of *Begriff*, translated as concept rather than notion, which was Turchiarulo's choice.[29] Beyond their various differences, it appears clear that the first Italian Hegelians found Hegel's philosophy of history highly attractive because of the notion of freedom as the liberation of humanity through the struggle of Spirit in its historical existence, combined with an idea of progress addressed to all nations. Recognising the revolutionary potential of Hegel's thought, Italian intellectuals during the Risorgimento discerned in his philosophy of history the certainty of Italy's future liberation. A dialectical philosophy of history helped Italians to look into the future in order to confirm the promise of a new age.

There were important differences between the North and the South of the peninsula where Hegel's reception was concerned. As Eugenio Garin once observed, before 1848 Hegel's *Philosophy of History* was more widely read among intellectuals in northern Italy, while in the South, thanks to Francesco De Sanctis (1817–1883) and Bertrando (1817–1883) and Silvio Spaventa (1822–1893), Hegel's lectures on aesthetics and *The Phenomenology of Spirit* were better known.[30] It was in the South that Hegelianism assumed the guise of an actual philosophical movement, commonly referred to as Neapolitan Hegelianism, which over the years assumed an important role also on the national stage.

1.2 The Neapolitan School

The city of Naples has always attracted the interest of novelists and historians, and quite recently the intellectual context of the city, in particular during the eighteenth century, has been the object of a number

[29] On this, see Federica Pitillo, 'Una rivoluzione silenziosa: Storia e diritto nelle edizioni preunitarie di Hegel (1840–1848)', in *La fortuna di Hegel in Italia nell'Ottocento*, ed. Marco Diamanti (Naples: Bibliopolis 2020), pp. 17–37.

[30] Eugenio Garin, 'La "fortuna" nella filosofia italiana', in *L'opera e l'eredità di Hegel*, ed. G. Calabrò (Bari: Laterza 1972). On this, see F. Gallo and A. Körner, 'Challenging Intellectual Hierarchies. Hegel in Risorgimento Political Thought: An Introduction', *Journal of Modern Italian Studies*, 24, no. 2, 2019: 209–225.

of brilliant historical enquiries. Mention should be made of John Robertson's fine study, *The Case of the Enlightenment: Scotland and Naples 1680–1760*, which focuses on the Neapolitan Enlightenment, as well as the very recent *Companion to Early Modern Naples* edited by Tommaso Astarita, or John Davis' seminal work *Naples and Napoleon: Southern Italy and the European Revolutions (1780–1860)*, which explores the nineteenth-century historical context of the city within the general 'Southern Question', investigating the main narrative of Southern Italian pre-modern backwardness. Even a cursory survey of the secondary literature gives the impression of a historiographical consensus to the effect that after Giambattista Vico and the Neapolitan Enlightenment, Naples as a city has had very little to contribute to the intellectual history of modern Europe. This section challenges this view by focusing on the peculiar amalgamation of Vico and Hegel's philosophies of history taking place in Naples between 1830 and 1848.[31]

In the Kingdom of Two Sicilies during the first Restoration (1815–1821), the main strategy of the crown was to 'protect' the Catholic religion from the 'assaults' of the 'free thinking': schools were in the grip of the Society of Jesus, censorship was reinforced, and incarceration was often used to silence intellectual opponents. The 'French decade' (1806–1815) had brought about a profound social transformation, promulgating new laws, eradicating the feudal system, stimulating civil and political interests in society at large, and enhancing public spirit. However, the reforms were realised very slowly, and the period was too brief to have a deep impact at an intellectual level. After the revolution, in 1821 and alongside the Giunta della Pubblica Istruzione, which oversaw teaching programmes and licenses to teach in private and public schools, the crown created four more *Giunte* to scrutinize all the works published in the Kingdom together with the syllabuses taught in private and public schools. The bill of the 2nd of June of 1821 states: 'Experience has shown that the gravest wounds to public morality have been inflicted through the reading of pernicious books, and that these latter, diffused through the unsuspecting hands of superficially educated youths, became fatal to the tranquillity

---

[31] On this, see Melissa Calaresu, 'The Patriots and the People in Late Eighteenth-Century Naples', *History of European Ideas*, 20, nos. 1–3, 1995: 203–209; John Robertson, *The Case of the Enlightenment: Scotland and Naples 1680–1760*. (Cambridge: Cambridge University Press, 2005); Tommaso Astarita (ed.), *Companion to Early Modern Naples* (Leiden: Brill, 2013); John Davis, *Naples and Napoleon: Southern Italy and the European Revolutions (1780–1860)* (Oxford: Oxford University Press, 2006).

and honour of a good number of cultivated nations.'[32] Liberal and constitutional demands were the main obstacle that the crown sought to overcome by repressing intellectual production.

There was a line of continuity between Ferdinando I and his son
Francesco I di Borbone (1777–1830), who reigned from 1825 to 1830.
In 1830, when Ferdinando II di Borbone (1810–1859) ascended the
throne, a series of economic, financial, and political reforms were enacted.
In an attempt to mitigate social discontent, he permitted a relaxation of
political control over intellectual production and teaching activities and
abolished the penalties for those declared guilty of acts against the State
(*reita' di Stato*). This served to reinforce the political and administrative
structures of the Kingdom and thereby to enlarge the support for the
monarchy. However, the temporary loosening of political control allowed
for what Francesco De Sanctis described in his memoirs *La Giovinezza* as a
temporary interval of tolerance conceded by the Bourbon reaction to
intellectual development.[33] The amnesty enabled many exiles to come
back to the Kingdom and political prisoners to regain their freedom.
The intellectual debate in the city of Naples, where most of the intellectuals from the provinces also converged, was not slow to revive. Among
these intellectuals there was Ottavio Colecchi, who after his time in
Königsberg moved to Naples and launched his own private school, teaching his students about Kant, supporting them in learning the German
language with a view to their gaining access to these texts, and discussing
with them how Kant should be interpreted by drawing his thought closer
to that of Vico. Towards the end of his life, Colecchi went on to study
Hegel's *Aesthetics*. As teacher in his private school, he educated the majority of the Hegelians who would be the key protagonists of the 1848 revolution in Naples and who would seek to align Hegel's philosophy with
some of the less or non-metaphysical aspects of Vico's thought.

During the 1830s, Neapolitan culture revived, the city boasting more
than eight hundred private schools. Their activities were independent of
the government and they enjoyed quite unrestricted freedom to teach

---

[32] *Collezione delle leggi, de' decreti e di altri atti riguardati la pubblica istruzione*, Naples 1861–63, II,
pp. 4–6 (decreto 2 Giugno). Translation in English in A. De Arcangelis, 'Hegelians on the Slopes of
Vesuvius: A Transnational Study in the Intellectual History of Naples, 1799–1861', PhD thesis,
University College London, 2018, p. 131. On the context of Naples in the first half of the
nineteenth century, see Guido Oldrini, *La cultura filosofica napoletana dell'Ottocento* (Bari:
Laterza, 1973); John Davis, *Naples and Napoleon: Southern Italy and the European Revolutions,
1780–1860* (Oxford: Oxford University Press, 2008).
[33] See Francesco De Sanctis, *La Giovinezza: Frammento autobiografico* (Naples: Morano, 1889),
pp. 24–37, 123–137.

(methods, syllabuses, etc.), promoting a substantial engagement with foreign ideas. As Settembrini highlights in his *Ricordanze*: 'Science was not learned from the official professor who taught as [our] superiors wished, but from private teachers who in their own houses taught as they wished: method, books, system.'[34] The same period also saw the launch of many new journals in Naples. In the space of a few years, the number of Neapolitan periodicals rose to around forty, a tally that, per head of population, was higher than that of any other Italian or European centre of the time.

A new engagement with Giambattista Vico's thought in Naples was linked to this philosophical resurgence, which aimed at proving the utility of history by defining and understanding history scientifically, as the *New Science* of Vico had prescribed. The latter highlighted the need to investigate the connections between events as well as the theoretical justification of their succession and eventually to identify the laws and the principles that drive the 'ideal eternal history of the nations'. These historical ideas are a product of humankind and, as such, can be known and understood by human investigation. The circulation of Vico's ideas in Naples in the period of the Restoration exerted a profound influence upon the study of law, in particular regarding the understanding of the relationship between *verum* (truth) and *factum* (certainty), that is, the universal principle of reason, on the one hand, and legal concepts, on the other. The Neapolitan juridical school interpreted Vico by highlighting that laws (certainty) are in relationship with the science of law (truth), in much the same way as history relates to the philosophy of history.

It has to be highlighted that in Naples Vico had never been forgotten. Antonio Genovesi (1713–1769), for instance, who was professor of Ethics and Commerce at the University of Naples between 1746 and 1769, and attended Vico's classes in rhetoric, declared himself to be Vico's 'discipulus' already in 1751.[35] It remains unclear to what extent Genovesi's direct mediation of Vico's work influenced his own students, although he certainly passed on to the latter a sense of the *New Science*'s 'interest and significance'.[36] 'Genovesi's school' was constantly engaging with Vico's

---

[34] Luigi Settembrini, *Ricordanze della mia vita e scritti autobiografici* (Turin: Einaudi, 1961), p. 58.

[35] Antonio Genovesi, *Elementa Metaphysicae Matematicum in Morem Adornatorum*, Editio secunda Neapolitana multo auctioret correctior (Napoli: typis Benedicti, et Ignatii Gessari, 1751–1752), pp. 276–277.

[36] Robertson, *The Case for the Enlightenment*, p. 253. On this, see Felix Waldmann, 'Antonio Genovesi, the "Scuola Genovesina", and Philosophy in the Kingdom of Naples, 1743–1792', PhD disseration, Faculty of History, University of Cambridge, 2016, pp. 219–248. Parts of this study are published in Felix Waldmann, 'Natural Law and the Chair of Ethics in the University of Naples, 1703–1769', *Modern Intellectual History*, 19, 2022: 54–80.

philosophy and among these students were also some of the key protagonists of the 1799 Neapolitan revolution, men and women who contributed greatly to the Neapolitan Enlightenment.[37]

One of their number, Francesco Mario Pagano (1748–1799), funded the so-called historical school of law and drafted the constitutional project for the new Neapolitan republic.[38] This *Costituzione della Repubblica Napoletana* banned torture and capital punishment and instituted the 'body of ephors', which is considered the precursor of the modern constitutional court. Participation in the revolution cost him his life: he was hanged by the Bourbon police in Mercato square in Naples, dying there in October 1799. Pagano had engaged conspicuously with the *New Science* in his *Saggi politici* (1783–1785; 1791–1792), extolling there Vico's attempt to formulate 'the new and unknown thought of bringing philosophy into history . . .. None had formed a philosophy out of history before'.[39] The identification of Vico's legacy in Pagano's work was particularly highlighted by Vincenzo Cuoco (1770–1823) in his *Saggio storico sulla rivoluzione napoletana del 1799* (1801): 'In the sublime career of the eternal history of the human race, you find that only the footsteps of Pagano may guide you to reach the height of Vico.'[40]

In Naples in the 1830s and 1840s, the re-elaboration of Vico's philosophy in light of the reading of Hegel was especially important in the juridical debate, where the attempt was made to forge a brand of liberalism defined by Neapolitan thinkers as civil philosophy. This philosophy, by focussing on the study of the evolution of the laws and institutions of human society, provided the intellectual tools to overcome the traumas of the revolutionary experiances of 1799, 1806, and 1820. The law, secured on philosophical grounds, could reconcile political liberty with social stability, ensuring the establishment constitutional freedom. Vico had taught to Neapolitan intellectuals that natural law was not a metaphysical entity but rather a product of historical development.

During this period, alongside Vico's thought, it was the philosophy of Victor Cousin that was dominating the cultural debate in Naples. Two

---

[37] On the debate around the school of Genovesi, see Vincenzo Padula, *Elogio dell'abbate Antonio Genovesi* (Naples: Stabilimento Tipografico Androsio, 1869), p. 26; Giovanni Gentile, *Memorie italiana e problemi della filosofia e della vita* (Florence, 1936), p. 21; Giovanni Gentile, *Storia della filosofia italiana. Dal Genovesi al Galluppi* (Florence, 1942), I, p. 2; Franco Venturi, *Settecento riformatore*, I, p. 557. See also Franco Venturi, *Riformatori napoletani* (Ricciardi, 1962).

[38] Fulvio Tessitore, *Comprensione storica e cultura: Revisioni storicistiche* (Naples: Guida, 1979), p. 27.

[39] F. M. Pagano, *Dei Saggi Politici* (1783–1785), I (1), p. 11.

[40] Vincenzo Cuoco, *Saggio storico sulla rivoluzione di Napoli*, ed. Antonino de Francesco (Laterza: Bari/Rome, 2014), p. 504.

periodicals, in particular, hosted discussions about 'the French eclectic': *Il Progresso delle scienze, delle lettere, delle arti*, running from 1832 to 1847 and replacing the previously mentioned *Antologia*, directed by Vieusseux, which ceased publication around 1832–1833; and *Il Museo di letteratura e filosofia*, which ran from 1841 to 1862 and was funded with a critical intent regarding Cousin's eclecticism and has to be considered the key organon of the early development of Neapolitan Hegelianism. The shift from Eclecticism to Hegelianism in Naples was made possible by the diffusion of Kant's ideas in relation to Vico's philosophy at the private school of Colecchi, whose interpretation of Kant developed in contrast with that of another old liberal from a province of the Kingdom (Calabria), who was teaching philosophy at the University of Naples, Pasquale Galluppi (1770–1846).

In 1831, Galluppi was appointed to the Chair of Logic and Metaphysics at the University of Naples and in the same period published in Naples *La filosofia di Vittorio Cousin*, a translation of Cousin's *Fragments philosophiques* together with his own comments. Cousin became a philosophical celebrity in Naples, Marc Monnier later referring to him as the 'most popular writer in Naples'.[41] The pinnacle of his fame was reached around 1838, when his *Cours d'Introduction à l'Histoire de la Philosophie* was finally circulated in Italy, as well as the third edition of the *Fragments Philosophiques*, in which the French author addressed the main criticisms he had received. Cousin's eclecticism proposed to 'select in all systems what appears to be true and good, and consequently everlasting' and he believed the future of philosophy to be 'sustained by the history of philosophy'.[42] He considered Vico to be the father of the history of philosophy and introduced him to nineteenth-century readers as the forerunner of intellectual history.[43] History thereby became an essential part of the philosophical elaboration and construction of a philosophy of history, as the idea of a universal history of humanity, the main task for a philosopher as well as for a historian. This perspective found a very fruitful ground in the city of Vico.

During the 1830s, however, although the conditions for an intellectual debate had improved in the region, censorship on political matters was still

---

[41] Marc Monnier, 'Le movement italien à Naples de 1830 à 1860 dans la literature et dans l'enseignement', *Revue des deux mondes*, LVI, 1865.

[42] Victor Cousin, 'Préface' to the translation of the *Manuel de l'histoire de la philosophie de Tennemann*, I (Paris: Sautelet, 1829), pp XII–XIII.

[43] See Donald R. Kelley, 'Eclecticism and the History of Ideas', *Journal of the History of Ideas*, 62, 2001: 577–592.

very harsh. This deflected philosophical discussions to gnoseological and theoretical issues, hiding in those abstract arguments views about political communities, historical development, and revolution. Colecchi, for example, criticises both Galluppi and Cousin from his Kantian perspective. With a series of articles in the periodical *Il Progresso* between 1836 and 1837, he highlights how Cousin's gnoseology was analytic rather than synthetic: what Cousin called 'synthesis' was indeed a 'reconstruction of the parts into which the unity had been divided in order to be analysed'.[44] Kant's synthetic a priori judgement instead renders it possible, Colecchi maintained, to connect the parts into which the unity had been divided with new relationships between the parts, creating then new knowledge. This is the synthesis a priori, a function of the judgement that made all other experiences possible, the original condition of thinking. This demonstrates Colecchi's hermeneutic loyalty to the Kantian model of transcendentalism. He highlights the relevance of the 'Logic' as the science of the pure forms of thinking, without a specific content. Explaining mainly Kant's *Critique of Pure Reason*, Colecchi argues that logic can be a science: 'If it is contained within its own limits, it is true science; but it ceases to be such when from the form of the cognition it goes on to treat the object or material of cognition itself.'[45] Colecchi addresses in particular Galluppi who, presenting his system as close to the Kantian system, had defined the categories of 'space' and 'time' as empirical and psychological, rather than transcendental. Colecchi for his part insists that subjective forms, such as space and time, are necessary and universal, in the same way in which Kant had proved this in his 1781 *Critique of Pure Reason*. However, Colecchi's understanding of the Kantian 'transcendental' is reformulated by 'correcting' parts of Kant's doctrine on the ground of his own Vichian philosophy. Colecchi criticises Kant's doctrine of 'transcendental schematism' in order to avoid potential deviations into a formal-rationalist system or an idealistic one:

> We have thought to move from concrete judgement so as to ascend to the universal. There is therefore a very great difference between our method of philosophising and that of Kant: [namely], that Kant goes from the universal to the particular, and we, with a wholly opposite way of proceeding, go from the particular to the universal. It follows from this that we from the

---

[44] Ottavio Colecchi, 'Sull'analisi e sulla sintesi teorica di Vittorio Cousin. Suo esame', *Il Progresso*, XVII, 1837: 190–191; see also O. Colecchi, 'Se la sola analisi sia un mezzo d'invenzione, o s'inventi con la sintesi ancora', *Progresso*, XIV, 1836: 213–228.
[45] O. Colecchi, 'Sopra alcune questioni le piu' importanti della filosofia. Osservazioni critiche', Naples, 1843, p. 6.

object of experience ascend, by way of the schemas, to the category; Kant conversely descends from the category by way of the schemas to the knowledge of what is offered in experience. To put it briefly, our method of philosophising is inductive; that of Kant, deductive. We, from what sense[-perception] proposes, ascend by way of a pure synthesis of the category. Kant does the contrary.[46]

Colecchi's gnoseological revision of Kant's 'transcendental schematism' entails proceeding from history to philosophy, from the experience to the principle, without renouncing a universal knowledge (meaning a knowledge that is the same for everyone). Galluppi's gnoseology instead criticised Kant's transcendental apriorism because it implied, he argued, that only the subject has access to the knowledge of the object. Galluppi believed that the phenomenon is rather the interaction of subject and object: 'the phenomenon presupposes necessarily two realities', that of the subject and that of the object.[47] According to Galluppi, this interaction is guaranteed by consciousness, through which 'I perceive *myself*, which perceives *the outside of myself*.[48] Galluppi's interpretation of Kant was based on partial and incomplete translations of the three *Critiques*, as he did not know German. His criticism of Kant in his 'philosophy of experience' (*filosofia dell'esperienza*) was contested by Colecchi because, if the transcendental approach to knowledge were not applied, the only possible knowledge would have been a collection of historical experiences without their rational principle, a history without a philosophy of history, a revolution without an idea. However, according to Colecchi, this knowledge must begin with historical experience and not with the transcendental categories.

Colecchi's most original contribution to the understanding of Kant lies in the field of moral philosophy. He agrees completely with Kant's definition of the moral law:

> The moral law has its seat in the reason, which commands the action as a means to obtain an end, which is considered by reason itself to be good . . ..
> If the moral law has its seat in reason . . . it ought to follow from that that reason in this respect is legislative.[49]

---

[46] O. Colecchi, 'Saggio sul nostro metodo di filosofare', in *Questioni filosofiche*, III, p. 127–129.

[47] P. Galluppi, *Saggio filosofico sulla critica della conoscenza*, Naples 1832, IV, p. 350. For other works of Galluppi on Kant, see *Lettere filosofiche sulle vicende della filosofia relativamente ai principii delle conoscenze umane da Cartesio sino a Kant inclusivamente* (Messina: Pappalardo, 1838).

[48] P. Galluppi, *Elementi di filosofia*, 1820–1827, vol. I, 2001, p. 253.

[49] Ottavio Colecchi, 'Della legge morale', *Il Progresso delle scienze lettere ed arti*, XXIV, no. 47, 1839: 5–27, now in O. Colecchi, *Questioni filosofiche*, II, p. 70.

Moral law, therefore, is a synthetic a priori principle, is rational, and is the legislator. However, Colecchi further insists on the connection between ethical (inner) law and juridical (external) laws. Written laws cannot be based on the arbitrariness of experience but rather they must be anchored in moral objectivity. Here Colecchi is in polemic with Romagnosi's *Introduzione al diritto pubblico universale* (*Introduction to Universal Public Right*), where the latter highlights the natural origin of the law. In this text, 'natural' is used to indicate the empirical dimension of law, which is not based on the transcendental principle of the moral law. More generally, Colecchi supports the key Kantian principles of modern ethics: autonomy of moral action, universality of ethical reason in respect to individual freedom, the affirmation of 'human personality'. This ethical *persona* that characterises the Kantian system is, according to Colecchi, very similar to Vico's *degnita VI* and *VII*, where he distinguishes between a philosophical dimension, which investigates 'what ought to be', and a political, historical, and juridical dimension, which investigates 'what is', identifying a practical sphere of historical action. Colecchi insists on Vico's theory of law and the historical application of the theoretical connection *verum-factum* in order to expand Kant's criticism from gnoseology to the historical and social aspect. Vico's linking of *verum* and *factum* creates the possibility of a mediation between logic and history, between the norm and its concrete manifestation in societies and institutions, between the *truth* of a universal principle and the *certainty* of the historical objectification. Colecchi refers to Vico's concept of *Providence* as the law that realises 'divine things' in the historical world and the *New Science* as the demonstration of the 'historical fact' of *Providence*. The idea of natural right seems to Colecchi to foster the possibility of reconciling the thought of Vico and Kant in order to proceed from logic to history.

What lies at the heart of this discussion is Colecchi's understanding of the so-called *diritto naturale delle genti* (natural law of the peoples), which presents the tension between an ideal eternal law and the historical and juridical laws of the different nations. On the one hand, this led Colecchi to attempt to link Vico's legal philosophy to Kant's transcendentalism, by arguing that legislation, which considers humankind as it is, can direct actions in order to bring about what ought to be. On the other hand, he draws Kant closer to the historical terminology of Vico by arguing that although the moral law is eternal and rational, it can be recognised only through its historical realisation, where it has to deal with the autonomy of human free will. By virtue of the connection between Vico and Kant, the 'normativity' of Reason, the dimension of the *verum* (truth), encounters

the 'measure' of history, the individual objectification, the 'certainty'
(*factum*) of the common sense in which the 'natural right of the peoples'
finds its origin and manifests itself in the 'customs of the nations'.[50] The
verum of what ought to be is the object that philosophy must investigate,
while the *factum* of what is, is the object of legislation. By connecting Vico
and Kant, Colecchi grounds the Kantian philosophical 'revolution' of the
autonomy and freedom of the subject in the historical dimension of
humanity and its sociability. The metaphysical and the non-metaphysical,
gnoseology and history, logic and politics, ideas and practice start to come
together in the establishing of this connection between Vico and Kant: it
would be for Colecchi's students to undertake the further task of connecting Vico with Hegel and thereby overcoming the apparent contradictions
between these two dimensions of human existence.

Among the followers of Cousin in Naples were two intellectuals who
had been profoundly influenced by Colecchi, namely, Stanislao Gatti
(1820–1870) and Stefano Cusani (1815–1846), educated together with
Francesco De Sanctis at the private school of Basilio Puoti (1782–1847), a
representative of the purist grammatical school, which favoured a dialogical
pedagogy. Both Gatti and Cusani engaged critically with Cousin's philosophy and connected the Vichian and Hegelian philosophies. Thanks to
their personal relationship with Colecchi, they moved from linguistic
purism to German transcendentalism, though by way of the French
eclectic school as they did not know German.

When in 1838 Cousin's third edition of the *Fragments Philosophiques*
was published, Stanislao Gatti translated the *Avertissement* in *Il Progresso*
and was at pains to endorse Cousin's method: 'Eclecticism is more a
method of philosophising than a system of philosophy .... Perhaps I am
mistaken, but I sincerely desire that Italians should follow eclecticism both
in the sciences and in civil life.'[51] Stefano Cusani had also discussed
Cousin's methodology, likewise supporting the eclectic approach,
according to which 'the method of science is often the criterion of the
truth of philosophical solutions, and not these latter that of the method'.[52]

---

[50] G. Vico, *Opere* (Bari: Laterza, 1914), I, p. 136.

[51] Stanislao Gatti, 'Di una risposta di Vittore Cousin ad alcuni dubbi intorno alla sua filosofia', in *Il
Progresso delle scienze lettere ed arti*, XXI (Naples: Tipografia Flautina, 1838), pp. 34–52, 49.

[52] For Stefano Cusani's essays on this, see 'Del metodo filosofico e d'una sua storia infino agli ultimi
sistemi di filosofia che senso veduti uscir fuori in Germania ed in Francia', *Il Progresso delle scienze
lettere ed arti*, XXII, 1839: 176–178, 212–215; 'Della Scienza fenomenologica o dello studio dei
fatti di coscienza', *Il Progresso delle scienze lettere ed arti*, XXIV, no. 47, 1839: 28–83; XXV, 1840:
16–37, 187–205. On this, see also Luca Fonnesu and Barbara Henry (eds.), *Diritto Naturale e
filosofia classica tedesca* (Pisa: Pacini, 2003).

According to this method, Cusani observed, psychology represented the starting point of knowledge, which would then move beyond the phenomenological experiences of consciousness – the analysis of sensible objects and human activities – to engage subsequently with the understanding of 'necessary, infinite, absolute ... Reason'.[53] The main problem to address according to both Gatti and Cusani is the legitimacy of the shift from knowledge of the subject to that of the object, from logic to ontology, which would be solved, they held, by transcendental logic.[54] This logic identifies universal laws of thinking, which are independent from the feeling and willing of the individual subject (the consciousness of psychology) and can lead to an objective knowledge: Reason lies far beyond individuality. Identifying the role of Reason and of transcendental logic had been the signal merit of Kant and of the idealist philosophy of Schelling and Hegel. Merging the psychologism of Cousin with the idealist philosophy became the main aim of Gatti and Cusani, who needed a new intellectual platform for this purpose.

In September 1841, they therefore funded a new periodical, *Il Museo di letteratura e filosofia*, whose first number presented its intellectual programme. The aim was to amalgamate the different cultural tendencies concerned to solve the philosophical problem of the relationship between the infinite principle of absolute reason with its finite manifestations:

> The present Work will discuss all the parts of the moral world, philosophy, literature, art, the most abstract and immediate manifestations of the spirit, binding them all to a common prin.ciple, showing them as subjected to one and the same law as the expression of a supreme idea from which, as [a] ray from its fire, everything derives *that does not die and that can die*, and accompanying them in all their works, in all their products, in all their applications, will be able to come secretly to show how beneath this continuous succession of mutable forms, their substance remains identical.[55]

It is from the pages of this periodical that Gatti investigates 'the progressive development of the philosophical idea in the history of humanity', referring to the understanding both of different historical stages in the development of the 'philosophical idea' (history of philosophy) and of the

---

[53] S. Cusani, 'Del reale obietto d'ogni filosofia e del solo procedimento a poterlo raggiungere', *Il Progresso delle scienze lettere ed arti*, XXIII, 1839: 27–60.

[54] On this, see S. Cusani, 'Della logica trascendentale', *Il Progresso delle scienze lettere ed arti*, XXVI, 1840: 161–187.

[55] Stanislao Gatti, 'Introduzione', in *Il Museo di letteratura e filosofia*, vol. I (Naples, 1841), p. 19.

immanence of that idea in the historical world (philosophy of history).[56] According to Gatti and Cusani, history is the product of the development of the spirit, which is the expression of rationality originating in consciousness. This implies that to understand the philosophy of history it is necessary to understand consciousness in itself so that we may grasp its realisation in social life (commerce, the State, art, religion, etc). With this view, Vico's *storia ideal' eterna* (eternal ideal history) appears closer to Hegel's absolute Reason whose laws are immanent in history, or rather in what Vico himself calls the *storia di tutte le nazioni* (history of all the nations). While Vico affirms that 'the order of ideas should proceed according to the order of things', subordinating the history of nations to the ideal eternal history, the influence of Eclecticism and Hegelianism leads Gatti and Cusani to invert this hierarchy.

Because of their eclectic formation, both Cusani and Gatti interpreted the development of consciousness and that of history as one and the same problem on account of their common origin in the principle of reason. However, under the influence of Colecchi, they both realised that this common origin, the unity of consciousness and history, is a synthetic unity of opposites. The Kantian concept of a priori synthesis of finite empirical world and infinite absolute reason that had been introduced into Italy by Colecchi, serves as a self-criticism of their own eclecticism as they turn to what they call 'transcendent idealism'. The *Museo* is actually the platform on which this change happens, around 1841–1842, with many essays on German idealism featured there. The latter appears to them to represent the philosophy best suited to grasping the ontological problem: eclecticism demonstrates that the empirical world exists and that we can come to know it; German idealism demonstrates how the empirical world exists:

> We accept that one cannot proceed to the knowledge of beings, unless our means of knowing have first been examined, and as human intelligence passes legitimately from the subjective to the objective. But it being declared once upon a time that we can know beings in a mode [that is] absolute in relation to existences, and that the science of beings is not at all impossible for us to reach, it remains the case that we learn so to speak their construction, and we set out from the absolute in order to descend to the world and to man.[57]

---

[56] See S. Gatti, 'Del progressive svolgimento dell'idea filosofica nella storia', in *Il Museo di letteratura e filosofia*, vol. I (1841), pp. 99–112; III (1842), pp. 3–11, 97–105; S. Cusani, 'Idea d'una storia compendiata della filosofia', vol. I (1841), pp. 113–135 and vol. II (1842), pp. 3–8; 97–120.

[57] S. Cusani, 'Del modo di trattare la scienza degli esseri. Disegno di una metafisica', *Rivista napolitana*, III, no. 2, 1842: 21–22.

As Gatti clarified a year later: 'We accept the works of the eclectic school of France in matters of psychology, but we cannot help but separate ourselves from it with respect to ontology, being reconciled to Germany.'[58] By the early 1840s, reflecting on the scientific foundations of knowledge, and therefore on ontology, Cusani defined this scientific knowledge as *scienza assoluta* (absolute knowledge), which is 'the active and living substance determined as spirit', thereby moving Neapolitan philosophical culture from eclecticism to Hegelianism and the dialectic.[59] Gatti, for instance, was persuaded that the Hegelian philosophy of history, whose dialectical method placed 'unity in variety', could be associated with Vico's intuition of the 'individuality of the people' as the mediation between people and individuality.[60] The realisation of the Spirit had to be understood through its finite manifestations, such as language, in order to graft Hegel's abstract logic upon the philological praxis emerging from the *New Science*.[61]

Between 1843 and 1848, years in which Bourbon censorship became more restrictive and the police more aggressive towards intellectuals, Gatti and Cusani acquired a deeper knowledge of German in order to gain access to Hegel's texts in the original language. Engaging with Hegelian ideas in the same period in Naples were also the Spaventa brothers, Giuseppe Tari, Camillo De Meis, Gian Battista Ajello, and Francesco De Sanctis, who for his part was particularly impressed by Hegel's *Aesthetic* and began teaching this text and Hegel's theory in his private school. In the 1840s, the regime's censors suspended many periodicals, the *Rivista Napolitana* among them; the publication of many others was never approved, such as Silvio Spaventa's proposal in 1844 for the publication of a philosophical journal; a number of books were not allowed to be published, such as Colecchi's third volume of the *Questioni filosofiche* in 1843; private teaching was suspended, Bertrando Spaventa's private school, for example, being closed down in 1847. The general anxiety of the Bourbon government regarding the spread of liberal and revolutionary ideas just before 1848 resulted in a violent attack on the Neapolitan cultural milieu. In the

---

[58] Cusani, 'Del modo di trattare la scienza degli esseri', p. 18. For a similar philosophical analysis, see also S. Gatti, 'Fichte e la dottrina della scienza', *Museo di scienza e letteratura*, I, 1843: 93–94. Note that because of the restrictions of censorship in the early 1840s and the government's mistrust of philosophers, Gatti and Cusani were led to change the name of the periodical, removing the term philosophy from the title in 1843.

[59] S. Cusani, 'Della scienza assoluta' (discorso I), *Museo di letteratura e filosofia*, IV, 1842: 110–126.

[60] S. Gatti, 'La filosofia della storia', in *Scritti vari di filosofia e letteratura* (Naples: Stamperia Nazionale, 1844), vol. I, p. 140.

[61] Gatti, 'La filosofia della storia', p. 158.

1840s, official teaching programmes were stringently controlled and it was therefore in the private schools that the merging of local and foreign philosophical ideas was fostered.[62] Bertrando Spaventa later recalled this period in a letter to his brother Silvio:

> In Naples, starting in 1843 [when Silvio and Bertrando Spaventa began attending Colecchi's private school], the Hegelian idea penetrated the minds of the young cultivators of science, who, uniting fraternally, took to advocating it in speech and in writing as if moved by saintly love. Neither the early suspicions of the police, motivated by ignorance and religious hypocrisy, nor their threats and persecutions could dampen the faith of these daring defenders of intellectual independence. The numerous students who deserted the old universities gathered in the great capital city from all corners of the kingdom; they rushed in throngs to hear the new word. It was an irresistible and universal urge impelling [them] toward a new and wonderful future, toward an organic unity of the different branches of human knowledge. Students of medicine, natural scientists, law students, mathematicians, and students of literature participated in this general movement, and their main ambition was, as it was with the ancient Italians, to turn into philosophers .... It was a cult, an ideal religion, in which those young people demonstrated themselves worthy descendants of the wretched Bruno [understood as a reference to the modern spirit of the Renaissance].[63]

De Sanctis' first private school remained open for about a decade from 1839 to 1848 and made a key contribution to the amalgamation of Vico and Hegel's philosophies in Naples. In the first two academic years, De Sanctis taught mainly courses of grammar because of his collaboration with his older master, the purist Basilio Puoti. He probably taught his courses on aesthetics between 1842 and 1844 together with his courses on the different literary genres. It is in 1845–1846 that we have evidence of a course taught on Hegel as well as on the philosophy of history, designating what he would describe as the 'historical school' (*la scuola storica*) to indicate a historicist approach to literary criticism. According to De Sanctis, Vico was the founder of this approach, which led him to seek out the historical causes of artistic representations: 'Vico replaces the life of the authors with the life of the people and societies, biography with

[62] On the private schools in Naples, see Alessandro De Arcangelis, 'Hegelians on the Slopes of Vesuvius: A Transnational Study in the Intellectual History of Naples, 1799–1861', PhD thesis, University College London, 2018; Nicola Capone, *Libertà di ricerca e organizzazione della cultura: crisi dell'Università e funzione storica delle Accademie* (Naples: Scuola di Pitagora, 2013).

[63] Silvio Spaventa, *Dal 1848 al 1861. Lettere, scritti, documenti* (Bari: Laterza 1923), p. 322.

history.'[64] De Sanctis then identifies a further step in the development of this school in Cousin's method, which he summarised as an approach through which 'science is resolved into history'.[65] Eclecticism represents the subjective consideration of art, whereby meaning is connected to the individual. However, the objective understanding of art, its understanding outside space and time, is possible thanks to the Hegelian dialectic: 'through Hegel history itself becomes a form, and the idea and art are developed in different moments of humanity, and a particular form corresponds to every moment of the idea'.[66]

After the courses on the historical school and aesthetics, De Sanctis goes on to compare Vico and Hegel's philosophies of history: 'The philosophy of history is not the whim of one man, but the need that all feel at a certain time to give value to the facts . . .. Vico did indeed try to substitute society for the individual', while according to Hegel 'reason governs history . . . progressively . . . this progress is subordinated to the progress of humanity.'[67] According to De Sanctis, Vico produced an idea of history that did not include in a convincing fashion a progressive pattern, although it had the merit of envisaging anti-metaphysical laws of historical development. Hegel, however, had developed an aprioristic logic that remained abstract and could be understood only when it unfolded in historical development. De Sanctis invites his readers to think the unity of philosophy and history, of idea and fact: on the one hand, philosophy will prove the rationality unfolding in history as absolute and necessary, on the other hand, the intelligibility of history is observable in human actions and the history of all the nations. By merging Hegel with Vico, De Sanctis will begin his intellectual development, a development that will conclude with a practical understanding of Hegel's ideas summarised in his own philosophical category of 'life'. Life was indeed violently forcing its way into philosophical reflection: Europe was on the verge of one of the most transformative

---

[64] F. De Sanctis, 'Le lezioni sulla storia della critica, in *Teoria e storia della letteratura: Lezioni tenute in Napoli dal 1839 al 1848*, vol. II (Bari: Laterza, 1926), pp. 73–77. For an accurate reconstruction of De Sanctis' courses in his first private school, see B. Croce, 'Introduction' to F. De Sanctis, *Teoria e storia della letteratura: Lezioni tenute in Napoli dal 1839 al 1848*, vol. I (Bari: Laterza, 1926), pp. 17–36. For a more recent study on De Sanctis' first school, see Anya Ciccone, 'National Character in Restoration Naples: Francesco De Sanctis between Schlegel, Hegel and Bozzelli', and A. De Arcangelis, '*Geschichte, Histoire*, Storia: Stefano Cusani, Stanislao Gatti e la circolazione transnazionale dell'Hegelismo, 1838–48', both in *Gli Hegeliani di Napoli: Il risorgimento e la ricezione di Hegel in Italia*, ed. F. Gallo (Naples: Scuola di Pitagora, 2020) pp. 87–117; 61–86.

[65] De Sanctis, 'Le lezioni sulla storia della critica', p. 77.

[66] De Sanctis, 'Le lezioni sulla storia della critica', p. 97.

[67] F. De Sanctis, 'Lezioni sulla filosofia della storia e la storia', in *Teoria e storia della letteratura: Lezioni tenute in Napoli dal 1839 al 1848*, vol. II (Bari: Laterza, 1926), pp. 131–144, 137–138.

periods in modern times and the revolutionary change brought about by the 1848 'springtime of the peoples' was about to mark out a different intellectual path for the Neapolitan Hegelians.

1.3   Nationality and Revolution

On 25 August 1847, on the hill of Poggioreale cemetery at the entrance to the ancient city centre of Naples, a group of revolutionaries were paying their last respects to their old teacher Ottavio Colecchi. The police, who had kept the liberal Kantian scholar under surveillance for most of his life, had suppressed all notices in the press of his death. His students, therefore, decided to turn his funeral into an anti-Bourbon protest. These young Hegelians – among them Bertrando and Silvio Spaventa, Francesco De Sanctis, Luigi Settembrini, and Stanislao Gatti – were also being watched by the Bourbon chief of police Francesco Saverio Del Carretto (1777–1861), on the grounds that they were conspiring against the Bourbons. At the outset of the 1848 revolution, the Hegelians were burying, together with their venerated master, the belief that a compromise between liberalism and the Bourbon monarchy was possible.

The two different generations experienced two very different constitutional revolutions. Colecchi had been a supporter of the 1820–1821 Neapolitan revolution, which had hoped to establish a constitution modelled on the Cadiz Constitution of 1812, one that mediated between liberalism and the Catholicism, parliament and monarchy. The failure of this political negotiation and the repression of the 1820–1821 revolution led to the rupture between the two political communities and, later on, to the end of the Kingdom of Two Sicilies.[68] After 1848, Neapolitan liberals believed a constitution possible only within the process of attaining national unification and winning independence from foreign domination. It was indeed during the 1848 revolution in Naples that the liberal parliamentary majority led by the Hegelians attempted for the first time to achieve a constitutional and pro-Italian mediation. After the repression on the 15th of May 1848 and the Restoration, it was clear that liberals' political and cultural aspirations were incompatible with the very existence of the old Kingdom.[69] In the troubled years around the 1848 revolutions,

---

[68] Carmine Pinto, '1820–21. Revolución y Restauración en Nápoles. Una Interpretación Histórica', *Barceo. Revista Riojana de Ciencias Sociales y Humanidades*, 179, 2020: 51–66.

[69] See Viviana Mellone, 'La rivoluzione napoletana del 1848. Fonti e metodi per lo studio della partecipazione politica', *Meridiana*, no. 78, 2013: 31–51.

Southern Italy represents a privileged vantage point from which to understand the permeable boundaries of the intellectual life in the 1830s and 1840s, masterfully described by Christopher Clark in his recent volume *Revolutionary Spring*.[70] This context had been characterised by political arguments that could be infiltrated in unpredictable ways by economic discourses, patriotic claims, and the language of religious belief. The Hegelians perceived the world around them as a place where traditional identities were dissolving, and a brutal rupture was occurring, and where nonetheless a new world, a new 'shape of the spirit', was about to emerge, as memorably described by Hegel in his *Phenomenology of Spirit*:

> It is not difficult to see that ours is a birth-time and a period of transition to a new era. Spirit has broken with the world it has hitherto inhabited and imagined, and is of a mind to submerge it in the past, and in the labour of its own transformation. Spirit is indeed never at rest but always engaged in moving forward. But just as the first breath drawn by a child after its long, quiet nourishment breaks the gradualness of merely quantitative growth – there is a qualitative leap, and the child is born – so likewise the Spirit in its formation matures slowly and quietly into its new shape, dissolving bit by bit the structure of its previous world, whose tottering state is only hinted at by isolated symptoms. The frivolity and boredom which unsettle the established order, the vague foreboding of something unknown, these are the heralds of approaching change. The gradual crumbling that left unaltered the face of the whole is cut short by a sunburst which, in one flash, illuminates the features of the new world. (§11)

Hegel represented this kind of fracture as a 'qualitative leap' since a completely new normative order was replacing an older settlement. As Richard Bourke has recently highlighted while commenting on Hegel's idea of revolution, 'a more conducive reconstruction of political values presupposed an alignment between insurgent moral energy and the received norms of social life'.[71] His Italian followers shared the German philosopher's conviction that 'the actual Revolution' emerges from an '"inner" revolution' and they for their part contributed both to this inner revolution of the consciousness and to the actual political upheaval.[72] This new world in the making was the one the Hegelians were determined to inhabit.

---

[70] See Christopher Clarke, *Revolutionary Spring: Fighting for a New World, 1848–49* (London: Penguin, 2023), especially chapter III.
[71] Richard Bourke, *Hegel's World Revolutions* (Princeton: Princeton University Press, 2023), p. 102.
[72] Hegel, *Phenomenology*, §§582–583. Hegel's word here is *Umwälzung* (upheaval) rather than *Revolution*.

The story begins in Calabria, the toe of the boot and thus the Southernmost province of the Kingdom, where, on the 29th of August 1847, the brothers Domenico and Giannandrea Romeo raised the Italian tricolour in Santo Stefano square in Aspromonte, Calabria, proclaiming the outbreak of an insurrection that sought to seize power in Reggio Calabria, instituting a new provisional government. The revolt was suppressed by the Bourbon army after a few days and Domenico Romeo was brutally killed and decapitated. A wider repression ensued, with Silvio Spaventa being hunted by the police and accused of taking part in the insurrection in Calabria. He was forced to flee Naples on a ship bound for Livorno, heading then to Florence. It was during this first exile that the correspondence between the two Spaventa brothers began, providing one of the main sources through which to understand the complicated network of relationships and political affiliations within the Neapolitan Hegelian group. In the first letter to Silvio, sent together with money to support his brother in exile, Bertrando describes the turmoil in Naples during the week before Christmas 1847 and the many arrests and perilous escapes of those in their immediate circle, protesting to the cry of *Viva l'Italia*.

King Ferdinando II had commanded his generals to point the cannon of Castel Sant'Elmo, the fortress high up on the hill dominating the city, towards the main street of the centre, Via Toledo, rather than in the direction of the sea, from where enemies were usually expected.[73] The whole Kingdom was on the verge of a revolution and it was in January 1848, under one of the most repressive regimes in all of Europe, on the island too often kicked by the Italian boot, that the Sicilian revolution precipitated the wave of revolutions of the so-called Springtime of the Peoples. The Sicilian news travelled swiftly across Europe: in France *La Réforme*, a radical republican Parisian daily, offers the outlook of some of those most actively involved in the February revolution and its aftermath.[74] From 23 January 1848, when the first report of the Palermitan insurrection appears, there is not a single issue without a lengthy account

---

[73] Marco Diamanti, Marcello Mustè and Maria Rascaglia, *Epistolario (1847–1883): Bertrando Spaventa* (Rome: Viella 2020), p. 22.

[74] Among the editors and contributors of *La Réforme* appeared Alexandre Ledru-Rollin, who became Minister of the Interior in the Provisional Government established after the February Revolution; the socialist Louis Blanc, who also joined the Provisional Government; the former Carbonaro and insurgent of 1832 and 1834, Etienne Arago, who became the Director of Postal Services; and the journalist Félix Pyat, who served as a 'commissary' of the Provisional Government. For an account of the engagement of *La Réforme* with the wider European debate, see Christopher Clark, *Revolutionary Spring*.

of the latest news from Sicily.[75] The issue of 26 January contained extensive reporting on Sicily and Naples and a serialised excerpt from Settembrini's *Protest of the Neapolitan People*.[76] The Sicilian revolt against the Bourbons was immediately followed by a similar uprising in Naples, and the King was forced to grant the Constitution on the 29th of January 1848. But it was too little and too late, as the people in the Kingdom itself and in Europe were not as they had been in the 1820s. Silvio returned immediately to Naples and on the 1st of March published the first issue of *Il Nazionale*, the short-lived periodical, where Neapolitan Hegelians commented on current political issues, and that had among its collaborators also the translator of Hegel's *Philosophy of Right*, Antonio Turchiarulo. The main aim of *Il Nazionale*'s political programme was a democratic constitutionalism and the establishment of a new national state under Piedmontese leadership, while in Sicily, for instance, revolutionaries were far more sympathetic to a federalist programme.[77]

The Constitution granted by King Ferdinand II was markedly less progressive than the one with a unicameral system conceded in 1820–1821, modelled on the Cadiz constitution. It was instead an adaptation of the 1830 French constitution and with a bicameral system. Sicilians decided not to participate in the elections and to constitute an autonomous Kingdom with its own constitution, thus continuing on the autonomist constitutional path already marked out by the constitution of 1812, developed during the British protectorate.[78] On 15 April 1848, Silvio Spaventa was elected to the Parliament. A few days earlier he had been commenting in the pages of *Il Nazionale* that the 'principle of nationality' had to be understood as concrete liberty. Monarchy, Spaventa insists, has to grasp that its very survival requires relinquishing absolute power and accepting the constitution, otherwise 'the peoples will do it by themselves' (*I popoli faranno da se*). The newly elected members of Parliament would sit on the day of the opening, the 15th of May, in the *Chiostro di Monteoliveto*, the same rooms in which fifty years earlier the

---

[75] L'insurrection en Sicile', 'L'Italie', 'Nouvelles Diverses', 'Dernière nouvelles de l'Italie', in *La Réforme*, 23 January 1848, pp. 1–3.
[76] 'Le Soulèvement en Sicile', 'Nouvelles Diverses', in *La Réforme*, 26 January 1848, pp. 1–2.
[77] A. Körner, A. *America in Italy. The United States in the Political Thought and Imagination of the Risorgimento, 1763–1865* (Princeton:Princeton University Press, 2017), pp. 146–160.
[78] On this, see Giuseppe Grieco, 'British Imperialism and Southern Liberalism: Re-Shaping the Mediterranean Space, c. 1817–1823', *Global Intellectual History*, 3, 2018: 202–230; Angelo Grimaldi, 'La Costituzione Siciliana del 1812', *Revista de Derecho*, 48, 2017: 208–233; Diletta D'Andrea, 'Great Britain and the Mediterranean Islands in the Napoleonic Wars – the "Insular Strategy" of Gould Francis Leckie', *Journal of Mediterranean Studies*, 16, 2006: 79–90.

State had put on trial the few Jacobins from the Neapolitan Republic of 1799 to have survived the bloodthirsty repression. In Naples, the ferocious counter-revolution began, demonstrating to the rest of Europe that the repression of the revolutionaries was not only possible but also desirable as it would win the backing of broad swathes of the lower classes, the so-called *lazzari*. As Engels explained in an article published in the *Neue Rheinische Zeitung* on the 1st of June 1848, the Neapolitan *Lumpenproletariat* together with the army of Ferdinando II crushed the revolutionary forces and sacked the city. Engels highlighted how the Neapolitan plebs were fervently attached to Monarchy and Church, acting once again as 'sanfedisti', referring to the support they had given to the army of the Cardinal Fabrizio Ruffo (1744–1827), which in 1799 had brought down the Neapolitan Revolution and the republican government.

It was indeed among the republicans that the protest against the Bourbons had started: many members of Parliament did not wish to swear on the Constitution proposed by the King, who thereupon decided to dismiss the two Chambers. This led to fresh elections in June with a first session scheduled for the 10th of July but postponed until March 1849, when the King dismissed the chambers for the last time. Immediately afterwards, Silvio Spaventa was arrested by the chief of police Campagna, while making his way home from princess Della Rocca's house, where he had had lunch in celebration of Saint Joseph's day. Ten whole years would pass before Silvio Spaventa would again enjoy a walk along the alleyways that connect Via Toledo to the hill dominated by the fortress of Sant'Elmo. After two hours of interrogation in the police station, he was locked up in a Bourbon prison together with 841 other political prisoners detained in the prisons of the Kingdom of Two Sicilies.

While Silvio Spaventa was languishing in jail, his brother Bertrando left Naples on a British vessel on October 1849, to avoid being imprisoned, or worse still, killed, a fate suffered by their little brother Tito, who died at the age of fifteen under the cannon of the Bourbons during the repression of May 15th. That morning, while the members of Parliament were trying to negotiate some modifications to the Constitution with the King, the general population was building barricades on the main street. At 11:00 in the morning, the Bourbon soldiers were already firing with their cannon on the general population. This day is described by Settembrini in his *Ricordanze della mia vita* (*Memories of My Life*, 1879) as a terrible wound in the history of Naples, where for a population that was finally emerging from a long servitude, freedom brought on a sort of carnival mood, and, as he concluded: 'May 15th was the work of fools, the wise could not prevent it, and a cunning man profited from it. In other words: the people were fools, governments were indecisive, the king evil and mendacious.'[79] The soldiers were indeed cruel, and he describes their marching through the streets to the chilling cry *Viva il Re! Mora la Nazione!* (Long live the King! May the Nation die!). The 'Nation' to which the soldiers were referring was national sovereignty, the same 'Nation' that Neapolitan Hegelians were describing in the pages of *Il Nazionale*, while delineating a form of liberalism based on the principle of nationality, freedom and statehood.

In his articles, Silvio Spaventa mentions several times 'the principle of nationality', which, he believed, was 'constituted by free institutions, the rule of law and the control of public opinion over politics'. The principle of nationality is an idea emerging from the connection between Giambattista Vico's search for the universal laws regulating civil society and Hegel's philosophy of history conceived as the realization of freedom. Spaventa's national liberalism presented a theory of the state that identified freedom and nationality, without asserting the primacy of the nation. Spaventa disagreed with Hegel's theory that a single nation could embody the 'spirit of the world' in a given historical epoch. Closer to Giuseppe Mazzini's earlier views of a 'cosmopolitanism of the nations', Spaventa recognised that the rights of each nationality had to be limited by the mutual recognition of all the nationalities. This view would be later diffused by the Southerner jurist Pasquale Stanislao Mancini with his famous 1851 speech 'Della nazionalità come fondamento del diritto delle genti' (On Nationality as Foundation of the Right of the Peoples).

During 1848 in Naples, with the publication of Silvio Spaventa's periodical, *Il Nazionale*, and the translation of Hegel's *Philosophy of Right* by Antonio Turchiarulo, the theoretical connection between freedom and nationality seemed established. Turchiarulo had already published translations of Friedrich Carl von Savigny's (1779–1861) works, and in his introduction to the translation of the *Philosophy of Right*, he argues that free nationality is realised in the State through the evolution of law. In the Neapolitan reading of Hegel in 1848, is the actualisation of nationality in the State that represents the realisation of the Reason in the 'world spirit'. Therefore the 'principle of nationality' could only be realised in the unitary Italian State. Within this perspective, Italian unification becomes the outcome of the rational and necessary development of the Spirit, rather than the result of a social contract. Around 1848, Spaventa's Hegelian understanding of the State as an ethical substance begins to be delineated, clarifying as he

---

[79] L. Settembrini, *Ricordanze della mia vita* (Naples: Morano, 1906), pp. 48–49.

does that the State is not dependent on any arbitrary will and that it represents the progressive development of liberty and the consciousness of the 'Infinite of Society'. He wrote in *Il Nazionale* during the revolution:

> The idea of the State, which is that of the Infinite of Society, cannot be joined together with the concept without spirit, which the Infinite should seek here in an extrinsic and particular part of the whole. Naples has found beneath the government [that has] fallen an empty sepulchre, because the union of Neapolitan society with the Eternal is not here . . . .. There is only the form of the State here, the spirit is in the whole of Italy.[80]

This 'Infinite of Society' is in contrast with the Church, clearly indicating its ethical ground, although the theory of the ethical State is not yet fully developed. A few days later, Spaventa reflects again on the idea of the State and criticises contractarian theories of the State and the individualist atomism to which they are connected:

> The state is the people, considered not as a collection of individuals but as their universal and concrete unity. The State is the true image of the people, inasmuch as in the State every individual recovers himself, as a person, as a moral being, and obtains in it an infinite satisfaction. Only in the State can the individual say, I am, inasmuch as he attributes to himself that which is above his individuality, that which has a true value, the being of the State . . . .. One would wish to make an essential distinction between the State and the Government, [for] not always where there is Government is there State. Sometimes behind the Government, there is State. Sometimes behind the Government there is emptiness or a corpse.[81]

Il Nazionale thus presents a theory of the State that by merging Vico with Hegel, was based on the ethical ground of the principle of nationality – the realisation of national freedom and self-consciousness. According to Vico, the eternal ideality is the rationality of human beings, which is manifested as the infinite and divine element in history.

Vico's philosophy, Kant's transcendentalism, and Victor Cousin's eclecticism together with Hegel's philosophy of history helped Neapolitan intellectuals to envisage a philosophical foundation for law based on universal principle and derived from the study of society. That universal principle, as Hegel argues, is the actualisation of the spirit that dialectically unfolds in history: it is the realisation of a universal reason that is acknowledged as the idea of freedom. This universal law guides the progress of all nations.

---

[80] *Il Nazionale*, no. 41, 22 April 1848.   [81] *Il Nazionale*, no. 42, 26 April 1848.

In conjunction with the revolutions in Calabria, Sicily, and Lombardy, Silvio Spaventa and the other contributors to *Il Nazionale* instituted the Società dell'Unità Italiana, a secret sect that sought to perpetuate the legacy of the Carboneria and of the Mazzinian Giovine Italia (Young Italy, 1831). However, differently from those republican sects, the programme of the Società dell'Unità Italiana did not propose a specific form of government, having as its key objective the unity of the Italian State and putting an end to the political power of the Bourbons. Following the example of the Carboneria and Giovine Italia, the society also had an oath of a religious character in which each member swore 'to use all my strength to free Italy from any internal and external oppression'.[82] This association with Giovine Italia has led some scholars to identify a connection between Mazzini and Spaventa's early political thought. However, from these early writings onwards, the influence of the Hegelian concept of the State appears clear: Spaventa highlights how the revolution is 'fatal' when there is a contradiction between the state and the society as this represents 'a contradiction [of the State] with its own concept'.[83] The development of the State 'on the one side ensures the progressive unfolding of liberty, on the other side it founds the nationality'.[84] Spaventa incorporates Hegel's interpretation of the revolution by arguing that the State overcomes the abstract idea of freedom that emerged from the French Revolution because it is the idea of this revolution, therefore its rationality. However, this rational principle, liberty, unfolds in history in the immediate form of nationality, which in its infinite form is the State. Therefore, according to Spaventa 'the concept of our revolution [the 1848 revolution] is the concept of Italian independence'.[85] In 1848, Hegel incorporates Vico, and the dialectical process in history is thereby fully embraced by the Neapolitan Hegelians, who believed that the inner revolution – the idea of the revolution – unfolds in the historical revolution: liberty unfolds in its ethico-practical determinations of nationality and State:

> The idea is the rationality of the revolution: through it the revolution is and lives, has power and dignity, pulls down every obstacle, imposes itself on every mind, enthralls every heart, overturns what exists, positions itself in place of it and takes on an organic actualisation: inasmuch as reason alone

---

[82] The programme, statute, and oath of the Società dell'Unità Italiana are in S. Spaventa, *Dal 1848 al 1861*, pp. 49–54, 53.

[83] S. Spaventa, 'Idea del movimento italiano', *Il Nazionale*, 2, 5 March 1848.

[84] S. Spaventa, 'L'Italianità', *Il Nazionale*, 38, 18 April 1848.

[85] S. Spaventa, 'Il fine ultimo delle rivoluzioni e il fine proprio della rivoluzione italiana', *Il Nazionale*, 41, 22 April 1848.

governs the world and has an infinite right to existence. Reason is [a] purpose by itself, and this purpose is liberty.[86]

The dialectical connection between 'inner' and political liberty is further clarified by Bertrando Spaventa a few years later, when in June 1851 in exile in Turin he published a series of articles entitled 'La Rivoluzione e l'Italia' in the Piedmontese journal *Progresso*, where he explains: 'We wished that every Italian might be persuaded that political liberty is impossible without liberty of feeling and thought.'[87] The role of the philosophers is therefore revolutionary, inasmuch as they have grasped the rationality of the idea of the revolution and can therefore guide the revolutionary movement: 'Without the philosophers the revolution would be blind, indeterminate, lacking in purpose .... The philosophers give to the instinct and feeling of the masses the rational baptism of the idea, of right.'[88] Therefore, following on from the philosophical revolution that was inaugurated by the principles of 'liberty, equality and fraternity', there will come the political revolution in the form of 'democracy, social reform, and solidarity of the people'.[89] Popular sovereignty, expressed in the principle of nationality, represents the realisation of equality in the concrete existence of the State, a kind of state in which, echoing Engels and Marx's *Communist Manifesto*, 'in it there will no longer be either noble or plebeian, bourgeois or proletarian; but in it there will be man.'[90] Bertrando Spaventa's interest in social reform had been expressed as early as 1850, when he attempted to collect funds for his plan to publish in Italian a translation of Lorenz von Stein's *Der Sozialismus und Communismus des heutigen Frankreich. Ein Beitrag zur Zeitgeschichte* (*Socialism and Communism of Today's France: A Contribution to Contemporary History*), although we have no proof that this project was eventually realised.[91]

---

[86] S. Spaventa, 'Programma', *Il Nazionale*, 1, 1 March 1848.

[87] B. Spaventa, 'La Rivoluzione e l'Italia' *Progresso*, 3–15 June 1851, now in B. Spaventa, *Le Utopie*, in *Bertrando Spaventa pubblicista (giugno-dicembre 1851)*, pp. 89–90. On the relationship between intellectual and political revolution, see also R. Racinaro, *Rivoluzione e Stato in alcuni momenti della riflessione di Bertrando Spaventa e Francesco de Sanctis*, in AA.VV., *Gli hegeliani di Napoli e la costruzione dello Stato unitario*, Rome: Istituto poligrafico e Zecca dello Stato, 1989, pp. 179–200.

[88] B. Spaventa, 'La Rivoluzione e l'Italia', cit., p. 69.

[89] B. Spaventa, 'La Rivoluzione e l'Italia', pp. 89–90.

[90] B. Spaventa, 'La Rivoluzione e l'Italia', p. 71.

[91] On this, see Bertrando Spaventa, *Il Socialismo e il Comunismo in Francia*, in 'Rivista Italiana', n.s., Turin, I, Settembre 1850, pp. 332–333, republished in B. Spaventa, *Scritti inediti e rari (1840–1880)*, cit., pp. 27–29. This same text is also in the essay by Sergio Landucci, *Il giovane Spaventa fra hegelismo e socialismo*, Annali dell'Istituto Giangiacomo Feltrinelli, anno VI, 1963, pp. 647–707, reprinted in full at pp. 693–695: Landucci states that he found this text in the Florentine periodical 'Il Nazionale' for 14 September 1850. The translation announced by

The political revolution had to be spread through the wider society, but the philosophical idea of revolution was its premise. The revolutionary idea was the Hegelian idea, the Hegelian understanding of history: 'Hegel is the Aristotle of the new civilization.' However, Hegel was a difficult philosopher who, by contrast with Aristotle, could not simply be translated but would need to be 'popularized', and 'rendered intelligible' to Italian readers: 'Hegel cannot be translated in the same way as Aristotle, one needs to understand him, to render him intelligible without superficiality, render him *popular*, not *vulgar*.'[92] There was therefore a need to merge Hegel with the Italian intellectual context; and with this purpose in mind, Vico seemed the best candidate.

In his 1850 essay *Studii sopra la filosofia di Hegel* (*Studies on the Philosophy of Hegel*), Spaventa clarifies this connection with Vico. Whereas in the seventeenth century political theories had been either mechanistic (life is subject to natural law and man and society are simply machines) or based on the law of arbitrariness (society and the state are the result of a contract), Vico affirmed the principle of the 'free nationality of the people'. The *ideal eternal history* was 'the moral universe free and governed by a rational law, which is realised in the national life of each people and in which all the peoples have [their] unity and common destiny'.[93] According to Vico, the eternal ideality is the rationality of human beings, which manifests the infinite and divine element in history. This notion, in Spaventa's judgement, had engendered a science of history that the other political theorists had excluded. When in 1850 Pasquale Villari wrote to Spaventa in a letter: 'if we could only get Italians to understand Hegel, Italy would be regenerated', what he meant was that the new Italian State would arise if they interpreted Hegel in such a way as to render his thought familiar to Italian readers. In other words, they should draw Hegel closer to Vico's philosophy. But why was it so

---

Bertrando refers to the second edition of Stein's book (Leipzig: Verlag von Otto Wigand, 1848), as is evinced by the fact of its presence in the Spaventa brothers' library, housed now in the Biblioteca Civica 'A. Mai' in Bergamo. In this regard, see D. D'Orsi *Prefazione*, in B. Spaventa, *Scritti inediti e rari (1840–1880)*, cit., p. 23 n. 1; and also AA.VV., *Silvio Spaventa politico e statista dell'Italia unita nei documenti della Biblioteca Civica 'A. Mai' di Bergamo*, Proceedings of the bibliographical and documentary exhibition held at Bergamo from 26 April to 31 May 1990, edited by S. Ricci and C. Scarano, Bergamo 1990, pp. 89–91. As regards Spaventa's study on Stein, see also F. M. De Sanctis, *Lorenz Von Stein e il giovane Bertrando Spaventa*, in *Gli hegeliani di Napoli e la costruzione dello Stato unitario*, Proceedings of the Conference held in Naples, 6 and 7 February 1987 at the Istituto italiano per gli Studi filosofici and at the Biblioteca Nazionale di Napoli (Rome: Poligrafico e Zecca dello Stato, Libreria di Stato, 1989), pp. 169–178.
[92] B. Spaventa, *Studii sopra la filosofia di Hegel*, in *Scritti inediti e rari (1840–1880)*, cit., p. 506.
[93] Spaventa, *Studii sopra la filosofia di Hegel*, 291.

important to amalgamate Hegel with Vico? Here the role of philosophy, even in its abstract metaphysical form, emerges with clarity:

> Without philosophy, one cannot become a nation, and today there is no Italian philosophy, nor is there any hope [of there being one], unless some bold young person presses forward: [unless] he dares. Italy should not follow in the footsteps of anyone, it needs to find a system that represents the whole nationality, that gathers together whatever elements of life there are in the whole of the peninsula; but, first and foremost, it needs to recover the consciousness of itself, and no system is more capable of this than the Hegelian.[94]

By drawing on Hegel and Vico, the Neapolitan Hegelians were endeavouring to establish the principle of nationality as the expression of both inner liberty and the political liberty that unfolds within historical institutions. However, in the first half of the nineteenth century in Italy, various different ideas of the nation were competing with each other. The prevailing understanding of the idea of nation during the Risorgimento is linked to the debate on 'national character', a term used as an 'explanatory category' by nineteenth-century European historians.[95] The political culture of the national movement in the first half of the nineteenth century was far from uniform and the different definitions offered of the Italian national character were connected to the diverse interpretations of the origins of the nation. Vincenzo Cuoco's works – for example, his *Saggio storico sulla rivoluzione napoletana del 1799* (1801) or his *Giornale italiano* (1804–1806) – were among the first attempts in Italy to *create* a public spirit. During the period in which he wrote, 'the point was to lift the minds of the Italians, to mould the inhabitants of provinces into citizens of a state'.[96] The diverse nationalisms and political perspectives on display were connected to different interpretations of the origins of Italian culture and to contrasting definitions of Italian national character. As Giuseppe Ferrari pointed out in 1844, it was not simply a question of responding to the national cause, since patriots had to decide which national cause to respond to.[97] From the publication of Cuoco's

---

[94] Letter from Villari to B. Spaventa in S. Spaventa, *Dal 1848 al 1861*, p. 78 (October 1850).

[95] Varouxakis, Georgios, 'The Discreet Charm of "Southernness"', *Journal of Modern Italian Studies*, 17, no. 5, 2012: 547. On this, see also Roberto Romani, *National Character and Public Spirit in Britain and France, 1750–1914* (Cambridge: Cambridge University Press, 2002).

[96] Bruce Haddock, 'State, Nation and Risorgimento', in *The Politics of Italian National Identity*, ed. G. Bedani and B. Haddock (Cardiff: University of Wales Press, 2000), pp. 11–49, 16

[97] Giuseppe Ferrari, 'Le révolution et les réformes en Italie', *Revue des Deux Mondes*, 16, 1844: 573–614; 17, 1845: 150–194.

Platone in Italia (1806) and Giuseppe Micali's *L'Italia avanti il dominio de' i romani* (*Italy before the Domination of the Romans*, 1810) it is possible to discern a number of different approaches to the task of defining the ancient features of Italian nationality.

The central role of historical discourse in the construction of the identity of the nation is clarified by the debate on the origins of Etruscan culture and ancient Italian wisdom.[98] The autochthony of the Italian people became 'the myth of its perpetual presence in [a] country that by attesting its antiquity supposedly also substantiates its cultural primacy'.[99] The existence of the mythical Pelasgian culture was championed by, among others, Vincenzo Gioberti (1801–1852), who, in his widely read *Primato morale e civile degli italiani* (*On the Moral and Civil Primacy of the Italians*, 1843) connected this myth to the Catholic roots of Italian culture. This idea of 'primacy' was the idea of an Italian philosophy that derives from a native antiquity, untainted by foreign 'deviations'.[100]

Another relevant narrative traced the origins of the Italian nation to the 'communal age of freedom' during the early Middle Ages. This 'Medieval revival' saw in the Italian Renaissance a moment of decadence and backwardness, due to the fall of the *comuni* and the demise of political freedom.[101] This negative judgement of the Renaissance among Risorgimento intellectuals reflected a wider definition of the paradigm of modernity in nineteenth-century European historiography. This was informed by Hegel's *Philosophy of History*, which had underlined the decisive role of Protestantism in the origins of modernity, implying an evaluation of Catholicism as a retrograde factor. Catholic countries were thus considered to be backward and in a subordinate and peripheral position. This thesis was advanced in celebrated works by influential nineteenth-century intellectuals, such as Madame de Staël in her *Corinne ou l'Italie* (1807) or Simonde de Sismondi in his *L'Histoire des Républiques Italiennes du Moyen Age* (1807–1818), and it permeated the consciousness of a significant sector of the Italian intellectual elite.

---

[98] Paolo Casini, *L'antica sapienza italica. Cronistoria di un mito* (Bologna: Il Mulino, 1998); Axel Körner, *Politics of Culture in Liberal Italy: From Unification to Fascism* (London: Routledge, 2009).

[99] Antonino De Francesco, *The Antiquity of the Italian Nation: The Cultural Origins of a Political Myth in Modern Italy, 1796–1943* (Oxford: Oxford University Press, 2013), p. 17.

[100] On the debate on Italian primacy during the Risorgimento, see Antonino De Francesco, *The Antiquity of the Italian Nation. The Cultural Origins of a Political Myth in Modern Italy, 1796–1943* (Oxford: Oxford University Press, 2013); Paolo Casini, *L'antica sapienza italica: Cronistoria di un mito* (Bologna: Il Mulino, 1998).

[101] Axel Körner, *Politics of Culture in Liberal Italy: From Unification to Fascism* (London: Routledge, 2009), pp. 103–122.

Concerns about the absence of a Protestant Reformation in Italian history were accompanied by the idea that the Renaissance had been a moment of moral decadence and corruption, or so the majority of prominent Risorgimento intellectuals believed. This conception of modernity reinforced the perception of boundaries between a modern and civilised northern Europe and a backward and barbaric southern Europe. This division does, indeed, still affect intellectual history: 'The North-South divide is [now] a category of thought, a device for the assessment of national histories, cultural products, and individual or collective personalities.'[102] The association of modernity with Protestantism was denounced also by Silvio Spaventa in the pages of *Il Nazionale*, where he wrote:

> Everyone claims: it is Luther who inspires Descartes; modern philosophy stems from Protestantism. This can only be true to a certain extent. Yet, having not had Protestantism, should we be prevented from having modern philosophy? This would be a very strange consequence in the general course of human affairs. We shall demonstrate that the entire philosophical movement, which currently ignites entire peoples, has likewise developed in our country among philosophers, men of letters and thinkers.[103]

Silvio Spaventa was clearly engaged in a debate here with the French intellectual François Guizot, who maintained that Italy, like other Catholic countries, could not have known modernity and progress because of the absence of the Protestant Reformation and its liberating consequences.[104] Silvio Spaventa answered that critic by writing:

> The French eclectic, following on behind the Berlin school, has gone so far as to say, that in the South, where perhaps it also pleases him to represent his immobile idea of Unity, one would be hard pressed to find an attitude appropriate to modern civilisation, nowadays flowering in more or less the whole of the North, in which he sees objectivised the opposite idea of the multiple, active, revolutionary and recalcitrant with the former.[105]

The understanding within the broader European Protestant milieu that Italy was a backward country and the Renaissance a moment of political

---

[102] Roberto Romani, *National Character and Public Spirit in Britain and France, 1750–1914* (Cambridge: Cambridge University Press, 2002), p. 79.

[103] Spaventa, *Dal 1848 al 1861. Lettere, scritti, documenti*, 8. On Silvio Spaventa's experience with the journal *Il Nazionale*, see Spaventa, *Dal 1848 al 1861*. For a general understanding of his thinking and life, see Paolo Romano, *Silvio Spaventa. Biografia politica* (Bari: Laterza, 1942); Raffaele De Cesare, *La fine di un Regno* (Milan: Longanesi, 1969); Saverio Ricci and Cesare Scarano (eds.), *Silvio Spaventa politico e statista dell'Italia unita nei documenti della Biblioteca Civica 'A. Mai'* (Bergamo: Secomandi, 1990).

[104] See Guizot, *Cours d'histoire moderne*.

[105] Spaventa, *Dal 1848 al 1861. Lettere, scritti, documenti*, p. 6.

decadence strongly influenced the Italian intellectual elites and in particular the Hegelians.

After the repression of the 1848 revolution, the Neapolitan Hegelian group was dispersed for about ten years with individual members behind bars or stranded in exile in Turin, Zurich, or Paris. During this decade it is possible to trace a common attempt within this circle of intellectuals to delineate a new perspective on the Italian philosophical tradition and national character by focusing on the rediscovery of the political thought of the Italian Renaissance. The Hegelians agreed as to how modernity should best be defined, following in this regard Hegel's philosophy of history but at the same time proposing an *Italian version* of that original structure. They searched in the Italian philosophical, political, and scientific thought of the Renaissance for that same principle of the Reformation, namely, the unity of divine and human nature, the infinite and the finite, spirit and form. They applied the Hegelian scheme of the philosophy of history but, while Spaventa and Marianna Florenzi Waddington focused on Giordano Bruno as the central figure of modernity, De Sanctis and Pasquale Villari conferred that role on Machiavelli, the 'Italian Luther'.[106]

The re-evaluation of the Italian intellectual tradition of the Renaissance in connection with the reinterpretation of Hegelian philosophy in its connections with Vico's political thought imparted a new energy to the Neapolitan intellectual context. The importance of the phenomenon in Naples was clear also to foreign observers. Between 1864 and 1865, the German Hegelian Theodor Sträter (1833–1910), professor at the University of Bonn, was in Naples as a correspondent for the Berlin-based periodical *Der Gedanke*. He was close to Spaventa and the other local Hegelians, including Antonio Tari (1809–1884) and Felice Tocco (1845–1911), whose lectures at the University of Naples he attended. Reporting on the cultural and political debate in Naples to the editor of the periodical, Karl Ludwig Michelet (1801–1893), he wrote:

> If modern philosophy is ever to have a future ... this will not take place in Germany, France, or England, but in Italy, and in particular on these marvellous shores of the Mezzogiorno. What distinguishes the manner of philosophising here from the ever more stifling, bookish erudition that smells [so] closed off in Germany, is its characteristic vitality, intense energy, vivacious temperament: in all these Italians who are now dedicating themselves to the queen of sciences, in particular however in professor

---

[106] Francesco De Sanctis, 'L'uomo di Guicciardini', in *Opere. L'arte, la scienza e la vita*, ed. M. T. Lanza (Turin: Einaudi, 1969), pp. 93–117.

> Spaventa and in his disciples, philosophy has become truly what it should
> be from the time of Fichte: life, action, personal character, I mean religion
> of the heart and not just one mental occupation among others[107]

During his stay in Naples, Sträter was present at the inauguration at the
University of Naples of the statues of Thomas Aquinas, Pietro della Vigna,
Giambattista Vico, and Giordano Bruno, erected with a view to celebrating the Neapolitan intellectual contribution to the history of Italian
political thought. He was attending Bertrando Spaventa's lectures at the
University of Naples and was well aware that the choice of those statues
was a consequence of Spaventa's teaching:

> The historical importance of Spaventa consists precisely in the fact that he,
> like no other hitherto in Italy, has expounded with clarity to his fellow
> citizens this relationship of Italian thought with European philosophy, and
> is thus now beginning to found a completely genuine school ... the impact
> and influence exerted by Spaventa over the studious youth of Naples, who
> always flock in their hundreds to his lecture hall, is incalculable ....
> Spaventa's personality does in fact have a Socratic quality: he knows how
> to find in the soul of his young listeners the point at which there should
> arise a pure sensitivity towards the complete and entire dialectical truth of
> the modern consciousness of modern knowledge.[108]

At the heart of Spaventa's lectures in the early 1860s was the philosophy of
Giordano Bruno, its key role in the development of Italian philosophy,
and its connection with European philosophy and with German Idealism
in particular. When Pope Pius IX published in December 1864 the
Syllabus complectens praecipuos nostrae aetatis errores and the Encyclical
Quanta Cura – condemning modern political ideologies, such as liberalism, socialism, and nationalism, as well as philosophies such as pantheism,
naturalism, and rationalism – the Neapolitan students burned both documents in front of the statue of Giordano Bruno in the courtyard of the
University of Naples. Sträter witnessed this episode and was persuaded that
this gesture was mainly the consequence of Spaventa's influence on his
students:

> I find myself at present in the happy circumstance, at the moment at which
> the Encyclical came out, of living in a place where the studious youth has
> solemnly burned this just issued Encyclical in the courtyard of the

---

[107] Theodor Sträter, 'Briefe über die Italianische Philosophie', in *Der Gedanke. Sieben Studien zu den deutchen-italienischen Beziehungen in Philosophie und Kunst*, ed. Wolfgang Kaltenbacher (Würzburg: Könighausen & Neumann, 2004), p. 210.

[108] T. Straeter, *Lettere sulla filosofia italiana*, 1987, pp. 15–16 (*Der Gedanke*, 5 December 1864).

University, at the foot of the beautiful statue of our immortal Giordano Bruno. On the enraged face of the great martyr of liberty there seemed to hover a conciliatory smile, when the flame from the fire, sending its glow up towards him, pronounced its definitive judgement precisely upon that system whose representatives abandoned by God did once upon a time condemn this soul of fire to the stake.[109]

A long intellectual journey lay behind the recognition of Giordano Bruno as a key legacy for the modern Italian nation, and the Neapolitan Hegelians played a central role in the rediscovery of this Southern philosopher of the Renaissance.

---

[109] Straeter, *Lettere sulla filosofia italiana*, pp. 20–27.

CHAPTER 2

The Renaissance

If we could only get Italians to understand Hegel, Italy would
be regenerated

Letter of Pasquale Villari to Bertrando Spaventa, October 1850

On the eve of the tricentenary of the death of Giordano Bruno
(17 February 1900) (Figure 2.1), Antonio Labriola gave a public lecture
in the courtyard of the University of Rome 'La Sapienza', as part of his
course in the philosophy of history. On this occasion, Labriola depicted
Bruno as the 'martyr of the freedom of thought', the philosopher of the
'revolution', representing the spirit of the 'Renaissance' and of 'modern
science'.[1] While denouncing Pope Leo XIII (1810–1903) for his refusal
to authorise access to the documents pertaining to Bruno's trial, Labriola
recounted the story of his unfortunate fate.[2] Arrested as a heretic in
Venice on the 23rd of May 1592 and then transferred to the Inquisition
in Rome, where the trial began only in 1599, he was imprisoned in a
dungeon in the Tor di Nona. Bruno was tortured and called upon to
mend his ways but he refused and was sentenced to death on the 8th of
February 1600. He was then transferred to the cell known as *'prigione di*

---

[1] The public lecture by Antonio Labriola was taken down in shorthand by one of his students in the
audience and the MS is preserved in the Fondo Dal Pane (Carte Labriola, 18.1) and annotated by
Benedetto Croce, who clarifies that in that year Labriola had also taught a course on Giordano
Bruno. The critical edition of this manuscript has been edited by Stefano Miccolis and Alessandro
Savorelli: Antonio Labriola *Da un secolo all'altro: 1897–1903* (Naples: Bibliopolis, 2012), pp. 89–94;
now in Antonio Labriola, *Giordano Bruno nella ricorrenza del terzo centenario dell'arsione in Campo
de' Fiori*, in *Tutti gli scritti filosofici e di teoria dell'educazione*, ed. l. Basile and L. Steardo (Milan:
Bompiani, 2014), pp. 1577–1585.

[2] The *Sommario* of Bruno's trial was probably identified for the first time by cardinal Joseph
Herganröther (1824–1890) in the mid-1880s but kept secret by the Vatican until 1942, when
mons. Angelo Mercati published the summary of the trial: Mercati, *Il sommario del processo di
Giordani Bruno: con un'appendice di documenti sull'eresia e l'Inquisizione a Modena nel secolo XVI*,
Biblioteca Apostolica (Vaticana: Città del Vaticano, 1942). On this see L. Firpo, *Il processo di
Giordano Bruno* (Rome: Salerno, 1993).

Figure 2.1   Statue in bronze of Giordano Bruno by Ettore Ferrari, Campo de' Fiori,
Rome, 1889. To Bruno/the age forseen by him/here/where the pyre burned

vita', reserved for those who had received a death sentence.[3] It was still dark and very cold when, on the morning of the 17th of February 1600, the brothers of the confraternity of San Giovanni Decollato processed in their black hoods, having lit their lamps, and intoned their prayers as they walked alongside the condemned man from the prison to Campo de' Fiori. Bruno was silenced by the Sant'Uffizio first with the *mordacchia* (a muzzle of iron and wood used by the Inquisition to block the tongue of irredeemable heretics) and then by burning him alive. At dawn, the executioner lit the fire on the south-eastern side of Campo de' Fiori, and Giordano Bruno died amidst the ruins of the Theatre of Pompey, on the very spot where Caesar was assassinated on the Ides of March of 44 BCE. In exile for most of his life, a heretic in the eyes of every church, always on the run, extremely brave, Giordano Bruno dies as a martyr at the hands of an authoritarian and oppressive Church that negates freedom of thought: this favoured a process of identification of Risorgimento patriots with the Renaissance martyr. Indeed, when Silvio Spaventa was sentenced to death in October 1852 for his participation in the 1848 revolution in Naples, he quoted Giordano Bruno in front of the jury, pronouncing the very same words that Bruno reserved for his executioners: 'probably you judges pronounce the sentence against me with more fear then I have in hearing it'.[4] The document describing Bruno's execution had first been published a few years before Labriola's lecture, found hidden in the archives of the confraternity of San Giovanni Decollato during the requisition ordered by the prime minister Francesco Crispi.[5] While describing these events and the anticlerical role of Giordano Bruno, Labriola recalls the importance of the statue inaugurated in Campo de' Fiori a few years earlier, in June 1889, as a symbol of the 'regenerated nation'.[6]

---

[3] The prison Tor di Nona appears on the map by Antonio Tempesta from 1593. In the second half of the seventeenth century, after the construction of the new prison Carceri Nuove, Tor di Nona was transformed into the *Apollo* theatre, where Giuseppe Verdi's operas *Il Trovatore* and *Un ballo in Maschera* were first performed. In the 1880s, the prison was demolished. On this, see Eugenio Canone, 'L'editto di proibizione delle opere di Bruno e Campanella', in *Bruniana e Campanelliana*, I, nos. 1/2, 1995: 43–61, 51 n. 21.

[4] 'Maiori forsan cum timore sententiam in me fertis quam ego accipiam'. See L. Firpo, *Il processo di Giordano Bruno* (Rome: Salerno, 1993), p. 351.

[5] The document was published by A. Pognisi, *Giordano Bruno e l'Archivio di San Giovanni Decollato. Notizia* (Turin: Paravian, 1891).

[6] Antonio Labriola, *Al Comitato per la celebrazione di Giordano Bruno in Pisa*, in *Tutti gli scritti filosofici e di teoria dell'educazione*, ed l. Basile and L. Steardo (Milan: Bompiani, 2014), pp. 1569–1575, 1572.

It was thanks to the initiative of a group of university students in Rome, led by the journalists and politicians Alfredo Comandini (1853–1923) and Adriano Colocci (1855–1941), that in 1876 was formed the first committee to erect the statue of Bruno on the very spot where he had been executed. This initiative was backed by university students in Naples and Pisa who then merged into a single committee, which in 1885 collected the funds needed to realise the statue. The committee was made up of students, professors, and European intellectuals and politicians such as the Italians Antonio Labriola, Bertrando Spaventa, Silvio Spaventa, Francesco De Sanctis, Giuseppe Bovio, the Russian Michail Bakunin, the Norwegian Henrik Ibsen, the British Herbert Spencer, the German Kuno Fisher and Eduard Zeller, the French Victor Hugo and Armand Lévy, the latter being a socialist journalist and lawyer, one of the main supporters of the project, who had escaped from Paris after the 1871 Commune and found refuge in Rome. There was a great deal of resistance from the municipality in Rome but in 1887 the support of the Prime Minister Crispi, who had removed the mayor of Rome, Leopoldo Torlonia, on account of his pro-clerical policy and sympathies, and the popular demonstrations in favour of the statue, played a crucial part in the eventual realisation by Ettore Ferrari of Giordano Bruno's statue, which was completed on the 9th of June 1889. Only a few weeks after the French government had celebrated Republican freedom with the inauguration of the Eiffel Tower on the centenary of the Revolution, Italy was celebrating its own statue of liberty. However, the celebration revealed a deep fracture in the political culture between a secular and radical Italy and a clerical one.[7]

The statue in Rome represents the friar with his head slightly bowed, the face partly covered by the hood, while his arms are crossed around a book and his leg protrudes from his cloak as if he were about to walk. The severe and austere gaze of Giordano Bruno points in the direction of the Vatican, as a reproach to his executioner. Beneath the statue there is the following apothegm, composed by the philosopher and politician Giovanni Bovio: To Bruno/ the age foreseen by him/ here/ where the pyre burned.[8] Since 1889, every year, on the 17th of February, under Bruno's statue in Campo de' Fiori, there has been a demonstration celebrating freedom of thought and opposition to arbitrary authority. This tradition was interrupted only by the Fascist government, which,

---

[7] On this conflict and the vicissitudes that led to the erection of Bruno's statue, see Massimo Bucciantini, *Campo dei Fiori; storia di un monumento maledetto* (Turin: Einaudi, 2015).
[8] In the original Italian: A Bruno / il secolo da lui divinato / qui / dove il rogo arse.

after signing the Patti Lateranensi (Lateran Treaty) in 1929, banned the demonstration. Pius XI asked Mussolini to remove the statue but, thanks to the intervention of Giovanni Gentile, this did not happen. Mussolini found another way, however, to belittle the revolutionary and anti-authoritarian figure of Bruno, setting up in Campo de' Fiori the local market, whose stalls still obscure Bruno's severe gaze, hidden by the crates of fresh fruit and vegetables.

From Spaventa's quoting of Bruno's words in 1852 to Labriola's public lecture in 1900 about fifty years had passed. The recasting of the legacy of the Italian Renaissance and the rediscovery of its key figures, Giordano Bruno and Niccolo' Machiavelli among them, took a long time and followed a winding path. It was thanks to the commitment of the Italian Hegelians that the philosophy of the Renaissance and some of its main protagonists found a new glory in the second half of the nineteenth century and served as a common ground for the new Italian nation. As Labriola reminds us in his lecture, 'the last disciple of Bruno was Hegel'. However, Hegel himself, as well as many other Italian and European intellectuals at the time, would have begged to differ.[9]

Hegel argues that the rebirth of the modern spirit is represented by the Reformation, which is the 'old and continually preserved inwardness of the German people'.[10] He maintains that the philosophers of the Italian Renaissance, such as Bruno and Vanini, belonged to the Middle Ages and the only reaction to that epoch was the Reformation, as the real glorification of the human dimension. Hegel considers the Renaissance to be a period of religious indifference, a moment of dissolution with a vague and indefinite spirituality and without moral vigour.[11] More in general, within the wider Protestant cultural milieu, the Italian Renaissance was seen in a negative light, because it had lacked the Protestant Reformation, which was conceived as the real beginning of the modern European spirit. French interpreters likewise tended to judge the Italian Renaissance harshly. For example, the doctrinaire François Guizot maintained that Italy, like the other Catholic countries, for want of the Protestant Reformation and its liberating consequences, could not have known modernity and progress.[12] The Genevan Jean-Charles-

---

[9] Labriola, *Giordano Bruno nella ricorrenza del terzo centenario dell'arsione in Campo de' Fiori*, p. 1584.

[10] 'Die alte und durch bewharte Innigkeit des deutschen Volks', in Hegel, *Vorlesungen über die Philosophie der Geschichte*, in *Säntliche Werke* (Stuttgart: 1949), vol. XI, p. 524.

[11] Ref. to Hegel, *Vorlesungen über die Geschichte der Philosophie*.

[12] François Guizot, *Cours d'histoire moderne: Histoire générale de la civilisation en Europe depuis la chute de l'empire romain jusqu'à la révolution française* (Paris: Pichon et Didier, 1828).

Léonard Simonde de Sismondi for his part traced the origins of the Renaissance to the Italian *comuni,* where individual virtues were nurtured but argued that the nation had not evolved with those virtues because of the absence of the Reformation.[13] The idea of modernity encapsulated in the Protestant Reformation greatly appealed to Italian liberals during the Risorgimento, a fair number of them in exile and far afield even going to such lengths as to convert to Protestantism.[14]

Just as European culture beyond Italy had tended to consider the Renaissance to be a pre-modern cultural movement because of the absence of any religious reformation, so too did most Italian intellectuals of the nineteenth century judge the period harshly, due to the lack of political liberty and the absence of national unity and independence. For instance, one of the most important political leaders of the Risorgimento, Cesare Balbo (1789–1853), offers a negative interpretation of the Renaissance because of the absence of political liberty and the repeated foreign invasions:[15]

> And thus there arose what we formerly called a Bacchanal, but that here we shall call a highly elegant bacchanal of culture; a mixture of iniquities and sufferings and entertainments, by virtue of which the whole of sixteenth-century Italy bears comparison with the merry band telling their tales, singing and philandering in the midst of Boccaccio's plague; were it not for the fact that, in addition to the plague, there were also the repeated foreign invasions, the wars, the sackings [of cities]; every disgrace, every elegance, every contrast.[16]

Balbo also delivers a negative judgement on the philosophy of the Renaissance, observing that it was not only an interpretation of the politics of the Renaissance but also of its culture:

> The works of Vanini, Bruno and Campanella continue to demonstrate that Italian spiritual philosophy was mediocre, if one would wish to acknowledge as mediocre also the philosophies that were ingenious, acute, bold, and even in part progressive, but logically flawed, badly put together, not firm, failing to combine their constituent parts, and indeed retrograde in

---

[13] Jean-Charles-Léonard Simonde de Sismondi, *Histoire des républiques italiennes du moyen âge* (Paris: Furne et Cie, 1840).

[14] On this topic, see the magisterial work of Giorgio Spini, *Risorgimento e protestanti* (Turin: Il Saggiatore, 1989); on the relations between liberty and religion in the Risorgimento, see also Maurizio Viroli, *As If God Existed: Religion and Liberty in the History of Italy* (Princeton: Princeton University Press, 2012).

[15] Cesare Balbo, *Della storia d'Italia dalle origini fino ai nostri tempi. Sommario,* ed. Giuseppe Talamo (Milan: Giuffré, 1962).

[16] Balbo, *Della storia d'Italia dalle origini fino ai nostri tempi,* pp. 258–259.

many parts; philosophies that advance by going close to but not treading the path of truth.[17]

The most influential philosopher of the Risorgimento, Vincenzo Gioberti, likewise had a negative attitude to the Renaissance, on account of his Catholic morality, even going so far as to partially condone the persecution of those accused of scandals and promiscuity. Of course, he was convinced that these problems were exacerbated by the absence of national unity and independence.

Catholic moderate Italian culture did not consider the Renaissance to be modern, nor indeed a period of cultural efflorescence, tracing the Italian right to participate in modern Europe to its Catholic roots instead. It is interesting to note that within the democratic and progressive sector things were not markedly different. The patriot and political leader Giuseppe Mazzini (1805–1872) thus maintained that from a moral, political and civil perspective the Renaissance should be considered 'infertile' for Italy because of the absence of political liberty and the diffusion of tyranny, while the Reformation was 'a favourable renovation':

> [The Renaissance] imparted a swifter motion to intelligences, a greater independence to opinions, a fervour to initiatives, a tireless commitment to enquiry, a spirit of reflection and examination ... generous deeds, but [undertaken] by individuals; glory, but in art; fruitful discoveries that often [nurtured] European progress, revelations in philosophy and especially in the sciences, [imbued] with an intellectual potency that naturally fostered initiatives among the nations, but [proved] sterile in Italy because of tyranny.[18]

So even if Mazzini condemns Protestantism because it was confined to the Church, he supports the general reform movement in its opposition to the Pope and its affirmation of the principle of individuality. The republican and democratic federalist Giuseppe Ferrari (1811–1876) also highlights the problem, during the Renaissance, of political division and foreign invasions, and criticises an epoch that was focused only on the arts and aesthetic life:

> The sixteenth century is an inexhaustible source of sympathy and disgust for every Italian, it is an epoch of bizarre episodes and contradictions, it is a

[17] Balbo, *Della storia d'Italia dalle origini fino ai nostri tempi*, pp. 401–402.
[18] Giuseppe Mazzini, *Scritti editi ed inediti*, Edizione Nazionale (Imola: Galeati, 1906), vol. I, pp. 211 and 347. Regarding Mazzini's relationship with Protestantism, see Eugenio Biagini, 'Mazzini and Anticlericalism: The English Exile', in C. A. Bayly and E. Biagini, *Giuseppe Mazzini and the Globalization of Democratic Nationalism, 1830–1920* (London: British Academy, 2008), pp. 145–166.

strange mixture of heedlessness and reflection, of Paganism and of Catholicism, of inspiration and pedantry, of luxury and barbarism: a throng of artists presses forward, merges with a throng of pedants; there are men of genius who abandon honest dreams of divine idealisation and stab their enemies . . .. The spectacle of the splendid horde of poets, artists, princes, cardinals, writers, villains, assassins, who rioted and rampaged in the cinquecento, resembles one of those festivals created through the religious frenzy of a barbarous people, from which we do not know if everyone will escape with their lives.[19]

These conceptions of modernity among Italian intellectual elites served to reinforce the perception of boundaries between Northern Europe, modern and civilised, and Southern Europe, backward and barbaric, contributing thereby to the idea of a fractured continent, based on a dialectic of centre-periphery. At the same time, they confirm the thesis that ideological and political motivations prompted Italian nineteenth-century historiography to posit a contrived identification between the Renaissance and the Risorgimento, recognising in them a common revolutionary character.[20] Neapolitan Hegelians amalgamated the widespread criticisms regarding the 'missed Reformation' in Italy with the rediscovery of the Italian philosophers of the Renaissance, their aim being to recast this period as the Italian path to modernity, or as 'the Italian version of the Reformation'. They brought to light the works of Giordano Bruno and Niccolo' Machiavelli, judging them to be the lynchpin of Italian modernity since, they argued, their ideas had brought about the same profound cultural revolution as the Protestant Reformation had championed in northern Europe. In their judgement, Machiavelli and Bruno had affirmed the autonomy of conscience and the infinite value of human dignity by reformulating existing notions of moral and political liberty. The historiographical debate that the Neapolitan Hegelians initiated and the variety of interpretations offered regarding these two pivotal figures of the Renaissance contributed greatly to the wider diffusion of Bruno and Machiavelli's works in Italy and in Europe alike.

---

[19] Giuseppe Ferrari, *La mente di Giambattista Vico* (Milan: Società tipografica dei classici italiani, 1837), p. 3.

[20] See, for example, Benedetto Croce, 'La crisi italiana del Cinquecento e il legame del Rinascimento col Risorgimento', in *Poeti e scrittori del pieno e del tardo Rinascimento* (Bari: Laterza, 1958), pp. 1–16; Giovanni Gentile, *I profeti del Risorgimento* (Florence: Vallecchi, 1923); Russo, *Francesco De Sanctis e la cultura napoletana*; Tiziana Provvidera, 'Note su Gioberti, Bruno e il panteismo', in *Brunus redivivus. Momenti della fortuna di Giordano Bruno nel XIX secolo*, ed. Eugenio Canone (Pisa-Rome: Istituti editoriali e poligrafici internazionali, 1998), pp. 279–287.

2.1   The Forerunner of Modernity

The rediscovery of the figure of Giordano Bruno comes from the margins of Italian Hegelianism, from the Hegelian female scholar, Marianna Bacinetti, better known as Marianna Florenzi Waddington (1802–1870) – these two surnames being those of her first and second husbands. She married Ettore Florenzi from Perugia in 1819 and the British Protestant expatriate Evelyn Waddington in 1836, two years after her first husband's death. When she moved to Perugia at the age of seventeen, she attended the university, studying physics and chemistry. In 1821, in Rome, she met Ludwig I of Bavaria. The two would fall in love and have a close relationship until the King's death. She travelled often to Munich, spending long periods there and learning German. During these stays, she met Schelling and in 1844 decided to translate his *Bruno oder über das göttliche und natürliche Prinzip der Dinge* (1802) into Italian.[21] As suggested by Rebecca and Brian Copenhaver, 'it was probably the appeal of Schelling's title to an Italian readership', that persuaded Florenzi Waddington to translate this work and then to publish it in the face of official resistance.[22] Schelling valued the translation highly, and in the second edition, promoted by Fiorentino and published in 1859, three letters from Schelling to Florenzi Waddington were also included. The persecution she suffered at the hands of the papal authorities was due to the backing she had given, since the 1830s, to the liberals, welcoming them to her villa *La Colombella* in Perugia, where she also hosted a salon. Because of her career and philosophical acuity, in 1865 Spaventa supported her election as the first woman to be admitted to the *Accademia delle scienze morali e politiche* of Naples. Her philosophical engagement ran as deep as her political commitment. Despite her first husband's official obligations to the papacy, in the city of Perugia, that was part of the Papal

---

[21]   See M. A. Degl'innocenti Venturini, 'Marianna Florenzi Waddington; una traduttrice di Schelling', *Archivio di Filosofia*, 1, 1976: 173–175. For more information on Marianna Florenzi Waddington, see F. Bozzi, *Marianna allo specchio. Spigolature sulla vita e i pensieri della marchesa Florenzi Waddington in forma di racconto* (Perugia: Era Nuova, 1995); and A. Pieretti and C. Vinti, *La riflessione filosofica di Marianna Florenzi Waddington: Dimensioni storiche e teoretiche*, Introduction to M. Florenzi Waddington, *Saggio sulla natura* (Perugia: Fabrizio Fabbri Editore, 2000), vii–liv; I. Degli Oddi, *Marianna Florenzi Waddington: Dalla vita di una donna alla storia di un paese* (Perugia: Edizioni Guerra, 2001). On Florenzi's philosophy and her role in Italian philosophical culture, see G. Gentile, *Le origini della filosofia contemporanea in Italia*, in *Opere* (Florence: Sansoni, 1957), pp. 36–49; and E. Garin, *Storia della filosofia italiana* (Turin: Einaudi, 1967), vol. III, pp. 1239–1240.

[22]   R. Copenhaver and B. P. Copenhaver, *From Kant to Croce: Modern Philosophy in Italy 1800–1950*. (Toronto: University of Toronto Press, 2012), p. 69.

state, she had long shared the anti-clerical ideas of the liberal circles she frequented. She disputed the Pope's claims to temporal power and supported Italian nationalism and constitutional monarchy, as her 1850 pamphlet *Sulle cose attuali d'Italia (On the Current State of Things in Italy)* made plain, although in another work that same year, *Alcune Riflessioni sopra il Socialismo e Comunismo (Some Reflections on Socialism and Communism)*, she considered Italy unready for democracy. A few years after Florenzi Waddington's translation of Schelling's *Bruno*, Spaventa drafted (but did not publish) the first modern Italian monograph on Bruno, casting him as the Italian Spinoza.[23] To follow up a monograph on Bruno's pantheism – dedicated in fact to Florenzi Waddington – Francesco Fiorentino for his part also planned a major study of *Giordano Bruno and His Times*, which sadly he did not live to see in print.[24]

Bertrando Spaventa began his study of the philosophers of the Renaissance while he was in exile in Turin, where he spent almost a decade.[25] Spaventa had left Naples in 1849, together with Francesco Pignatelli Prince of Strongoli (1775–1853) and his family, having been hired as tutor to the prince's son. The Pignatelli family relocated to Florence, where Bertrando spent ten tedious months, living in intellectual isolation and having difficulties in finding Hegel and Kant's books, which seemed to be absent from Tuscany's libraries and bookshops: 'I must confess, much to my chagrin, that in Tuscany, not to speak of the works of Hegel, I have not even managed to find those of Kant.'[26] In August 1850, Spaventa decided to move to Turin, quitting a job that

---

[23] The notes for this publication project written between 1853–1854 have been collected and published: Bertrando Spaventa, *Lettera sulla dottrina di Bruno. Scritti inediti 1853–54*, ed. Mariolina Rascaglia and Alessandro Savorelli (Naples: Bibliopolis, 2000).

[24] See Friedrich Schelling, *Bruno. Dialogo di Federico Schelling*, ed. Marianna Florenzi Waddington (Florence: Le Monnier, 1859); Francesco Fiorentino, *Il panteismo di Giordano Bruno* (Naples: La Scuola di Pitagora, 2008). On the figure of Marianna Florenzi Waddington, see Fabiana Cacciapuoti, 'Marianna Florenzi Waddington tra panteismo e hegelismo nelle carte napoletane', *Archivio per la storia delle donne*, I, 2004: 219–226; F. Duranti, 'La Marchesa Florenzi, Terenzio Mamiani e una traduzione italiana dello Schelling', *Rassegna storica del Risorgimento*, no. XXIX, 1942: 421–426.

[25] For the latest reconstruction of Spaventa's work on the Renaissance, see Bertrando Spaventa, *Scritti sul Rinascimento (1852–1872)*, ed. Giuseppe Landolfi Petrone (Rome: Fabrizio Serra, 2011). On Spaventa's interpretations of Bruno and, more in general, on the nineteenth-century interpretations of the philosopher from Nola, see Saverio Ricci, *Dal 'Brunus redivivus' al Bruno degli italiani* (Rome: Edizioni di Storia e Letteratura, 2009); Bertrando Spaventa, *Lettera sulla dottrina di Bruno. Scritti inediti 1853–54*, ed. Mariolina Rascaglia and Alessandro Savorelli (Naples: Bibliopolis, 2000); Giuseppe Cacciatore, *Giordano Bruno e noi. Momenti della sua fortuna tra Settecento e Ottocento* (Salerno: Edizioni Marte, 2003); Canone, *Brunus redivivus*.

[26] B. Spaventa, *Studii sopra la filosofia di Hegel; Le prime categorie della logica di Hegel*, ed. E. Colombo (Milan: CUSL, 2001), p. 38.

made him miserable and reaching what was then perceived to be the Italian capital: 'Here [in Turin] is the Idea of our country, here is Italy, here is freedom.'[27] This was a very difficult decision to take, as his job as tutor was the only source of funds he could provide for his brother Silvio, incarcerated in Naples. Once in Turin, he started to seek employment and began writing for a number of different journals and newspapers. His intellectual interests between 1851 and 1856 concerned the philosophy of the Renaissance and that of Giordano Bruno in particular. He maintained that the new idea of freedom that emerged from Giordano Bruno's works represented a deeper change than the Reformation, because it was not only a religious reform but also a philosophical and political one. He recognised the urgent need to rekindle in Italian citizens the ancient idea of moral freedom that had been framed during the Renaissance. More especially, the idea of moral freedom that emerges from Spaventa's interpretation of Bruno was to provide the political input for the 'creation' of Italians. Indeed, Spaventa maintains that Bruno's idea of the fundamental principle of Christianity, as the union of infinite divine nature and finite human nature, implies that every human being has an inestimable value and dignity and that no earthly authority can rightfully coerce their conscience. Spaventa insists that this concept of moral freedom was the only idea suited to bringing about the cultural and moral revolution that the Italian people needed in order to attain political union.

The objective of Bertrando Spaventa is to demonstrate that what Luther had forged in German culture was equivalent to what Bruno achieved in Italy with his principle of moral liberty. Indeed, Spaventa goes so far as to assert that Bruno's idea was even more radical than the Reformation's idea of moral freedom and that the Renaissance was the 'Italian version of the Protestant Reform'. He also demonstrates that the Italian philosophical revolution of the sixteenth and the early seventeenth century had affirmed the principle of freedom of thought and the infinite reality of God, that is, God's immanence. The main protagonist in this revolution was Giordano Bruno, and for this reason Spaventa inaugurated a fruitful season in the study of his thought, in order to demonstrate that 'Italy, that is, Catholic Rome, burning Bruno alive and not understanding Vico, has renounced the substance of modern life'.[28] Bruno's idea of moral freedom is indeed

---

[27] Bertrando Spaventa, *Epistolario di Bertrando Spaventa (1847–1860)*, ed. Mariolina Rascaglia, vol. I (Rome: Istituto Poligrafico e Zecca dello Stato, 1995), p. 73.

[28] Spaventa, *Epistolario*, p. 97.

based on the belief that a human being has an infinite value. For, as Spaventa wrote:

> for Bruno the sphere of the inner conscience is a sanctuary, that no human power may legitimately penetrate and invade; in it a man may freely develop all the riches of his nature, without any other law than his own conviction, without any other judgement than his own approval. Man, as inner man, has an infinite, absolute, unlimited value.[29]

So, if a human being has, in their inner life, an infinite value, and the inner life is the moral life, then 'the truly moral man is God's image on earth', God is realised in the works of man'.[30] Human moral activity has to abide by the civic virtues: prudence, wisdom, and justice. Justice is the most important virtue because it has to correct external actions that breach the laws but cannot punish intentions or thoughts:

> Thought is not [an] object of punitive justice, because whatever may be its movement and development, it does not offend against any law (it has no other law but itself): thought is absolutely free. The same may be said of speech, save where this latter may come to shed the respect by which the res publica is sustained. Thought and speech, since they cannot offend the law, nor harm the res publica, do not offend God, nor do they cause him pleasure or displeasure, sadness or delight.[31]

According to Spaventa, the new principle of modernity expressed by Bruno is the divine commandment: do not persecute people for their thoughts and their works, their ideas and their words. Let them be the owners of their own consciousness. This divine command must be known and followed by the majority and it is possible only if this kind of 'religious sentiment' is widespread. This religious sentiment is a new idea of freedom based on the inner moral life and the autonomy of consciousness.[32] Bruno's thought maintains the principle of the Reformation, that is, the absence of mediation between God and human beings, and this was the principle that had produced freedom of religion. The difference is that, while the Reformation had revolutionised the religious sphere, Bruno's notion of the autonomy of consciousness, free from religious and secular authorities, had a number of other consequences in various different domains. Spaventa wrote that:

---

[29] Bertrando Spaventa, 'Principii della filosofia pratica di G. Bruno', in *Saggi di critica filosofica, politica e religiosa* (Naples: Scuola di Pitagora, 2008), p. 152.

[30] Spaventa, 'Principii della filosofia pratica di G. Bruno', pp. 145 and 155.

[31] Spaventa, 'Principii della filosofia pratica di G. Bruno', p. 151.

[32] Spaventa, 'Principii della filosofia pratica di G. Bruno', p. 171.

The new principle led in political life to the assertion of the lay power (of whatever nature, be it civic or royal), and to its separation from the power of the Church; in religious life to the dissolution of Catholic unity, to the advent of the Reformation and to the limiting and decline of papal authority; in the particular life of the [various] nations to the formation of national unity through political unity (e.g. in France); and in practical life to the assertion of the importance of the particular ends of human activity as means to a higher end.[33]

The other important philosopher of the Renaissance that Spaventa rediscovered in the 1850s was Tommaso Campanella, who shared with Bruno a life of persecution: while Bruno was burned at the stake for his ideas, Campanella spent twenty-seven years in jail. According to Spaventa, Campanella's thought is divided between the Middle Ages and Modernity, or rather between magic and science:

In Campanella there are as it were two men: the man of the Middle Ages, the Dominican, the disciple of St. Thomas [Aquinas], and the new man, with new instincts and tendencies, who always fears to contradict the former, and simply means to resolve this opposition, which had already arisen at that time and which is one of the principal features of the emancipation of the spirit of the Middle Ages, between the new science, especially the knowledge of nature, and ecclesiastical beliefs.[34]

The modern aspect of Campanella's philosophy, which is more interesting for us, is the recognition of the value of the senses and experience, which establishes the principle of self-consciousness and the spontaneous activity of the spirit. Through this identification, Campanella posits subjectivity as first principle, anticipating, according to Spaventa, Descartes' philosophical revolution, which established modern philosophy on the principle of the autonomy of consciousness:

To Descartes has been attributed the glory of having been the first to found philosophy upon self-consciousness, to have restored certainty to the contents of cognition, by positing a principle, in which thought and being, form and contents, the certain and the true are immediately identified with each other, that is, the *cogito ergo sum:* but to Campanella also is this glory due.[35]

[33] Bertrando Spaventa, 'Del principio della riforma religiosa, politica e filosofica nel secolo XVI', in *Saggi di critica filosofica, politica e religiosa* (Naples: Scuola di Pitagora, 2008), pp. 304–305.
[34] Bertrando Spaventa, 'Tommaso Campanella', in *Saggi di critica filosofica, politica e religiosa* (Naples: Scuola di Pitagora, 2008), p. 19.
[35] Spaventa, 'Tommaso Campanella', p. 59.

Spaventa's study of Campanella and Bruno must not be assessed for its historiographical accuracy nor for the methodology, which rests on the typical nineteenth-century category of the 'forerunner',[36] but must rather be understood in terms of his philosophical and political commitment. It was of fundamental importance to Spaventa to recognise the same two principles – the autonomy of consciousness and the infinite value of human dignity – that characterised modernity, and not only in the Protestant Reformation, but also in the Italian Renaissance, in order to participate in the general philosophical modernity of Europe.

The real modern revolution was the one that had founded philosophy on the observation of nature and the autonomy of thought. Studying Bruno and Campanella's thought and the philosophy of the Renaissance was not simply an intellectual amusement for Spaventa, or an attempt to offer a precise historiographical reconstruction, but was primarily the expression of his determination to respond to the moral and intellectual decline of his country. For Spaventa, the only way to create a free nation was to rekindle in Italian citizens the ancient idea of moral freedom and the autonomy of thought, which had been formulated during the Renaissance. Spaventa was intent on rediscovering a moral and religious reformation in Italian political thought, being convinced that '[we] Italians, to a greater extent than the Germans or the English, need inner moral, religious, scientific and philosophical freedom in order to be free politically, externally, in the open air. We need it because we have at home, as a thing or person that is our own, our greatest enemy, the enemy of the free spirit, infallible spiritual authority'.[37]

There is a close link between Italian Hegelianism and the study of the philosophy of the Renaissance, namely, the connection with both the theory of 'national revolution' and the problem of 'national tradition'.[38] As Sergio Landucci stresses: 'The Hegelianism of Spaventa was not only a theory of national revolution, but also, in connection with this, the posing of the problem itself of "national tradition' . . .. Of the concrete Spaventian reconstruction [of that problem] there subsist indications that are no

[36] The category of 'forerunner' is an interpretation that is characteristic of the philosophy of history of the nineteenth century and points to some Italian authors as having anticipated the most important European philosophers: for example, Spaventa identifies in Bruno the precursor of Spinoza and in Campanella intimations of Descartes.

[37] Bertrando Spaventa, 'Paolottismo, positivismo, razionalismo', in *Opere*, vol. I (Florence: Sansoni, 1972), p. 485.

[38] On this important connection, see also Tessitore, 'La cultura filosofica tra due rivoluzioni (1799–1860)'; Ricci, *Dal 'Brunus redivivus' al Bruno degli italiani*.

longer denied: Bruno, Campanella, Vico.'[39] As a consequence, the Hegelianism of Spaventa, who interprets the moment of self-consciousness from a practical point of view, ascribes a radical moral dimension to the logic and theory of knowledge. Reading history as the development of freedom, and at the same time interpreting the philosophy of right in terms of the philosophy of history, rendered Spaventa's interpretation of Hegelianism both a theory of 'national revolution' and an interpretation of the 'national tradition'. The interpretation of the Renaissance is precisely the moment when the issue of national revolution intersected with the reconstruction of national tradition.

In 1860, Spaventa publicly expounded his ideas regarding the Renaissance in an account that summarises his various publications on the topic through the 1850s. In his inaugural address as professor of philosophy of law at the University of Bologna entitled *The Nationality of Philosophy*, he thus argued that modern philosophy could not be restricted to a specific nationality but had to be understood as the circulation of European ideas: 'modern philosophy is no longer only British, nor [is it] French, nor Italian, nor German but European'.[40] At the heart of this circulation of ideas lay, in Spaventa's view, the philosophy of the Renaissance, which represented the modernity both of Italian and of European culture:

> To recover the sacred thread of our philosophical tradition, to revive the knowledge of our free thought in the study of our greatest philosophers, to research in the philosophies of other nations the seeds received by the founding fathers of our philosophy and then returned to us in a new form and with a more fully developed system, to understand this *circulation of Italian thought* . . .to know in short what we were, what we are and what we should be in the movement of modern philosophy, not as members isolated and split off from the universal life of the peoples, nor as bound to the triumphal car of a particular people, but as a free and equal nation in the community of nations: such, Sirs, has always been the aspiration and the occupation of my life.[41]

Spaventa's theory of the circulation of Italian and European thought was intended first of all to demonstrate that the philosophical revolution of the Italian Renaissance was based on the same principles as the Reformation.

---

[39] Landucci, 'L'hegelismo in Italia nell'età del Risorgimento', p. 620.

[40] Bertrando Spaventa 'Carattere e sviluppo della filosofia italiana dal secolo XVI sino al nostro tempo', in *La filosofia del Risorgimento. Le prolusioni di Bertrando Spaventa*, ed. Nicola Capone (Naples: Scuola di Pitagora, 2005), p. 8.

[41] Spaventa 'Carattere e sviluppo della filosofia italiana dal secolo XVI sino al nostro tempo', p. 69.

The advocates of this revolution, Giordano Bruno and Tommaso Campanella, had affirmed the immanence of the divine nature in human nature, the dignity and sanctity of the individual, the autonomy of consciousness, and liberty from any kind of authority whatsoever.

Spaventa's studies on the Renaissance flowed into his theory of the circulation of Italian and European thought, in which he argues that the principles of modernity, suppressed in Italy on account of the violence unleashed by the Counter-Reformation, which had not hesitated to burn heterodox thinkers at the stake, flourished in other regions that were experiencing periods of political or religious liberty:

> Italian philosophy was not smothered on the pyres of our philosophers; rather, it took its leave and went on to develop in a freer country and in freer minds. Thus, to look for it in its new fatherland is not to engage in a servile imitation of the German nationality. Rather it amounts to a reclamation of what belonged to us, of what, under different guises, has become a property of universal spirit, the essential condition of our civilisation and of all peoples. It is not our philosophers of the last two centuries, but Spinoza, Kant, Fichte, Schelling, and Hegel who are the true disciples of Bruno, of Vanini, of Campanella, of Vico and other illustrious thinkers.[42]

Thanks to the integration of Giambattista Vico's ideas, Spaventa understands that these two principles have to become *mores*, a real determination, to establish the state. To obtain this, however, it is necessary that Italians become aware of themselves and of the history of their own philosophical tradition.[43] This lack of self-awareness is, according to Spaventa, one of the main causes of the servitude of Italians.[44] More in general, his theory sought to demonstrate firstly that the philosophers of the Italian Renaissance were the forerunners of modern philosophy and, secondly, that the Italian philosophers of his time – Pasquale Galluppi, Antonio Rosmini (1797–1855), and Vincenzo Gioberti - were, in the results of their thinking, in harmony with European thought, in particular German idealism. With this theory, Spaventa tried to build a bridge between the two traditions to which he was most closely linked: Renaissance philosophy and German Idealism.

The three key authors Spaventa considers in his assessment of contemporary Italian philosophy were all grappling in different ways with the

---

[42] Bertrando Spaventa, 'Logica e Metafisica', in *Opere*, ed. Giovanni Gentile, III (Florence: Sansoni, 1972), p. 21.
[43] Bertrando Spaventa, 'Ms. XXXI – Lettera', D.1. Carta 21, Società di storia patria, December 8, 1861.
[44] Spaventa, 'Ms. XXXI – Lettera'.

problem of the immanentisation of the transcendence and, more generally, with the challenge to find a middle term between rationalism and empiricism. They all engaged with Kant but did not find his philosophy wholly satisfactory. We have already discussed Galluppi's sensism in Chapter 1, when comparing his understanding of Kant with Colecchi's and the proposition that the foundation of the knowledge of the external world is based on 'self-perception'. According to Spaventa, Galluppi was a 'Kantian against his own will' because, by distinguishing counsciousness and the senses he established the foundation of knowledge not on the senses but on the conscious self-perception.[45]

Abbot Antonio Rosmini was also dealing with the Kantian system, but his reading tended towards spiritualism. Born in Rovereto under Habsburg control he studied as a priest and concluded his ecclesiastical education in 1819, proceeding then to discuss Kantian gnoseology in his first important philosophical work, *New Essay on the Origins of Ideas* (1830), where he reduced Kant's categories to one only: Being. This category is also the one on which moral principles are based, as described in his *Principle of Moral Science* (1831). Rosmini's doctrine of the 'Ideal Being' presents itself as a psychologism by which Being does not originate from the experience of the senses, as in Galluppi, but is innate. This innate idea is the condition of the possibility of knowledge, and according to Spaventa this claim represented a Kantian influence on Rosmini.[46]

It is on the interpretation of Being that Rosmini and Gioberti diverged. We have already encountered the author of the famous pamphlet on the *Moral and Civil Primacy of the Italians* (1843), in which Gioberti delved deeply into the remote Italic, Pelasgic origins of Italian intellectual identity, connecting it to the Pythagorean school and maintaining that Italians' proximity to Catholic institutions made them the privileged custodians of this mode of thought. He was the inspiration behind neo-Guelphism, a political movement that supported the unification of Italy in the guise of a federation under the aegis of the Pope. This name refers to the more famous medieval Guelphs, the faction that supported the Pope in opposition to the Ghibellines, who were aligned with the Holy Roman Emperor in the struggles for supremacy over the Italian city-states during the twelfth and thirteenth century. In contrast to Rosmini, Gioberti's 'Ideal Formula' does not isolate Being from reality. His theory that 'Being creates the Existent, and the Existent returns to Being' insisted rather on the point

---

[45] Spaventa, *Epistolario*, p. 207 (13 July 1857).
[46] Spaventa, *La filosofia di Kant e le sue relazioni con la filosofia italiana*, p. 560.

that Universal Reason is determined in reality, and reality aims at the rationality of the idea. This ontologism presented a dialectical understanding of the relationship between Being, which is the mode of God, and Existence, which is the mode of human beings. In this, Spaventa discerns similarities with Hegel's philosophy. Gioberti, Spaventa observed, had thus identified 'the *creation* in a mode that is similar to the Hegelian', presenting the 'identification of world and God'.[47] However, Gioberti had failed to grasp the power of the *Aufhebung* and therefore to develop a proper dialectical understanding of the relationship between the rational and the real.[48]

Spaventa indicates how the development of the principles of modernity conceived by the philosophers of the Italian Renaissance, 'the real infinity of God and the spontaneity of human thought', will not be fully developed in nineteenth-century Italy by Galluppi, Rosmini, and Gioberti, but rather by the philosophers of German idealism, and Hegel in particular. This movement of ideas is presented in the theory of the 'circulation of Italian thought', outlined during the course that Spaventa taught in Bologna and then developed in its entirety at the University of Naples in 1861, published the following year with the title *Prolusione ed introduzione alle lezioni di filosofia nella Università di Napoli. 23 Novembre – 23 Dicembre 1861*.[49] That thesis made Spaventa a well-known figure among historians of philosophy, who generally have studied his thinking from this perspective.

The idea of nation that emerged from this definition of 'national character' described the nation not simply as a natural and 'immediate' unity (e.g., language, religion, customs) but as the 'project' of a juridical personality that was the product of the free consciousness and awareness of the people. Spaventa's modern nation, founded on the revolutionary philosophy of the Renaissance, presupposed the refusal of authority, of a concept of religion founded on dogma. This revolutionary philosophy was founded instead on the inwardness of individual religious sentiment, on the autonomy of the State, and on the re-evaluation of the worldly and finite dimension, that has in itself a spark of divinity, of the infinite.

---

[47] Benedetto Croce, *Silvio Spaventa*, p. 263 (2 September 1858).
[48] Bertrando Spaventa, *La filosofia di Gioberti* (Naples: Morano, 1863).
[49] Giovanni Gentile republished the text of the Inaugural Address in 1908 with the title that made it well-known: *La filosofia italiana nelle sue relazioni con la filosofia europea*. Gentile's intention was to highlight with the new title the originality and philosophical autonomy of Spaventa's thesis. For the latest edition of this work see Bertrando Spaventa, *La filosofia italiana nelle sue relazioni con la filosofia europea*, ed. Alessandro Savorelli (Rome: Edizioni di Storia e Letteratura, 2003).

2.2   The Philosopher of the Renaissance

Spaventa's rediscovery of Giordano Bruno's work inaugurated a fruitful season of studies on the philosopher from Nola, who became one of the main protagonists in the building of a unified Italian culture.[50] Among Spaventa's pupils, Francesco Fiorentino and Antonio Labriola carried on this tradition of study on the Renaissance and Bruno. Indeed, Fiorentino dedicated most of his life to the study of Renaissance philosophers, while Labriola studied the work of Giordano Bruno between 1888 and 1900.[51]

When Fiorentino arrived in Naples in 1861, after being appointed professor of philosophy at a school in a small town on the periphery of the city (Maddaloni), he drafted his first scientific work entitled *Il panteismo di Giordano Bruno* (*The Pantheism of Giordano Bruno*), composed as an entry to be submitted to an essay competition.[52] In this work, focused on Bruno's dialectic and the relationship between infinite and finite, the influence of Gioberti's thesis regarding the ancient origins of Italian philosophy is clear, and in fact the first chapter of the book is dedicated to the dialectic in the schools of Crotone, Elea, and Alexandria:

> Then I wrote the Essay on Giordano Bruno. Gioberti was still my Ideal . . ..
> Inasmuch as my Gioberti was not a sacrestan, he was militant: he was
> Catholic, yes, but he would not have bowed before the baseness of the
> *Sillabo*; And I was Catholic in his manner, writing against the popes, and in
> favour of the independence of thought.[53]

Gioberti's concern to establish links between philosophy and the 'national cause', his understanding of philosophy as an instrument in the fight for national unity and independence, appealed greatly to the young Fiorentino: 'The captivating pages of Vincenzo Gioberti's *Primato degli Italiani* were the novel of our youth.'[54] Gioberti's influence gradually

---

[50] Carlo Ossola, 'E Aby scoprì Bruno', *Il Sole 24 ore*, July 9, 2008. On this topic see also Canone, *Brunus redivivus*; Ricci, *Dal 'Brunus redivivus' al Bruno degli italiani*.

[51] See Antonio Labriola, *Giordano Bruno: Scritti editi e inediti, 1888–1900*, ed. Stefano Miccolis and Alessandro Savorelli (Naples: Bibliopolis, 2008).

[52] Fiorentino, *Il panteismo di Giordano Bruno*. On Fiorentino's intepretations of the Renaissance, see Fabiana Cacciapuoti, 'Bruno nelle ricerche sul Rinascimento di F. Fiorentino', in *Brunus Redivivus. Momenti della fortuna di Giordano Bruno nel XIX secolo*, ed. Eugenio Canone (Pisa-Rome: Istituti editoriali e poligrafici internazionali, 1998), pp. 191–230; see also Ricci, *Dal 'Brunus redivivus' al Bruno degli italiani*.

[53] Francesco Fiorentino, *La filosofia contemporanea in Italia, risposta di Francesco Fiorentino al professore Francesco Acri* (Naples: Morano, 1876), p. 151.

[54] Fiorentino, *La filosofia contemporanea in Italia, risposta di Francesco Fiorentino al professore Francesco Acri*, p. 9.

decreased after the encounter between Fiorentino and Spaventa in 1861, which the author describes as the rebirth of his mind:

> I came to know Spaventa belatedly, and shortly before that his books. Having read his books, I glimpsed another world, and I seemed to be reborn. I was then a professor at Maddaloni, and was [living in] Naples. I was one of the many getting ready to combat [his ideas]; but having read him, I felt myself drawn to him, and I understood that his adversaries were not even worth[y to tie] his shoelaces.[55]

From that moment, Fiorentino and Spaventa remained very close and collaborated until Spaventa's death, in 1883:

> I knew B. Spaventa in the years of his maturity, I was no longer in the first flush of youth, it was 1861, when he, having returned from Bologna, had come to this university, of which he was a splendid ornament for twenty-two years; and before [knowing] him I had known some of his critical articles, which had disclosed to my mind something like a new world.[56]

Like Spaventa's treatment of the topic, Fiorentino's study of the Renaissance is civic in tone, interweaving as it does historiographical, political, and philosophical reflections, especially on the philosophy of the Renaissance. Indeed, Fiorentino considered the question of the Italian philosophical tradition to be fundamental to the fashioning of a good citizen: 'Clarifying and ascertaining the task of the Risorgimento in the [context of the] History of Philosophy therefore appears to me to be the task of a good citizen. I call this recovering the thread of our tradition.'[57] If we suppose a close correspondence between the philosophy of the Renaissance and modern philosophy – this being the chief insight Fiorentino owed to Spaventa – the study of the Renaissance becomes something more than an intellectual caprice. Indeed, it then serves as an exhortation to rediscover the origins of the 'Italian character'. In Fiorentino's studies on the Renaissance there was raised a theoretical structure that combined the Hegelian interpretation of the history of philosophy and Spaventa's thesis regarding the connection between the Renaissance and modern thought.

---

[55] Fiorentino, *La filosofia contemporanea in Italia, risposta di Francesco Fiorentino al professore Francesco Acri*, p. 150.
[56] Francesco Fiorentino, 'Bertrando Spaventa', in *Ritratti storici e saggi critici*, ed. Giovanni Gentile (Florence: Sansoni, 1935), p. 299.
[57] See Francesco Fiorentino, 'Dedica al Cav. A. C. De Meis', in *Bernardino Telesio ossia studi storici sull'idea della natura nel Risorgimento italiano* (Naples: La Scuola di Pitagora, 2008), pp. 1–6.

By contrast with Spaventa, however, Fiorentino's civic sense led him to extend the chronological period of his analysis to the centuries before the sixteenth century. In addition to the recognition that the philosophy of the Renaissance is the vital core of modern philosophy, developed through the European *peregrinatio*, Fiorentino is searching for the specific features of the Italian nation, qualities that might sustain the future Italian battle for unity and independence. He focused, with more philological accuracy than Spaventa, on the different *stations* of the circulation of thought, deepening the thinking of the various philosophers and intellectuals of the Renaissance.[58] He is convinced that in relation to Italy one should identify three different *Risorgimenti*: the artistic one, which occurred during the fourteenth century through the poetry of Dante and Petrarch, and the prose of Boccaccio, which also influenced Italian philosophy; the scientific one, which took place during the sixteenth century; and finally the political one, realized through the Italian unification of the nineteenth century.[59]

However, Fiorentino's interpretation of Bruno's philosophy, if we compare his first work, from 1861, *Il panteismo di Giordano Bruno*[60] with his essay on *Le opera latine di Giordano Bruno* of 1879,[61] reflects a marked shift in his understanding of the Renaissance, one that occurred between the period closest to Italian unification and the second half of the 1870s. We should also note how the influence of Spaventa had come to prevail over that of Gioberti. In the book written in 1861, Fiorentino describes the Renaissance as a period of a new life called *Risorgimento*:

> The sixteenth century is labelled with the name of Risorgimento, as if the nations of Europe, weary of the long struggle of the Middle Ages, had got to their feet in order to regain the interrupted road through that fearsome night. A new life began to wind through that man who emerged reshaped by the elements for so many contending centuries . . . . Up until that time authority had reigned over the Middle Ages, and on its own held the field, invading, and binding property, law, and faith . . . . Human intelligence, impatient to free itself from the incomparable servitude, turned in hope to classical antiquity, and sought to revive that cadaver in which were preserved, without the vital breath, [but] still inviolate the beauties of form.[62]

[58] Francesco Fiorentino, *Pietro Pomponazzi. Studi storici sulla scuola bolognese e padovana del secolo XVI* (Naples: La Scuola di Pitagora, 2008), p. 6.

[59] On this topic, see Francesco Fiorentino, 'La filosofia del Petrarca', in *Scritti varii di letteratura, filosofia e critica per Francesco Fiorentino* (Naples: Morano, 1876), pp. 101–125.

[60] Fiorentino, *Il panteismo di Giordano Bruno.*

[61] Francesco Fiorentino, 'Le opere latine di Giordano Bruno', in *Il panteismo di Giordano Bruno* (Naples: La Scuola di Pitagora, 2008), pp. 13–49.

[62] Fiorentino, *Il panteismo di Giordano Bruno*, pp. 1–2.

Like Spaventa, Fiorentino maintains that the philosophical revolution of the Italian Renaissance had been more profound than the Protestant Reformation, which for its part had not been as free as Italian critical thinking of the sixteenth century:

> The malignity of the times and the unchecked ardour of his mind rendered it impossible for Bruno to dwell in Naples, or in any other of our cities. He therefore abandoned, albeit reluctantly, Italy, and crossed the Retic Alps in 1580, still young and in his thirties. Switzerland was reputed then to be the asylum of the boldest intelligences of the day, so much so indeed that the Protestants were wont to hail it in the most emphatic of terms as the land of Canaan. On the shores of Lake Leman, in flourishing Geneva, he therefore believed himself to have found the golden breezes of liberty, which a threefold contagion tainted in his native land. But the Protest had shaken the yoke of Rome in order to impose another burden, not a heavier, but a more shameful one, inasmuch as the wicked voice of liberty jeered at the poor wretches disappointed and in their high-sounding chains. In Geneva one had to think in conformity with the venerable Consistory, just as in Rome one was obliged to speak the language of the Holy Office. Bruno, impatient with the former, as with the Roman yoke, reckoned it would be best for him to leave, and seek refuge in England, [therefore] taking the road to France.[63]

During the years around Italian unification, the Hegelians felt a sort of identification with the period they called *Risorgimento* and believed that they had a mission to accomplish. It was, they firmly believed, their duty to regain the long and arduous path to Italian Modernity, which had begun with the Renaissance and matured through three centuries:

> The designs of providence have matured in our own age, and after the slow and arduous toil of three centuries, [and ever] since the modern age emerged from the middle ages, we have felt such national pride at seeing that to the list of martyrs of science Italy [has] add[ed] the most renowned and honoured names [Telesio, Campanella, Galileo, Sarpi, Bruno and Vanini]. But from the iniquitous acts of pillage, from the sending into exile, from the prisons, from the tortures [inflicted], from the scoffing, from the dagger and from the burnings at the stake, there has always risen up an immortal and invincible athlete, triumphant thought.[64]

There was a sentiment of responsibility towards the martyrs of science who had died in the early modern age, who could be honoured only by fighting

---

[63] Fiorentino, *Il panteismo di Giordano Bruno*, pp. 5–6. On this topic, see Cantimori, *Eretici italiani del Cinquecento-Prospettive di storia ereticale italiana del Cinquecento*.
[64] Fiorentino, *Il panteismo di Giordano Bruno*, pp. 14–15.

for Italian independence. The difference that Fiorentino underlines is that, while the free thinkers of the Renaissance had struggled for individual autonomy and freedom of conscience, the patriots of the nineteenth century were striving for national independence. Furthermore, Fiorentino enhances the proposed identification by arguing that through the celebration of the martyrs of national unification, Italians would finally be able to honour the unknown martyrs of the liberty of thought who had died during the Renaissance:

> Whereas before the fight was by the few with syllogisms and speech in order to free individual thought ... now on the other hand there are many who demand in the open field, with their weapons in their hands, not their own but national independence. The obscure and despised martyrs of science have been replaced by those glorious ones who fall fighting for the fatherland. And on the field you did indeed fall, Santorre Santarosa, Alessandro Poerio, and Leopoldo Pilla; great by virtue of your intelligence, great above all else for your envied death[s]. With your names therefore it is only just that there should be passed on to the future generations, those more unhappy, but no less to be commended, who were more able to suffer than to act for their fatherland. Whence I am overjoyed that Naples should have remembered her Giordano Bruno.[65]

By the end of the 1870s, the overall approach to the study of the Renaissance and its protagonists had changed: if, on the one side, interest in the topic remained strong, on the other, there was perceptible a shift from the concern to promote an identification between that period and the modern age to a preoccupation with historiographical and philological scrutiny. The case of Fiorentino exemplifies this change because in different periods his studies of Giordano Bruno evince a markedly different sensibility. When, in 1878, Francesco De Sanctis was once again appointed Minister of Public Education, he entrusted Fiorentino with the task of completing the edition of Bruno's Latin works, which was concluded only after the philosopher's own death in 1891. He published two volumes, in 1879 and 1884, and his introduction to the work, in marked contrast to the study he had published in 1861, manifests a historiographical and philological interest rather than a civil passion.[66] This work does indeed offer a scholarly reconstruction of Bruno's Latin books, one involving an appraisal of the influence of the contemporary literature upon Bruno, and, more especially, it reflects the editor's concern to bring to light a number of his

---

[65] Fiorentino, *Il panteismo di Giordano Bruno*, p. 15.
[66] See Fiorentino, 'Le opere latine di Giordano Bruno'. For the role of Spaventa in the editing of Bruno's Latin works, see Cacciapuoti, 'Bruno nelle ricerche sul Rinascimento di F. Fiorentino'.

neglected writings. In this introduction, Fiorentino chose not to underline the identification between the national cause and the rediscovering of the philosophy of the Renaissance, even if he was at pains to welcome De Sanctis' idea as an altogether honourable initiative.

Fiorentino's interest in the philosophy of the Renaissance pervades his oeuvre. Indeed, surveying his most important studies, such as *Pietro Pomponazzi* (1868), *Bernardino Telesio* (1872–1874) and the third volume of his *Manuale di storia della filosofia ad uso dei licei* (1879–1881), or those published posthumously, such as *Il risorgimento filosofico nel quattrocento* (1885) and *Studi e ritratti della Rinascenza* (1911), we can note that the common thread running through his entire intellectual production was the accurate and precise rediscovery of Renaissance philosophy, while being mindful for our part of the political range of the philosophical thesis connecting the philosophy of the Renaissance to modern thought.[67] The appreciation of Renaissance thinking, so characteristic of Italian Hegelians during the Risorgimento, should be considered a cultural activity with a political and patriotic purpose, which was the definition of Italian identity and the realisation of Italian consciousness in order to complete the process of unification and liberation. In 1862, Fiorentino, in his *Prolusione al corso di storia della filosofia*, elevates philosophy to being a weapon of national redemption and affirms that: 'Science can perhaps be an adornment and a decoration; for we Italians it is a desire for redemption, it is an indispensable condition of life [itself].'[68] The political character thus ascribed to the interpretation of Renaissance philosophy is reinforced by Spaventa's philosophical thesis, which had connected the philosophy of the Renaissance to modern philosophy. Fiorentino clearly acknowledges his intellectual debt to the Hegelian when dedicating his study on *Telesio*: 'Without your stupendous *Saggi critici sul Bruno e sul Campanella*, I would have had great difficulty in orienting myself in that muddle, the philosophy of the Risorgimento [Renaissance].'[69]

---

[67] Francesco Fiorentino, *Pietro Pomponazzi. Studi storici sulla scuola bolognese e padovana del secolo XVI* (Naples: La Scuola di Pitagora, 2008); Francesco Fiorentino, *Bernardino Telesio ossia studi storici sull'idea della natura nel Risorgimento italiano*, 2 vols. (Naples: La Scuola di Pitagora, 2008); Francesco Fiorentino, *Manuale di storia della filosofia ad uso dei licei. Parte terza. La filosofia moderna*, vol. III, IV vols. (Naples: La Scuola di Pitagora, 2007); Francesco Fiorentino, *Il risorgimento filosofico del Quattrocento* (Naples: La Scuola di Pitagora, 2008); Francesco Fiorentino, *Studi e ritratti della Rinascenza*, ed. Luisa Fiorentino (Naples: La Scuola di Pitagora, 2008).

[68] Francesco Fiorentino, *Prolusione al corso di Storia della Filosofia, letta nella Regia Università di Bologna il 25 Novembre 1862* (Bologna: Vitali, 1863), p. 17.

[69] Fiorentino, *Bernardino Telesio ossia studi storici sull'idea della natura nel Risorgimento italiano*, I, p. 2.

Furthermore, Fiorentino attributes to the philosophy of the Renaissance, which in his view had had the merit of integrating the divine nature within humanity with the finite and historical world, a creative role comparable to that of modern philosophy. The one epoch deriving from the other, it was necessary to grasp 'in what [respect] the modern age is dissimilar to the period of the Renaissance, and in what way the former was born from the other'.[70] Like Spaventa, Fiorentino applied the historiographical category of the 'forerunner' and saw in the philosophy of the Renaissance intimations or anticipations of Hegelian philosophy, because the latter was the supreme affirmation of the immanence of the divine: 'It seems to me that it is in the Hegelian philosophy that there shines clearly and deeply the trace of Italian thought developed in the interminable polemics of the sixteenth century.'[71] Conversely, and in contrast to Spaventa, Fiorentino underlines the important role of the new method of natural sciences elaborated during the Italian Renaissance:

> The Italian Risorgimento sought to inaugurate the new philosophy, in which the natural sciences had to break away from speculative research, and thereby seal that complete independence of the idea of nature, for whose emancipation the preceding age had laboured.[72]

While Spaventa had argued that beside Bruno and Campanella's ideas and the works of Vico there had not been original thinking in Italy, Fiorentino insists on the importance of the inheritance represented by the natural philosophy of the Renaissance, rejecting any such gap in the history of Italian philosophy.

Beyond Spaventa and Fiorentino's differences regarding the account one should give of the Renaissance's protagonists and ideas, it is important to note that for both the study of the Renaissance involves a need to clarify the philosophical aspects that characterise the nation. In other words, it was precisely through the rediscovery of the philosophy of the Renaissance that they and their contemporaries might hope to play their part in the 'redemption of our fatherland'.[73]. Fiorentino traces the history of the concept of the State, illustrating the characteristics of the modern State, which he differentiates from a religious one (like Jewish theocracy), a warrior State (such as Egypt or Persia), and the Greek and Roman one. The most important comparison he draws is between the rule of law

---

[70] Fiorentino, *Pietro Pomponazzi*, p. 474.   [71] Fiorentino, *Pietro Pomponazzi*, p. 487.

[72] Fiorentino, *Bernardino Telesio ossia studi storici sull'idea della natura nel Risorgimento italiano*, p. 254.

[73] Fiorentino, *Prolusione al corso di Storia della Filosofia, letta nella Regia Università di Bologna il 25 Novembre 1862*, p. 17.

(*Rechtsstaat*) and the modern State as he conceives it: the limit of the *Rechtsstaat* is the idea that liberty is a boundless will and the State is the sum of all such abstract and single free wills; on the other side, the importance of the rule of law is its negating of the divine origin of the State, which is a human product, and its sustaining of the idea that the State is founded on the free consciousness of persons and not on natural strength.

Fiorentino maintains instead that the peculiarity of the modern State is that it is founded on nationality, which adds to the definition of the State an ethical aspect. The modern State indeed has acquired a spiritual dimension, which in the past was a prerogative of the Church, and in this way it has freed itself from any external interference. So the State is no longer a boundless and blind power but one with limits that determine it. Fiorentino criticises the conception of the State as an atomistic aggregation of individuals, whereby it is the guarantor of individual rights. Indeed, he is convinced that the modern State has an ethical dimension that derives from nationality, which is a natural and moral bond expressed by culture and language.

Like Spaventa, Fiorentino is thus interested in the connection between the modern State and the concept of nationality, his argument being based on a specific interpretation of the history of Italian philosophy and Italian modernity, one that is centred on Renaissance thought. Fiorentino clarifies that 'the State is therefore nowadays the realisation of the human ideal in the individuality of a nation.'[74]. That bond with nationality gave to the State an ethical dimension, on which is built the political consciousness of the people:

> The modern State essentially therefore has an ethical foundation: the natural element of place and of origin only features insofar as it has an influence upon the determination of national genius, which does not reveal itself otherwise than in language, in art, in religion, in science, and in a greater or lesser aptitude for this or for another form of work.[75]

The modern state thus conceived is the product of Italian history and is the collective consciousness of the nation. It was an ideal born during the Renaissance and guarded through the centuries by Italian poets, historians, and statesmen. As Fiorentino wrote:

---

[74] Francesco Fiorentino, 'Lo Stato moderno. Due lettere a Silvio Spaventa', in *Ritratti storici e saggi critici*, ed. Giovanni Gentile (Florence: Sansoni, 1935), p. 40.
[75] Fiorentino, 'Lo Stato moderno', p. 41.

> Our soil having been ridden over and overrun by foreign conquerors has
> never caused us to lose this consciousness: our statesmen, our historians,
> our poets, have jealously guarded this tradition, and initiated the hope:
> three decades ago we felt in ourselves the strength to put into effect that
> ideal and our State, having lived for five centuries hidden in the penetralia
> of our consciousness, as a pure ideal, passed in a full and vigorous [condi-
> tion] into the reality of history.[76]

So Fiorentino also traces a link between the Renaissance and the
Risorgimento and, like the majority of the Hegelians, he thought that
the first epoch had had a positive influence on the second. In other words,
he was at pains to identify in both epochs a concern to celebrate the ideal
of Italian independence and liberty. These two historical periods are thus
in his view representative both of the heroes of thought (Telesio,
Campanella, Galilei, Sarpi, Bruno, Vanini) and of the heroes of action
(Santorre di Santarosa, Alessandro Poerio, and Leopoldo Pilla). That is
why, in opposition to the widespread view of the Renaissance as a period of
decadence, Fiorentino maintains that:

> If the sixteenth century began on the one hand the ill-starred epoch of
> foreign domination in our home; Italy on the other hand, as if to remake
> itself, spent all of its inexhaustible energy in science, and called this century
> (a boldness truly to be remembered!) the epoch of the Risorgimento.[77]

Furthermore, he argues that the Renaissance as well as being a period of
elaboration of a new concept of the world, also expresses intellectual strength
and moral solidity, much as the Risorgimento would in its turn do:

> The energy of the individual and of the many, translated into glorious deeds
> and into the sufferings of the martyrs of science and of those glorious
> [heroes] who fell fighting for the fatherland, serves to delineate the precious
> physiognomy of an Italy vital in thoughts and in actions, with a history
> woven from great ideals capable of assuming a positive form.[78]

The idealist approach of Fiorentino, together with his national sentiment,
established the peculiar character of his studies on the Renaissance and
bestowed a patriotic awareness on his historical researches.

Fiorentino's reflections are especially concerned with the new-born
Italian State, which has to be a modern State founded on a national
constitution and on citizens who have already acquired their political

---

[76] Fiorentino, 'Lo Stato moderno', p. 42.

[77] Fiorentino, *Prolusione al corso di Storia della Filosofia, letta nella Regia Università di Bologna il
25 Novembre 1862*, p. 4.

[78] Manieri, *Il 'ritorno a Kant' e lo studio del Rinascimento in Francesco Fiorentino e Felice Tocco*, p. 76.

consciousness and an awareness of their independence. The author is mindful of the fundamental role of public schools in a new, modern State because it is based on nationality, that is to say, on art, science, and language. There is a need, in other words, to know deeply the culture of the nation, both scientific and literary, and the guaranteeing of public instruction is thus one of the most important duties of the State.[79]

Unlike Spaventa, Fiorentino did not propose a systematic consideration of the theory of the State nor a direct comparison with Hegel's political thought, but they were agreed that an understanding of Renaissance philosophy was needed in order to sustain the founding of the new Italian State. This approach, which strictly links philosophical historiography and politics, is characteristic of the Italian Hegelians: while Spaventa insists on the circulation and connection of Italian philosophy with the European, Fiorentino enhances this argument by reflecting both on the links between the Middle Ages and the Renaissance and on the interpretation of the history of Italian philosophy as the history of freedom, using philological studies and deeper archival research. Again, by contrast with Spaventa, Fiorentino returns to the sources and redefines in detail the relevant debates and contexts. His avowed purpose is to describe the essential character of Italian thinking, which in his judgement is, as Spaventa also maintains, focused on the connection between moral and political freedom. An ideal of this sort is to be kept alive and pursued also during the Risorgimento. In Fiorentino, we note that philological accuracy and the historiographical approach sustain an interpretation of the Renaissance as a moral ideal to follow in building the new State. The very same ideal and the same identification are evident in Spaventa.

2.3 The Anti-clerical

In order to understand Antonio Labriola's interest in Bruno, we should bear in mind his Hegelian formation and his interest in modern Italian philosophy, nurtured at the school run by Spaventa, where he also learnt that the relationship between State and Church is a key factor in Italian history. The figure of Bruno is very important to Labriola also because it represents the development of this relationship: it is not a coincidence that he focuses on Bruno and not on other protagonists of the Renaissance. Indeed, according to Labriola, Bruno represents the long-term condition

---

[79] See Francesco Fiorentino, 'L'educazione politica e l'università', in *Ritratti storici e saggi critici*, ed. Giovanni Gentile (Florence: Sansoni, 1935), pp. 50–64.

of Italian servitude (*servaggio*) in which the Catholic Church had placed the Italian people, which also accounted for the weakness of the State. It means that a monument remembering Bruno is important as a symbol of the new Italy and the new State in which the nation is reborn:

> Let us therefore raise the monument to Giordano Bruno in Campo dei Fiori, so as to expiate the guilt of our forefathers, whose cowardly morality was the reason for our delayed political progress, because it serves as a symbol to the masses of liberty of conscience . . . . If it is true that man does not live by bread alone, in the growing material prosperity of our country, let us take care not to forget *the ideas*, for which we have risen up, and without which we cannot continue the civil work of a free and progressive state.[80]

Labriola locates Bruno four-square in the Renaissance, even if in terms of strict chronology he belongs to a later period: 'Bruno was humanist, and although belatedly, had living within himself, and this more than any other writer of the Renaissance, that sense of nature, from which then germinated the new science of experiment.'[81] Labriola cannot be considered an expert on Giordano Bruno and the presence of the author in his books remains marginal, but his interpretation has attracted the interest of scholars in recent years because, in contrast to his contemporaries, he had an active attitude towards the sources and he distinguished Bruno's work from his fortune and fate. Labriola's Brunian writings all belong to the period between the turbulent two years 1888–1889, linked to the question of the monument in the Campo de' fiori, and the tricentenary of his being burnt at the stake, celebrated in February 1900. Two very different circumstances: the first serving as a conclusion, in a theatrical form, of the liveliest cycle of studies of the philosopher from Nola in the nineteenth century; the second, at the end of a long construction of the *myth* of Bruno over the previous decades and a stasis in historical research.[82]

In Labriola's interpretation of Bruno, we can also note an attitude bearing a marked resemblance to that of Spaventa and Fiorentino, regarding the connection between the understanding of the Italian history of philosophy, especially the period of the Renaissance and the theory of the State. It is clear, indeed, that the interpretation of the Renaissance is a

---

[80] Antonio Labriola, 'Al comitato per la commemorazione di G. Bruno in Pisa', in *Giordano Bruno: scritti editi e inediti, 1888–1900*, ed. Stefano Miccolis and Alessandro Savorelli (Naples: Bibliopolis, 2008), pp. 36–38.

[81] Antonio Labriola, 'Nola a Giordano Bruno', in *Giordano Bruno: Scritti editi e inediti, 1888–1900*, ed. Stefano Miccolis and Alessandro Savorelli (Naples: Bibliopolis, 2008), p. 43.

[82] Labriola, *Giordano Bruno*, pp. 16–17. See Alessandro Savorelli, *L' aurea catena. Saggio sulla storiografia filosofica dell'idealismo italiano* (Florence: Le Lettere, 2003); Canone, *Brunus redivivus*.

key point in understanding the political philosophy and the theory of the State of the Italian Hegelians in general and of Labriola in particular. First of all, he recognises the important role of religious sentiment in sustaining moral sentiments, especially as regards the lower classes: the withering of religious sentiment results in a withering of moral sensibility.[83]

The first sign of Labriola's interest in Bruno's thought was indeed an ironical comment on Fiorentino's commitment to the edition of Bruno's Latin works, featured in a letter to Angelo Camillo De Meis: 'Fiorentino is working very hard on the Bruno edition, and this will be De Sanctis' best work!"[84] Labriola's interest in the figure of Giordano Bruno was prompted, it should be understood, by civic passion, and he began to study him chiefly for political motives, during the second half of the 1880s, even as he was coming to adopt a democratic-radical position. This is the reason why he interprets the scientific movement, ending with Bruno's death, as the beginning of a social movement for the emancipation of the people: 'But there in Campo dei Fiori ... and in that effigy documented in bronze [the people] may see not the end of a scientific movement but the beginning of a social movement, a sign, a stage in the arduous way that they will have to traverse, in order to achieve their complete emancipation.'[85]

During the course in the philosophy of history inaugurated with the public lecture on the tricentenary of Bruno's death in 1900, Labriola gave two lectures on the philosopher from Nola, in which he clearly underlines his debt to Spaventa, concerning his interpretation of the role of Bruno in the history of philosophy: 'Nor have I waited until 1889 to honour the philosopher from Nola because I come, even though I do not follow its ideas, from the school in which shone Bertrando Spaventa, who thought that the study of German philosophy would have been open to rebuke if it had not continued the Brunian tradition.'[86] Labriola describes Spaventa as the 'first truly to vindicate Bruno philosophically in Italy', and he high-lights the important role of the Hegelian in the interpretation of modern philosophy, for, as he wrote to Engels in 1894: 'Spaventa (the best of them all, and I will pass over the others in silence), wrote about dialectic in an exquisite manner, rediscovered Bruno and Campanella, delineated the

[83] See Antonio Labriola, 'Morale e religione (1873)', in *Tutti gli scritti filosofici e di teoria dell'educazione*, ed. Luca Basile and Lorenzo Steardo (Milan: Bompiani, 2014), pp. 785–830.

[84] Antonio Labriola, *Carteggio. I. 1861–1880*, ed. Stefano Miccolis (Naples: Bibliopolis, 2000), p. 638.

[85] Antonio Labriola, 'Giordano Bruno e la democrazia (1889)', in *Giordano Bruno: Scritti editi e inediti, 1888–1900*, ed. Stefano Miccolis and Alessandro Savorelli (Naples: Bibliopolis, 2008), p. 47.

[86] Labriola, *Giordano Bruno*, p. 127.

useful and utilisable part of Vico, and found by himself (in 1864!) the link between Hegel and Darwin.'[87]

On the other hand, it is only because Labriola does not deem Bruno to be the 'forerunner' of either Spinoza or German idealism that he does not share Spaventa's general perspective on the philosopher from Nola. He does not accept Spaventa's interpretation of the unity of Bruno's philosophy, rejecting the idea that its vital core is the same as the Hegelian dialectic. Whatever his differences with the Hegelians regarding both interpretations and political vision, throughout his life Labriola recognised the importance of that revolutionary movement, while at the same time emphasising its shortcomings:

> [The Hegelians] were in part epigones pure and simple, but some were vigorous thinkers. All in all they represented a revolutionary current of considerable importance, despite the traditional scholasticism, the spiritual-ism in the French mode and the philosophy of so-called common sense . . . . All trace and memory of the whole movement has been lost to us here, in the span of so very few years. The writings of these thinkers are only found in the hands of those concerned to vindicate antiquarian stuff and trifles from bookshops. This dispersal into nothingness of a whole scientific activity, and certainly one not without importance . . . has more intrinsic reasons. Those Hegelians wrote and taught, and disputed, as if they stood, not in Naples, but in Berlin, or heavens knows where. They were convers-ing mentally with their *Camarades d'Allemagne* . . .. They did not manage to mould their treatises and their dialectic into books that might appear to be a new intellectual acquisition of the nation.[88]

Labriola stresses his Hegelian formation and the influence that it had on his philosophical approach:

> In reading the *Heilige Familie* [of Marx and Engels], I remembered the Hegelians of Naples, in whose midst I lived from my earliest youth, and it seems to me that I had understood and savoured that book, more than many manage to, lacking at present as they do the typical and intuitively [understood] details of that curious humorous approach . . . I too lived

---

[87] Labriola, *Giordano Bruno*, p. 127; Valentino Gerratana, 'Per una corretta lettura di Labriola. Precisazioni e rettifiche', *Critica marxista*, XI, 1973: 264–265. The most important testimony of the intense relationship between Bertrando Spaventa and Antonio Labriola is their correspondence: see Antonio Labriola, '123 lettere inedite di Antonio Labriola a Bertrando Spaventa', ed. Giuseppe Berti, *Rinascita* 12, 1953: 714–736; Labriola, *Giordano Bruno*; Antonio Labriola, 'Dodici lettere inedite di Antonio Labriola a Bertrando Spaventa', ed. Giuseppe Vacca, *Studi Storici* 7, no. 4, 1966: 757–766; Labriola, *Carteggio*.

[88] Antonio Labriola, 'Discorrendo di socialismo e filosofia. Seconda edizione ritoccata ed ampliata (1902)', in *Tutti gli scritti filosofici e di teoria dell'educazione*, ed. Luca Basile and Lorenzo Steardo (Milan: Bompiani, 2014), pp. 1429–1430.

when young in that sort of gymnasium, and I do not regret it; I lived for years with my mind divided between Hegel and Spinoza: of the former I defended, with youthful ingenuity, the dialectic against Zeller who initiated *neo-Kantianism;* of the latter [that is, Spinoza] I knew his writings by heart, and expounded them, with an understanding born of love, the theory of the affects and of the passions. Now all such things come back into my memory as the most distant prehistory.[89]

He even admitted that he became a Marxist because of his Hegelian background, which had taught him the dialectical conception that is the foundation of scientific socialism:

I did not even ask Marxism for knowledge of that philosophy, which it presupposes, and, in a certain sense, continues, overcoming it, through *dialectical inversion*; and it is *Hegelianism*, which did indeed flower again in Italy in my youth, and in which I was as it were raised. As chance would have it, my first philosophical composition, dated May 1862 is the *Difesa della dialettica di Hegel contro il ritorno a Kant iniziato da Ed. Zeller* (*Defence of Hegel's Dialectic against the Return to Kant Initiated by Ed. Zeller*). In order to understand scientific socialism, I therefore did not need to approach for the first time the dialectical, evolutionary or genetic conception, call it what you will, having always lived in this circle of ideas, ever since I thought thoughtfully.[90]

Labriola recognises the strength of religious sentiment, 'one of the most intimate and deepest needs of human nature', and, insofar as it represents a religion 'purged' of superstition and clericalism, a thing that may therefore serve to sustain Italian civic life.[91] Like Spaventa, Labriola seeks a new, widely diffused religious sentiment, founded on the concept of moral liberty formulated by Giordano Bruno and the philosophy of the Renaissance, which is free from dogmas and from the hegemony of the confessional. He also regards it as a precondition for durable political stability in the new-born Italian State, which is 'always exposed to the danger of falling apart, if the gains of thought and liberty, which now a few of the privileged enjoy, do not become the common inheritance of people redeemed from superstition through culture'.[92]

[89] Labriola, 'Discorrendo di socialismo e filosofia', pp. 1430–1431.
[90] Labriola, 'Discorrendo di socialismo e filosofia', p. 1457.
[91] See Labriola, 'Morale e religione (1873)', p. 814; Antonio Labriola, 'La quistione religiosa e l'Italia. II', *Il Piccolo*, October 7, 1871.
[92] Antonio Labriola, 'Al comitato di Terni per le onoranze a Giordano Bruno (1888)', in *Giordano Bruno: scritti editi e inediti, 1888–1900*, ed. Stefano Miccolis and Alessandro Savorelli (Naples: Bibliopolis, 2008), p. 33.

According to Labriola, the absence of a popular religious and moral culture is also the reason for the weakness of the risorgimental State and its lack of popular support. On the other hand, in his judgement the great achievement of the risorgimental process, its historical importance and political originality, lay in the destruction of the temporal power of the Church, which was a fundamental event for all European states. To honour Giordano Bruno was to honour the figure who symbolised modern secular culture, which was itself, in Labriola's opinion, intrinsically linked to the progressive risorgimental tradition. By virtue of that tie, the nation had been regenerated in a new form of State, which was a new *patria*.

It is not hard to discern the influence of Spaventa's Hegelianism upon this interpretation of the relationship between moral and political liberty, for example, upon the understanding of the State. There is, in particular, a brief work by the young Labriola, written in 1864–1865, in which he expounds Spaventa's theory of the State and of the relationship between politics and religion: *Della relazione della Chiesa allo Stato* (*On the Relation of the Church to the State*).[93] It was probably written at the request of his colleague Giovanni Angarano in order to introduce him to Spaventa's classes. On one hand, he illustrates Spaventa's trenchant distinction between the Church and religion, whereby he warns against the mistaken affirmation of the superiority of the Church, infinite and above the world, to the State, finite and worldly; on the other hand, he underlines the importance of the role of the State. While the Church, as an institution, has those guarantees and liberties that each body in civil society has, the State (which represents the totality of ethical relationships) has to defend the religious and ethical sentiment that characterises human life in a society and not just a specific religious institution:

> The relation of the Church to the State rests upon the principle of religious liberty, not as a conception of a *legislative power*, but as emerging from *religious conscience* itself. The true Church is thus the *many Churches*, diverse expressions of just one principle, in the accidental form of *symbolism*, and of *worship*. [The State] is the ultimate expression of liberty in the sphere of right.[94]

If we do not conceive the State as based on ethical and religious sentiment, the risk we run is that of engendering the decadence of the modern State, which has to be understood as the 'domination of the optimum':

---

[93] Antonio Labriola, 'Della relazione della Chiesa allo Stato', in *Tutti gli scritti filosofici e di teoria dell'educazione*, ed. Luca Basile and Lorenzo Steardo (Milan: Bompiani, 2014), pp. 475–480.
[94] Labriola, 'Della relazione della Chiesa allo Stato', p. 479.

The state, the greatest human institution, thus threatens to go into decline: because its strength can only consist of the domination of the optimum: and here, it seems to me, it begins to lose every opinion of the optimum, or it believes that excellence is so natural in every man, that all should be able to find it by themselves.[95]

The religious sentiment is what imparts strength to the inner life of those who are not excellent but can be moved in their moral judgement by it. Widely diffused religious sentiment and the moral inner life are the only viable support to political liberty:

> Political liberty, which was our starting point, therefore does not have value without the moral efficacy of character: and when the state is not, or does not do its utmost to be [the] form and coordination of educative institutions, liberty turns out to be the negation of itself.[96]

Religion also has a part to play in supporting moral consciousness and thus in sustaining political liberty, which is represented by the modern State:

> Religion does not have a foundation if, instead of sharpening moral sentiment, and developing real strength of character, it transports [us] into a world beyond the ideal of perfection . . .. Because the real force of religion can only consist in this: that is to say, that it presents in the idea of divine perfection, and in the representation of the ideal figure of the saviour . . . a real stimulus to human impotence.[97]

On the one hand, the attention Labriola pays to religion and to the relationship between moral and political liberty is an additional confirmation of the importance of those themes in the culture of Italian Hegelianism and of their derivation from a particular interpretation of the philosophy of the Renaissance. On the other hand, in Labriola's analysis of Bruno's thought, there is no trace of the risorgimental identification with the protagonists of the Renaissance: his works are characterised by accurate evaluations of the 'political implications' of Bruno's thought, an active approach to the historical sources and a critical judgement of nineteenth-century interpretations, his concern being to distinguish the philosopher of Nola's ideas from his fortunes in the scholarly literature.[98] Labriola represents indeed the new attitude of the final years of the nineteenth century, in which there is manifested a historiographical interest rather than an identification.

---

[95] Labriola, 'Della libertà morale (1873)', p. 670.
[96] Labriola, 'Della libertà morale (1873)', p. 783.
[97] Labriola, 'Della libertà morale (1873)', p. 783.   [98] See Labriola, *Giordano Bruno*, pp. 9–28.

Labriola does however underline the bond between the Renaissance and the Risorgimento, between Italian moral, cultural, and political emancipation. This is the reason why he associated the inauguration of Bruno's statue in Campo de' Fiori with the celebration of Giuseppe Garibaldi.[99]

> Therefore, inaugurated in Campo di Fiori in [the] temple of truthfulness, with the banners of the democratic and workers' societies we moved across the summit of Campidoglio in order to bring there the auspices of the future in the name of Giuseppe Garibaldi, hero of the popular cause and all too human apostle of universal fraternity.[100]

Labriola refers to that bond between Renaissance and Risorgimento but not exactly as Spaventa and Fiorentino had done, since they had identified fully with the Renaissance and imagined themselves as protagonists of that time. In the pages of Labriola, we can discern a disjunction between the historian and the historical moment of the Risorgimento. Even if he acknowledges that bond, which he surely observed in all those who had formed part of his original cultural and intellectual context, he felt at a distance from it.

The relationship between religious sentiment and political liberty is also the point of view from which Labriola analyses the Risorgimento. As we have already underlined, the most important event of the Risorgimento was, in his judgement, the destruction of the temporal power of the Church, which was the precondition for the founding of the new, modern State. On the other hand, Labriola criticises the liberal elite of the Risorgimento, who had not bridged the gap between the majority of uneducated and the minority of educated people created by the 'missed Reformation'. Indeed, according to Labriola, the very existence of that gap was due to the absence of a Protestant Reformation, since the educated elite had founded its moral sentiment on the principle, formulated by the philosophy of the Renaissance, of the liberty of conscience, which was less accessible to the masses. The elite's aristocratic indifference to the religious question and its focus upon a strictly civil renewal of the State were the main causes of the distance between the masses and the ruling class after the national revolution:

---

[99] On the 9th of June 1889, the statue of Giordano Bruno was inaugurated in Campo de' Fiori in Rome, promoted by various different university student committees. Considering that on the 10th of June there should have been the ceremony for the seventh anniversary of Giuseppe Garibaldi's death, student organisations decided to celebrate the two ceremonies on the same date. It also attested how widespread was the idea of a close connection between the Renaissance and the Risorgimento.

[100] Labriola, 'Giordano Bruno e la democrazia (1889)', pp. 47–48.

The Italian *Risorgimento* unfolded wholly within the nineteenth century; but it unfolded within it rather in the sense of *passive* history than in that of *active* history. The effectively active [history] begins in 1870 . . . . That Italy was in a certain sense historically active even in the time of its preparation for national unity, and especially in the moments of the revolts and the wars, no one would deny: but here in this argument, where we seek to take everything back to the detailed report of the end of the century, we must consider as relatively passive the condition of Italy in all the years prior to 1870, in which the other leading nations laid the premises and gave the first powerful start to the present expansion and truly global competition.[101]

On the one hand, the dialectic between the State, or rather modern thinking, and the Church, that is, the dogmatic principle of authority, had had a fundamental part to play in distracting the masses from superstition; on the other, the new Italy, politically regenerated, could base its moral and intellectual rebirth only on modern culture and the principle of the liberty of conscience. The latter is the principle on which the new nationality was based and that, according to Labriola, was symbolised by the figure of Giordano Bruno. That was also, as for Spaventa, the principle on which the Italian Renaissance had been founded and this is the reason why both authors consider the Counter-Reformation to be the cause of Italian decadence, as Stefano Miccolis maintains: 'But Bruno's personal tragedy brings us back to a still greater tragedy – the decadence of Italy . . . . The reformation that drove other nations and most notably Holland and England on to the paths of progress merely had with us the effect of reaction . . . the ruin of the south begins – and the decadence of every seed of liberty and of progress.'[102]

The analyses of Labriola and Spaventa, and Fiorentino's interpretation thus serve to differentiate the problem of the 'missed Reformation' from that of Italy's 'moral decadence'. Whereas De Sanctis and Villari had dated the 'decadence' earlier and saw it as arising from the internal contradictions of Renaissance Italy, Labriola for his part believed that the caesura in Italian history was situated at the height of the Counter-Reformation. For him, Bruno was the symbol of 'the entire revolution of the modern world', the 'herald of liberty'. Indeed, the philosopher of Nola was

---

[101] Antonio Labriola, 'Da un secolo all'altro. Considerazioni retrospettive e presagi. Frammento (1901)', in *Tutti gli scritti filosofici e di teoria dell'educazione*, ed. Luca Basile and Lorenzo Steardo (Milan: Bompiani, 2014), pp. 1684–1685.

[102] Antonio Labriola, 'Il destino storico di Bruno', in *Giordano Bruno: scritti editi e inediti, 1888–1900*, ed. Stefano Miccolis and Alessandro Savorelli (Naples: Bibliopolis, 2008), p. 65.

emblematic of the heritage of the Renaissance as against Italy's decadence, the latter being represented instead by the poet Torquato Tasso:

> Torquato Tasso is the psychological symbol of the decadence. More note-worthy therefore [is] the figure of Bruno, who precisely in the second half of the sixteenth century gathers together the inheritance of the Renaissance, and as a precursor of science – that is, as a philosopher of the Copernican intuition goes into battle against the pedants – the misoneists – the orthodox of every kind – has his lungs of speculative respiration open to every sort of adaptation – is the herald of the *cosmocentric* conception that reduces [the] pleasure and pain of everyday experience to a relative measure. And for this reason too he is a *dreamer*. Genius is long-sighted. He remains *Italian* though migrating throughout the whole world because Italy is civilisation – he still remains *Catholic,* because Catholicism had been the *work* of history inasmuch as it is not the emptiness of subjective faith.[103]

Decadence arrived after the sixteenth century, or so Labriola insists, and the national revolution is the answer to that decadence: 'Our recent revolution does not consist ... in the *bourgeoisie* coming to dominate over society. This revolution has admittedly been made chiefly under the direction of the bourgeois spirit, but the Italian bourgeoisie already existed for centuries, and it had had not only its glories, but its terrible downfall at the end of the sixteenth century, and its prolonged decadence up until the French Revolution.'[104]

Antonio Labriola's interpretation of Giordano Bruno's work and more in general of the Renaissance therefore offers a privileged point of observation on the process of Italian national emancipation, reaffirming that peculiar bond between historiography, philosophy, and politics that characterised Italian culture during the nineteenth century. This bond emerges clearly also when we explore the different approaches that Neapolitan Hegelians had towards the work of Niccolo' Machiavelli.

---

[103] Labriola, 'Il destino storico di Bruno', p. 67.   [104] Labriola, 'Da un secolo all'altro', p. 1686.

CHAPTER 3

The Risorgimento

Great men are honoured neither with statues, nor otherwise; but by
reevaluating their spirit and causing it to live again.

Francesco De Sanctis, *Conferenze su Niccolò Machiavelli*, 1869

During the nineteenth century, Italian political language underwent a
radical transformation: while the term *Risorgimento* had generally indicated
a specific period of early modern history (approximately from the fourteenth to the sixteenth centuries), by the end of the century that term

Figure 3.1   Statue of Niccolò Macchiavelli (Series 'the Great Florentines') by Lorenzo
Bartolini, Uffizi Gallery, Florence, Italy, 1845–1846

began to be identified with the Italian struggles for national emancipation.[1] At the same time, the word *Renaissance* began to be used to indicate
the period of early modern history between the fourteenth and the
sixteenth centuries, also identified with the birth of 'Modernity'. This
change in language represents a shift from an interpretation that highlights
the religious and moral dimensions of the principle of Italian modernity to
one that stresses its historical characteristics. Such a shift from an ethico-
political meaning to a historiographical one consists of an interpretative
transformation of the origins of modern national culture: initially, the
Renaissance was considered a political and moral model, to emulate or to
condemn, but it then assumed the guise of a historiographical category.
The transformation of the language represents a change of ideas or rather,
in this case, of the way the intellectual and political leaders of the
Risorgimento interpreted the failed religious and moral reformation in
the Italy of the early modern period. While recent scholarship has highlighted how the term *Risorgimento* came to mark a 'symbolic repositioning
from the religious to the political' dimension of the term, it was still
confused with the *Renaissance* as then understood.[2] Linguistic studies have
traced a semantic history of the two terms, *Risorgimento* and *Renaissance*,
illustrating how political and ideological factors conditioned their use and
the meanings they carried.[3] It is thus interesting to note that the word
Renaissance became widespread in Italian culture only after 1876, when the
Italian translation of Burckhardt's well-known book *Civilization of the
Renaissance in Italy* (*Die Kultur der Renaissance in Italien*, 1860) began to
circulate.[4]

Canonical studies concerning the interpretations of the Renaissance agree
that with Burckhardt's work, together with Jules Michelet's *Histoire de
France* (1855), the *Renaissance* asserted itself as a historiographical category.[5]

---

[1] On the complex debate on the dating of the Renaissance, see Delio Cantimori, 'La periodizzazione dell'età del Rinascimento' (1955), in *Storici e storia* (Turin: Einaudi, 1971), pp. 553–557.

[2] Banti et al., *Atlante culturale del Risorgimento. Lessico del linguaggio politico dal Settecento all'Unità*, p. 33.

[3] Alessio Cotugno, 'Rinascimento e Risorgimento (sec. XVIII–XIX)', *Lingua e Stile*, 2, 2012: 265–310.

[4] See Jacob Burckhardt, *Die Kultur der Renaissance in Italien* (Basel, 1860). The first Italian translation was published in 1876: Jacob Burckhardt, *La civiltà del Rinascimento in Italia, con aggiunte e correzioni inedite fornite dall'autore*, trans. Domenico Valbusa (Florence: Sansoni, 1876). On Burckhardt's interpretation of the Renaissance, see also John Burrow, *A History of Histories* (London: Penguin: 2007), pp. 414–423.

[5] Jules Michelet, *Histoire de France au seizieme siecle: Renaissance* (Paris, 1855). On the history and the influence of this book, see also Lucien Febvre, 'Comment Jules Michelet inventa la Renaissance', *Le Genre Humain*, 1, no. 27, 1993: 77–87.

In the literature, Burckhardt's work is of central importance in modern historiographical studies on the Renaissance. Insomuch as in Wallace K. Ferguson's monumental study *The Renaissance in Historical Thought*, Burckhardt's work is the cornerstone of both previous and subsequent historiographical interpretations of the Renaissance:

> It is true that nearly all the separate materials for the creation of Burckhardt's synthesis were already present by the middle of the nineteenth century . . .. Yet Burckhardt's Italian Renaissance was nonetheless, in its integrated entirety, an original creation, the masterpiece of a great historical artist.[6]

Indeed, Ferguson maintains that the Swiss scholar was the first to have defined the Renaissance as a specific historical period and as a peculiar Italian experience. Ferguson maintains that Burckhardt's writing is a 'coherent synthesis' that unified the different interpretations that he identified as characteristic of 'modern progress': 'The growth of individual freedom of thought and expression, the full development of self-conscious personality, and the evolution of moral autonomy founded upon a high conception of the dignity of man.[7] Ferguson's analysis is not particularly concerned with the interpretation of the Renaissance during the Italian Risorgimento, especially because he centers his study on Burckhardt's *Civilization*, which circulated in Italy itself, as we have already noted, only after Italian unification. Although he does consider, along with the majority of scholars, the patriotic spirit that led some Italian intellectuals, Pasquale Villari and Francesco De Sanctis among them, to their interpretation of the Renaissance, he makes no attempt to account for the influence that those interpretations had on the process of Italian unification.

The Italian historian Federico Chabod, in his *Gli studi di storia del Rinascimento* (*Studies on the History of the Renaissance*), likewise recognised the role of Burckhardt's book in establishing a separation between cultural and political history, and in confirming the Renaissance as a 'historical category', a 'specific period' and an 'organic bloc' from the fourteenth to the beginning of the sixteenth century:

> It is altogether true that the historian of Basel's work opened with a broad picture of Italian political society: but it was no longer the society of

---

[6] Wallace K. Ferguson, *The Renaissance in Historical Thought. Five Centuries of Interpretation* (Cambridge, MA: Riverside Press Cambridge, 1948), p. 179.
[7] Ferguson, *The Renaissance in Historical Thought*, p. 182.

freedom, the age of the comuni, of the powerful individualities, the strong ideals, the harsh clashes, but rather the society of the 'tyrannies', of states as a 'work of art', a society that no longer signifies, in the fashion of Sismondi, the resurgence of liberty in Europe, but indeed the diminution of the sense of liberty and the affirmation of 'entirely special political forms' typical of Italy and based on the cold and precise calculation of all the [available] means …. The comune was thrown back into the Middle Ages and the Renaissance had its beginnings with the seigneuries: and here the contrast with Romanticism's way of seeing could not be clearer.[8]

Chabod's thesis is that during the nineteenth century the historiographical question of the Renaissance had to do with the origins of modern thought and other important aspects of modernity, such as the understanding of life and history and the human–God and human–nature relationships. At that date, the European dimension of the Renaissance began to transcend its narrowly Italian connotation. Whereas the link between cultural and political history had served to restrict the meaning of the Renaissance to the problem of Italian national emancipation, the Renaissance, like other historical categories such as Romanticism or Enlightenment, now became one of the historical periods of spiritual life in Europe:

If the Renaissance has become a historical category, it is – on a par with the other, similar concepts of the Enlightenment and Romanticism – in the only sense possible, and that is as a historical moment in European spiritual life, as a philosophical, literary, artistic period, that originates certainly in a determinate new social and political reality, but which, at a certain moment, unfolds so to speak in an autonomous fashion and, having drawn from that reality the vital sap upon which to feed, then elaborates it conceptually and imaginatively.[9]

According to Chabod, Burckhardt's work changed the characteristics of the organic approach to risorgimental historiography, as it separated the political and cultural element that had instead been kept together by the idea of the nation.[10] That kind of historiography was used as a criterion to evaluate the moral life of individuals and patriotic virtues, such as 'amor patrii', liberty, and independence.[11]

---

[8] Federico Chabod, 'Gli studi di storia del Rinascimento', in *Cinquant 'anni di vita intellettuale italiana'. 1896–1946, Scritti in onore di Benedetto Croce per il suo ottantesimo anniversario*, ed. Carlo Antoni and Raffaele Mattioli (Naples: Edizioni Scientifiche Italiane, 1950), pp. 10–11.
[9] Chabod, 'Gli studi di storia del Rinascimento', p. 14.
[10] Federico Chabod, *L' idea di nazione* (Bari-Rome: Laterza, 2008).
[11] Chabod, 'Gli studi di storia del Rinascimento', p. 3.

The problem of the intrinsic bias of nineteenth-century Italian histori-ography was also remarked upon by Delio Cantimori, who stressed the need to reformulate the prevailing historiographical interpretations of the Renaissance: 'There is a need to free historiography from the concepts, myths or categories of a false presentism, [be it] political, pedagogical or propagandistic, which have been passed down to it by the earlier historiog-raphy.'[12] Cantimori moreover considers the work of Burckhardt to be absolutely central to the analysis of the Renaissance. This said, he seeks to differentiate the approach of the Swiss historian from that of Hegel, who was concerned to describe the manner in which the history of the Renaissance had developed.[13] Furthermore, Cantimori maintains that most of the Italian interpretations of the nineteenth century derived from Burckhardt's reading, which had established the Renaissance as a historical category.[14]

Benedetto Croce likewise reckoned that Italian historiography during the Risorgimento had been too passionate and therefore devoid of any objective historical perspective. In his pioneering *La crisi italiana del Cinquecento e il legame del Rinascimento col Risorgimento* (*The Italian Crisis of the 1500s and the Link of the Renaissance with the Risorgimento*, 1939) he thus observed that 'the passion of the Risorgimento ... overlooking and not caring to establish the real conditions of the spirits of the 1500s, spun novels and dramas and poems out of the events of those days, infusing them with their own ideals. The same goes for their histories'.[15] Thanks to Croce, scholars began to focus on the link between the Renaissance and the Risorgimento and, furthermore, on the meaning this assonance might bear, centered as it was on the themes of rebirth or revival. For example, Giovanni Papini noted that the coexistence of the words *Renaissance* and *Risorgimento* had tended to mislead even the Italian educated classes:

> 'Rising up again' is not strictly speaking 'being born again'. Rising up again is what those who have fallen low do, or those who have regained their lost sanity or their lost power and wealth or even certain qualities of the soul

---

[12] Delio Cantimori, 'Sulla storia del concetto di Rinascimento', *Gli Annali della R. Scuola Normale Superiore di Pisa* 1, no. 3, 1932: 230.

[13] Cantimori, 'Sulla storia del concetto di Rinascimento', p. 241. On this topic, see Biscione, *Neoumanesimo e Rinascimento. L'immagine del Rinscimento nella storia della cultura dell'Ottocento*; Michele Biscione, 'Hegel e il Rinascimento', in *Incidenza di Hegel*, ed. Fulvio Tessitore (Naples: Morano, 1970), pp. 437–451

[14] Cantimori, 'Sulla storia del concetto di Rinascimento', p. 243.

[15] For the English tranlsation by Michael Subialka, see B. Croce, 'The Italian Crisis of the 1500s and the Link between the Renaissance and the Risorgimento', in *The Renaissance from an Italian Perspective: An Anthology of Essays, 1860–1968*, ed. Rocco Rubini (Ravenna: Longo Editore, 2014), pp. 161–170, 162.

that seemed to have gone astray: Leopardi's *Risorgimento* comes to mind. Being born again is something more and recalls Christ's famous words to Nicodemus: 'Except a man be born again, he cannot see the kingdom of God.' Being born, then, a second time. After death or rather during this life which in truth is similar to death.[16]

Croce's analysis goes deeper than a merely terminological study, however. He thus maintains that the missed Reformation in Italy was one of the most important elements behind the sixteenth-century crisis: 'The Italian crisis and decadence of the 1500s amounted to ... the inability to embrace, with transformative and purifying consequences, the principles and suggestions deriving from religious reform of the evangelical and Pauline kind.'[17] Croce suggests a connection between Renaissance and Risorgimento:

> The object of these considerations of mine has been to demonstrate that, in fact, the Risorgimento was substantially a reawakening of the Renaissance, or, rather, a reawakening of its rational and religious kernel. Thus, even the *hiatus* between these two periods, the intermediate age of decline, should not be understood as marking a total detachment or decline.[18]

Croce identifies a subtle and continuous connection between the Renaissance and the Risorgimento, kept alive by those whom he called the *Apostles of the future*, such as the religious dissidents, philosophers, and historians of the sixteenth and the seventeenth centuries, because they insisted on the rational principle, which is also a religious one, that links these two historical periods.[19] He was persuaded that Risorgimento political thought had been more influenced by the period of free Italian city-states than by the Renaissance, and he was therefore more interested in the analysis of the connections between these two periods than in understanding how the idea of the Renaissance might have influenced nineteenth-century Italian political thought:

> By transporting its loves and hatreds into the past, the passion of the Risorgimento contributed not only to placing a *hiatus* between the

---

[16] Giovanni Papini, 'Rinascimento e Risorgimento', in *Politica e civiltà* (Milan: Mondadori, [1943] 1965), p. 654.

[17] B. Croce, 'The Italian Crisis of the 1500s and the Link between the Renaissance and the Risorgimento', p. 164.

[18] Croce, 'The Italian Crisis of the 1500s and the Link between the Renaissance and the Risorgimento', p. 170. Leopardi's *Risorgimento* is an individual poem within his poetry collection *Canti* (no. XX), published in 1835. For an English translation, see Giacomo Leopardi, *Canti: Poems. A Bilingual Edition*, trans. Jonathan Galassi (New York: Farrar, Straus and Giroux, 2010).

[19] Croce, 'The Italian Crisis of the 1500s and the Link between the Renaissance and the Risorgimento', p. 165.

Renaissance and the Risorgimento but above all to making the two ages mutually estranged. As such, when people searched for an ideal re-connection to the past, the majority found it in the Middle Ages and the communal age. The Renaissance appeared to be the age of paganism and of Italian materialism – it was a sensual, pleasure-loving, literary, and retorical Italy against which the new Italians had a duty to react.[20]

Croce stressed the importance of the moral and religious dimension of the Renaissance and, above all, the fact that 'decadence', during the sixteenth century in Italy, had been caused by 'the lack or the weakness of an idea'.[21] He noted that patriots had tended to interpret the Renaissance as a failed religious and moral reformation, which they for their part were determined to bring about successfully during their own lifetimes. If this were still possible, it was because decadence had not destroyed every vestige of those ideals. The author conceded that there was a hiatus between the two periods, the Risorgimento having been in the main inspired by the Italian free republics. Nevertheless, he had identified a connection between the Renaissance and the Risorgimento by virtue of the work of the 'Apostles of the future'. But this connection was deeper than he supposed: Italian patriots aspired to reconstruct this connection and place the polit-ical and cultural emancipation of the Italian people in continuity with this process of liberation, working to build the nation upon the ideal of the 'religion of liberty' that had inspired those Apostles.[22]

Carlo Dionisotti, in his study *Rinascimento e Risorgimento: La questione morale* (*Renaissance and Risorgimento: The Moral !uestion*), confirms Croce's thesis that Italian intellectuals had been more interested in the republican *umanesimo* of the Middle Ages, as described, for example, by the Swiss historian Simonde de Sismondi in his *Histoire des républiques italiennes du Moyen Âge* (*History of the Italian Republics of the Middle Ages*, 1807–1818), than in the philosophical, scientific, and artistic Renaissance of the six-teenth century. He maintains that the foreign contributions and the attention paid to the study of the Italian Renaissance had had more impact than the Italian ones:

> In Italy the men involved in the Risorgimento enterprise had neither the time nor the will nor the means – had they even wished for it – for a historical retrieval of a past that was by then remote. This was especially

---

[20] Croce, 'The Italian Crisis of the 1500s and the Link between the Renaissance and the Risorgimento', p. 170.

[21] Croce, 'The Italian Crisis of the 1500s and the Link between the Renaissance and the Risorgimento', p. 166.

[22] Benedetto Croce, *Storia d'Europa nel secolo decimonono* (Bari: Laterza, [1932] 1972), pp. 7–21.

true of an age like the Renaissance, which foreign scholars and tourists had
loved and loved still, but which Italians – intolerant of foreign supremacy –
could not entirely love for equally valid reasons . . ... from the monographic
studies of great figures of the Renaissance, interest rose only after a long
lapse, in the second half of the century, when the direction of Italian studies
in the new unified state fell to people who had played little or no part in the
Risorgimento . . .. In the nineteenth century, and especially in the years
immediately after the fulfilment of political unity, there was a tendency to
accept the Renaissance as the age in which Italy had primacy in literature
and artistry in Europe, but there was a preference for the medieval and
modern periods as representative of Italy, old and new, that had given proof
of her progressive force.[23]

If Dionisotti criticised Croce's thesis of Italian decadence, it was because he
was more concerned to comprehend the deconstruction of the concept of
the Renaissance produced during the Risorgimento. Several factors could
be held in his opinion to account for this – dismantling, incompatibility,
historical distance, and insufficient knowledge among them.

The main goal of historians such as Croce, Cantimori, Chabod, or
Dionisotti was to analyse the interpretations of the Renaissance without
taking into account the politically oriented passions of the patriots of the
nineteenth century, and this prevented them from understanding the role
that these biased interpretations had had in the process of Italian political
emancipation. Indeed, the writings of intellectuals of the nineteenth
century must be considered not for their historiographical accuracy but
for their political meaning. I am thus persuaded that, in order to understand the use of the idea of the Renaissance in the Italian historical and
political debates of the nineteenth century, we have to consider the
peculiar connection between philosophy, history, and politics that characterised what Renan called 'la vie publique de l'histoire'.[24]

The shift from the word *Risorgimento* to a word still in use today,
Renaissance (Rinascimento), to indicate the same historiographical category,
brings to light the relationship between the nineteenth-century construction of the idea of the Renaissance and the years in which Italian

[23] Carlo Dionisotti, 'Rinascimento e Risorgimento: la questione morale', in *Il Rinascimento
nell'Ottocento in Italia e Germania/ Die Renaissance im 19. Jahrhundert in Italien und Deutschland*,
ed. Auguat Buck and Cesare Vasoli (Bologna: Mulino; Berlin: Duncker & Humblot, 1989),
pp. 157–169, 160–166. For the English translation by Cosette Bruhns and Silvia Guslandi, see
Carlo Dionisotti, 'Renaissance and Risorgimento: The Moral Question', in *The Reaissance from an
Italian Perspective: An Anthology of Essays, 1860–1968*, ed. Rocco Rubini (Ravenna: Longo Editore,
2014), pp. 235–245, 238–243.

[24] Ernest Renan, 'M. Augustin Thierry', in *Essais de morale et de critique. Œuvres complètes*, vol. 2
(Paris: Calmann Lévy, 1910), pp. 117–118.

unification unfolded. Indeed, this process established a new representation of the *Risorgimento*, requiring a comparison with early modern Italian history and not only for terminological reasons. If we consider the meta-phorical meaning of the term *Risorgimento*, two main lines of interpret-ation come to mind: on one hand, the political-civil understanding, which reveals a general moral or aesthetic 're-raising' of a civilization after a fall; on the other hand, a delimited historical-political sense, which suggests a 're-raising' of the national spirit. The metaphor of 're-raising' indicates a semantic recasting of the political meaning of the word *Risorgimento*. By the end of the nineteenth century, the first meaning had come to be contained within the word *Renaissance*, while the most delimited political understanding had been absorbed by the word *Risorgimento*. The process through which the word *Risorgimento* passed from the generic meaning of 'rising', or 'rising again', to that specific historical sense that the nineteenth century gave it, covers an essential stage in the revolutionary triennium (1796–1799). The word presupposed the perception of decadence, the threat of which was presented by the revolutionaries in terms of a 'theo-logical damnation'. This sense of damnation reflected the hybridisation of the religious and the political characteristics of Jacobin language (later also carried by the term *regeneration*), the pronounced democratic-republican connotations of which would cause it later to disappear, to the decided advantage of the Risorgimento, which inherited this clear determination of the term in the political sense.[25] If there were numerous exhortations to a political resurgence of Italy, especially at the turn of the Napoleonic period (1799–1800), the political meaning of the word would still run parallel to the historiographical one, in the broad sense (civil, literary, artistic). Between 1848 and 1900, the terms *Risorgimento* and *Renaissance* basically coexisted, and starting from 1847–1848, the name of Risorgimento took on a decidedly political meaning, to designate the process of Italian political liberation.

The idea of the regeneration of the nation implies the return to a human essence, forgotten or suppressed, and this is possible only through a revolution. Revolution, in short, offers the promise of emancipation, which has shifted from the religious to the political sphere, involving as it does what Jaume calls a *transfert de religiosité(s)*.[26] This definition

---

[25] Cotugno, 'Rinascimento e Risorgimento (sec. XVIII–XIX)', pp. 279–281.

[26] Lucien Jaume, *Le Religieux et le politique dans la Révolution française. L'idée de régénération* (Paris: PUF, 2015), p. 7; on this debate, see also Josep R. Llobera, *The God of Modernity: The Development of Nationalism in Western Europe* (London: Bloomsbury, 1996); Anthony W. Marx, *Faith in Nation: Exclusionary Origins of Nationalism* (Oxford: Oxford University Press, 2003).

highlights the inner, subjective tension within the general aspiration towards regeneration, entailing something other than the merely external dimension of ceremonies and symbols related to the new cults. In Italian the two terms 'regeneration' (*rigenerazione*) and 'resurgence' (*risorgimento*) coexisted during the first half of the nineteenth century, while in its latter half the word 'Risorgimento' took precedence.[27]

The idea of the need for a regeneration (or resurgence) of the moral and intellectual life of Italians was connected to the widespread assumption among European and Italian intellectuals that the Italian character suffered from a backwardness, laziness, and indolence.[28] In order to assume a new role as a modern nation, the Italians needed first, or so it was supposed, a moral and intellectual revolution: the incessant references to the regeneration of the nation in Italian political discourse, from the republicans to the most conservative political groups, demonstrates a process of self-othering among the national elites.[29]

Between the 1850s and 1870s, there was a fluctuation in the Italian language between the terms *Risorgimento* and *Renaissance*, each being used as a synonym for the other, until in due course *Renaissance* replaced *Risorgimento* to indicate the early modern period. The analysis of Francesco De Sanctis' *Storia della letteratura italiana* (1870–1872) exemplifies this fluctuation.[30] The traditional term *Risorgimento* is used by De Sanctis nineteen times in nine chapters of his work, and the chapter where he uses this term most often is the one on Machiavelli (six times), which is also the most representative for the variation in the meaning of

---

[27] See Erasmo Leso, *Lingua e rivoluzione: Ricerche sul vocabolario politico italiano nel triennio rivoluzionario 1796–1799* (Venice: Istituto veneto di scienze lettere ed arti, 1991), pp. 153–154. By language here I refer mainly to the notion elaborated by J. G. A. Pocock, 'Introduction: the State of the Art' in *Virtue, Commerce and History: Essays on Political Thought and History, Chiefly in the Eighteenth Century* (Cambridge: Cambridge University Press, 1985), pp. 1–34.

[28] For a more specific analysis of these stereotypes on the Italian national character, see Silvana Patriarca, 'Indolence and Regeneration: Tropes and Tensions of Risorgimento Patriotism', *The American Historical Review*, 110, no. 2, April 2005: 380–408.

[29] Lucy Riall, 'Which Italy? Italian Culture and the Problem of Politics', *Journal of Contemporary History*, 39, no. 3, 2004: 437–446, 438.

[30] See Pasquale Sabbatino, 'Letteratura e "risurrezione della coscienza nazionale". Le occorrenze di Risorgimento e Rinascimento nella Storia di Francesco De Sanctis e il Rinnovamento dei tempi moderni', in *La nuova scienza come rinascita dell'identità nazionale: La Storia della letteratura italiana di Francesco De Sanctis (1870–2010)*, ed. Toni Iermano and Pasquale Sabbatino (Naples: Edizioni Scientifiche Italiane, 2012), pp. 53–88; Pasquale Sabbatino, 'Rinascimento, Risorgimento e Alto Evo Moderno nella storiografia letteraria tra Otto e Novecento', *Studi Rinascimentali*, 8, 2010: 37–55; Toni Iermano, 'Era il popolo men serio del mondo e meno disciplinato': Risorgimento e

the word.[31] Machiavelli, indeed, is, on one hand, the 'negation of the Risorgimento', 'not the ecstatic and contemplative face of the middle ages nor the tranquil and idyllic face of the Risorgimento', because he is the modern man who judges things for what they are and not for what they ought to be: he considers only the *verità effettuale* (effectual truth).[32] On the other, Machiavelli is also 'a bourgeois of the Risorgimento', 'an ironical spirit of the Risorgimento', who represents completely the spirit of modernity.[33] While, in the first case, De Sanctis, using the word 'Risorgimento', means the period of moral decadence, the age of Italian *corrutela* (corruption), which is, for this reason, distinguished from Modernity; in the second, he means the reformation of the modern world, based on the autonomy of the spirit and the observation of nature. This meaning more nearly resembles the use made of the word *Rinnovamento* (*Renewal*), which is also very important in De Sanctis' *Storia*, but, while the *Rinnovamento* indicates the regeneration of the moral spirit happening during De Sanctis' time and requiring to be completed, continuing the process started during the sixteenth century, the Risorgimento, in the second meaning analysed here, is the period when the roots of the new spirit of *Rinnovamento* began to appear, and Machiavelli is the pivotal figure in this passage. Therefore, De Sanctis traces a line between the *Risorgimento* and the *Rinnovamento*, that is, a line between Italian modernity and the Italian process of political and moral emancipation. The variation in De Sanctis' use of the two words now becomes clearer: while he defines Italian moral decadence and the missed moral and religious reformation of the Italian modern age, he also searches in that period for the elements of that reformation, which are useful as a basis for the *Rinnovamento* that Italians needed in the nineteenth century.

Rinascimento nella'Storia della letteratura italiana', in *La prudenza e l'audacia. Letteratura e impegno politico in Francesco De Sanctis* (Naples: L'ancora del Mediterraneo, 2012), pp. 75–104; Toni Iermano, "Francesco De Sanctis, La storia della letteratura italiana," *Studi Rinascimentali* 8 (2010): 15–35; Antonio Palermo, "Il 'Rinascimento' e l'invenzione della 'Storia della letteratura italiana,'" *Studi Rinascimentali* 1 (2003): 161–67; Biscione, *Neoumanesimo e Rinascimento. L'immagine del Rinscimento nella storia della cultura dell'Ottocento*; Cantimori, 'De Sanctis e il "Rinascimento".

[31] The term 'Risorgimento' is used: once in chapter IV *La prosa*; three times in XI *Le Stanze*; once in XII *Il Cinquecento*; three times in XIII *L'Orlando furioso*; six times in XV *Machiavelli*; once in XVII *Torquato Tasso*; once in XVIII *Marino*; once in XIX *La nuova scienza* (but in the lower case: risorgimento); twice in XX *La nuova letteratura*.

[32] De Sanctis, 'Storia della letteratura italiana', p. 488.

[33] De Sanctis, 'Storia della letteratura italiana', pp. 488 and 496.

In contrast to other important works of De Sanctis, where the word *Rinascimento* does not appear, in his *Storia* it appears fourteen times, nine of which are in the last chapter, chapter XX, *La nuova letteratura*.[34] De Sanctis was suspicious of the *Renaissance* as a historiographical category, which was how Burckhardt used it.[35] In De Sanctis' hands, the word 'Renaissance' served as a temporal indication of a phase of Italian intellectual history and not as a categorisation of the development of the history of culture and art, as in Burckhardt. With the term 'Renaissance', De Sanctis does not mean a concept; instead, he refers to a period that is 'an age that is developed and complete in itself in all its gradations, like an individual', and it is not a conventional and restricted time.[36] It is the same attitude as this author has towards the division of history into centuries: to him a century refers only to an important phase in human history:

> We call a century not the conventional and restricted space of a hundred years; but one of the great ages of humanity; a century appears when another world appears. When a new nature comes to form part of humanity, then there begin the great epochs, which are not artificially created, but are produced by a slow elaboration of humanity, which is founded upon the past.[37]

According to De Sanctis, the process of renewal that characterised the Italian Renaissance had failed because it was overly radical in its denial of faith and religious authority, by contrast with the Protestant Reformation, which had been founded upon a religious and moral spirit. In this sense, the connection that De Sanctis posits between the Rinascimento and the political Risorgimento or Rinnovamento to be accomplished during his own time is also a warning to learn from history and not to repeat the same mistake: an inner and moral reformation was the only way to bring about the cultural and political revolution that the Italian people needed in order to attain a

---

[34] See, for example, Francesco De Sanctis, 'La scienza e la vita', in *Opere. L'arte, la scienza e la vita*, vol. XIV (Turin: Einaudi, 1972), pp. 316–340; Francesco De Sanctis, 'La giovinezza', in *Opere*, ed. Niccolò Gallo, vol. 56 (Rome: Riccardo Ricciardi, 2004); Francesco De Sanctis, *La letteratura italiana nel secolo XIX. Scuola liberale – scuola democratica*, ed. Benedetto Croce and Francesco Torraca (Naples: Morano, 1902). The term 'Rinascimento' is used: once in chapter XI. *Le Stanze*; three times in XIII *L'Orlando furioso*; once in XIX *La nuova scienza*; nine times in XX *La nuova letteratura*

[35] Cantimori, 'De Sanctis e il "Rinascimento"', p. 326.

[36] Cantimori, 'De Sanctis e il "Rinascimento"', p. 384.

[37] Francesco De Sanctis, 'Conferenze su Niccolò Machiavelli', in *Opere. L'arte, la scienza e la vita* (Turin: Einaudi, [1869] 1972), p. 42.

durable political liberty. Machiavelli represents the spirit of Renewal, he is the 'Italian Luther', as De Sanctis defined the Florentine secretary.

3.1 The Italian Luther

As one of the main protagonists of the 1848 revolution in Naples, Francesco De Sanctis proposed a series of educational reforms, but the tide of reaction in 1849 forced him to flee the city. In December 1850, he was imprisoned on a fabricated charge of plotting to kill the king. Once released, De Sanctis travelled to Turin, where he spent his days with Bertrando Spaventa, Pasquale Villari, and Diomede Marvasi. They usually had Sunday lunch together at Spaventa's house and supported each other during the hardship of exile, creating a little community of Southerners that was in close contact with the intellectual elites in Turin. In 1856, De Sanctis was invited to become professor of Italian literature at the Polytechnic in Zurich. The need for regular employment, hard to find in Turin, and the prestige of the appointment, led De Sanctis to accept the post, despite his fear of the probable isolation he would suffer. He taught in Switzerland until 1860, returning then to Italy and to political activity, working first to reform the University of Naples and then being appointed as Minister of Public Education of the new State. During the 1850s and his period of exile in Turin and Zurich, De Sanctis, like the other Hegelians, refined his ideas on the Renaissance and on the central role of Niccolo' Machiavelli and his republican thought.

De Sanctis was influenced by the prevailing 'Luthercentric approach', while at the same time trying to understand why the Reformation had failed to establish itself in Italy. The general consensus at the time, as Cantimori highlights, was that: 'Italy was weak, corrupt and devoted to the cult of form; no moral and intellectual reform could therefore thrive in the educated [parts of] our society.'[38] In his *L'uomo di Guicciardini*, De Sanctis gives a clear account of what was indeed the unanimous judgement of the critics at the time. The causes of Italian decadence during the Renaissance, or so the argument went, had much to do with the religious dimension. For some interpreters, the weakening of religious sentiment was of paramount importance, while for others the doctrinal stance of the Catholic Church of Rome had been chiefly to blame:

---

[38] Delio Cantimori, 'De Sanctis e il "Rinascimento"', in *Studi di storia* (Turin: Einaudi, 1959), p. 323. On De Sanctis' interpretation of the Renaissance, see also the recent article by Emma Giammattei, 'Idea e figura del Rinascimento fra De Sanctis e Carducci', *Intersezioni*, XXXV, no. 1, 2015: 35–61.

One and all were convinced that the country was corrupt, though some derived the corruption from the weakened religious sentiment, and others traced it back to religion as it had been interpreted and practised by the court of Rome. The former saw the remedy 'in returning society to its [first] principles', with a religious and moral reform that would serve to restore the religious beliefs and amend the customs: which reform, the priests pressed by friar Savonarola and later by friar Luther, realised in their own fashion at the Council of Trent. The others conversely saw the remedy as lying in the emancipation of conscience from every religious authority, which would bring with it the abolition of the papacy, which they judged to be the principal enemy of liberty and of national unity.[39]

Much like Spaventa, De Sanctis clearly had in mind Hegel's interpretation, which saw the origins of modernity as lying in the Protestant Reformation, and he also attempted to reassess the role of Italy in modern history through the notion of Machiavelli as the Italian Luther: 'In a theological form, that is to say, in the guise of a return to Christian origins, Italy could no longer have it [the Reformation]; and as for free examination and participation in the founding of the modern age, Italy has had Machiavelli.'[40] Machiavelli represented 'the spirit of a moral and intellectual renewal', and the problem of the Renaissance in De Sanctis appears as the problem of the missed Italian moral Reformation. As Cantimori suggests, to have a concept of the Renaissance implied a positive evaluation of the period, which De Sanctis for his part lacked.[41] By contrast with Spaventa, indeed, De Sanctis did not identify the philosophical principle of moral liberty as the characteristic of Italian philosophy of the sixteenth century.

As Cantimori goes on to argue, De Sanctis connects the Hegelian and the Republican interpretations of European history, which both take the Protestant Reformation to be the origin of modernity. The connection between these two views is the history of the Church: 'The common link is precisely the history of the Church, since an interpretation of the Hegelian type is protestant, and the "republican" interpretation is for the most part full of protestant sympathies when not directly protestant, and it then along with other elements converged with the "liberal" interpretation.'[42] In the pages of De Sanctis, the problem of the moral and intellectual

[39] Francesco De Sanctis, 'L'uomo di Guicciardini', in *Opere. L'arte, la scienza e la vita* (Turin: Einaudi, 1972), p. 96.
[40] Cantimori, "De Sanctis e il "Rinascimento"", p. 325.
[41] Cantimori, 'De Sanctis e il "Rinascimento"', p. 330.
[42] Cantimori, 'De Sanctis e il "Rinascimento"', p. 322.

reform of the Italians serves to intensify this relationship. De Sanctis' interest in the Republican tradition was particularly strong during his Swiss exile in Zurich, and closer analysis of this experience may serve to shed light on the connection between these two interpretations of history.

De Sanctis worried more about Italian moral *corrutela* than he did about the oppressive political power wielded by the Counter-Reformation. Concerned though he was to salvage the reputations of some of the key figures of the Renaissance, such as Machiavelli and Ariosto, he considered that period to have been in general a moment of 'splendid moral decadence', because of the absence of a religious and moral reformation. In this regard, he was plainly closer than Spaventa to the Hegelian scheme and to the current European historiography. Indeed, De Sanctis was more deeply stirred by the idea of the Reformation than by that of the Renaissance, the former representing for him the principle of intellectual, religious, moral, and political *Rinnovamento* (renewal) of Italian consciousness. De Sanctis' *Rinnovamento* is the 'great movement of the spirit, that marks the dawn of modern times'; it is a movement of opposition, and the history of this Italian opposition is 'the slow reconstruction of the national consciousness'.[43] The idea of *Rinnovamento* as opposition represents both Hegel's dialectical conception and republican or radical attitudes: this idea helps De Sanctis to overcome the antithesis between the Renaissance and the Protestant Reformation, finding common ground between reformed people and Italian philosophers:

> Machiavelli, Bruno, Campanella, Galileo were not solitary beings. They were the product of new times, the bigger stars around which moved swarms of free men, animated by the same spirit. What did they want? To seek out the being behind appearance, as Machiavelli said; to seek out the spirit through the forms, as the Reformation said; to seek out the real and the positive, as Galileo said; or, as Bruno and Campanella said, to seek out the one through the multiple, to seek out the divine in nature. They are different formulae for one and the same concept. Reformers and philosophers by virtue of their [intrinsic] tendencies meet on a common ground.[44]

The central point that De Sanctis and Spaventa have in common in their interpretations of the Renaissance, despite all the differences, is their agreement on the definition of the principle of the modern age, which, on the one hand, represents the Hegelian structure of philosophy of history and, on the other, is the 'Italian version' of that same structure,

---

[43] De Sanctis, 'Storia della letteratura italiana', p. 693.
[44] De Sanctis, 'Storia della letteratura italiana', p. 693.

because it searches in Italian philosophical, political, and scientific thought for the same principle: the unity of divine and human nature, infinite and finite, spirit and form.

In the chapter dedicated to Machiavelli in his *Storia della letterature italiana* (*History of Italian Literature*), De Sanctis applied the Hegelian philosophy of history, using as the epitome of progress the figure of Machiavelli. The Florentine *secretario* allows him to introduce the parallelism between citizens who love their country and nations that fulfil their duties towards humanity:

> Just as individuals have their mission on earth, so too do the nations. Individuals without a fatherland, without virtue, without glory, are lost atoms, *numerus fruges consumere nati*. And by the same token there are idle and empty nations, that leave no trace of themselves in the world. Historic nations are those that have fulfilled a task in humanity, or, as was then said, in humankind, such as Assyria, Persia, Greece and Rome. What renders nations great is virtue or temperament, intellectual and corporeal vigour, which forms character or moral strength. But as with individuals, so too the nations have their old age, when the ideas that have constituted them grow weak in their consciousness and the temperament becomes worn out. And the guidance of the world escapes from their hands and passes to other nations.[45]

We can note that what Spaventa regards as the Risorgimento is to all intents and purposes identical with what De Sanctis terms the *Rinnovamento* (renewal) but, while De Sanctis yearns for a moral and religious reformation that never in fact happened, Spaventa for his part describes the philosophical and moral reformation actually accomplished by Bruno and Campanella but obstructed, stifled, and in the end destroyed by the political power of the Counter-Reformation. However, while Spaventa considers the *Risorgimento filosofico* a deeper reformation than the Protestant Reformation, for De Sanctis the only remedy for the *corrutela*, and the only hope for the regeneration of the people, remains an actual reformation: 'And all those who had looked deeply [into things] asked themselves if there were a remedy: When corruption has spread to all the social classes, must a society perforce die? There is indeed a remedy; reformation; the peoples can be regenerated, if they have the virtue of reformation.'[46] Closely scrutinising De Sanctis' thought, we note that he

---

[45] De Sanctis, 'Storia della letteratura italiana', pp. 493–494. The Latin tag, *Nos numerus sumus, fruges consumere nati*, is from Horace, Epistles, I, II, l. 27: 'We are but numbers, born to consume resources.'

[46] De Sanctis, 'Conferenze su Niccolò Machiavelli', p. 48.

traces a sort of reformation also during the Renaissance, even if it is scientific and philosophical in nature, rather than moral:

> This [the reformation] can be born either from enthusiasm and faith or from science and thought. The former is possible when not all classes are corrupt; even ignorant, those classes are not corrupt, and they do not wish to resign themselves to being alive among the dead; those produced the French Revolution. When corruption has infiltrated everywhere, the reformation does not at a stroke give life but it can prepare the resurrection; and this is the reformation of science. There arise the thinkers, solitary, misunderstood, persecuted; who ask themselves whether society can be recast on other foundations: they entrust their ideas to books composed in part of phantasies and in part of thoughts. Until the hour of the resurrection arrives, the country feels [that] in it there is a thing that *is not called it*; but is called Bruno, Campanella, Galileo, Giannone, Machiavelli.[47]

While for Spaventa the philosophical reformation was deeper and more important than the religious one, De Sanctis for his part considers the moral one to be more important. Yet, in his view, the scientific and philosophical reformation was to inaugurate the moral reformation, one that had to be enacted in his own lifetime. Indeed, Machiavelli's utopia was what De Sanctis wished to see realised through unification:

> Here [then] is Machiavelli's utopia. He imagined: let us give the Italian people political institutions, let us give them a leader and we shall make them into a nation. But he does not see that the institutions themselves are effects, not causes; that it was necessary to recreate the people, recreate thought, in short recreate man, the Roman man of whom he dreamt; or rather, he did all this; but not for [his] contemporaries. In Italy there only remained a residue of life ... the vibration in the brain of the thinkers; which gave Europe the last fruits of the vital part of the nation, with Columbus, Galileo, Giannone, Vico and Machiavelli![48]

The rediscovery of Italian character in order to recreate the Italian people and Italian thought was a preoccupation common to De Sanctis and Spaventa, and by the same token they both, notwithstanding Hegel, championed the originality and importance of Italian philosophical thought of the sixteenth century, which likewise represented for them both the beginning of the process of Italian emancipation.

---

[47] De Sanctis, 'Conferenze su Niccolò Machiavelli', p. 48.
[48] De Sanctis, 'Conferenze su Niccolò Machiavelli', p. 91.

Both Spaventa and De Sanctis thus considered it their duty to reconnect Italy with its glorious past and overcome Italian moral torpor, because the modern seeds sown in Italy had borne fruit in other countries:

> The Italian intellectual type, after great struggles [has] become the type, the physiognomy of the whole of civil Europe. This power and energy produced works that bore fruit in other lands, assisted human progress, and remained sterile where they had been born. Galileo, Columbus, Vico, and many other powerful intellects, who played so large a part in European civilisation, had barely any virtue or efficacy in the civilisation of their own country, where there was no longer the material suited to receiving and engendering.[49]

De Sanctis' analysis of the Renaissance is more complex perhaps than that of Spaventa and cannot simply be reduced to the idea of moral decadence. He considers also certain figures from that period, and in particular Machiavelli, as the Italian source of modernity and as the intellectual instrument for overcoming Italy's moral weakness. De Sanctis searches in the Italian Renaissance for the disease of and cure for moral weakness, the greatest obstacle to Italian political and moral freedom also in his own day: 'The Italian race is not yet cured of this moral weakness, and there has not yet disappeared from its brow the mark that the history of duplicity and simulation has impressed upon it.'[50]

Considering the ambivalence of De Sanctis' interpretation, we can note more similarities with Spaventa's understanding of the Italian *Risorgimento filosofico*, because both thinkers insist on the importance for attaining political liberty and unification of rediscovering the concept of moral liberty in the Italian thinking of the sixteenth century. De Sanctis is not really interested in the problem of the Renaissance as a specific historical period because he is more focused on the general character of modernity, while Spaventa associates modernity with the *Risorgimento filosofico*.

It is interesting to note that both Spaventa and De Sanctis apply the Hegelian scheme of philosophy of history but, while Spaventa focuses on Giordano Bruno as the central figure and the initiator of modernity, De Sanctis confers that role on Machiavelli, the most representative figure of the Italian republican tradition. This important difference between the two Hegelians – who shared, together with their friends Pasquale Villari, Camillo De Meis, and Diomede Marvasi, exile in Turin from 1853 to 1856 – derives also from De Sanctis' Swiss exile and the republican ethos that prevailed in Zurich.

---

[49] De Sanctis, 'L'uomo di Guicciardini', p. 109.   [50] De Sanctis, 'L'uomo di Guicciardini', p. 117.

3.2 The Republican

De Sanctis was in exile in Zurich between 1856 and 1860, and the seeds of the most powerful pages on the republican tradition from the *Storia della letteratura italiana* (1870–1872) are to be found in the years he spent there, inspired by the all-pervasive Swiss republican ethos.[51] Yet canonical studies on republicanism, including even those regarded as contemporary milestones in the field, do not consider the Swiss republican experience as a relevant intellectual reference.[52] This lacuna in the literature has now been filled thanks to the important study by Thomas Maissen, *Die Geburt der Republik*, which clearly shows that the connection between the historical development of modern Switzerland and the ideal of republican political liberty is very strong.[53] In the history of Italy, exile has always played a fundamental role, and the Risorgimento was the first important political experience also made possible through the contribution of exiles. They often chose the Helvetic Confederation as a destination, especially from 1815 onwards, when the poet Ugo Foscolo was the first to cross the Alps voluntarily, and, moving to Switzerland, he 'gave to Italy, leaving the fatherland of his own accord, a new institution: exile'.[54]

During their stay in Switzerland, Italian exiles found possibilities for free expression and a flourishing republican culture as, for example, Ugo Foscolo observed: 'The Holy Confederation of the Swiss Republics' represents the favourite destination for 'men unable to serve.'[55] Carlo Cattaneo for his part was likewise strongly convinced that 'Swiss liberty is an institution that can protect the neighbouring nations from the effects of their

---

[51] Critics have emphasised, especially in recent years, the importance of biographies and individual stories of exiles. This attitude has led to several publications of collections of letters and diaries of prominent figures, as, for example, the study of Carlo Moos, *L' 'altro' Risorgimento: L'ultimo Cattaneo tra Italia e Svizzera* (Milan: Franco Angeli, 1992). Especially through this biographical perspective, De Sanctis' exile in Zurich inspired different studies: the most relevant source is his letters from Zurich, which Benedetto Croce began to publish: see Francesco De Sanctis, *Lettere da Zurigo a Diomede Marvasi (1856–1860)*, ed. Benedetto Croce (Naples: Ricciardi, 1913); Francesco De Sanctis, *Lettere dall'esilio (1853–1860)* (Bari: G. Laterza & Figli, 1938). Then this work was continued until the publication of the whole collection of his letters in different volumes in the complete edition of De Sanctis' *Opere*, which appeared from 1956 to 1993, edited by different scholars.

[52] See Philip Pettit, *Republicanism: A Theory of Freedom and Government: A Theory of Freedom and Government* (Oxford: Oxford University Press, 1997); Quentin Skinner, *Liberty before Liberalism* (Cambridge: Cambridge University Press, 1998); Maurizio Viroli, *Republicanism* (New York: Farrar Straus and Giroux, 2002).

[53] Thomas Maissen, *Die Geburt Der Republik*, Auflage: 2 (Göttingen: Vandenhoeck & Ruprecht, 2006).

[54] Carlo Cattaneo, 'Ugo Foscolo e l'Italia', in *Scritti letterari*, vol. I (Florence: Treves, 1981), p. 536.

[55] Ugo Foscolo, *Della servitù d'Italia* (Florence: Le Monnier, 1852), p. 230.

own errors and from their passing frenzies'.[56] Giuseppe Mazzini too underlined the importance of Switzerland for Italian political liberty:

> Switzerland was and is an important country not only for itself, but also notably for Italy. Since 1 January 1338 that little people has [had] neither master nor king. Consequently, for over five centuries, uniquely in Europe, ringed by jealous and conquering monarchies, a republican banner shines, almost as a stimulus and an omen to all of us, on the heights of the Alpine region. Charles V, Louis XIV, Napoleon passed [through]: that banner remained motionless and sacred. There is in that fact a promise of life, a pledge of Nationality [that is] not destined, as others think, to disappear.[57]

Italian patriots found in Switzerland a fitting climate for free people, one that materially and ideally helped them to specify or modify their political thought and practice: often in collaboration with Swiss intellectuals and politicians, Italian exiles founded newspapers, reviews, and presses, or contributed to their growth, particularly by translating and distributing important European books. Italian patriots, persecuted political figures, and refugees found beyond the Alps not only a shelter but also a laboratory for the theory and the practice of political liberty. What deserves to be brought to light is their connection with the republican practice of political freedom.

Regarding the impact of Swiss political and religious ideas on the Italian Risorgimento, we have a number of still very useful classic studies, such as the contribution, for example, of Romeo Manzoni and the work of Reto Roedel.[58] These works reconstruct the connections between the most prominent Italian political and intellectual leaders, Cavour and Manzoni in particular, and Swiss intellectual life. More recent works like Maurizio Isabella's *Risorgimento in Exile* have accurately described the complex intellectual interplay in the nineteenth century between Italian patriots

---

[56] Carlo Cattaneo, *Opere edite e inedite*, ed. Agostino Bertani, vol. V (Florence: Le Monnier, 1881), p. 230.

[57] Giuseppe Mazzini, *Note autobiografiche*, ed. Roberto Pertici (Milan: Rizzoli, 1986), p. 267.

[58] See Francesco Ruffini, *La vita religiosa di Alessandro Manzoni* (Bari: Laterza, 1931); Adolfo Omodeo, *Studi sull'età della restaurazione* (Turin: Einaudi, 1970); Romeo Manzoni, *Gli esuli italiani nella Svizzera* (Lugano-Milan: Libreria Arnold, 1922); Reto Roedel, 'I rapporti fra Italia e Svizzera nel Risorgimento', *Archivio Storico Ticinese*, no. 7, 1961: 347–358. On Italian exiles during the Risorgimento and particularly in Switzerland, there are several studies such as Agostino Bistarelli, *Gli esuli del Risorgimento* (Bologna: Il Mulino, 2011). On the exiles in Switzerland, see Giovanni Ferretti, *Esuli del Risorgimento in Svizzera* (Bologna: Zanichelli, 1948); Alberto M Ghisalberti, 'Esuli italiani in Svizzera nel Risorgimento', *Il Veltro*, XI, nos. 3–4, 1967: 387–394; Fabrizio Panzera, 'Gli esuli italiani nelle città svizzere tra Otto e Novecento', in *Città e pensiero politico italiano dal Risorgimento alla Repubblica*, ed. Robertino Ghiringhelli (Milan: Vita e Pensiero, 2006), pp. 321–323.

and European cultural and political life: 'Between 1799 and 1860 [exile] was a phenomenon which affected a significant section of the Italian educated classes, if not in quantitative terms, then in terms of the importance that this group of exiled intellectuals had in Italy and continued to have abroad in the creation of a national movement and a national identity.'[59] Unlike other scholars, Isabella emphasises the 'migration of ideas from the host country into Italian thinking by way of the exiles, thus "decontextualizing" it from the milieu in which it was originally conceived'.[60] The Risorgimento involved a dialogue with other cultures, in which we may discern the reciprocal engendering of different identities: 'As a form of displacement, the experience of exile invites us to focus on how culture moves, on the relations that were established between Italy and the diasporic community, and between the diaspora and the cultures encountered in the host countries.'[61]

Despite the relevance of the Swiss republican experience and the steady stream of Italian exiles making their way to Switzerland during the Risorgimento, the scholarly literature fails to consider the influence of the Swiss republican ethos on the Italian exiles. In this regard, the case of Francesco De Sanctis is particularly illuminating: he arrived in Zurich, in 1856, from Turin, where he had been in exile with his closest friends Diomede Marvasi, Angelo Camillo De Meis, and Bertrando Spaventa, all Southern Italian Hegelians like him. For the exiles, the community that they managed to create was very important, and, by going to Zurich, De Sanctis had lost his dearest companions. Even if he had been considered an exile in Turin, the experience in Switzerland was very different. For he had felt Piedmont to be his *patria*, because it was in Italy, even if Italy was still divided. This is the reason why, when he was invited to go to the Polytechnic of Zurich to teach Italian literature, he explained that he did it only from necessity: 'It grieves me, my dear friend – to leave Italy and so many of my beloved friends; but what choice do I have? I shall use this opportunity to complete my studies. And then? Then we shall see, my heart tells me that we shall see each other again and in happier circumstances. I would prefer the least college in Italy to all the Universities of Europe' (Turin, 18 January 1856).[62] When he was appointed professor in Zurich he wrote to his dear friend Pasquale in Turin:

---

[59] Isabella, *Risorgimento in Exile*, p. 1. [60] Isabella, *Risorgimento in Exile*, p. 2.
[61] Isabella, *Risorgimento in Exile*, p. 6.
[62] The letters are cited from Francesco De Sanctis, 'Epistolario (1856–1858)', in *Opere*, ed. Giovanni Ferretti and Muzio Mazzocchi Alemanni, vol. XIX (Turin: Einaudi, 1965); Francesco De Sanctis, 'Epistolario (1859–1860)', in *Opere*, ed. Giuseppe Talamo, vol. XX (Turin: Einaudi, 1965).

I have been informed of my appointment. It seems to me as if I am dreaming. I was born to dwell in a quiet corner between young people and friends. And here I am for a second time breaking my heart; here I am [faced with] another exile! It seems almost as if I am moving away from you for a second time. I obey necessity: I know all the advantages of my new circumstance, but my heart resists it. Oh, it will be a sad day on which I shall have to separate from Diomede, from Spaventa, from Camillo, from my dear Camillo, whom I leave just when he has most need of being comforted! Do you know what consoles me? There is within me a secret thought, that tells me that you all will come to Zurich, where life costs ever so little, where it is possible to give private courses at the University, where at long last ... we shall be together. (Turin, 18 January 1856)

His friends Diomede Marvasi and Camillo De Meis went with De Sanctis to Bellinzona and then he continued his trip to Zurich alone. Loneliness was the heaviest burden for De Sanctis, especially at the beginning, but he took comfort from the beauty of the city, which reminded him of Naples:

Zurich, my dear Diomede, is more beautiful than I had anticipated. The promenade of around two miles along the lake calls to mind the road from Castellamare to Vico [Equense], or the Posillipo Riviera. The eye sweeps to right and to left, within a boundless horizon: bright green of the fields, and then little houses on two floors with the most pleasant gardens around them, and then little hills that gently rise, and reveal further on yet other fields, without ever shutting off the horizon as in Turin. (Zurich, 2 April 1856)

Despite the wonderful city, he felt alone and he sought out other Italian exiles in Zurich, trying to recreate the sort of community he had known when in Turin:

I thought it better to go out, see the city, embrace adventure, ask barbers, cafe owners, tobacconists, for addresses of Italians. I wasted four hours without getting anything. Being quite out of breath I asked about eating something and was told that in Zurich you dine at midday, and at that hour everything was closed, and that you had to wait until half past six for dinner. Endowed with a tried and tested patience I shrug my shoulders, and approach my birds, for whom I had only just bought a very beautiful cage; and what do I see? A crowd of people planted beneath the window with their eyes wide open and staring at my canaries, birds rare in these parts: – *Sie sind schön!* – I cried out. – *Ja! Ja!* – I heard on all sides. They were the ones who were made welcome, who were fêted, and I was stood there, like a dog, without a bite to eat, and with no one looking at me. (Zurich, 2 April 1856).

In the mid-nineteenth century, Zurich was an open, expanding, and progressive city and was becoming the centre of Swiss liberalism and progressive thinking. Liberal artists and intellectuals fled there after the collapse of the 1848 revolutions in Germany and Italy, Richard Wagner, Theodor Mommsen, or Gottfried Semper among them.[63] De Sanctis was one of their number and was welcomed as an important Italian intellectual in the local press, where he was defined as the 'creator of a new literature in Italy'. Despite this handsome treatment, he felt himself to be a stranger:

> There is something dark inside me, that casts a veil over this nature and these men. What would you? Even the children here, of whom I am fond, with whom I am so happy to joke, cause me to take a step backwards, when I hear issuing from those terrible mouths the horrible sounds of a jargon which is neither German, nor French, nor Italian, a mixture of I know not what, with certain aspirations of so formidable a nature that it seems as if, when they speak, they want to spit in your face. (Zurich, 2 April 1856, to Virginia Basco).

When De Sanctis arrived, the Polytechnic had already been open for a few years, and since 1855 the Federation had introduced the teaching of moral, literary, and philosophical subjects, being persuaded that the development of technical skills also required a humanistic education. He represented an important part of the history of the Polytechnic and it is not by chance that a large number of the studies on De Sanctis' Swiss exile were promoted by this university and its professors.[64] De Sanctis was also struck by the differences in teaching style in Italy and Switzerland and between him and his new colleagues, in particular professors Friedrich Theodor Vischer and Jacob Burckhardt:

> Applause is banned, as in all the Germanic universities: the professors would believe themselves to be stooping to the trade of actors; the university is not a theatre, they say . . . . I do not love rhetoric; but, in truth, I now understand, because Vischer's style is so harsh and colourless. It is another extreme; it is thought reduced to algebraic form. He speaks of the beautiful without one having any sense of it, without any pose liable to produce it. The professor in his chair never gets animated; he does not gesticulate, he

---

[63] See Lionel Gossman, *Basel in the Age of Burckhrdt* (Chicago: Chicago University Press, 2000), pp. 234–236.

[64] See Guido Caligari, *L'arrivo e il soggiorno del De Sanctis a Zurigo* (Zurich: Edizioni Poligrafiche Zurigo, 1956); *Omaggio a Francesco de Sanctis: Discorsi di Giuseppe Zoppi [u.a.] pronunziati in occasione dell'inaugurazione d'una lapide a Francesco de Sanctis . . . il 23 maggio 1948 e preceduti da un messaggio di Benedetto Croce* (Zurich: Ed. poligrafiche, 1948); Giuseppe Zoppi, *Francesco de Sanctis a Zurigo: Prolusione letta nel Politecnico federale il 16 gennaio 1932* (Sauerländer, 1932); Dante Isella, *Per Francesco De Sanctis, nel centenario della morte: atti del convegno di studi, 2 dicembre 1983, Politecnico di Zurigo* (Bellinzona: Casagrande, 1985).

does not show his hands; he is a machine that speaks. (Zurich, 23 April 1856, to Diomede Marvasi).

Impressed though De Sanctis certainly was by the different teaching methodology, what struck him most was the complete freedom of professors and the notice that was taken of students' opinions when formulating academic policy:

> There is considerable liberty . . . . You can utter as many heresies as you like: no one will pass comment on it . . . . Furthermore there is a counterweight in the young: their opinion is decisive. Their judgement is instinctive and sure, and they brook no appeal: the government abides by it. They wished to appoint such and such a person; the young did not want him and he has been rejected. (Zurich, 6 May 1856 to Marvasi).

As Rocco Rubini has recently demonstrated, in the wake of Spaventa's writings, Italian intellectuals insisted on the philosophical meaning of the Renaissance, defining an *Other Renaissance* that has provided 'an account of the Renaissance in "philosophical" rather than "historical" thought'. This 'historical' thought refers to the tradition initiated by the Swiss historian Jacob Burckhardt's *Die Kultur der Renaissance in Italien* (*Civilization of the Renaissance in Italy*, 1860), which 'has informed our view of the Renaissance so far'.[65] Martin Ruehl has recently demonstrated how Burkhardt's work marked, in particular in Germany, the beginning of 'a new aesthetic orientation and with it a new perception of the Italian as well as the European past', defining the Renaissance as the 'mother of modernity'.[66] The 'Burckhardt effect' – as described by Ruehl, which distinguishes the Renaissance from the Reformation and the Middle Ages and made it the exclusive intellectual property of Italy – had certainly influenced De Sanctis. Although the two scholars were together at the University of Zurich between 1856 and 1858, it is not clear if they ever developed an intellectual relationship. Burckhardt's biographer, Warner Kaegi, reports that during De Sanctis' first year in Zurich, in 1856, they had developed a 'friendly relationship' (*freundschaftlicher Verkehr*): 'A witness from Zurich recounts that it was not uncommon for the two to

---

[65] Rocco Rubini, *The Other Renaissance: Italian Humanism between Hegel and Heidegger* (Chicago: Chicago University Press, 2014), p. 24. See Jacob Burckhardt, *Die Kultur der Renaissance in Italien* (Basel, 1860). The first Italian translation was published in 1876: Jacob Burckhardt, *La civiltà del Rinascimento in Italia, con aggiunte e correzioni inedite fornite dall'autore*, trans. Domenico Valbusa (Florence: Sansoni, 1876).

[66] Martin A. Ruehl, *The Italian Renaissance in the German Historical Imagination, 1860–1930* (Cambridge: Cambridge University Press, 2015).

be seen walking and talking; occasionally Burckhardt sat among the audience in the auditorium of [his] Italian friend ... one could assuredly recognize suggestions made by De Sanctis in Burckhardt's later view of Petrarch.'[67] Kaegi also highlights that this friendly relationship hardly outlasted that first year: the Swiss historian's private and guarded nature kept De Sanctis away from his research project as it unfolded. It seems quite clear though that De Sanctis' *Storia della letteratura italiana* (*History of Italian Literature*), published in 1870, addresses Burckhardt's work, seeking in fact to 'correct' it, although the Italian never refers explicitly to the *Civilization* in his work.[68] What emerges as a clear difference is that Burckhardt's engagement with Italy's Renaissance was an engagement with that country's past undertaken in order to answer the 'questions that vexed the [German] bourgeois consciousness',[69] while De Sanctis was looking in Italy's past for the answers to Italy's current challenges. De Sanctis identifies in materialistic thinking the greatness of the Renaissance: 'Italy could no longer have the [Reformation]; and with regard to freedom of conscience and participation in the founding of the modern age, Italy has had Machiavelli.'[70] De Sanctis is more Hegelian than Burckhardtian: whereas the Italian thinker considers the panaestheticism of the Renaissance a problem, his Swiss colleague holds it to be a virtue. De Sanctis is suspicious of the historiographical category proposed by the Swiss historian, because it is a purely intellectual concept, which captures an aesthetic and cultural moment but is morally empty.[71] Indeed, for De Sanctis, and in marked contrast to Burckhardt, we cannot identify a concept of the 'Renaissance as such, because he is not interested in the history of culture (civilisation) but rather in the history of the Italian intellectual and moral consciousness: for De Sanctis it is not the civilisation that revived but the Italians themselves who were reborn.[72]

---

[67] See Werner Kaegi, *Jacob Burckhardt: Eine Biographie*, VII vols. (Basel/Stuttgart: Schwabe, 1949), vol III, pp. 598–600. This friendship is also confirmed by Lionel Gossman, *Basel in the Age of Burckhardt* (Chicago: Chicago University Press, 2000), pp. 234–236.

[68] For the connection between Burckhardt's *Die Kultur der Renaissance in Italien* and De Sanctis' *Storia della letteratura italiana*, see Riccardo Fubini, 'Considerazioni su Burckhardt. Il libro sul Rinascimento in Italia; De Sanctis e Burckhardt', *Archivio Storico Italiano*, 158, no. 583, 2000: 85–118.; Cantimori, 'De Sanctis e il "Rinascimento"'; Arminio Janner, 'Problemi del Rinascimento', *Nuova Antologia*, no. XI, 1933: 3–8.; Arminio Janner, 'Jacob Burckhardt und Francesco De Sanctis', *Zeitschrift für schweizerische Geschichte*, XII, no. 2, 1932: 210–233.

[69] Martin A. Ruehl, *The Italian Renaissance in the German Historical Imagination, 1860–1930* (Cambridge: Cambridge University Press, 2015), p. 53.

[70] Delio Cantimori, 'De Sanctis e il "Rinascimento"', in *Studi di storia* (Turin: Einaudi, 1959), p. 325.

[71] Cantimori, 'De Sanctis e il "Rinascimento"', p. 326.

[72] Cantimori, 'De Sanctis e il "Rinascimento"', p. 328.

De Sanctis made Hegel's philosophy of history the lynchpin of his own theory by proposing an 'Italian version of the Protestant Reformation', conferring a central role upon Machiavelli, the most representative figure of the Italian republican tradition. This derived in part from De Sanctis' Swiss exile and the republican ethos he had imbibed while in Zurich (1856–1860). It was during this phase of his life that De Sanctis focused on Machiavelli's republican thought and defined his concept of the modern Renaissance on the basis of republican values. More importantly, De Sanctis saw in the Renaissance a sort of reformation that had been scientific and philosophical rather than moral. He was adamant that, when corruption is ubiquitous, reformation can prepare a resurrection through science, thanks to individual and isolated thinkers who are usually persecuted but who firmly trust in their own thoughts, such as Bruno, Campanella, Galileo, Machiavelli, and Giannone.[73]

Besides the general observations of De Sanctis about the city of Zurich, the university and his own feelings, what is particularly interesting are his notes on the Swiss people, who are *citizens of a free republic*. De Sanctis usually refers to the host country as *the free Switzerland*, especially because he had the opportunity to observe how Swiss republicans differed from their Italian counterparts. For example, in 1856, he witnessed the preparations for the war in Zurich over the 'Neuchâtel question', and wrote as follows:

> How beautiful Zurich has become! I feel myself coming to life again. The formerly deserted streets are swarming with soldiers running in from the countryside. And here! Citizens who the other day were sitting quietly in their workshops and on their benches, run to get their weapons. In the theatre the national anthem is sung, and at concerts and balls, they sing Körner's hymn; They speak of the fatherland with the sort of interest that our plebs manifests in their private affairs .... I go every morning to attend the military exercises. That, Camillo, is what a free and serious people is. I can hardly believe my eyes.[74]

It was a high moment of civic passion and the first important challenge for the new Switzerland, regenerated after the promulgation of the liberal Constitution of 1848. The armies of the different Cantons were eager to participate and De Sanctis looked on admiringly at people of different social classes, from the towns and the countryside, joining together in a republican and democratic ferment, which united young and old, students and workers. This experience, which showed him the union of culture and

---

[73] Francesco De Sanctis, 'Conferenze su Niccolo` Machiavelli', in *Opere: L'arte*, p. 48.
[74] Zoppi, *Francesco de Sanctis a Zurigo*, p. 18.

moral duty, and the loyalty that a republic could inspire, left him still more convinced that human virtues come before technical prowess. For this reason, in his speech *Ai miei giovani*, delivered at the time to the students at the Polytechnic, he underlined the importance of studying humanities even in a technical Faculty because 'before being engineers, you are men'.[75] During his stay in Zurich, he also attended the beautiful celebrations for the centenary of Friedrich Schiller's birth and he noted the fundamental role of civil celebrations in a republic, complaining that no such ceremonies had ever been staged in Italy to renew the memory of figures such as 'Columbus, or Dante or Vico or Alfieri' (Zurich, 13 November 1859, to Diomede Marvasi). Classical republican theorists had after all insisted that civic rituals were one of the most powerful means to encourage citizens to participate in the life of the republic and make them proud of their *patria*, to inspire the loyalty that is needed to defend it, especially in war.

More evidence of De Sanctis' appreciation of the Swiss republican ethos is provided by the letters that, during the spring of 1861, he wrote to Johannes Gustav Stocker, secretary of the academic board of the Polytechnic, and Johann Karl Keppler, president of the federal academic board and the Polytechnic. In that period, he was already the Minister of Public Education in Italy but he had not forgotten his Swiss experience nor the contribution its educational system made to political liberty; so in these letters he asked 'if you would be so kind as to send me the laws regarding public instruction that are in vigour in Switzerland' (Turin, 21 May 1861, to Johann Karl Keppler). De Sanctis was convinced that public education was the only means available to turn proletarians into proud and free citizens like the Swiss. De Sanctis was Minister only for a limited period, having just enough time to harmonise the scholastic administrations of the different kingdoms, although he took care to recognise, as an aspect of his policy, the autonomy accorded the local directors of studies, which was also a characteristic of the Swiss system.[76]

During his stay in Zurich, De Sanctis gave lectures, which have become renowned, and published studies on Dante and Petrarch, Schopenhauer,

---

[75] Francesco De Sanctis, 'Ai miei giovani. Prolusione letta all'Istituto Politecnico di Zurigo', in *Saggi Critici*, ed. Luigi Russo, vol. II (Bari: Laterza, 1960), p. 56.

[76] De Sanctis was Minister of Education in different brief moments: 17 March 1861–12 June 1861 (Government Cavour); 12 June 1861–3 March 1862 (Government Ricasoli I); 24 March 1878–19 December 1878 (Government Càiroli I); 25 November 1879–2 January 1881 (Government Càiroli III). See Giuseppe Talamo, *De sanctis politico e altri saggi* (Rome: E. De Santis, 1969).

and Leopardi.[77] One of the figures, indeed, on which De Sanctis focused his attention was Niccolo' Machiavelli, who plays a fundamental role in any understanding of the Italian Renaissance, for, as he wrote in the *Storia della letteratura italiana*: 'If then we want to undertake a serious study of this century (the sixteenth century), we should seek out its secrets in the two great men who are its synthesis: Ludovico Ariosto and Niccolò Machiavelli.'[78] De Sanctis believed that 'a people is always mature [enough] to live freely. Liberty is learnt through liberty'.[79] This ideal of 'living freely' was clearly a republican legacy, as he quite rightly underlined in the chapter on Machiavelli in his *Storia della letteratura italiana*, where he explained that in Florence, during the time of Machiavelli, the Roman republican idea of liberty and the love of 'living freely' was widely diffused:

> Florence was still the heart of Italy; the lineaments of a people were still there, the image of the fatherland was there. Liberty did not yet wish to die. The Ghibelline and Guelph idea was exhausted, but there was however the republican idea in a Roman guise, an effect of classical culture which, fortified by the traditional love of living freely, and by the glorious memories of the past, resisted the Medicis. The use of liberty and the political struggles kept the temper of the soul firm, and rendered possible Savonarola, Capponi, Michelangelo, Ferruccio and the immortal resistance to the papal imperial armies. The independence and the glory of the fatherland and the love of liberty were moral forces in the midst of that Medicean corruption [and they were] rendered sharper and livelier by the contrast. [80]

Even if the book was published between 1870 and 1872, in two volumes, the seeds of that study, especially the pages on the most important modern republican thinker, namely, Machiavelli, were sown during the years in Zurich.[81] The strongest evidence that the Swiss exile was a fruitful time for De Sanctis' republican studies is that, from October 1859 to March 1860, he taught a course called *Machiavelli e i suoi tempi*, as the loan register of the Stadtbibliothek in Zurich proves.[82] In that semester, De Sanctis

---

[77] See Francesco De Sanctis, *Saggio critico sul Petrarca* (Naples: Morano, 1869); Francesco De Sanctis, 'Schopenhauer e Leopardi', *Rivista contemporanea*, XV, no. VI, 1858: 369–408.

[78] De Sanctis, 'Storia della letteratura italiana', p. 424.

[79] Francesco De Sanctis, *Il Mezzogiorno e lo Stato unitario* (Turin: Einaudi, 1972), p. 348.

[80] De Sanctis, 'Storia della letteratura italiana', p. 483.

[81] The studies of De Sanctis in Zurich were probably useful also for the lectures he gave in Naples in 1869. See Francesco De Sanctis, *Machiavelli. Conferenze*, in *Saggi critici*, ed. L. Russo (Bari: Laterza, 1853), vol. II, pp. 349–379.

[82] The titles of all the courses that De Sanctis taught in Zurich are, in chronological order: *Storia della letteratura italiana del XIV secolo*; *L'Inferno*; *Il Purgatorio e il Paradiso*; *Il Petrarca*; *il Petrarca e il Poliziano*; *Storia dei poemi cavallereschi in Italia*; *Il Tasso e la sua scuola*; *Il Machiavelli e i suoi tempi*; *il seicento in Italia: Il Marino e il suo tempo*. A final course was announced but never taught because he

borrowed some books from the library that would shed light on Florentine life during the sixteenth century: the *Istorie fiorentine* (*Florentine Histories*) by Giovanni Villani (22 October 1859), *Vita e pontificato di Leone X* (*Life and Pontificate of Leo X*) and *Vita di Lorenzo de' Medici* (*The Life of Lorenzo de' Medici*) by Guglielmo Roscoe (29 October 1859). When reading the chapter on Machiavelli in the *Storia della letteratura italiana*, we immediately sense that the connection between Lorenzo de Medici and Machiavelli was probably formulated in that period and owing much to the study by William Roscoe. Indeed De Sanctis wrote: 'There is visible in Niccolò Machiavelli the sceptical and mocking spirit of Lorenzo, impressed upon the brow of the Italian bourgeoisie in that period. And he also had that practical sense, that understanding of men and of things, that rendered Lorenzo eminent among princes.'[83] It is also interesting that along with Machiavelli's *Principe* and *Discorsi* (in the edition of the *Società tipografica dei Classici Italiani*, Milan, 1804), De Sanctis borrowed Paolo Paruta's *Discorsi politici* (on 21 November 1859) and in his *Storia* De Sanctis suggests a connection between Paruta and Machiavelli: 'Paolo Paruta, closest in spirit and wit to Niccolò Machiavelli .... In his *Discorsi politici* you find the successor to Machiavelli and the precursor of Montesquieu, Venetian practical sense and Florentine insight.'[84]

While De Sanctis insists on the republican aspect of Machiavelli's thought, Hegel, in his essay on *The German Constitution*, had focused on Machiavelli's *Prince*:

> Deeply conscious of this state of universal misery, hatred, upheaval and blindness, an Italian statesman, with cool deliberation grasped the necessary idea of saving Italy by uniting it into a single state. With rigorous logic, he mapped out the way forward which both the country's salvation and the corruption and blind folly of the age made necessary, and appealed in the following words to his prince to assume the exalted role of saviour of Italy and to earn the fame of bringing its misfortune to an end.[85]

---

returned to Italy: *Introduzione alla storia della letteratura italiana odierna: Metastasio e Alfieri*. See Ottavio Besomi, 'De Sanctis "in partibus transalpinis" ma non "infedelium": Letture zurighesi', in *Per Francesco De Sanctis*, ed. Dante Isella (Bellinzona: Casagrande, 1985), pp. 89–116.

[83] De Sanctis, 'Storia della letteratura italiana', pp. 482–483.

[84] De Sanctis, 'Storia della letteratura italiana', pp. 687–688. De Sanctis also borrowed the volume of Machiavelli's *Legazioni* on the 12th of March 1860. For a similar interpretation of the relationship between Paruta and Machiavelli, see J. G. A. Pocock, *The Machiavellian Moment: Florentine Political Thought and the Atlantic Republican Tradition* (Princeton: Princeton University Press, 2003), pp. 272–330.

[85] Wilhelm Friedrich Hegel, 'The German Constitution', in *Political Writings* (Cambridge: Cambridge University Press, 1999), p. 79.

Hegel had identified as the most important principle in Machiavelli the idea that 'freedom is possible only when people are legally united within a state'.[86] He was not interested in the controversy over Machiavelli's morality, which was hotly debated in that period. De Sanctis, like Hegel, considers the debate surrounding Machiavelli's morality to be of limited importance, indeed fruitless, and he is not particularly attracted by Machiavelli's *Prince* but rather by his other works. So De Sanctis differentiated himself from the philosopher from Stuttgart, who in that period had become hard for him to study, as he wrote to his friend Camillo De Meis in 1857: 'I would now find the reading of Hegel intolerable.'

Furthermore De Sanctis underlines the republican aspects of Machiavelli's thought and the central role of the concept of *patria*:

> Niccolò actually advocates the constitution of a large Italian state, which would be a bulwark of Italy against the foreigner. The concept of the fatherland is thereby enlarged. The fatherland is not only the little comune but it is the whole nation. Italy in the Dantean utopia is the garden of the empire; in Machiavelli's utopia it is the fatherland, an autonomous and independent nation.[87]

It is precisely by dint of his having suffered for his *patria* that the Hegelian De Sanctis is tied to the Republican Machiavelli, as the exile confessed to Camillo De Meis:

> The reading of Machiavelli deeply saddens me: today it is the same, with hypocrisy to boot. But what there is that has changed, is precisely this hypocrisy, a homage rendered to certain ideas, ridiculed and adopted as vile in the upper [reaches of society], but persistent and widening from below: the future seems to me to be full of light, the present is sad, and as for we who belong to this present, suffering is all that remains. (Zurich, 27 November 1859).

De Sanctis is influenced more than the other Italian Hegelians by republican culture, especially because of his Swiss experience. The Hegelian does not abide by the 'Exhortation to exiles' of the nationalist Gioberti, who had urged his compatriots not to blend their ideas and habits with those of other peoples but rather to preserve their 'Italian purity':

> Take heed [cautioned Gioberti] not to assume the customs and the errors of the land in which you are living: do indeed study the men and their affairs;

---

[86] Hegel, 'German Constitution', pp. 60, 69–70, 79, G. W. F. Hegel, *Jenaer Systementwürfe III: Naturphilosophie und Philosophie des Geistes*, ed. Rolf-Peter Horstmann (Hamburg: Felix Meiner Verlag, 1987), p. 236.

[87] De Sanctis, 'Storia della letteratura italiana', p. 491.

but preserve intact the [native] genius of the fatherland, and preserve yourselves unsullied by foreign opinions and usages. Know yourselves to be frank and free Italians, thinking and feeling in an Italian way even amidst the barbarians: in that resisting foreign flatteries is the best proof you could ever give of your great soul in its love for your native land.[88]

De Sanctis, for his part, considered his experience in Switzerland very precious and his appreciation of the republican tradition is one of the *souvenirs ineffaçables* that the Helvetic Confederation had bequeathed to him. When he came back to Italy, he underlined this special connection with his host country, writing to Johann Karl Keppler: 'Sir, Switzerland has left me with *certain memories that cannot be erased*. After my own fatherland, it is Switzerland that I love. In Naples I had the opportunity to do several Swiss a good turn; I said to myself: this is a debt that I'm paying: for I will never forget the generous welcome I received in Zurich' (Turin, 21 May 1861).

The Swiss experience was of fundamental importance for De Sanctis' elaboration of the *Storia della letteratura italiana* and for his political commitments. His letters show that he developed in Switzerland a 'republican awareness' he had not had before. This awareness led him to focus on Machiavelli as the greatest Italian republican thinker and the main figure, along with Ludovico Ariosto, of Italian 'Modernity'. The link between the Hegelian philosophy of history and the Republican scheme of history identified above becomes even clearer: it concerns not only method or strictly philosophical matters but also De Sanctis' life experience and sensibility.

Despite this link, the scholarly literature has underestimated the relationship between Hegelianism and Republicanism: while there are a handful of studies on Republicanism – considered as 'the practices and institutions of citizenship as integral to the experience of freedom'[89] – and Hegel's philosophy,[90] especially in its Left Hegelian interpretation[91], the influence of the republican historiographical approach on nineteenth-century Italian Hegelianism has been utterly neglected.[92] On this topic,

---

[88] Gioberti, *Del primato morale e civile degli italiani*, vol. II, p. 4.

[89] Douglas Moggach, 'Hegelianism, Republicanism and Modernity', in *The New Hegelians. Politics and Philosophy in the Hegelian School* (Cambridge: Cambridge University Press, 2011), p. 5.

[90] James Bohman, 'Is Hegel a Republican? Pippin, Recognition, and Domination in the Philosophy of Right', *Inquiry*, 53, no. 5, 2010: 435–449. See also Alan Patten, *Hegel's Idea of Freedom* (Oxford; New York: Oxford University Press, 2002). On this topic, refer also to Moggach, 'Hegelianism, Republicanism and Modernity'.

[91] Douglas Moggach (ed.), *The New Hegelians. Politics and Philosophy in the Hegelian School* (Cambridge: Cambridge University Press, 2011).

[92] It is absent, for example, in Gareth Stedman Jones and Gregory Claeys (eds.), *The Cambridge History of Nineteenth Century Political Thought History of Ideas and Intellectual History* (Cambridge: Cambridge University Press, 2011).

the analysis of De Sanctis' ideas, especially of his interpretation of the Renaissance and his Swiss experience, allows us to understand more deeply the circulation of ideas in Europe during the nineteenth century. The Italian Hegelians did not appreciate the political republicanism represented in Italy, during the Risorgimento, by Giuseppe Mazzini, but this does not mean that they rejected republican culture as such. They did indeed, like the Left Hegelians in Germany, 'seek to find in Hegel, and in the critique of Hegel, resources for grasping the central theoretical issues of modernity', and for them these issues were surely connected with the interpretation of the Renaissance and the idea of inner freedom.[93]

Recent scholarship has set out to reconstruct the sheer complexity of the ideas and political ambition of Risorgimento political thought and the attendant plurality of concepts of nationalism. By re-evaluating the philosophy of the Renaissance and the role of Bruno, Campanella, and Machiavelli, Italian Hegelians had traced in modern Italian history a reformed conception of the individual. This new and modern individual was deemed to have had a consciousness independent of the state and of any other political or religious authority. It is this new individual that is the subject of the sentiment of nationality, which is for its part a product of their autonomous consciousness and of their actions.

3.3   The Splendid Decadence

De Sanctis' ideas were embraced by his pupil Pasquale Villari (1827–1917), who, after the struggles of 1848, fled to Florence, where he studied in particular the figure of Girolamo Savonarola. He was appointed as professor of history at the University of Pisa and then he transferred to the chair of modern history at the Istituto di Studi Superiori in Florence. He was for several years a member of Parliament, in 1884 was appointed senator, became vice-president of the Senate in 1887, and in 1891–1892 was Minister of Public Education. Villari is a central figure in the passage from Hegelian culture to Italian positivism:

> From Naples Villari had emerged a Hegelian . . . . In '54 he still exalts
> Hegel, though acknowledging the links between philosophy of history and

---

[93] Moggach, 'Hegelianism, Republicanism and Modernity', p. 2; see Alessandro Casati and R. Foà, 'Mazzini e gli Hegeliani di Napoli', *La Critica. Rivista di Letterature, Storia e Filosofia*, 10, 1912: 73–79.

positive sciences; in '57 he condemns Spaventa, not on account of love for Hegel whom he calls 'great, very great', but for his having reduced himself to being Hegel's annotator . . . in '66, in the fourth series of the *Politecnico*, there appears 'La filosofia positiva e il metodo storico" in which Ardigò recognised the dawn of Italian positivism'.[94]

Villari was something of an oddity within the Hegelian cultural milieu, inasmuch as he became attracted to the new positivist theories and then contested the Hegelian approach. Nevertheless, he can plausibly still be considered a student of De Sanctis and, like his master, he judges the Renaissance to have been a period of splendid decadence: he was particularly fascinated by the figure of the friar Girolamo Savonarola and therefore moved to Florence in order to write his *La storia di Girolamo Savonarola e de' suoi tempi* (*The History of Girolamo Savonarola and of His Yimes*, 1859–1861).[95] His stay in Florence was very important for his biography and he was considered, together with Gino Capponi, one of the most eminent figures in the city's cultural life.[96] Villari's interpretation of the Renaissance should indeed be understood within the Florentine cultural context.[97] Villari's interest in the Renaissance begins with Girolamo Savonarola, in whom he recognises a particular greatness:

> For us, however, the historical greatness of Savonarola lies in his having dared to believe; when everyone doubted; in his having, against the scandals of the Borgias and the sceptical cynicism of the philosophers, affirmed the then forgotten and derided rights of Christianity, together with those of liberty and of reason. He knew how to think upon the moral renewal of man, when everyone thought only about his intellectual renewal; he saw in virtue the sound foundation of religion and the true source of liberty, when everyone seemed convinced that political virtue and Christian [virtue], the fatherland and religion, were [locked] in an inevitable and irreconcileable conflict.[98]

Villari was particularly fascinated by the religious spirit of the Renaissance, in his judgement the only viable way to achieve the moral renewal that Italy needed. That kind of faith, which characterised Savonarola and led him to the ultimate sacrifice, was a faith in virtue, which was sustained by

[94] Eugenio Garin, *Un secolo di cultura a Firenze. Da Pasquale Villari a Piero Calamandrei* (Florence: La Nuova Italia, 1960), pp. 7–8.
[95] Pasquale Villari, *La storia di Girolamo Savonarola e de' suoi tempi*, 2 vols. (Florence: Le Monnier, 1910).
[96] On the Florentine cultural context during the Risorgimento, see Giovanni Gentile, *Gino Capponi e la cultura toscana nel secolo XIX* (Florence: Sansoni, 1973).
[97] Luigi Russo, *Francesco De Sanctis e la cultura napoletana* (Rome: Editori Riuniti, 1983), pp. 202–248.
[98] Villari, *La storia di Girolamo Savonarola e de' suoi tempi*, 1910, vol. 1, pp. xiv–xv.

religion, with both supporting freedom: 'To this faith in virtue, sanctified by religion, and serving to sanctify liberty, [Savonarola] dedicated his whole life, and for it he died.'[99] Despite this new religious spirit that guided Savonarola's actions and thoughts, Villari refused the putative connection between the Florentine priest and Luther: there were many differences between the two doctrines, and Savonarola and his disciples always professed to be Catholic. Villari distinguished Savonarola from Luther because he was concerned to analyse the reformation of Christianity, not the Protestant Reformation, and furthermore he held Savonarola to have been the first of the 'genuinely original men of the Renaissance'.[100] Despite the presence of an important and modern Renaissance figure such as Savonarola, Villari was aware that the Renaissance could not itself be defined as modern:

> The Renaissance is not yet modern civilisation, nor does it resemble its entrance-hall; it had a character that was universal, and yet still indefinite and indeterminate. The men who truly deserve to be called new in that period, foresee that civilisation is advancing towards a larger synthesis of humankind, and feel themselves to be closer to God .... They know only that they are advancing, they feel that in their course they are dragging the world behind them: nothing else. They are breaking up the shadows; they are opening up the paths to the new road, more by force of will and of faith than by force of reason. They have the mind of prophets, the heart of heroes and the destiny of martyrs. The world is in fact terrified of this new species of Titans, who are rising up to combat the old idols, and it straightway starts to oppress them. Then the Renaissance gives way to modern civilisation ...: Savonarola, Telesio, Campanella, Bruno, are succeeded by Galileo, Bacon, Descartes, who come with their powerful genius to render the ground more fertile, to gather the crop already sown .... Such was the character of the true Renaissance, and two Italians first initiated it. Columbus opened the paths of the seas, Savonarola those of the spirit.[101]

Unlike Spaventa and, in some respects, De Sanctis, Villari maintains that the Renaissance is not Modernity, and, even if there are figures that might be deemed modern, they do not represent the *Zeitgeist*. Modernity begins after the Renaissance, when Galileo, Bacon, and Descartes follow on from Savonarola, Telesio, Campanella, and Bruno. Villari analyses the Renaissance as a historiographical category that defines a period between the Middle Ages and Modernity and for this reason it is a moment of

---

[99] Villari, *La storia di Girolamo Savonarola e de' suoi tempi*, 1910, vol. 1, p. xvi.
[100] Villari, *La storia di Girolamo Savonarola e de' suoi tempi*, 1910, vol. 2, p. 257.
[101] Villari, *La storia di Girolamo Savonarola e de' suoi tempi*, 1910, vol. 2, pp. 257–259.

'splendid decadence', or rather a moment of moral and political decadence, which was paradoxically accompanied by the flourishing of the arts and culture. Nonetheless, his studies of Savonarola persuaded him that a reformation of Christianity was necessary in order to bring about a rebirth of Italian civilisation and that it was assuredly still necessary:

> [Savonarola's work] aspires to that Christian and Catholic reformation that was the eternal desire of the great Italians, of some among the greatest thinkers in the whole of the civil world. And when this reformation, which has already become a conviction, a general desire, will have begun to become a fact; then will Christianity revived by faith, fortified by reason, receive in the world its true and full development, and Italy will not be last in the renewed civilisation.[102]

Several years later, after Italian unification, Villari completes his work on *Niccolò Machiavelli e i suoi tempi* (1877–1882).[103] Here, like De Sanctis, Villari recognises both the brilliance of Italian art and the weakness of the moral consciousness:

> A feeling for the beautiful was then, one would say, the only and the surest guide for human life, which, it seemed, sought to identify itself with art. In Castiglione's *Cortegiano* we see just how far the gentleman of the sixteenth century could, by this path, refine and ennoble himself; but we see still what a weak foundation his moral conscience had .... At a stroke the foreign invasions stifled every [trace of] political life among us, and the Italian Renaissance remained as if instantaneously petrified before our eyes, with all its uncertainties, its contradictions.[104]

In this work, Villari identifies as the cause of moral decadence the absence of a religious sentiment and the importance given to the external forms of worship at the expense of inner moral sentiment; this is the reason why he even defines the history of the Renaissance as the history of a catastrophe:

> [In the Renaissance] they worked with relentless energy; they sought out and they found all the literary forms; they won a great truth and rendered things easier in prose and in poetry; they created oratorical, diplomatic, historical, philosophical language and style; but religious sentiment disappeared; moral sense grew weak, and the cult of form grew and often at the expense of substance, a defect that persisted for many centuries in Italian literature. Upon seeing this prodigious intellectual activity, which in a thousand different forms reproduces itself as ever richer and more splendid,

---

[102] Villari, *La storia di Girolamo Savonarola e de' suoi tempi*, 1910, vol. 2, pp. 260–261.
[103] Pasquale Villari, *Niccolò Machiavelli e i suoi tempi*, 3 vols. (Milan: Hoepli, 1912).
[104] Villari, *Niccolò Machiavelli e i suoi tempi*, 1912, vol. 1, p. 228.

yet always accompanied by a social and moral decadence, the historian who studies these times, remains dismayed, feeling himself to be in the presence of a mysterious contradiction, that causes one to foresee future miseries. When the evil that afflicts this people internally shall come to the surface, a catastrophe will be inevitable. Its slow and continuous advance, in the midst of so much intellectual progress, is precisely the history of the Renaissance.[105]

According to Villari, the absence of religious sentiment is the main cause of the moral decadence during the Renaissance. Nonetheless, he recognises the greatness of Italian culture and art, manifested in some of its key figures:

The man of the Italian Renaissance, dominated as he was by a profound egotism, without the moral guidance of a general interest, amidst the crumbling away of all the medieval institutions, preoccupied always and only with *his own particularity*, would have reduced everything to anarchy and to ruin, had not his intelligence, the greatness of the culture, the love of art and of science, the objective study of reality saved him, at least in part, along with the society to which he belonged.[106]

Villari considers the absence of religious sentiment and the prevailing moral decadence to have likewise been the cause of the defeat of Girolamo Savonarola in Florence:

Savonarola's faith, his love for the universal good, his abnegation had been heroic; his eloquence and his political judgement great; the religious zeal that he believed himself to have stirred up in the Florentine people had however been ephemeral. The latter's exaltation had been solely due to its love of liberty, and it had listened with enthusiasm to the Friar's religious word only so long as it had reinforced the popular government. But once it saw in him a danger to the Republic, without hesitating overmuch it abandoned him to the Pope. And in truth when the poor Friar breathed his last, the dangers threatening on all sides the government founded by him completely disappeared.[107]

Both De Sanctis and Villari maintained that Machiavelli had devoted himself to the national redemption of his *patria* and that his dream was realised only with Italian unification:

Italy had become incapable of [implementing] a religious reformation, such as followed in Germany and in England. Instead of soaring up towards God, as Savonarola had formerly preached; instead of seeking out strength in a new concept of faith, as Martin Luther preached, it turned to the idea

[105] Villari, *Niccolò Machiavelli e i suoi tempi*, 1912, vol. 1, pp. 26–27.
[106] Villari, *Niccolò Machiavelli e i suoi tempi*, 1912, vol. 2, pp. 273–274.
[107] Villari, *Niccolò Machiavelli e i suoi tempi*, 1912, vol. 1, pp. 290–291.

of State and fatherland, which only with the sacrifice of one and all to the common good could be firmly constituted. It seemed that this was then the only way possible among us for [achieving] a genuine national redemption. The unity of the risen fatherland would have rendered necessary, inevitable the reconstruction of morality, rekindled faith in virtue public and private, and led to some way being found of once again sanctifying the goal of life. This concept, which we find vaguely and weakly felt by very many of our greatest writers and statesmen in that period, was Machiavelli's dominant thought, the ideal to which he sacrificed his whole life. But national decadence had become inevitable, events followed on inexorably, and he [Machiavelli] at his death was faced with the spectacle of Italy going to its ruin, invaded by foreigners. His great thought therefore remained a dream, and he was the least understood and most slandered man known to history. Now that today the Italian people has begun to redeem itself politically, now that the fatherland has constituted itself according to the prophecy of Machiavelli, whose dream became a reality, the moment has come in which at last justice can be done to him.[108]

Villari considers, on one side, the Renaissance as the period of the 'emancipation of secular society and of reason';[109] on the other, he recognises that the Renaissance is also the period of the building of a new era, 'with the fragments of antiquity the Italian Renaissance built a new world'.[110] According to Villari, the causes of moral decadence are the absence of religious sentiment and the absence of political liberty. By contrast with De Sanctis, he also maintains that the absence in Italy of political liberty is caused by the lack of a unitary State and of a national army. It means that the problem of religious sentiment is strictly linked to the problem of political liberty, both during the Renaissance and in the nineteenth century.

By identifying the Renaissance as the main category of modernity, the Neapolitan Hegelians were able to contest two distinct narratives regarding the Italian national character. Spaventa challenged the myth of the antiquity of the Italian people, championing rather the philosophy of the Renaissance as the true origin of the Italian nation, which, in his opinion, ought to be considered as European from the outset. In contrast to the great majority of the patriots and intellectuals of the Risorgimento, a positive meaning of the Renaissance was elaborated by the Neapolitan Hegelians. The main protagonists of this philosophical movement, despite their differing perspectives, forged a conception of the Renaissance as the idea of modernity and not as a cultural epoch, as Burckhardt's *Civilization*

---

[108] Villari, *Niccolò Machiavelli e i suoi tempi*, 1912, vol. 3, pp. 384–385.
[109] Villari, *Niccolò Machiavelli e i suoi tempi*, 1912, vol. 2, p. 285.
[110] Villari, *Niccolò Machiavelli e i suoi tempi*, 1912, vol. 2, p. 279.

affirmed. The Hegelians insisted on the philosophical meaning of the Renaissance as the affirmation of the immanence of the divine nature in human nature, of the dignity and sanctity of the individual, of the autonomy of consciousness and moral liberty regarding any moral and political authority. It represents the demand that the individual be granted autonomy with regard to the State and any political and religious power whatsoever. It defines a concept of modernity that traces in Italian history some of the same principles as prevailed in protestant Europe and offers an idea of Europe at odds with the main narrative of the 'Protestant Supremacy'. Hence, the rise of the Renaissance as a concept of modernity elaborated by the Neapolitan Hegelians, must be understood within this broader transnational debate regarding the origins of modernity as a reflection on the European heritage and within the general context of Hegel's reception in Italy.

Neapolitan Hegelians had fashioned a dialogue between Giordano Bruno and Niccolo' Machiavelli, a dialogue that served to recast ideas of moral liberty and political liberty arising from the philosophy of the Renaissance and that could still serve the purpose, or so they judged, of creating the consciousness that any modern nation needed to develop in order to become fully aware of its identity, as described by Hegel. The Hegelians took to heart the pain and suffering, and the manifold anxieties of their Renaissance thinkers. It is not by chance that Machiavelli's statue, sculpted by Lorenzo Bartolini and placed in a niche in the colonnade of the Uffizi Gallery, originally designed by Giorgio Vasari, was created in the mid-nineteenth century (1845–1846) (Figure 3.1). Bruno's warning to his executioner turned into the ironic smile of Machiavelli, when with the *Breccia di Porta Pia* the Italian troops entered Rome in September 1870, De Sanctis wrote: 'Let us be proud of our Machiavelli. His is the glory when any part of the ancient edifice collapses. And his is the glory when any part of the new one is built. Even as I write, the bells ring continuously, and they announce the entry of the Italians into Rome. The temporal power is collapsing. And people cry 'Viva' to the unity of Italy. Glory be to Machiavelli.'[111] That old world was about to collapse and the new State had to be built, and this was the main political role of the Neapolitan Hegelians, who formed part of the Italian government from 1860 to 1876.

---

[111] Villari, *Niccolò Machiavelli e i suoi tempi*, 1912, vol. 2, p. 525. On this topic, see Maurizio Viroli, *Machiavelli's God* (Princeton: Princeton University Press, 2012), pp. 281–284.

CHAPTER 4

The Ethical State

The human being will always be infinite and free even if [it] is trapped in chains.

Marianna Florenzi Waddington, *Saggio sulla Filosofia dello Spirito*, 1867

The painting by Franz Wenzel Schwarz reproduced here (Figure 4.1) represents the tumultuous celebrations in the city of Naples on the 7th of September 1860, when Garibaldi and his Red Shirts entered the city, completing the conquest of the Kingdom of Two Sicilies. The latter had

Figure 4.1   *Entry of Garibaldi into Naples on 7th September 1860*, Franz Wenzel Schwarz, 1860–1875, Museo Civico, Naples

begun on the 11th of May, when Garibaldi's volunteer army, the Thousand, disembarked in Marsala, Sicily, to support the local revolts against the Bourbon Monarchy and defeated the King's troops. The King, Francesco II, had already abandoned the capital of the Kingdom, escaping to Gaeta, so Garibaldi on his entrance into the city met with no significant resistance. In the meantime, in central Italy, a number of different plebiscites were held to ratify the annexation of the various states to the Kingdom of Sardinia. A simple 'yes' or 'no' was to be the answer to the question 'Do you wish to unite with the constitutional monarchy of the King Vittorio Emanuele?'[1] Cavour was suspicious of Garibaldi's almost legendary fame in Sicily and did not favour the continuation of the war on the mainland.[2] However, in Naples, Garibaldi declared his loyalty to the King Vittorio Emanuele, while Cavour sent the Piedmontese army to Naples to share the victory with the Red Shirts. In order to reach Naples, the troops had to pass through Umbria and Marche in central Italy, thus conquering part of the territories of the Catholic Church. In October, plebiscites in the Kingdom of Two Sicilies and in the ex-papal states confirmed the growing support given to the unitary cause. On the 26th of October, Giuseppe Garibaldi and King Vittorio Emanuele met in Teano, north of Naples, and the General handed over the South to the new King of Italy. It was from the balcony of Doria d'Angri Palace, built by Luigi Vanvitelli and portrayed in the painting reproduced above, that Garibaldi had declared the annexation of the Kingdom of Two Sicilies to the Kingdom of Italy in November 1860, an event considered so important as to lead to the renaming of the Square of the Holy Ghost (Piazza Santo Spirito) as

[1] On the use of plebiscites during the Risorgimento, see G. Fruci, 'Democracy in Italy: From Egalitarian Republicanism to Plebiscitary Monarchy', in *Re-imagining democracy in the Mediterranean 1750–1860*, ed. J. Innes and M. Philp (Oxford: Oxford University Press, 2018); A. S. Chambost, 'Socialist Visions of Direct Democracy, The Mid-Century Crisis of Popular Sovereignty and the Constitutional Legacy of the Jacobins', in *The 1848 Revolutions and European Political Thought*, ed. Gareth Stedman Jones and Douglas Moggach (Cambridge: Cambridge University Press, 2018); Alex Körner, *America in Italy: The United States in the Political Thought and Imagination of the Risorgimento* (Princeton: Princeton University Press, 2017), chs. 2–3.
[2] Denis Mack Smith considered the tension between Cavour and Garibaldi to be of central importance: see Denis Mack Smith, *Cavour e Garibaldi nel 1860* (Turin: Einaudi, 1962). Recent studies have highlighted how the importance of the personal contrast was amplified a posteriori in order to accentuate the ideological opposition between a radical and democratic stance (Garibaldi and Mazzini) and the moderate, institutional approach of the Piedmontese government. For a discussion on this, see Gilles Pécout, *Il lungo Risorgimento: La nascita dell'Italia contemporanea (1770–1922)* (Milan: Mondadori, 2011), pp. 164–180.

Seventh September Square (Piazza Sette Settembre), the name it still bears today.

The process of Italian unification has often been portrayed in the historiography as a process of royal conquest, whereby its principal architect, Cavour, together with the King Vittorio Emanuele, imposed Piedmontese rule on the rest of the Peninsula. Moreover, the representation of Southern Italy in many Northern Italian accounts as a backward and uncivilized land, has led historians in recent years to portray the South through the 'logic of coloniality'.[3] Studies by Jane Schneider, John Dickie, Nelson Moe, and Silvana Patriarca have thus explored the widespread proliferation of stereotypes representing Southern Italy in the aftermath of unification, in the process often going beyond the analysis of the so-called 'Southern Question' – which investigates instead the economic and political differences between the North and the South of the Peninsula.[4] Very recently, scholars such as Roberto Dainotto, Luigi Carmine Cazzato, and Claudio Fogu have considered the process of Italian nation-building through the lens of postcolonial critical studies, applying the logic of Edward Said's Orientalism to Southern Europe, and Southern Italy, and so proposing a discursive construction of the 'Souths' of Europe dubbed 'Meridionism'.[5] Although the key role of Piedmont in the unification process is beyond dispute, these approaches tend to overshadow local and popular participation in the patriotic effort, in particular within the Kingdom of Two Sicilies, as well as the work of Southern Italian political representatives in the new Parliament. This section of the book explores the contribution of the political thought and political praxis of Italian Hegelians, most of whom were from the South, to the building of the new Italian State. Many of them had first served the Kingdom of Italy in the Southern provinces during the delicate transition period, then in the

---

[3] Claudio Fogu, *The Fishing Net and the Spider Web: Mediterranean Imaginaries and the Making of Italians* (London: Palgrave, 2020), p. 17.

[4] On this, see Silvana Patriarca, *Italian Vices: Nation and Character from the Risorgimento to the Republic* (Cambridge; New York: Cambridge University Press, 2010); Jane Schneider (ed.), *Italy's 'Southern Question': Orientalism in One Country* (London: Bloomsbury, 1998), parts 1 and 3; Nelson Moe, *The View from Vesuvius: Italian Culture and the Southern Question* (Berkeley: University of California Press, 2002), especially pp. 187–223; John Dickie, *Darkest Italy: the Nation and Stereotype of the Mezzogiorno, 1860–1900* (London: Macmillan, 1999).

[5] Roberto Dainotto, *Europe (in Theory)* (Durham, NC: Duke University Press, 2007); Fogu, *The Fishing Net and the Spider Web*; Luigi Carmine Cazzato, 'Fractured Mediterranean and Imperial Difference: Mediterraneanism, Meridionism, and John Ruskin', *Journal of Mediterranean Studies*, 26, no. 1, 2017: 69–78. On this, see also Matthew D'Auria and Fernanda Gallo, 'Ideas of Europe and the (Modern) Mediterranean', in *Mediterranean Europe(s): Rethinking Europe from Its Southern Shores*, ed. Fernanda Gallo and Matthew D'Auria (London: Routledge, 2022), pp. 1–19.

central government and parliament in the early years of state-building, between 1861 and the 1880s, serving as representatives in both of the main parties, the Historical Right (Destra Storica) and the Historical Left (Sinistra Storica). This section will explore the reshaping of the Hegelian theory of the State, reinterpreted as it was by Italian Hegelians, and how it served the new Italian political context and contributed to the understanding and designing of the new Italian State.

4.1   The Philosophy of Right

Hegel's *Philosophy of Right* was translated into Italian for the first time by Vito Antonio Turchiarulo and published in 1848 in Naples. As described in Chapter 1, Turchiarulo's philosophical understanding of Hegel was somewhat limited, and the translation was as a consequence not particularly good either. The clarification of Hegel's political thought to the Italian public should be attributed to two texts appearing in the 1860s as a commentary upon, and explication of, Hegel's complex political philosophy: Marianna Florenzi Waddington, *Essay on the Philosophy of the Spirit*, published in 1867, and Bertrando Spaventa, *Studies on Hegel's Ethics*, published in 1869. They both had access to the original German text in the edition by Eduard Gans, and they published a commentary upon Hegel's ethical and political ideas by connecting them with key concepts from the Italian philosophical tradition. In order to clarify the novelty of Hegel's thought as well as its relevance for the Italian context, both authors refer constantly to Giordano Bruno's pantheism, Giambattista Vico's understanding of history, as well as Vincenzo Gioberti's ontology. In this section, we will explore their reading of Italian philosophy in the light of Hegel's political ideas, whereas in Section 4.2 we will compare Spaventa's theory of the State with Hegel's understanding of the 'Ethical State'. In Section 4.3, we will consider the legacy of the theory of the Ethical State in early twentieth- century Italian political thought.

Just as Giovanni Gentile did much to promote the thought of Bertrando Spaventa, so too did he bear a great responsibility for the underestimation of Florenzi Waddington's contribution, defining her, somewhat condescendingly, as 'a refined writer, who, if she did not contribute to the progress of speculative thought ... nonetheless had a virile sense of philosophical problems'.[6] In more recent years, her place in

---

[6] Gentile, *Le origini della filosofia contemporanea in Italia*, p. 36.

nineteenth-century Italian philosophical culture has been cautiously re-evaluated by scholars such as Claudio Cesa, who have highlighted the difference between her philosophical production and 'the *otium* of a noblewoman'.[7] It is anyway due to the pioneering efforts of Fabiana Cacciapuoti, Maria Alessandra Degl'Innocenti Venturini, and Ippolita Degli Oddi that the work of this interesting female thinker has now been investigated thoroughly, her published and unpublished work dissemin-ated, and her dignity as a philosopher restored to her. These scholars identify four main areas of interest in Florenzi Waddington's thought: her initial reflections, which represent an attempt at autonomous thinking, such as in her translation of Schelling's *Bruno* and her *Lettere Filosofiche* (*Philosophical Letters*, 1848), her works on Leibnitz's *Monadology* and interest in cosmology and rationalism, her Hegelian works and her reflec-tions on religion. However, her key role within the maturation of Hegelianism in Italy has still to be assessed and, in this book, we present her as one of the main exponents of Italian Hegelianism.

Marianna Florenzi Waddington's interest in pantheism stems from her work in 1844 on Schelling's *Bruno*. She read and discussed the works of Spaventa and Fiorentino on Giordano Bruno, and in her correspondence with Fiorentino she commented on topics such as the identification of world and God, as well as the immortality of the soul – on which topic she published an essay in 1868 entitled *Dell'immortalità dell'anima umana*.[8] She had also cultivated an interest in eclectic philosophy during her stay in Paris in 1842, and yet, to judge by their correspondence, it was only in 1862 that she met Victor Cousin himself.[9] Like the Neapolitan Hegelians, Florenzi at first engaged with German idealism through the mediation of French philosophy and especially of Cousin's work. It was by virtue of her relationship with the French philosopher that she developed her

---

[7] C. Cesa, 'Introduzione', in Maria Alessandra Degl'Innocenti Venturini, *Dalle carte di Marianna Florenzi Waddington. Scritti inediti sul panteismo* (Naples: Bibliopolis, 1978), p. 16.

[8] On her interest in pantheism, see Alessandro Poli, 'Idealismo platonico e filosofia della natura nel pensiero di Marianna Florenzi Waddington. Note sull'edizione della *Monadologia* di Leibnitz', in *Voci dell'Ottocento*, ed. I. Pozzoni (Villasanta: Limina Mentis, 2010), pp. 15–56; Fabiana Cacciapuoti, 'Marianna Florenzi Waddington: Tra panteismo ed hegelismo nelle carte napoletane', *Archivio per la storia delle donne*, 2004: 219–225. On Florenzi Waddington, see also Maria Alessandra Degl'Innocenti Venturini, 'Marianna Florenzi Waddington: Lo Svolgimento del suo pensiero filosofico', *Annali dell'istituto di filosofia*, 2, 1980: 311–350; 'Marianna Florenzi Waddington e il Risorgimento Italiano', *Rassegna storica del Risorgimento*, 68, 1981: 273–302; Ippolita Degli Oddi, *Marianna Florenzi Waddington: Dalla vita di una donna alla storia di un paese: Manoscritti ed inediti* (Perugia: Guerra, 2001).

[9] See 'Corrispondenza inedita di Vittorio Cousin con la marchesa Florenzi Waddington', in *La Rivista Europea* (1870), vol. I, pp. 493–498.

engagement with German idealism and in particular with Hegel. However, her close friendship with Fiorentino during the 1860s drew her near to the Neapolitan Hegelian cultural milieu and, in this period, she published a series of philosophical essays commenting on Hegel's philosophy: *Saggi di psicologia e di logica* (1864), *Saggio sulla natura* (1866), and the *Saggio sulla filosofia dello spirito* (1867). These works were all added in 1875 to the *Index of Prohibited Books* by the Catholic Church, which had harried her ever since her support for the liberals manifested itself for the first time in the 1830s.

In her *Essay on the Philosophy of the Spirit*, which is dedicated to Angelo Camillo De Meis, Florenzi Waddington devotes its first part to Hegel's absolute spirit. The essay features a section on each aspect: Art, Religion, and 'Scienza' (meaning 'philosophy'). In the second part, she discussed Hegel's philosophy of right, presenting there three sections on Law, Morality, and the State. Here, while explaining some of the fundamental concepts of Hegel's political thought – such as liberty, universality, the dialectic and the *Aufhebung*, the differences with Kant and his categorical imperative – she connects these ideas with the reflections of Italian philosophers. For instance, Giordano Bruno's moral philosophy, she observes, highlights the autonomy of freedom, grounding it on the inner moral dimension, and posits the individual as an end in itself and not as a means, thereby underlining the infinite value of human beings. Only Hegel, though, or so Waddington maintained, would develop this moral philosophy into the objective concretisation of *Sittlichkeit* (*custom*) through the concept of the State, in which the particular passions of individuals become universal and rational.[10]

While discussing the different forms of government – democratic, aristocratic, or monarchical – and clarifying the role of constitutional monarchy in Hegel, she highlights how Giambattista Vico, in his *New Science*, had differentiated between the government of the *One*, the *Few*, or the *Many and All*, judging the 'monarchie civili' to be the best form, including as they did all the others.[11] She also distinguishes between the government and the State, and insists that Hegel's idea of the State in the form of constitutional monarchy serves not to curb liberty but rather to sustain freedom within civil and political institutions.[12]

---

[10] Marianna Florenzi Waddington, *Saggio sulla filosofia dello spirito* (Florence: Monnier, 1867), pp. 79–92.
[11] On this, see Giuseppe Giarrizzo, *Vico, la politica e la storia* (Guida: Naples, 1981).
[12] Giarrizzo, *Vico, la politica e la storia*, pp. 93–106.

Florenzi Waddington pays particular attention to the institution of marriage as regards the concept of the infinite dignity of the '*persona*', the individual. The latter, she insists, is not only related to its inner and moral dimension (as it is for Spaventa) but also to the body: 'freedom – she posited – and its infinite value, is also for the body and, together, [spirit and body] constitute the entire human being'.[13] Moral freedom and dignity constitute the entire *persona* (its internal and external dimension), and it is on this ground that she criticises the marriage contract. A contract, indeed, implies that individuals are considered things to be possessed. For the same reason, the State cannot be based on a contract, such as the social contract. It is love, and not the right of property, that determined marriage:

> [someone] who is in love is not looking in the beloved person for [a] means to realize him/herself: they feel united one in the other and this unity is given by nature in its immediacy, and it is not the product of a calculation. A person can never be the property of another person and the absence of clarity on this concept has led, within the family, to consider 'the *pater familias* as the lord of his wife and children, who can dispose of their lives and of their goods as an owner with his things'.[14]

According to Florenzi Waddington, this confusion is still the cause of 'many barbaric consequences in practical life nowadays', and this is why it is important to clarify the concept of the individual as a *persona*. Indeed, she believes that 'the human being will always be infinite and free even if [it] is trapped in chains'.[15] Spaventa's understanding of the ethical life of marriage is likewise based on the idea that the woman is a free *persona*, but the freedom she enjoys is restricted to her willing, which is weaker and therefore more inclined to domestic life.

It appears evident that connecting the philosophies of Vico and of the Italian thinkers of the Renaissance with Hegel represents a fundamental aspect of the attempts made to clarify the latter's political philosophy to Italian readers. This connection is also the product of the Hegelian understanding of history applied to the specific political context of the Risorgimento. Only following on from an intellectual revolution was a national revolution deemed to be possible. Endorsing Hegel's interpretation of the idea of revolution, Francesco Fiorentino explained how Kant in Germany had accomplished an intellectual revolution that was more

---

[13] Florenzi Waddington, *Saggio sulla Filosofia dello Spirito*, p. 104.
[14] Florenzi Waddington, *Saggio sulla Filosofia dello Spirito*, p. 103.
[15] Florenzi Waddington, *Saggio sulla Filosofia dello Spirito*, p. 103.

profound than the French Revolution of 1789.[16] The Hegelian philosophy for its part represented the intellectual revolution on which the Italian national revolution would have to be founded. It was with these ideas at the forefront of his mind that Bertrando Spaventa moved to Modena in October 1859 to teach legal philosophy at the university, invited by Luigi Carlo Farini (1812–1866), who had been nominated by Cavour 'Commissioner' of Modena after Savoy's conquest of the papal central states. In Modena, Spaventa gave the inaugural lecture of the academic year and pronounced a *Discorso filosofico*, which was not a 'biography of a great person', as the tradition required, but 'the biography of the nation'.[17] The oration was greeted with enthusiasm by the Modena public, not least because it coincided with the denouement of the political Risorgimento. The philosopher explains that only a nation that is conscious of itself, its history and its culture, can regenerate itself. He argues that the new and free Italian state must be based on a conception of freedom that Italian people can recognise as originating in their own history and traditions. Hegelian freedom is reinterpreted by Spaventa as 'the principle of nationality', which is freedom interpreted as awareness of national history. It is a form of patriotism that does not refer to a specific territory or ties of blood but to a common history and tradition and that welcomes anyone willing to follow the Socratic maxim Γνῶθι σεαυτόν (Know thyself). This gnoseological process rests upon an understanding of Italian intellectual tradition as mainly characterised by the philosophy of the Renaissance and the idea of infinite and divine human nature developed by Bruno and Campanella, Niccolo' Machiavelli's reshaping of the relationship between politics and ethics, and Giambattista Vico's *ideal eternal history* – and its

---

[16] See F. Fiorentino, *La filosofia contemporanea in Italia* (Naples: Morano, 1876), pp. 1–5. On Hegel's interpretation of the Kantian and the French revolutions, see the very recent work by Richard Bourke, *Hegel's World Revolutions* (Princeton: Princeton University Press, 2023).

[17] The *Discorso filosofico* was published together with an accurate historical reconstruction of the period in Modena by Benvenuto Donati, 'L'insegnamento della filosofia del diritto e l'attività didattica di Bertrando Spaventa all'Università di Modena nel 1859–60', *Rivista internazionale di filosofia del diritto*, XVIII,1938: 541–571. The citations we use come from a published transcription of an unpublished manuscript of Bertrando Spaventa, 'Una prolusione inedita di Bertrando Spaventa a un corso di diritto pubblico', ed. Augusto Guzzo, *Giornale critico della filosofia italiana*, V, 1924: 280–296. Yet another draft of the *Discorso filosofico* was edited by Domenico D'Orsi, 'Della libertà e nazionalità dei popoli', *Rivista abruzzese*, XVIII, no. 3, 1965: 97–156. A number of lectures that Spaventa delivered in Modena have been collected and published by Giuseppe Tognon, 'Bertrando Spaventa. Lezioni inedite di filosofia del diritto. Modena 1860', *Archivio Storico Bergamasco*, II, nos. I–II, 1982: 37–60, 279–290. Further lectures were edited and published by Augusto Guzzo, 'Lezioni inedite di Bertrando Spaventa', *Giornale critico di filosofia italiana*, VI, nos. II–IV, 1925: 198–222, 291–295, 360–369. See also Domenico D'Orsi, 'Bertrando Spaventa: Lezioni inedite di storia della filosofia greca', *Sophia*, XXXVIII, nos. I–II, 1970: 80–92.

objective form, the 'State'. The Italian Hegelians see it as their philosophical mission to elaborate a theory of the State that rests on the Italian intellectual tradition as well as on the Hegelian conception of the Ethical State, thereby equipping the national revolution with the necessary intellectual instruments:

> There are epochs in the history of a people in which the power itself of external circumstances brings it back again to the inwardness of its thought, and leads it to ask of itself: what am I? Only this awareness of one's own being is the living source from which every national movement springs; it alone is the stable base upon which the new civil institutions are founded. The Socratic dictum: *Know thyself* ... applies not only to the moral formation of individuals but especially to that of the nations .... It is a time this, and an especial duty of all those among us who revere knowledge, to interrogate once again ourselves, our history and our scientific and literary tradition, to remember ever more vividly what we are or were formerly, and to know what we must be, seconding and actuating the potency of our nature.[18]

Spaventa therefore was adamant that the study and interpretation of Hegel's philosophy of right would have a key role in supporting the foundation of the new Italian State. He focused in particular on the role of objective spirit and on those passages in which the Stuttgart philosopher analyses the family, civil society, and the State. However, Spaventa's reading of Hegel's theory of the State was inflected by his own philosophy of history. According to Spaventa, the Renaissance had brought about 'a revolution, not only in the sciences themselves, but also in the arts and in the form of practical life ... a revolution effected by the entire spiritual intuition of the universe'. He was convinced that in that period 'the culture of the new times' had arisen and that patriots had to take the Renaissance as a reference point because 'the first philosophers of the Risorgimento [Renaissance] ... were Italian'.[19] Emboldened by his course in Modena and the analysis of Vico's philosophy, he continued his cultural programme of study and dissemination of modern Italian philosophy, convinced that an awareness of the development of national consciousness was necessary for Italian emancipation:

> The nations, Gentlemen, have a spirit of their own which is no less sacred and inviolable than that of individuals. Woe betide whoever tramples upon this spirit, but woe too betide whoever allows it to languish and all but sleep

---

[18] Spaventa, 'Una prolusione inedita di Bertrando Spaventa a un corso di diritto pubblico', p. 281.
[19] Spaventa, 'Una prolusione inedita di Bertrando Spaventa a un corso di diritto pubblico', p. 283.

in the most remote hiding place of the soul. The spirit is light, movement and truth, and it only lives [by virtue] of truth, movement and light. If Italy is here and today risen again and strong in its immortal right and asserts as much before God and men, the principal merit is due to those who promoted the development of the national consciousness in all epochs of our history, and to this great endeavour sacrificed fortune and life.[20]

Spaventa knew that while he was holding his classes, patriots were fighting against the Austrian army, and he tried to explain to the citizens of Modena and to young students that, even for those who could not defend their homeland with weapons, there were other ways to support the movement of national unity:

'While others are valiantly defending the *patria* with arms, those who cannot participate with so much glory, are defending it with knowledge and with science. Foreigners, who before used to reproach us for being a people without a strong will, now reproach us for willing too much and for thinking little, as if strong willing, especially when it has as its end the holiest of causes, should not have its root in the energy of thought. They say that we are a people without inwardness, concerned only with the external aspects of life, and that we want the freedom that is outside without first possessing the one that is inside ourselves. Let us show that this accusation is no less false than the other. Let us show them the admirable temper of the Italian intelligence, which contents itself neither with empty inwardness, which is not mirrored in an external reality, nor with dead interiority without an external life; Or if I may be permitted to use a famous phrase, neither of faith without works, nor of works without faith. Faith and works, thinking and acting, such is our genius, Gentlemen, and if there is an epoch in our history that demonstrates this character, it is [assuredly] the present.[21]

The Hegelian maintained that the rebirth of Italians would only be possible if they could understand the inner dimension of political freedom. Without this knowledge, any external conquest would prove to be fragile and fleeting, and before too long they would lose their freedom once again. For this reason, exhorting his audience to action, he referred to two Italian philosophers, Vico and Gioberti, and identified as their mission the bringing of reality as close to the idea as possible. The relationship between these two terms was not, as it had been for Hegel, an identification but rather an indication as to how to act:

Let us study the visible universe but let us not neglect the invisible [one], which alone can make us understand what our eyes see and our hands

[20] Spaventa, 'Una prolusione inedita di Bertrando Spaventa a un corso di diritto pubblico', p. 292.
[21] Spaventa, 'Una prolusione inedita di Bertrando Spaventa a un corso di diritto pubblico', p. 292.

touch. Let us continue Vico's great concept, already extended by other foreign thinkers, and renewed by the author of the ideal formula and of the *Primato*. Only thus can we not so much build the consciousness of our right and duty as men and as a nation, but fulfil our mission in the world, which is to inaugurate the concord not yet found between reality and the idea, between what is and what should be. It is not without reason, Gentlemen, that Italy has never been dead in the world of nations, and if now the peace of Europe depends upon the decision of our future.[22]

While Spaventa was pronouncing these words in November 1859, the key role played by Italy on the European chessboard was clear. During the same month, there was, indeed, this raw and edgy judgement of Constance d'Azeglio on the situation after the Treaty of Villafranca: 'There is only one thing to be said, and it is that so long as there are Austrians in Italy, Italy [itself] will be in ferment and Europe will not be calm.'[23]

The urgency of the present, the leading role played by Italian patriots, the awareness that they had a mission to accomplish with both force and ideas: these were the arguments used by Spaventa to inflame and motivate his audience in Modena. He maintained that free thinking, as well as being what distinguishes humans from animals, is what makes human beings like God and is the way in which they create themselves as human beings:

> Man is not born thinking, and still less is he born philosophising. What he is at the time of his birth is a very sorry thing: between him and an animal there is fairly little difference . . . . Man, however, [as against the animal] creates and superimposes upon the already existing world of nature a new world, more various, more rich, and more beautiful than the first one; and this world is not a vain production, a superfluous display of activity, an external work that adds nothing to the being who makes it . . . but it is man himself who fashions himself, his own true existence, his own world, flesh of his flesh and bone of his bone: author and work are one and the same thing; the author is simply himself as his own work . . . . This creating oneself as man, and no longer as animal, is the true prize and the true dignity of man: the true resemblance that he has with divinity, the true image that he renders of God upon the earth . . . . this *autoctisis* is human liberty itself in its plain meaning, and that the indefatigable organ of this freedom, indeed freedom itself, is thought, the free reflection of man upon himself. Whoever does not think is not free, and where there is not freedom there is not thought.[24]

---

[22] Spaventa, 'Una prolusione inedita di Bertrando Spaventa a un corso di diritto pubblico', p. 293.
[23] Costanza D'Azeglio, *Lettere al figlio (1829–1862)*, ed. Maldini Chiarito, vol. II (Rome: Istituto per la Storia del Risorgimento, 1996), p. 19.
[24] Bertrando Spaventa, *La filosofia del Risorgimento. Le prolusioni di Bertrando Spaventa* (Naples: Scuola di Pitagora, 2005), p. 50.

Therefore, free life is determined by free thought, which exists when an individual does not depend on the arbitrary will of another individual. Spaventa's conception of freedom derives from Aristotle, who argues that 'a free man is someone who is for himself and not for others'.[25] From a legal perspective, this concept defines the law not as a natural product but as a free one of human spontaneity: it is, indeed, the middle term through which the spirit is freed from the bonds of natural forms and becomes intelligence and will: 'Right is therefore the development of the personality, of the individuality that knows, wills and works, from its maximal abstraction (private law) up to its maximal concreteness as a political personality (the State).'[26]

The study of the philosophy of right thus becomes central for the understanding of the broad spectrum of human activities, from the individual will to the collective will. The methods used by Spaventa's contemporaries were not, in his opinion, sufficient: the philosophy of right could not be understood either with empirical analysis, which is limited to the observation of what is or was; or with the rationalist method, which formulates an abstract system that pays no attention to the real life of the spirit; or with Savigny's historical school, which conceives the development of the national consciousness of people as separate and different national formations and not as moments of the unique life of human spirit. According to Spaventa, it was necessary to apply Hegelian philosophical method, which, 'harmonising universality and development, considers right as divine thought, that is to say, concrete and objective reason'.[27] The study of the development of the conception of law in the history of thought was the only convincing way to define a concept of freedom clearly manifested in the life of Italians.

For this reason, Spaventa divided his course in Modena into two separate parts: first of all, a historical analysis of the evolution of the concept of law and of the relationship between historical law and the philosophy of law in those years; secondly, a theoretical analysis of the concept of the philosophy of right. This second part was, he believed, the most necessary for '[we] Italians, who need to fortify ever more strongly our consciousness of our right both as men and as a nation, given that the consciousness of national right is founded upon the consciousness of human right, of the right of man as man'.[28] Only citizens aware of their rights, of their freedom, could create a nation: the right to which Italians

---

[25] Spaventa, *La filosofia del Risorgimento*, p. 51.　　[26] Spaventa, *La filosofia del Risorgimento*, p. 62.
[27] Spaventa, *La filosofia del Risorgimento*, p. 63.　　[28] Spaventa, *La filosofia del Risorgimento*, p. 65.

should aspire, in January 1860, was the right to be a free and independent state, a free people in the sense of the Aristotelian definition:

> The State, Gentlemen, is the true reality of right; and this it is that we aspire to, to being a State. We have natural nationality: no one has been able to take that from us; even our enemies have conceded that we can lay claim to being a geographical expression. Yet we have more than this. We have our nationality as custom, as language, as art, as literature, as sentiment and intention; what we lack is nationality as unique personhood, living, free and powerful: political nationality. Shall we have it? We shall have it, if we come to know it and to will it; for my part I can only hasten it with desires, if not with work, that day on which I shall be able to raise my voice, no longer as an exile, but as the *free citizen of a great country.*[29]

According to Spaventa, the State is a real State only if it is constituted by 'free speech and the universal participation of citizens in political power', and it is not just something delimited by geographical boundaries.[30] The divine aspect of the State derives from two factors: the free participation of citizens in political power and the free exercise of critical thought. This last element depended on a specific interpretation of God as creation, an idea that stems from Gioberti's work. In fact, Spaventa was making symbolic use of the figure of Gioberti here, for its speculative and its political weight: on the one hand, he had set out to trace the thread of Italian philosophy; on the other, he was performing a political operation that his brother Silvio describes clearly in the following passage:

> You need to hurry up and complete the work on Gioberti. You have understood, I believe, a crucial truth: that the Italians will never understand what sort of thing modern philosophy is unless by obtaining it from their own philosophers; and for this there is a powerful reason, for which they are not so much in the wrong since they understand nothing of a philosophy that they see fall down upon their heads as if from the sky. And such for them is the true modern philosophy. Your work on Gioberti could there-fore be the communicating link between ordinary philosophy, such as it is in Italy, and the one we would wish there to be. Don't be downcast, then, my dear Bertrando: I am certain that the Italians will end up understanding you and appreciating you at your true worth.[31]

[29] Spaventa, *La filosofia del Risorgimento*, pp. 65–66.
[30] Spaventa, *La filosofia del Risorgimento*, p. 66.
[31] On Spaventa's re-evaluation of Gioberti's thought, see Gentile, 'Bertrando Spaventa'; Cubeddu, *Bertrando Spaventa*. On Gioberti's interpretation of Bruno, who attracted his mature interest, even if not to the same degree as Vico did, see Ricci, *Dal 'Brunus redivivus' al Bruno degli italiani*, pp. 112–121; Provvidera, 'Note su Gioberti, Bruno e il panteismo'; Spaventa, *Dal 1848 al 1861. Lettere, scritti, documenti*, p. 313.

Spaventa underlines the necessity in Italy both of a State and of the formation of a national *costume* (custom), that is to say a national psyche, as Vico defined it, what Hegel would define as the ethical life, or second nature.[32] A national *costume* would be possible only with a free political sovereignty. The Hegelian philosophy of right is interpreted by Spaventa through Vico's positing of a connection between spirit and history and, above all, in the context of the struggles for Italian national emancipation. This is the reason why Spaventa studies the history of Italian philosophy and its connections with European philosophy, weaving together the philosophy of right and the history of philosophy.

The thesis of the 'circulation of Italian thought' was the aspect of Spaventa's thought that most preoccupied his contemporaries, concerning as it did the problem of the reconstruction of the 'sacred thread of the philosophical tradition'.[33] According to this theory, the two concepts on which Italy was built were the infinite value and dignity of every human being and the autonomy of human thought. These principles had formed modern philosophical consciousness, and for Spaventa they embodied the revolutionary argument and stance of Giordano Bruno and Tommaso Campanella. Thanks to the integration of Giambattista Vico's ideas within his own philosophy, Spaventa understood that these two principles had to become *mores*, a real determination, in order to establish the state on a firm foundation. To realise this outcome, however, it was necessary that Italians become aware of themselves and of the history of their own thought, because 'the lack of liberty for so long a time has made us a secret to ourselves'.[34] This lack of self-awareness was, according to Spaventa, one of the main causes of the servitude of Italians, who were 'prone to seeking always outside of themselves for what they can find only within themselves'.[35] The thesis of the 'circulation of Italian thought' was discussed again during the twentieth century thanks to Giovanni Gentile, who edited many works by Bertrando Spaventa between 1900 and 1925, within a project for the renovation of national culture promoted by Spaventa's nephew, Benedetto Croce, who did however work mainly on the writings

---

[32] See Giuseppe Tognon, 'Bertrando Spaventa e la "filosofia del diritto" di Hegel', in *Filosofia e coscienza nazionale in Bertrando Spaventa*, ed. Guido Oldrini (Urbino: Quattro Venti, 1988), pp. 61–71.

[33] See especially the polemic with the Giobertian school and with the orthodox Hegelians. For a reconstruction of this debate, consult Oldrini, *La cultura filosofica napoletana dell'Ottocento*; Oldrini, *Gli Hegeliani di Napoli*.

[34] Bertrando Spaventa, 'Ms. XXXI – Lettera' (D.1. Carta 21, Società di storia patria, December 8, 1861).

[35] Spaventa, 'Ms. XXXI – Lettera'.

of his other uncle, Silvio Spaventa. If, by the end of the nineteenth century, Bertrando Spaventa's work was largely neglected, this was, Gentile maintained, because he was a 'difficult philosopher'. He was convinced that the thesis of the 'circulation of Italian and European thought' was the most original concept that the Hegelian had developed, although he judged this theory to be insufficiently historical, a shortcoming due to the 'emptiness' and 'jumps' between the various moments of the circular pattern. In other words, the concept suffered from a lack of continuity, which was the very thing to which the Sicilian philosopher aspired.[36]

Gentile's criticism greatly influenced later interpretations of the theory of the 'circulation of Italian thought', which gradually reduced its role until it appeared to be proposing a different kind of 'primacy'. While Gioberti's 1843 best-seller *Del Primato morale e civile degli italiani* (*On the Moral and Civil Primacy of Italians*) had stressed Italian moral 'primacy' because of the Catholic roots of its culture, Spaventa called for a critical reconstruction of the national philosophical tradition, opposing Gioberti's 'theory of supremacy', and denouncing the historical and cultural marginalisation of Italy by reflecting on the historical and philosophical high points of the national culture.[37]

In order to understand the relevance of the theory of the 'circulation of Italian thought', its connection with the philosophy of right should be borne in mind. As Guido Calogero recognised, when writing in 1936 the entry 'Bertrando Spaventa' for the *Enciclopedia Italiana*, the philosophy of right was not based on a contractual understanding of human relationships but rather on an 'organic reading of the history of philosophy'.[38] Overcoming the contractual understanding of the State by grounding it in the Italian philosophical tradition was a goal shared by Spaventa and

---

[36] Gentile also believed that Spaventa had not gone beyond the naturalistic conception of the nation. On this topic, see Giovanni Rota, 'La "circolazione del pensiero" secondo Bertrando Spaventa', *Rivista di storia della filosofia*, LX, no. 4, 2005: 655–686. For Spaventa's influence on Gentile's interpretation of the Renaissance, see Andrea Scazzola, *Giovanni Gentile e il Rinascimento* (Naples: Vivarium, 2002), pp. 85–121.

[37] The difference between the theory of the 'supremacy' of Italian culture and the attempt at a definition of an Italian intellectual disposition is clarified by Cantimori: 'cominciarono le prime scosse a quella ingenua concezione di primato nazionalistico mentre dall'altra parte si chiariva il significato più specificamente nazionale, non nel senso di contenuto patriottico, ma nel senso della tradizione intellettuale e della definizione di un momento storico'; Delio Cantimori, *Eretici italiani del Cinquecento-Prospettive di storia ereticale italiana del Cinquecento*, ed. Adriano Prosperi (Turin: Einaudi, 2009), p. 12.

[38] Guido Calogero, 'Spaventa, Bertrando', in *Enciclopedia italiana di scienze, lettere ed arti*, ed. Giovanni Gentile (Roma, 1936), 313.

Florenzi Waddington. They considered this approach to be best suited to conveying Hegel's political thought to the Italian public and to applying the Hegelian understanding of history to the Italian political context.

Scholarship has recognised that the theory of the 'circulation of Italian thought' was essentially a 'venture of political pedagogy',[39] 'overwhelmed by the urgency of an ethico-political purpose',[40] it was only because of 'the political demand'[41] to which Bertrando Spaventa was responding that he brought his interpretation of Italian thought to the fore. However, the deeper meaning of the theory of 'circulation' involves the political instances and the urgency of a present situation: Spaventa synthesises the categories required for the development of a philosophy of right capable of founding the construction of the nation-state and so as to go beyond the historical event of Italian unification. Bertrando Spaventa presented some of the key ideas of the theory of circulation in his inaugural address, entitled 'The Character and Development of Italian Philosophy from the Sixteenth Century until Our Time', at the University of Bologna, where he held a professorship in the History of Philosophy for the academic year 1860–1861.[42] For the next academic year, he was invited by Francesco De Sanctis to take up a post as professor of Theoretical Philosophy at the University of Naples, where Spaventa would eventually return after twelve years of exile.

When approaching the port of Naples in 1861 on board of a ship that had sailed out from Genoa, Bertrando Spaventa wrote to his wife: 'I see the Vesuvius. After twelve years! – If only you were here! I enter the Bay of Naples. I see Naples and I recognize it. I stop writing to look.'[43] With his exile at an end, he was also able to take stock and collect together the ideas he had developed in the course of the previous decade. He organised his first two courses at the University of Naples in order to explore the connection between his theory of the circulation of Italian and European thought and Hegel's philosophy of right, focusing in particular on the section on the objective spirit (family, civil society, and the State).

---

[39] Spaventa, *La filosofia italiana nelle sue relazioni con la filosofia europea*, p. xiv.
[40] Bertrando Spaventa, *Saggi di critica filosofica, politica e religiosa*, ed. Biagio De Giovanni (Naples: Scuola di Pitagora, 2008), p. 19.
[41] Garin, *Filosofia e politica in Bertrando Spaventa*, p. 39.
[42] The inaugural address at the University of Bologna (20 April 1860) is the only Spaventa text ever to have been translated into English. See Bertrando Spaventa, 'The Character and Development of Italian Philosophy from the XVI Century Until Our Time', in *From Kant to Croce. Modern Philosophy in Italy 1800–1950*, trans. Rebecca Copenhaver and Brian P. Copenhaver (Toronto: University of Toronto, 2011), pp. 343–370.
[43] Spaventa, *Epistolario*, p. 322 (12 November 1860).

Spaventa's comments on Hegel's *Elements of Philosophy of Right* would be published only in 1869 with the title *Studii sull'etica di Hegel* (*Studies on Hegel's Ethics*) but the text matches almost word for word the manuscript of his lectures delivered at the University of Naples between 1862 and 1863.[44] Spaventa studied the *Elements of the Philosophy of Right* using his copy of Eduard Gans' edition of 1840, preserved in the Biblioteca Comunale Angelo Mai in Bergamo, where Spaventa's private library was housed after the death of his younger brother Silvio in 1894.

4.2 The Theory of the State

The theoretical turning point represented by the 'circulation of Italian thought' led Spaventa to undertake an analysis of Hegel's *Elements of Philosophy of Right*, which featured in the course he taught in Naples during the academic year 1862–1863, but was only published in 1869, with the addition of a Preface. That preface defended Hegel's thought from Terenzio Mamiani's attack on Hegelian ethics, published in 1868 with the title *Confessioni di un metafisico* (*Confessions of a Metaphysician*).[45]

The backdating of Spaventa's studies on Hegel's ethics may serve to delineate a new interpretation whereby the thesis of the 'circulation of Italian thought' and the philosophy of right, having both been formulated in the same years and having several features in common, are shown to be closely related. For instance, in his analysis of Italian philosophy, Spaventa identifies the new concept of modern philosophy in the *unità sintetica originaria*, which is based on the phenomenological process of the dialectic, itself the foundation of Hegel's philosophy of right. In fact, the

---

[44] Gentile changes the name of the book to *Principi di etica* to highlight Spaventa's originality: Bertrando Spaventa, *Principi di etica* (Naples: Scuola di Pitagora, 2007). For the cataloguing and organisation of Spaventa's manuscripts, see Alessandro Savorelli, *Le carte Spaventa della Biblioteca Nazionale di Napoli* (Naples: Bibliopolis, 1980); Alessandro Savorelli, 'Manoscritti spaventiani nella Biblioteca Nazionale di Roma', *Giornale critico della filosofia italiana*, II, no. 7, 2006: 276–295; Fernanda Gallo, 'Il manoscritto "De Anima" di Bertrando Spaventa', *Logos*, no. 6, 2011: 323–336. For some of the most important contributions to the publication of Spaventa's unpublished works, refer to Spaventa, *Epistolario di Bertrando Spaventa (1847–1860)*; Spaventa, *Lettera sulla dottrina di Bruno. Scritti inediti 1853–54*; Bertrando Spaventa, *Le 'lezioni' sulla storia della filosofia italiana nell'anno accademico 1861–1862*, ed. Francesca Rizzo (Messina: Siciliano, 2001); Bertrando Spaventa, *Lezioni di antropologia*, ed. Domenico D'Orsi (Florence-Messina: D'Anna, 1976); Bertrando Spaventa, *Scritti inediti e rari (1840–1880)*, ed. Domenico D'Orsi (Padua: CEDAM, 1966); Guzzo, 'Lezioni inedite di Bertrando Spaventa'; D'Orsi, 'Bertrando Spaventa; Tognon, 'Bertrando Spaventa'.

[45] Terenzio Mamiani, *Confessioni di un metafisico. I: Principi di Ontologia. II: Principi di Cosmologia*, 2 vols. (Florence: Barbera, 1865).

ethical subject is the one who has made the transition from consciousness to the spirit as *mind*, which is the last stage reached in the analysis of his philosophy of history. The term *mind* refers to the infinite power of knowledge, the infinite dignity of human beings, which is the principle traced by sixteenth-century Italian philosophy and which appears again as the basis of the moral world, because the 'ethical subject' is the one capable of this awareness.

The *Studii sull'etica di Hegel* have the dual purpose of presenting an original exposition of Hegel's ethical doctrine to the Italian public and of identifying the salient attributes of the modern state, keeping in mind both the Hegelian philosophy and the philosophy of the Italian Renaissance.[46] Spaventa re-elaborates the Hegelian philosophy of right through his philosophical and political position: 'This exposition will be neither a compendium, nor an extract, nor a paraphrase, but the *concept* – I would almost say the image – *that I have formed for myself of it,* explained and defined in the most essential forms in which the absoluteness of willing is ever more identified.'[47] Spaventa approaches Hegel's Ethics through the perspective of the *Phänomenologie des Geistes* (*Phenomenology of Spirit*) and in particular the Lord-Bondsman dialectic, to which his earlier *Studii sopra la filosofia di Hegel* (*Studies on Hegel's Philosophy*, 1850) were dedicated. In fact, the dialectic of recognition is the process of the spirit that pertains to the formation of the theoretical spirit and also the development of the practical one. There is an unequal struggle between the two self-consciousnesses, and in the slave, who preferred life to death, there is the 'cradle of freedom':[48] it is the trembling of the Bondsman before the Lord that disciplines and strengthens the former's will:

> And in truth *freedom* does not consist in doing what pleases us. This is the very freedom of the Lord. If I am not free within myself, if I am not free from my own natural egoism, I am not truly free ... obedience is, then, only the *negative* part of freedom. However, without it, freedom is not real, and from it is born the *positive* part.[49]

In the Lord-Bondsman dialectic, the latter gives himself his law, and in this way he becomes free. Through self-discipline, the Bondsman conceives his

---

[46] The confrontation with positivism, indeed, will concern Spaventa only in the 1870s and the backdating of *Principi di etica* demonstrates that the study was conceived before the elaboration of anti-positivistic argumentation.

[47] Spaventa, *Principi di etica*, pp. 36–37.   [48] Spaventa, *Principi di etica*, p. 180.

[49] Spaventa, *Principi di etica*, p. 180.

own will, while the Lord achieves *his* own will through his new object, the natural denial of the will forged by the Bondsman through his obedience. The formation of human consciousness has an immediate practical side and the relationship of recognition has to be interpreted as a struggle for freedom and *of* freedom. To Spaventa the real achievement of modern philosophy is precisely the discovery of the practical side of thought, which he defines as 'the humanity of the Absolute', that is, the divine aspect of human beings. The new metaphysics of mind, to which he referred in the theory of 'circulation', puts the ethical at the heart of theoretical speculation, because, as Hegel writes, 'in thinking, I *am free* because I am not in an *other*, but remain simply and solely in communion with myself'.[50]. So the *mind* is both the subject who knows (theoretical) and the subject who wills (practical) and the unity of both is the ethical subject, that is, the protagonist of the philosophy of law.

When Spaventa describes the ethical subject he uses the terms *ethos*, *mores*, *customs*, meaning the actual state of the consciousness of people. In the ethical spirit, the subject becomes a *person*, arising in connection with others and with the world, starting from itself and not from the object. This is the act of freedom. In order to define the concept of freedom, Spaventa refers to his studies on Bruno, taking up the distinction between freedom and free will, thus placing at the foundation of his philosophy of law the idea that freedom emerged during the sixteenth century:

> Free will operates and is conscious of being able to operate the contrary; freedom operates necessarily, but does not cease to be free; because this necessity is its essence, it is reason. In free will the purpose of the activity is finite, particular, determinate, and therefore extraneous to the essence of the activity itself; in freedom the purpose is absolute, necessary, infinite, it is the essence itself of the activity . . .. In freedom consists the true nature of man, the spirit. – I am entirely convinced, that by reducing freedom to free will and consequently reason to the discursive intellect, a merely quantitative difference between man and animal is posited.[51]

Freedom consists in the pursuit of higher and infinite purposes and not simply in the choice between specified options. It is intrinsically linked to human nature and it is what characterises and distinguishes human beings from animals. This concept of freedom was conceived by the philosophers of the Italian Renaissance, who maintained that the foundation of freedom and human dignity is the idea of the identity of human and divine nature. The manifestation of this concept of freedom is in the Hegelian objective

---

[50] Hegel, *Phenomenology of Spirit*, §197.   [51] Spaventa, *Principi di etica*, p. 79.

spirit, which is composed of law, morality, and politics (politics being Spaventa's translation for the Hegelian *Sittlichkeit*). Unlike Hegel, however, Spaventa relates the philosophy of the Italian Renaissance to the themes of modern German philosophy, thus innovating both in the philosophy of law and in the philosophy of history.

Through the conception of the subject as a free activity that can produce the object, and by deploying the logical categories of a synthetic unity a priori, Spaventa interprets the history of philosophy as a philosophy of history. He was convinced of the close link between philosophy and revolution and believed in 'that "civil religion" that ought to guide the process of national unity in Italy and the corresponding formation of the State'.[52] Only philosophy could guarantee that the Italian people not suffer separation from other peoples. It seems clear that the common thread that binds together the studies of the 1850s on the Renaissance, the formulation of the theory of the 'circulation of Italian thought', and Spaventa's philosophy of right (elaborated between 1859 and 1863) is the concept of freedom as an objective world, therefore the freedom that manifests itself in the politics of States, or rather in the Hegelian *Sittlichkeit*, composed of Law, Morality, and Ethics.

In his *Studi sull'etica di Hegel*, Spaventa had expressed unabashed criticisms of Hegel's more controversial arguments regarding the death penalty, the necessity of monarchy, and the inevitability of war between states. Analysing the copy of the Gans edition of the text in Spaventa's personal possession, it is possible to identify in the guise of annotations and marks the aspects of Hegel's philosophy of right on which he focused and that represent the most original parts of his thought compared to Hegel himself. In fact, the major sections of the work with annotations and underlining are the introduction; the passages where Hegel rejects Beccaria's theory of crime and punishment (§§ 98–100); the section III of Ethics (*Sittlichkeit*), which Spaventa calls Policy, in particular the part on domestic state law (from §260 to §308); and § 270, which covers the relationship between the State and Religion.

One of the most telling differences between Spaventa and Hegel was their stance on the death penalty. Spaventa refused to countenance the very notion of the death penalty and of life sentences because they were in stark contrast to the principle of human dignity elaborated by the philosophy of the Renaissance. Indeed, the concept of penalty was itself based on the assumption that the criminal had a moral inner life, thus a definitive or

---

[52] Spaventa, *Saggi di critica filosofica, politica e religiosa*, p. 18.

permanent sentence was in conflict with this idea. To assent to the imposition of an ultimate penalty would be tantamount to accepting the idea that there were some people incapable of a moral life, therefore incapable of humanity, thereby denying the principle of modernity that recognised an infinite dignity in each and every human being. Furthermore, Spaventa believed that the nature of the spirit is the unity of a duality, which is the theory that he called *teorica dell'ens geminum Siamese*, using the metaphor of Siamese twins to explain the concept of the spirit as a *medesimezza* (Io = Io/ I = I), or rather to be two in one:

> Without my theory of the *ens geminum Siamese*, what sense would confession, absolution, remission of sins, forgiveness have? What sense would the penalty itself have, which is the contrary? ... I think and [am prepared to] say that my theory leads straight to demonstrating the death penalty to be unjust and absurd, and [that my theroy] is at the same time the only way to found the right to punish.[53]

Hegel, by contrast, had believed in the death penalty, and in his *Elements of the Philosophy of Right* (§ 100) he criticised Beccaria's theory against it:

> As is well known, Beccaria denied to the state the right of inflicting capital punishment. His reason was that it could not be presumed that the readiness of individuals to allow themselves to be executed was included in the social contract, and that in fact the contrary would have to be assumed. But the state is not a contract at all ... nor is its fundamental essence the unconditional protection and guarantee of the life and property of members of the public as individuals. On the contrary, it is that higher entity which even lays claim to this very life and property and demands its sacrifice.[54]

Although Spaventa, like Hegel, did not consider the State to be the product of a contract, he rejected the death penalty even if he followed Hegelian logic as interpreted through the Italian philosophy of the sixteenth century. He believed, as had Hegel, that ethics arises from a particular condition of the moral subject, because ethics emerges when the moral subject is aware of having a 'common root' with evil: 'The origin of evil – Hegel writes – in general is to be found in the mystery of freedom (i.e. in the speculative aspect of freedom), the mystery whereby freedom of necessity arises out of the natural level of the will and is something inward in comparison with that level.'[55] According to Spaventa, the awareness of

---

[53] Bertrando Spaventa, *Dal Carteggio inedito di Angelo Camillo de Meis, Comunicati all'Accademia Pontaniana del socio B. Croce*, ed. Benedetto Croce (Naples: Giannini, 1915), p. 9 (June 1868).
[54] Hegel, *Elements of the Philosophy of Right*, §100.
[55] Hegel, *Elements of the Philosophy of Right*, §139.

the common root of good and evil leads the individual to total solitude: 'I am alone; I am [in a] deep inward forsaken solitude with myself.'[56] The moral subject, being wholly abstract, is an empty infinite, and by the same token the good towards which it tends is an infinite nullity. From this state of inner loneliness and emptiness of intentions arises 'the good as custom, habit, good actuality, the true good', what Spaventa calls policy.[57] In his *Principi di etica*, he thus maintains that the political setting, being based upon an inner bond between citizens, is not only related to the external life of a community:

> Those who do not have *custom*, – ethical habit, this second nature, – can be assumed to respect and abide by the law, but can also be assumed not to have *conviction* regarding the law; just as they can be assumed to have subjective conviction, but do not abide by the law. This unity is not the affair of a moment; but something *substantial, necessary, traditional, common* and *universal*; it is the community itself. Right and morality, taken in themselves are two abstractions; they have reality only in the *ethos*.[58]

Politics therefore had to be based on the recognition of laws by citizens and depend on the community, as much as the community would depend on them. Spaventa illustrated this relationship with a metaphor involving a hat:

> Similar in a certain way to the right to this hat is that of individuals against the Community, which is their living and active substance: their true selfhood. What right has the thing against the universal? Assuredly, without the thing the universal would simply be the universal; it would have no other place but the intellect (the I). But without the universal would the thing be truly known?[59]

It means that the community cannot exist without the citizen, who in turn only exists in the community and whose existence depends on it. The community that Spaventa refers to here is real and inward at one and the same time and is what Hegel calls 'the habitual practice of ethical living . . . as a second nature'.[60] The Italian philosopher explains that the community is not 'an individual among individuals, a subject among subjects, a person among persons', it is instead '*substance*, which is *subject*', because it is free and necessary as national spirit.[61] This analysis is evidently intended to evoke a paragraph from the Preface to the *Phenomenology of Spirit*, where Hegel writes:

[56] Spaventa, *Principi di etica*, p. 134.   [57] Spaventa, *Principi di etica*, p. 136.
[58] Spaventa, *Principi di etica*, pp. 138–139.   [59] Spaventa, *Principi di etica*, p. 82.
[60] Hegel, *Elements of the Philosophy of Right*, §151.   [61] Spaventa, *Principi di etica*, p. 139.

Everything turns on grasping and expressing the True, not only as *Substance*, but equally as *Subject* .... the living Substance is being which is in truth *Subject*, or, what is the same, is in truth actual only in so far as it is the movement of positing itself, or is the mediation of its self-othering with itself.[62]

The community is then present, actual, *wirklich*, as it is a creative unity of subjects. Spaventa differs from the 'vulgar' conception of community, which sees individuals, immediate ethical entities, as the cause and the community as the result. In fact, he believes that the relationship between cause and effect must be understood in this way: 'What is understood through an other, understood in itself brings about the understanding of this other.'[63] This logical circularity proves that the outcome acts on the principle and then establishes itself as both the cause and the principle. The cause is indeed the association of individuals and not the individuals *ut sic*. However, they participate in the association because they have something in common, and, in fact, they are ethical and free subjects only because they belong to the community: 'The community is therefore the *cause*, and the individuals are the *effects*.'[64] The individual is then the cause because he creates the community through his own activity, but, at the same time, he can produce it because it already exists in the individual itself and in its essence:

> The community is neither pure cause nor pure effect of the individual; and the individual is neither pure effect nor pure cause of the community. [The community is] *act* or *communicative energy*; and this act, if it is true that it is not purely individual, it is no less true that it is not without individual activity, [not] without the free activity of the individual. And on the other hand the individual is not a true individual or member of the community, if either it is *posited* only by it and does not posit itself, and therefore it, in it, posits itself as pure will, pure *choice*, abstract and formal reflection.[65]

Spaventa deepens and clarifies the Hegelian concept of community by analysing it through the logical category of cause–effect. To a greater degree than Hegel, he stresses the importance of the individual and insists that the community depends on citizens as much as citizens depend on the community. The community exists only if citizens recognise its laws. The mission of the community is to educate the individual to be 'a citizen of a state with good laws',[66] one that guarantees people security and common

---

[62] Hegel, *Phenomenology of Spirit*, p. 10.   [63] Spaventa, *Principi di etica*, p. 45.
[64] Spaventa, *Principi di etica*, p. 140.   [65] Spaventa, *Principi di etica*, pp. 141–142.
[66] Hegel, *Elements of the Philosophy of Right*, §153.

freedom. On the other side, he underlines that one of the most important characteristics of the modern State is that 'particular interests should in fact not be set aside or completely suppressed'.[67] Freedom and security are guaranteed by the State, which aspires to the common good: '[The State] is reciprocal trust, love, obedience, like the family; it is consciousness, reflection, the activity of willing that determines and operates by itself, like civil society ... it is the absolute ethical subjectivity of individuals. *Absolute* because it is substance; *subjectivity* because it is *known* and *willed* by individuals.'[68] It means that the State is founded on the community, on its national *ethos*, and that the *ethos* 'cannot help but objectivise itself in institutional, state forms: so that only in such objectivization does it in fact exist'.[69] In fact, Spaventa's interest is directed mainly towards domestic state law, or rather the public system through which the common interest can be achieved.

The State, as a '*national substance really and truly conscious* of itself; the *spirit* of a people in its true and perfect existence', is the modern liberal state that Spaventa would help to realise in Italy through national unification, which promoted the general interest, public safety, and the welfare of citizens.[70] If an individual or group of individuals use the power of the state for their own particular interests, then this leads to the struggle between social and political principles. This conflict can be contained only by the constitution, in which the state stands above social struggles in order to achieve the common good. Like Hegel, Spaventa takes into account the problem of political power within constitutional guarantees, but he insists more than Hegel does that an inner moral life for citizens is necessary to sustain political freedom. He maintains that constitutional guarantees can exist only if citizens develop the idea of moral freedom defined by the philosophers of the Renaissance. Indeed, the Constitution is not simply an exterior and artificial form of the organisation of the State, 'that can be adapted at will to a State, like a dress, a shirt'.[71] The constitution reflects the moral life of the people that Spaventa identifies in the specific concept elaborated by Giordano Bruno. This is, for Spaventa, the

---

[67] Hegel, *Elements of the Philosophy of Right*, §261.   [68] Spaventa, *Principi di etica*, pp. 156–157.

[69] Roberto Racinaro, 'Rivoluzione e Stato in alcuni momenti della riflessione di Bertrando Spaventa e Francesco de Sanctis', in *Gli hegeliani di Napoli e la costruzione dello Stato unitario. Atti del convegno di Napoli*, ed. Istituto Italiano per gli Studi Filosofici (Rome: Istituto poligrafico e Zecca dello Stato, 1989), p. 189.

[70] Spaventa, *Principi di etica*, p. 157. On Spaventa's theory of the State and his role in Italian liberalism, see Domenico Losurdo, *Dai fratelli Spaventa a Gramsci. Per una storia politico-sociale della fortuna di Hegel in Italia* (Naples: Città del Sole, 1997).

[71] Spaventa, *Principi di etica*, p. 161.

kind of legitimation of political power that the modern State requires, because the Constitution is 'the consciousness that the people has of itself, of its reason; and the reason of the peoples is their history. The true guarantee is in the real organism of this reason, adjusted to the consciousness that the people has of it.'[72]

According to Spaventa, on that inner life is based the State's sovereignty, and it determines the 'true divine law'. He reinterprets §270 of Hegel's *Grundlinien*, on the relationship between State and religion, and argues that the legitimacy of state power is founded on the divine, infinite dimension of the human being, which is the intimate sphere of consciousness, therefore it concerns all citizens. This is the conception of the State as divine, meaning that the innermost consciousness is immanent in all citizens. The State is ethical because it has 'as its ultimate goal universal interest, the common good',[73] which means that it is not a place of neutrality but the site of an interest, or rather of the collective interest. Spaventa argues that sovereignty is based on the will of the nation and not on divine right: it is therefore based on *consensus* and 'stands in need of legitimation coming from below':[74] it is the result of the free participation of citizens in policy. The author is aware of the difficulties raised by the concept of the State as ethical substance, since it has two elements: consciousness, which is a free and autonomous personality, and substantiality, which represents the universal interest.

The great difficulty for the formation of the modern State is precisely the reconciliation of universality with personality, and the author warns us against the possible risks of the predominance of one element: for example, in a constitutional monarchy, personality may well prevail. This is probably the reason why Spaventa is against the idea that only the king, by birthright, can represent the State. Even though a monarchist, Spaventa is still at pains to maintain that the State can be variously represented by a King, a president, or a committee: 'The solution up until now has been representative constitutional monarchy. Some also talk of a republic, of pure democracy; and that's fine.'[75] On the other hand, Hegel clearly writes that 'sovereignty is there as the personality of the whole, and this personality is there, in the real existence adequate to its concept, as the person of the monarch'.[76] Spaventa distances himself from Hegel on a fundamental

---

[72] Spaventa, *Principi di etica*, p. 162.   [73] Spaventa, *Principi di etica*, p. 160.

[74] Racinaro, 'Rivoluzione e Stato in alcuni momenti della riflessione di Bertrando Spaventa e Francesco de Sanctis', p. 189.

[75] Spaventa, *Principi di etica*, p. 160.   [76] Hegel, *Elements of the Philosophy of Right*, §279.

feature of the organisation of the institutions and clearly distinguishes his political affiliations, which were completely influenced by the historical conjuncture, from the broader theory of law. He was convinced that constitutional monarchy, which was the form of government he longed to see established in Italy, was accomplishing its historic mission, which was to ensure freedom. Yet he was open to other options and considered the debate on the best form of government to be a matter 'still under consideration'. Furthermore, while Hegel maintains the necessity of war between States in order to develop the *Weltgeschichte* (§333–342), Spaventa believes that the confrontation between States should not be in the dimension of the objective spirit but in the dimension of the absolute spirit. It means that the development of the *Weltgeschichte* happens in the realm of science, which moves to a peaceful and progressive human unification, instead of to a world war.

Hegel's unrelenting attempts, recently described by Ludwig Siep, to attain to a view of the state unifying the protection of individual freedom with a strong identity of the spirit of the people (*Volksgeist*), appear still more clearly in Spaventa's interpretation.[77] The experience of Germany had shown that 'freedom is possible only when a people is legally united within a state'.[78] Indeed, Hegel had sought to harmonise personal and group rights and to develop an ideal of constitutional monarchy, but his strong theory of the state, admitting the death penalty, might serve to justify the sacrifice – in certain circumstances – of an individual life. Moreover, Spaventa argues that republics and democratic governments are also viable solutions; and in so arguing, he shows his propensity to bring back the state to the individual, who should never be sacrificed. This individual is the new subject described by Renaissance philosophers, who, according to Spaventa, had insisted on the autonomy of consciousness and individual liberty. An individual of this sort had to be rediscovered, or so Spaventa maintained, in order to achieve Italian freedom and unification in a state based on an idea of nation and respectful of the liberty and autonomy of each and every citizen.

We can, therefore, affirm that the source of the difference between Hegel and Spaventa is their contrasting interpretations of the philosophy of the Renaissance. Spaventa's interpretation underlines that every human being has an infinite value and dignity and that no political authority can

---

[77] Ludwig Siep, 'Hegel's Liberal, Social, and "Ethical" State', in *The Oxford Handbook of Hegel*, ed. D. Moyar (Oxford: Oxford University Press, 2017), 515–534.
[78] Hegel, 'German Constitution', p, 80.

constrain human conscience. Accordingly, Spaventa reinforces the role of the individual in relation to the State. His philosophy of right aims to offer a political theory that goes far beyond the immediate historical context. In fact, Spaventa's reading of Hegel's ethics emphasises the essentially political aspect of ethics, rendering those lectures a model of patriotic and civic commitment. Delivered at the University of Naples between 1862 and 1863, they encapsulate the mission of Southern Hegelianism, namely, 'to give Italians a sense of the State', and, at the same time, they are a rallying call to the young people of a new-born, free, and independent nation.[79]

The forgetting of this tradition is probably due to the defeat of its political programme, a defeat that led some critics to interpret the *Principi di etica* as 'a disenchanted balance sheet of a lost battle',[80] to reduce the importance of this text to the interpretation of Hegel's logical categories,[81] and to underestimate the significance of *Principi di etica* within the corpus of Spaventa's works.[82] The tone of defeat that emerges from the pages of the preface has certainly misled the commentators. However, it was written as late as 1869, when the enthusiasm for unification had already faded and in Italy the new positivist culture was beginning to consolidate itself; moreover, it was referring to a controversy on the interpretation of the Absolute and the Relative in Hegel's thought. Once it is conceded that the text of *Principi di etica* should actually be backdated to 1862–1863, and the preface of the work thus excluded from consideration, it seems clear that those lectures did not preach words of defeat but of hope, that the most underrated work of Spaventa represents the hub of the ethics and civic aspiration of all of Southern Hegelianism and the most ambitious contribution to the science of the State to be found within the Southern political thought of the Risorgimento. Spaventa was full of hope that things might change and, at the end of the course, he exhorted his students to rally to the civic commitment of science:

> Thanking you for having listened to me thus far, this is my recommenda-tion to you: to be men pure [in heart], to not go in for tittle-tattle, to love science for its own sake, to take it to be a serious thing; the most serious thing that there is. And one takes it for a serious thing when one truly studies and has persuaded oneself that studying is not improvising, pre-tending, dreaming ... but having a conscience, loyalty, sincerity, unity:

[79] Tognon, 'Bertrando Spaventa e la "filosofia del diritto" di Hegel', p. 64.
[80] Tognon, 'Bertrando Spaventa e la "filosofia del diritto" di Hegel', p. 69.
[81] Gentile, 'Bertrando Spaventa', pp. 111–114.
[82] Garin, *Filosofia e politica in Bertrando Spaventa*, pp. 42–44.

towards oneself and a little also towards one's fellows (living and dead). If at present that is not wholly how it is, if our sky is not yet wholly calm – if all those who lead in Science are not serious men –, I hope that it will be thus, if not today, tomorrow, the day after tomorrow. That depends on you.[83]

When Spaventa reworked the text of these lectures for publication in 1869, he removed the final exhortation. We do not know for sure if this depended simply on the fact that he wished to eliminate those flourishes that were designed to appeal to a lecture room or because he was now convinced that he had lost his political battle. His position, in fact, was lost and post-unification governments did not design a State with the characteristics desired by Spaventa, but he was aware that policy was not the only ground upon which to fight. The new battlefield was that of the word, convinced as he was that '[there is] no political community without the word'.[84] According to Spaventa, the possibility of going beyond the arena of political battle lay in science because it was there that all discord, opposition, and difference might be reconciled. While Hegel had theorised the necessity of war between states for the development of the history of the world,[85] Spaventa believed that the combination of different national spirits was *humanity*, and he brought the confrontation to the land of the absolute spirit, that is, the realm of science, which moves towards a peaceful and progressive unification of human beings, where 'the mystery and the problem of *its* national life becomes for it the mystery and the problem *of* life, the problem of *its* world the problem of the world'.[86] So Spaventa indicated the new path to follow:

> There are two lives: the mundane and the supramundane. Hence two interests and two kinds of struggle: political interests and struggles and supramundane interests and struggles (struggles of the word: artistic, religious, philosophical). Evil lies in lowering the latter to the former. Spirit, weary and not fully content with the first, finds its asylum and its satisfaction in the second: in the purity of this sky. And the true purity is science .... Science is the true seriousness of life, and there is nothing worse than introducing into it, not only the interests, but the mundane tittle-tattle ... its true interest is *itself*, to be sought after and loved for itself, not for something else.[87]

---

[83] See Gallo, 'Il manoscritto 'De Anima' di Bertrando Spaventa', p. 335. See also Bertrando Spaventa, 'De Anima' (M.S. 28.3, Biblioteca Nazionale di Roma – fondo Rughini-Ghezzi, 1862, p. 63).

[84] Spaventa, *Principi di etica*, p. 169.   [85] Hegel, *Elements of the Philosophy of Right*, §§ 330–343.

[86] Spaventa, *Principi di etica*, pp. 167–168.   [87] Spaventa, *Principi di etica*, pp. 167–168.

Spaventa's theory of the circulation of ideas is his solution to the scientific conflict, and he is convinced that the most profound revolution is a philosophical and cultural, not a political, one, though the latter is nonetheless necessary. Spaventa's idea of the Ethical State affirms the Hegelian primacy of the political, thereby rejecting the theory of the minimal state and attributing to the state the function of champion of culture and education and also social regulator. The state not only administers justice and defends civil society but also promotes the well-being of citizens in order to achieve the common good and the interest of one and all. Despite this regulatory function of the state and its pedagogic purpose, Spaventa's theory of the Ethical State does not imply the suppression of fundamental individual rights, nor an organicist model, nor an authoritarian force. In his theory, the majority of the space at issue is occupied by *subjectivity* (called by him *moralità*), which, by contrast with Hegel, is not a negativity (antithesis) that has to be domesticated and subordinated to the sphere of ethics but is its ground. Therefore, according to Spaventa, the modern state is based on the principle of nationality, which is the product of the free and autonomous consciousness of the individual, the subject. This subject is the new individual of the Renaissance and nationality is its main sentiment, which leads to a modern and liberal state, far removed from the deeply authoritarian and illiberal vision of Hegel's philosophy of right.

This is the state of the new Italy, which faces the challenge of having at its disposal only newly founded and fragile institutions. Spaventa's political position changes through the 1850s. In 1851, he had argued in favour of the gradual extension of social classes and had thought to allow the State a regulatory function with regard to civil society, one based on democratic control. His later concern to empower the State as an ethical force over civil society was related however to the historical context of the years around unification (1861) and aimed rather at preserving the fragile new institutions from the threat posed by particular group and municipal interests. From this originated Spaventa's reaffirmation of the existence of social classes in general and more particularly of a class whose members might act as the interpreter of the rationality of the law and the moderator of social conflict. This class consisted of those who had actively participated in the country's political unification.

Analysis of Spaventa's theory of the Ethical State sheds new light on the debate regarding Hegel's liberalism, the understanding of nationalism during the Risorgimento, and the connection between liberalism and nationalism in Italy between 1848 and 1863. It enriches this debate, by questioning the extent to which Hegel's ideas came to be deployed in support of a specific concept of the liberal State rooted in the Risorgimento context. The signal originality of the Neapolitan Hegelians compared to Hegel concerns their elaboration of the concept of nationality as the expression of the concrete life of the state, and not, as in the Hegelian philosophy of history, a succession of prominent figures. This historical account of nationality implied a progressive cooperation between diverse populations, each of them equally engaged in the development of *Weltgeschichte*. Since the revolution of 1848 in Naples, Neapolitan Hegelians had modified their own sense of how 'nationality' should be identified with the idea of freedom: the concrete form of freedom was the realisation of the sentiment of nationality within the rational form of the state, united and independent.

4.3   The Ethical State and the Risorgimento

Scholarship on Italian Hegelianism has often sought to establish a direct connection between the Italian Renaissance tradition of civil philosophy and Gentile's theory of 'Ethical State', through the mediation of nineteenth-century Italian Hegelianism:

> Italian Hegelianism has always been bound up with two very different claims. On the one side there is the Neapolitan school, a legacy that has passed from Spaventa to Angelo Camillo De Meis (1817–1891), Francesco Fiorentino (1834–1884) and Donato Jaja to Gentile and that places primacy on the political community, leading to the natural, albeit very specific (given the historical circumstances) conclusion of the theory of the ethical state. This falls within the Italian tradition of civil philosophy, which from Machiavelli (1469–1527) to the present day has characterized the nation's philosophical stance.[88]

In part this is because, as we have clarified in Chapters 2 and 3, the Italian Hegelians were chiefly responsible for the rediscovery of thinkers such as Bruno and Machiavelli in the course of the nineteenth century. This approach tends also to draw a line from the political thought of the Italian Risorgimento to Fascism, both in the historiography and in strictly philosophical studies. De Federicis, for example, writes:

---

[88] De Federicis, 'Hegel in Italy (1922–1931)', p. 234. On the civil peculiarity of Italian philosophy, that is, the importance it accords to the political community and political freedom, see Roberto Esposito, *Pensiero vivente. Origine e attualità della filosofia italiana* (Turin: Einaudi, 2012). For the English translation, see Roberto Esposito, *Living Thought. The Origins and Actuality of Italian Philosophy*, trans. Zakiya Hanafi (Stanford: Stanford University Press, 2012).

If a place must be found in the history of the nation of Italy for this philosophical chapter, it must be concluded that Giovanni Gentile, and not Benedetto Croce, was the true follower of Italian Hegelianism, because his idea of philosophy binds together politics and knowledge, reflecting the main principles of the Italian Risorgimento. In other words Gentile elaborated on the political vocation that originally emerged from the treatment of Hegel by early contemporary philosophy in Italy.[89]

This section of the chapter will focus on highlighting the differences between Spaventa and Gentile's theory of the Ethical State.[90]

Of particular relevance within the scholarly literature on the Risorgimento is Alberto Banti's interpretation, which is based on the assumption that there is just one concept of nation, which is that 'the nation as a natural community, comprising kinship ties and a territorial heritage that belongs to it from time immemorial: this, then, is the image conveyed by the texts in the "canon"'.[91] Despite the importance that Banti accords discursive analysis, he fails to differentiate between a patriotic and a nationalist language, ascribing one common idea of community to all the intellectuals of the Risorgimento: 'Risorgimento intellectuals, developing their ideas with a much greater degree of autonomy, had given shape to the image of the ethnic and cultural community: a solid entity, endowed with its own blood, land, memories, culture, and consciousness.'[92] That absence of a distinction between patriotism and nationalism implies the identification of 'deep figures' shared by the Risorgimento and Fascism alike:

---

[89] De Federicis, 'Hegel in Italy (1922–1931)', p. 235.

[90] See also Giovanni Gentile, *I fondamenti della filosofia del diritto* (Florence: Sansoni, 1937).

[91] Alberto Mario Banti, *The Nation of the Risorgimento: Kinship, Sanctity, and Honour in the Origins of Unified Italy* (New York: Routledge, 2020), p. 63. See also Banti and Ginsborg, *Il Risorgimento. Storia d'Italia Annale 22*; Banti, *Risorgimento italiano*; Banti et al., *Atlante culturale del Risorgimento*. On Banti's interpretation, see also Riall, *Il Risorgimento*; Lucy Riall et al., 'Alberto Banti's Interpretation of Risorgimento Nationalism: A Debate', *Nations and Nationalisms*, 15, no. 3, 2009: 402–445; For a critique to Banti's intepretation, see Viroli, *For Love of Country*; see also Viroli's preface to Leone Ginzburg, *La tradizione del Risorgimento* (Rome: Castelvecchi, 2014). The importance of the differentiation between language of patriotism and language of nationalism is also recognised by Paul Ginsborg, *Salviamo l'Italia* (Turin: Einaudi, 2010). On the difference between patriotism and cosmopolitanism, see also the recent study of Martha Nussbaum, *Political Emotions. Why Love Matters for Justice* (Cambridge, MA: Harvard University Press, 2013). For a recent analysis of Banti's idea of Risorgimento nationalism within the broader discourse on nineteenth-century European nationalism, see Matthew D'Auria, *The Shaping of French National Identity: Narrating the Nation's Past, 1715–1830* (Cambridge: Cambridge University Press, 2020), pp. 1–25.

[92] Alberto Mario Banti, *Sublime madre nostra. La nazione italiana dal Risorgimento al fascismo* (Bari-Rome: Laterza, 2011), p. 92.

Family; blood; soil; culture; emotions; war; sacrifice; the sanctity of the fatherland. The same elements that helped to form the idea of the nation of the Risorgimento continue to live in D'Annunzio's words, just as they have come to life in the pages of Carducci or De Amicis, through school textbooks, through the marble or bronze of statues, through lithographic engravings, through the images of the new marvel of mass entertainment, the cinema.[93]

Even if Banti recognises a stiffening and a polarisation of Fascist discourse compared to that of the Risorgimento, he insists that the same references feature in both periods:

> [With the advent of] the fascist nation the elementary tropes of the original discursive matrix become more rigid and extreme. From being metaphorical figures, genealogy and blood are transformed into projections of a racist 'knowledge' and common sense which colonial and racist laws render tragically operative. The mystique of sacrifice, the votive offering of the psychic and bodily self – for the men – of the members of their families and of their own affective world – for the women – proceed along a trajectory already adumbrated by the martyrologies and christologies of the Risorgimento period. The centrality of reproduction, of sexual honour, of the racial integrity of women and men in their sexual relations, recurs with implacable biopolitical coherence, [being] the essence of gender relations as they were traced out by the nationalism of origins.[94]

Banti's work has been contested by Antonino De Francesco in his *The Antiquity of the Italian Nation*, an essential study for anyone seeking to understand the present debate on the Risorgimento, especially for those scholars who are not satisfied by the prevailing cultural approach. In particular, De Francesco disputes Banti's claim that there is only one kind of Italian nationalism, developing gradually in a linear fashion through the nineteenth century. Banti, De Francesco objects, 'insists explicitly on the relationship between the *Risorgimento* and Fascism', where 'the political movement leading to unification is represented as a kind of block, [and] where differences are in some way sacrificed to homogeneity'.[95] This is the consequence of an 'ideological prejudice' predicated upon the social and cultural backwardness of the Italian national character. De Francesco traces back this prejudice to the work of Giovanni Gentile

---

[93] Banti, *Subline madre nostra*, p. 93.   [94] Banti, *Sublime madre nostra*, p. 21.
[95] Antonino De Francesco, *The Antiquity of the Italian Nation. The Cultural Origins of a Political Myth in Modern Italy, 1796–1943* (Oxford: Oxford University Press, 2014), pp. 12–13.

and then to that of Giulio Bollati.[96] This interpretation has tended to locate in the nineteenth century the roots of Italian twentieth-century inequality, authoritarianism, Fascism, and racism. It is therefore of the utmost importance to situate the political ideas of the Risorgimento in their original context.

The most recent scholarship on the Risorgimento, illuminated by the transnational approach, has clarified that the political culture of the national movement in the early years of the nineteenth century was far from uniform and, consequently, that there was a plurality of nationalisms, challenging therefore the thesis of an Italian backwardness.[97] The relevance of De Francesco's study for our present argument lies in his analysis of how different nationalisms and political perspectives are connected to different interpretations of the origins of Italian culture (Antiquity, the Middle Ages, Renaissance, etc.). While he focuses on the myth of the autochthony of Italian people – that is 'the myth of its perpetual presence in the country that by attesting its antiquity supposedly also substantiates its cultural primacy'[98] – we discuss the myth of the Renaissance. More importantly, the Risorgimento in itself represented a contested legacy in the early twentieth century, in particular within the debates led by the two central figures of Italian Neo-Idealism, Giovanni Gentile and Benedetto Croce.

The connection between the Risorgimento and Fascism was delineated by Giovanni Gentile in his *Manifesto degli intellettuali fascisti agli intellettuali di tutte le Nazioni* (appearing in *Il Popolo d'Italia* and nearly every other major newspaper on the 21st of April 1925), written while he was Minister of Public Education:

> [The liberal State] was not even the State, the idea of which had operated powerfully in the heroic Italian period of our Risorgimento, when the State had emerged from the work of restricted minorities, strong in the force of an idea before which individuals had bowed and had been founded with the great programme of making Italians, after having given them independence and unity. Against such a State Fascism encamped, it too [possessed by] the force of its idea which, thanks to the fascination that is always exerted by every religious idea that invites sacrifice, attracted a rapidly growing number of the young and was the party of the young (just as after the insurrections of '31 from an analogous moral and political need the 'Giovane Italia' of

---

[96] Giulio Bollati, 'L'Italiano', in *Storia d'Italia. I caratteri originali*, vol. 1 (Turin: Einaudi, 1972), pp. 951–1022; on this topic, see also Patriarca, *Italian Vices*.
[97] See, for instance, Körner, *America in Italy*; Isabella, 'Nationality before Liberty?'.
[98] De Francesco, *The Antiquity of the Italian Nation*, p. 17.

Giuseppe Mazzini had arisen). This party too had its hymn to youth that came to be sung by the fascists with exultant joy in their hearts. And it began to be, like the Mazzinian 'Giovane Italia', the faith of all Italians [who were] scornful of the past and desirous of renewal. A faith, like every faith that comes up against a reality constituted by shattering and melting down in the crucible of new energies and recasting in conformity with the new ardent and intransigent ideal.[99]

This was the moment in which the Fascist regime was being reinforced in its totalitarian ambitions, following the crisis sparked by the assassination of the socialist MP Giacomo Matteotti ordered by Benito Mussolini. The so-called *Leggi Fascistissime* were being introduced, limiting the power of Parliament, and bolstering that of the Prime Minister, banning opposition parties, introducing censorship and the special Court that went by the name of Tribunale Speciale per la difesa dello Stato, as well as reintroducing the death penalty. In March of 1925 was organised the first conference of the Fascist cultural institutes. The *Manifesto* was conceived in this context, being a re-elaboration of Gentile's paper on *Liberty and Liberalism* designed to present the political and cultural grounds of Fascist ideology, as well as to justify Mussolini's violence through ostensibly liberal arguments. A few days after, on the 1st of May 1925, Benedetto Croce published in *Il Mondo* a *Manifesto degli intellettuali antifascisti*, where the author objects that the patriots of the Risorgimento would surely have been offended and upset by both the words and the actions of the Fascists:

> We turn our eyes back to the images of the men of the Risorgimento, of those who for Italy worked, suffered and died; and we seem to see their countenances offended and disturbed by the words that are uttered and the acts carried out by our adversaries, and grave as they admonish us to hold their banner firmly. Our faith is not an artificial and abstract excogitation or an obsession of the brain caused by ill ascertained and ill understood theories; but it is the possession of a tradition, become the arrangement of sentiment, a mental or moral conformation. The intellectual fascists repeat in their manifesto a trite phrase to the effect that the Risorgimento of Italy was the work of a minority; but they do not realize that therein lay precisely the weakness of our political and social constitution; and indeed they seem almost to delight in the present day at least apparent indifference of a large part of the citizens of Italy regarding the clashes between fascism and its opponents. The liberals [for their part] never did delight in such a state of affairs, and endeavoured with all their might to call an ever greater

---

[99] Giovanni Gentile, 'Manifesto degli intellettuali fascisti agli intellettuali di tutte le Nazioni', *Il Popolo d'Italia*, 21 April 1925.

number of Italians to public life .... But it never crossed their minds to keep the bulk of the nation in inertia and indifference, delivering such material needs to them, because they knew that, in this way, they would have betrayed the causes of the Italian Risorgimento and brought back the evil arts of the absolutist or quietist governments.[100]

At this point, the cultural collaboration between Croce and Gentile had already ceased, their correspondence having concluded in 1924, along with their shared work on the Neapolitan Hegelians. This breach was due to their philosophical disagreement. Giovanni Gentile's philosophy fashions a theory of the Spirit as 'Pure Act' (*Atto Puro*), attributing reality only to the pure act of thinking and not to nature, this last being Hegel's negativity or antithesis: the Spirit therefore possesses, in Gentile's view, an original negativity. Croce's philosophy, instead, fashions a theory of the 'Distinti', whereby he distinguished 'differences' within the Spirit from the Hegelian 'oppositions'. The four 'distinti' (useful or the *utile*, truth, beauty, the good), Croce insisted, did not negate each other.[101]

Gentile and Croce's clash was also political. Croce had initially supported the fascist party, voting for Mussolini in the elections of April 1924 and for his government in July 1924, after the crisis precipitated by the assassination of Matteotti. When in January 1925 Mussolini assumed responsibility for the assassination of the socialist MP and introduced censorship, Croce went over to the opposition, becoming one of the leading voices of Italian Antifascism. Gentile by contrast remained the main intellectual representative of Fascism, serving as Minister of Public Education from 1922 to 1924, being a member of the Fascist Grand Council from 1925 to 1929, and remaining loyal to Mussolini even after the fall of the Fascist government in 1943. He was killed in Florence in 1944 by a group of communists belonging to the Partito D'Azione.

The theme of the Risorgimento as a contested heritage has been widely discussed in the scholarly literature, but for our purposes it is of particular importance to note that the two authors who did most to rediscover the work of the nineteenth-century Italian Hegelians, Benedetto Croce and Giovanni Gentile, were respectively the representatives of liberal political thought and Fascist culture.[102] Croce edited the works of Silvio Spaventa,

---

[100] Benedetto Croce, 'Manifesto degli intellettuali antifascisti', *Il Mondo*, 1 May 1925. In 2023, both Manifestos have been published by Alessandra Tarquini and Giovanni Scirocco with the Studio editoriale Littera in Milan.

[101] On Croce's theory, see *Estetica come scienza dell'espressione e linguistica generale* (1902). On Gentile's theory see *Teoria generale dello spirito come atto puro* (1916).

[102] See, for example, Riall, *Il Risorgimento*. See also Davis, 'Rethinking the Risorgimento'.

while the purported prefiguring of Gentile's 'Ethical State' by Bertrando Spaventa led to the latter's reputation being for a time tarnished. However, comparing Bertrando Spaventa's book on the philosophy of right with Gentile's *I fondamenti della filosofia del diritto* (*The Foundations of the Philosophy of Right*) we can discern some important differences that distinguish Spaventa's interpretation of Hegel's theory of the State from that of Gentile.[103] In the course of elaborating his own theory of the Ethical State, Gentile did indeed identify three important limits to Hegel's theory of the State, all three being derived in his view from a methodological problem:

> These three limitations certainly diminish the spiritual and ethical character of the State in Hegelian doctrine. And they derive from the method of his philosophy, [which was] not yet wholly free from the phenomenal positions of empiricism. Which leads one to consider spiritual reality from the outside, where its forms appear in their irreducible multiplicity, but which does not allow one to discern the unity of the process, in which the spirituality of the spirit properly consists.[104]

First of all, Gentile criticises Hegel's recognition of the existence of a number of States, which are at war with each other in the development of *Weltgeschichte*, because, according to this idea, the State as an ethical substance is confused with empirical states and its 'spiritual reality' is confused with the 'historical reality'. Second, Gentile does not agree that the State is a part of the objective spirit, because this would mean that the absolute spirit is more than the State. He especially considers absolute spirit (art, religion, and philosophy) 'fictitious and artificial' because the State, as self-consciousness, is also a form of philosophy. Finally, the family and civil society are to be differentiated empirically from the State, and the family is not an immediate and natural form of the spirit. In particular, the description of the relationship between family and State helps us to understand the role of the individual with regard to the State according to Gentile:

> The State, known inasmuch as it is spiritually lived, is a form of knowledge of itself that is no longer comparable with the family because it is not realizable save on condition that it absorb and annul the family, in such a guise as to silence in the breast of man every discordant voice [expressing] different laws and to unify spiritual interests which would otherwise present themselves in an often conflicting manner.[105]

---

[103] Gentile, *I fondamenti della filosofia del diritto*.
[104] Gentile, *I fondamenti della filosofia del diritto*, pp. 114–115.
[105] Gentile, *I fondamenti della filosofia del diritto*, p. 120.

Spaventa, instead, as we have already demonstrated, criticised Hegel's insistence upon the necessity of war between states for the development of the *Weltgeschichte*, and he maintained that the confrontation between states should not be in the dimension of the objective spirit but in that of the absolute spirit, moving towards a peaceful and progressive human unification. He also recognised, as did Hegel, family and civil society as fundamental *moments* of the State, which, in his opinion, was ethical because it had as its final goal the common good, the universal interest. That kind of State required legitimation by the people and was the result of the free participation of citizens in politics.

I have noted that Hegel and Spaventa's different understandings of State theory derived from their interpretations of the philosophy of the Renaissance, so we have to consider also Spaventa and Gentile's differences in their interpretations of that philosophy. Gentile, following Burckhardt's approach, identified, as the defining feature of the Renaissance, individualism and, in this aspect, by contrast with Spaventa, he recognised an element of decadence: 'The Italian civilization of the Renaissance glowed with so vivid a light in all of Europe, while Italy was submitting to foreign arrogance, [and] was rapidly approaching that decadence, with which it paid for the high honour of having given so powerful an impulse to the whole of modern civilization.'[106]

Gentile's description falls well short of the enthusiastic words of Spaventa and is reminiscent rather of the pages of De Sanctis' *Storia della letteratura italiana* or Villari's studies of Machiavelli and Savonarola[107]. He also focuses on the indifference towards politics and the moral decadence of the Italian people, reflected in their inability to fight for their freedom. He also insists on the fact that the freedom of the Italian republican city-state was destroyed by the decadence of its individualistic customs:

> And on the ruins of communal liberties, in the prostration of the robust medieval religiosity, amidst the heedlessness and the decadence of individualistic custom, Italy stood out and shone as a luminous beacon in all Europe on account of its poets and artists ... and almost all came to be convinced that the Italians are the wonder of the world for intelligence but are also the

---

[106] Giovanni Gentile, *Giordano Bruno e il pensiero del Rinascimento* (Florence: Vellecchi, 1925), p. 11.
[107] See Pasquale Villari, *La storia di Girolamo Savonarola e de' suoi tempi*, 2 vols. (Florence: Le Monnier, 1859); Pasquale Villari, *I primi due secoli della storia di Firenze*, 2 vols. (Florence: Le Monnier, 1893); Pasquale Villari, *Niccolò Machiavelli e i suoi tempi*, 3 vols. (Florence: Le Monnier, 1877).

'disgrace of the world', in Machiavelli's phrase, for their incapacity to fight and win respect for their land, their life, their interests.[108]

Gentile considers the Renaissance, and other historical epochs, as a phenomenological itinerary of logic: he transfers the categorical structure of the spirit into the history of epochs, with the Renaissance representing the moment of subjectivity.[109] He maintains that the political and moral decadence of the Renaissance was caused by the dichotomy between formal elegance and political inferiority, and the difficulty he faces in arriving at an interpretation consists in the search for a stable equilibrium between a negative political aspect and a positive cultural one.

In contrast to Gentile, Italian moral decadence does not provide Spaventa with an explanation of the political crisis; he was, however, persuaded that the power that had prevented the moral and political emancipation of Italians during the sixteenth century was the Counter-Reformation, which had been

> an arrogant and unjust force, as inexorable as fate in the ancient world ... which persecuted and killed our philosophers, corrupted our artists, dispersed our reformers, weakened our States, spoiled the morality of the heart, violated free religious sentiment, and replaced science with ignorance, love with hatred, union with discord, freedom with blind obedience, virtue with hypocrisy, law with human will, spirit with matter, life with death.[110]

According to Spaventa's historical analysis, the Counter-Reformation is the origin of the Italian crisis of the sixteenth century. This helps us understand the link he posits between the Renaissance and the Risorgimento: Spaventa identifies the Catholic Church as the cause of Italian moral and political decadence in the sixteenth century and recognises in the Catholic Church and in its temporal power the prime enemy of Italian political and moral emancipation at that date. Deeply admiring the inner and religious dimensions of the philosophy of the Renaissance, Spaventa by the same token judged very harshly the Catholic Church and the ecclesiastical hierarchy, above all because of his interpretation of the Renaissance and his concept of moral liberty[111]. He disagreed with the Jesuit review *Civiltà*

---

[108] Gentile, *Giordano Bruno e il pensiero del Rinascimento*, pp. 21–22.

[109] For a nuanced interpretation of Gentile's notion of subjectivity, see Sasso, *Le due Italie di Giovanni Gentile*, pp. 95–146.

[110] Bertrando Spaventa, 'Frammenti di studi sulla filosofia italiana del secolo XVI', *Monitore Bibliografico Italiano*, nos. 32–33, 1852: 50.

[111] Spaventa's activity as a journalist in reviews such as *Il Progresso* and *Il Cimento* bears out this point. See Bertrando Spaventa, 'La politica dei gesuiti nel secolo XVI e nel XIX. Polemica con la "Civiltà Cattolica"', in *Opere*, vol. II (Florence: Sansoni, 1972).

Cattolica, writing several articles in rebuttal of its stance. The most important point that he contested was the role of the State:

> *Civiltà Cattolica* recognises no other purpose in the State than the external
> freedom of the individual and it therefore only considers it in its purely
> mechanical aspect . . . . The Church is a doctor that makes out prescriptions,
> while the State is the chemist who executes them . . . the Church is the
> *teacher*, the State the *pupil*; the Church is *learned*, the State *ignorant*; the
> Church is *right*, the State is *force*.[112]

The Jesuits' theory affirms that the State must guarantee the external action
of the laws, while the Church and its temporal authority, the Pope, decide
what justice is. This means that where there is a conflict between the Church
and the political power, the State must submit to the Church and compel
citizens to follow religious rules. This theory regarding the relationship
between State and Church is, for Spaventa, incompatible with the political
emancipation of Italy and the modern State. Spaventa thinks that the
struggle for the moral emancipation of Italian citizens from Catholicism is
also a struggle to liberate Italy from the pretension of the Catholic Church to
be the only soul of society and the supreme regulator of the State:

> Who defines what truth, honesty, morality, justice are? The Church, none
> other than the Church . . . . If the State in those actions having a moral and
> spiritual side does not heed the dictates of the Church, but seeks to decide
> for itself, in the light, as one might say, of natural reason, what is just and
> honest, it becomes of necessity iniquitous, usurpatory, sacrilegious.[113]

The only way to counter the power of the Church and to regenerate the
consciousness of Italians is to rediscover Bruno's idea of moral liberty,
which can teach Italians that to be free citizens and not just servants they
must preserve their moral dignity and their autonomy of thought.
Spaventa is persuaded that finding this concept of moral liberty in the
Italian philosophical tradition may prove more effective, in that Italians
recognise there ideas that belong to their own past:

> It is now time for the Italians to enter frankly and boldly into the field of
> intelligence; to break the old chains, and become free thinkers, prior to
> becoming free citizens. Only then will they be able to remember that they
> are sons of Bruno, of Galileo, of Machiavelli; only then will the memory of
> our past cease to be, as it is at present, a [source of] shame.[114]

---

[112] Spaventa, 'La politica dei gesuiti nel secolo XVI e nel XIX', p. 773.
[113] Cited by Garin, *Filosofia e politica in Bertrando Spaventa*, p. 30.
[114] Spaventa, 'Frammenti di studi sulla filosofia italiana del secolo XVI', p. 54.

The interesting thing about the difference between Spaventa and Gentile's interpretations of the origins of Italian decadence, which are respectively the Counter-Reformation and individualism, is that it implies two different analyses of Bruno's death and Campanella's imprisonment. Gentile maintains that the abstract and immediate individuality of the philosophy of the Renaissance was the cause of these two episodes and the 'necessary conclusion' of their respective philosophies:

> Why marvel at Bruno ending up at the stake? It is the necessary conclusion of his philosophy: the concept of an infinite void, outside of which there remains history, in which should however live the man who fixes himself in the infinite. And why marvel that Campanella, with his ardent faith in his own strong individuality and in the bold design of his City of the Sun, should succumb to the power of the Spanish.[115]

Spaventa, instead, considers these two episodes to be the consequence of the oppression of the Counter-Reformation and the reason for the end in Italy of the modern spirit: 'Italy, that is, Catholic Rome, by burning Bruno alive ... renounced the essence of modern life.'[116] Spaventa's theory of the State has to be understood in the context of the Risorgimento, where the meaning of nation, *patria*, and individual dignity were completely different from Gentile's references. If it is possible to identify an important connection between Spaventa and Gentile's logic, it cannot properly be extended to their political thought.[117]

Spaventa's interpretation of the Counter-Reformation as the cause of Italian decadence also strongly influenced his pupils Francesco Fiorentino and Antonio Labriola, who themselves developed this thesis further, underlining the responsibility of the temporal power of the Catholic Church for Italian decadence and moral weakness, ascribing no blame therefore to the aesthetic individualism and the superficiality of external life during the Renaissance. Gentile, for his part, does not consider the Counter-Reformation to be the cause of Italian decadence. The issue for him, rather, is the persistence of medieval residues and the oppressive weight of traditional culture: 'Our spiritual spontaneity has always been (we can say without immodesty up until today) hindered and suppressed by our traditional and official and disastrous culture.'[118] In this perspective, the Renaissance is more a period of transition then a triumphant

---

[115] Gentile, *Giordano Bruno e il pensiero del Rinascimento*, 30; for Gentile's studies on the Renaissance, see also Giovanni Gentile, *Studi sul Rinascimento* (Florence: Sansoni, 1966).

[116] Spaventa, *Epistolario di Bertrando Spaventa (1847–1860)*, vol. I, p. 98.

[117] See Cubeddu, *Bertrando Spaventa*; Nuzzo, 'An Outline of Italian Hegelianism (1832–1998)'.

[118] Giovanni Gentile, *I problemi della scolastica e il pensiero italiano* (Florence: Sansoni, 1963), p. 25.

moment of the new modern epoch. We can note an evolution, however, in Gentile's interpretation of the Renaissance: his early studies are more influenced by Spaventa's philosophical interpretation – his interest in Bruno and Campanella, the recognition of the autonomy and dignity of the individual and the immanence of the divine as a fundamental principle of the epoch – and by Fiorentino's teaching – especially on the philological method and the interest in the entire epoch and not just, as with Spaventa, in a number of prominent figures.[119] However, in Gentile's works during the critical period of the 1920s, the interpretation of the Renaissance as a period of decadence, a representation of the 'old Italy', became more pronounced:

> We see two Italies before us: one old and one new: the Italy of centuries past which is our glory but it is also a sad legacy, which bows our shoulders and weighs upon our soul: and it is also, let us frankly admit it, [cause for] shame, which we wish to wash off ourselves, for which we must make amends. And it is precisely that great Italy, which has such a prominent place, as I have said, in the history of the world. The only Italy, one could say, that is known and studied and investigated by all civilized peoples, and whose history is not a particular history but an epoch in universal history: the Renaissance. In which there is so much light, indeed, and there are so many reasons for national pride: but there is so much shadow too.[120]

Nineteenth-century Italian Hegelianism exerted a profound influence on Italian Neo-Hegelianism, in particular because of the central role played by Benedetto Croce and Giovanni Gentile in Italian culture at the turn of the century. Their work as the principal editors and commentators on Italian Hegelians' works, as well as their deep knowledge of Hegelian philosophy and their engagement with the task of defining an Italian national culture has contributed to the diffusion of Italian Hegelianism. This intellectual connection has often also led to the reinforcing of the historiographical interpretation that connects Risorgimento political thought with early twentieth-century political theories. This chapter has sought to demonstrate the peculiarities of Risorgimento political ideas by presenting the differences between Spaventa and Hegel's theory of the State as well as between Spaventa and Gentile's Ethical State. Now that the philosophical ground has been explored, we will move on to the political actions of the Italian Hegelians and their contribution to the new Italian State.

---

[119] For a complete overview on the evolution of Gentile's interpretation of the Renaissance, see Scazzola, *Giovanni Gentile e il Rinascimento*.

[120] Giovanni Gentile, 'Che cosa è il fascismo. Discorsi e polemiche', in *Politica e cultura*, vol. I (Florence: Le Lettere, 1990), p. 12.

CHAPTER 5

Hegelians in Charge

If weapons are good for destroying and, ... maintaining States, the true unity of a nation, the freedom and the greatness of a people are only obtained through great ideas.

B. Spaventa, *False Accusations against Hegelianism*

In January 1859, after the sentence imposed upon sixty-six political prisoners had been commuted to perpetual exile in the United States,

Figure 5.1 'Arrival of Neapolitan Exiles at Paddington Station', *Illustrated London News*, Saturday, 2 April 1859

Silvio Spaventa boarded the ship *Stromboli*, together with his friends Luigi Settembrini and Carlo Poerio, ready to sail to New York. These prisoners were the ones considered to be the most dangerous political convicts, whose freedom 'could endanger public order'; they were therefore included in the decree issued by Ferdinand II, who changed their sentence to permanent exile from the Kingdom (December 1858).[1] The ship was hijacked and re-routed to Irland, thanks also to the intervention of Raffaele Settembrini, son of Luigi. The ship arrived in Cork Bay, where the political prisoners were warmly welcomed on the quayside.[2] The story was also covered by the *Times*, which organised a petition with a view to raising funds for the exiles. After the exciting escape, Silvio Spaventa spent a few weeks in London, where the 'Neapolitan Exiles' were welcomed with the warmest sympathy and offered financial support through a public subscription. An image published in the *Illustrated London News* on the 2nd of April shows Silvio Spaventa, Giuseppe Pica (1813–1887), and Carlo Poerio (1803–1867) at Paddington station being greeted by the crowd (Figure 5.1). The article highlights their 'delicacy and discretion' and their 'good taste and gentlemanly feeling that endeared them to all who have had the pleasure of their acquaintance'.[3] British public opinion was very supportive of the Italian patriotic cause. The memory of William Gladstone's furious denunciation of the conditions of the prisons and penal system of the Kingdom of Two Sicilies was still very influential, especially in liberal, Whig circles.

Between October 1850 and February 1851, Gladstone had accompanied his daughter Mary to Naples, in the hope that the city's salubrious climate would improve her health. There he met the advisor to the British Embassy in Naples, Giacomo Filippo Lacaita. They discussed the dire state of the prisons in the Kingdom, and more specifically the plight of political prisoners, and they both attended various political trials, those of Luigi Settembrini and Carlo Poerio among them.[4] Gladstone also visited the *Vicaria* prison in Naples and collected letters from several political

---

[1] Archivio di Stato di Napoli (hereafter ASN), fondo Pironti-Poerio, b. 13, n. 40.
[2] The National Archive, Home Office, 45/6872, *Letter from George Sandes Gravet to the Inspector General*, 6 March 1859.
[3] *Illustrated London News*, 2 April 1859.
[4] Gladstone attended some of the hearings relating to the lawsuits against the political sect Unita' italiana. On this, see M. R. D. Foot and H. C. G. Matthew (eds.), *The Gladstone Diaries*, vol. IV, 1848–1854 (Oxford: The Clarendon Press 1974), p. 303, 9 February 1851; p. 297, 3 and 4 January 1851.

prisoners, including Silvio Spaventa, describing the conditions of their detention. Lacaita himself was subsequently arrested by the Bourbon police, accused of having illicitly supplied Gladstone with confidential information on the government, though he was released after a week thanks to the timely intervention of the British Embassy. Gladstone was deeply shocked by the penal system of the Kingdom and by the callous treatment reserved for its political opponents and in particular for gentlemen. On his return to London, in April and July 1851, he published *Two letters to the Earl of Aberdeen on the State Prosecutions of the Neapolitan Government*, addressed to the Secretary of the Conservative Party and soon to be Prime Minister of the United Kingdom. Gladstone highlights the iniquity of having imposed prison sentences upon about 20,000 subjects of the Kingdom for mere crimes of opinion, often moderate opinions at that. Secondly, the author denounced the injustice of the entire procedural process, noting how even the most minimal legal protection was not respected: 'It is incessant, systematic, deliberate violation of the law by the Power appointed to watch over and maintain it. It is such violation of human and written law as this, carried on for the purpose of violating every other law, unwritten and eternal, human and divine.'[5] The last aspect examined was the actual condition of prisoners who, in some cases, had also been tortured. He describes how the prisoners were chained in pairs. Each prisoner had a leather belt around his hips, to which the upper ends of two chains were attached. The first of them, composed of four long and heavy rings, ended in a double ring fixed around the ankle. The second chain was made up of eight rings and connected the two prisoners, so that they could not move more than six feet away from each other. None of these chains were removed either by day or by night. Gladstone concluded his invective in the famous hyperbole that the Bourbon government in Naples was 'the negation of God erected into a system of Government'.

The *Two Letters* were widely read and shocked European public opinion. Within a month of their first publication, they had gone through eight editions, and were then reproduced, translated, and discussed in the pages of all British papers, several French ones, and the *Allgemeine Zeitung*. Above all, the scandal generated a debate in the House of Commons on the relationships between the British government and the Kingdom of Two Sicilies. The government in Naples presented an official reply, *Rassegna degli errori e delle fallacie pubblicate dal sig. Glasdstone in due sue*

---

[5] Letter 1, 7th of April 1851.

lettere indiritte al Conte Aberdeen sui processi politici nel Reame delle Due Sicilie (*Review of Errors and Fallacies Published by Mr. Gladstone in Two Letters from Him to Earl Aberdeen on Political Trials in the Kingdom of the Two Sicilies*), published anonymously on the 25th of August 1851 and probably authored by Salvatore Mandarini, judge of the Criminal Court. This elicited a response from Gladstone, who published a 'third letter' in January 1852, *An Examination of the Official Reply of the Neapolitan Government*, where he found himself obliged to retract certain assertions and confess to having been somewhat misled by his informants – for example, regarding the accusation of torture. Considering the prominence of this debate in British public opinion, it does not come as a surprise to observe both the call for a public subscription to assist the 'Neapolitan exiles' and their warm welcome by the crowds in London in 1859.

5.1 The End of a Kingdom

Silvio Spaventa was 'dazed, amazed, and exhausted' after the social whirl into which he had been pitched in London. After ten years of prison, the fame he experienced as an Italian liberal in exile was completely new to him. He described in letters to his brother Bertrando Spaventa, in Turin at the time, his *soirées* with Palmerston, Russell, and Gladstone, complaining about his 'need for rest and peace' and the difficulty of finding those in London, 'the most industrious and restless city in the world'.[6] However, the real worries of Silvio Spaventa were related to his understanding of the British opposition to Cavour's politics. London sought to prevent an alliance against Austria between the Kingdom of Sardinia and France, so as to avoid bolstering the latter on the European stage. The widespread influence of Giuseppe Mazzini's ideas in London and his opposition to the politics of Cavour served the interests of those British politicians who were suggesting to Spaventa and the other Neapolitan exiles that the Italian cause would benefit from British backing. Spaventa described the prevailing political mood to his brother: 'Arriving in this country, we found British public opinion as generally contrary to Piedmont [i.e., the Kingdom of Sardinia] and its politics – that, as you know, we mostly love and approve with all our heart – but very favourable, as you know, to us and to the cause of Neapolitan liberty, that we in a certain way represent.'[7]

---

[6] Silvio Spaventa, *Dal 1848 al 1861*, p. 243 (15 March 1859).
[7] Silvio Spaventa, *Dal 1848 al 1861*, p. 245 (12 April 1859).

As Elena Bacchin has recently highlighted, 'Neapolitan political activists incarcerated in Naples after the 1848 revolution aroused the interest of both public opinion and the world of diplomacy' and were perceived as a humanitarian cause.[8] They thus became spokespersons of their national and political cause abroad and contributed to the de-legitimisation of the Kingdom of the Two Sicilies in the international context.

These discussions between Neapolitan exiles and British politicians were broached just as Cavour was trying to secure Napoleon III's backing in the war he was hoped to provoke against Austria (the so-called Second War of Independence). Meanwhile, London was trying to avoid war, negotiating with Vienna the autonomy of Lombardy-Venetia and the independence of the Duchies of Modena and Parma. Austria demanded in return the disarmament of Piedmont. In April, France too was supporting the solution of Piedmontese disarmament, with Cavour consequently being about to resign, when Austria issued Turin with an ultimatum. The resulting war thus appeared not to have been promoted by France, which eventually entered the conflict on the side of Piedmont. Cavour's plan worked despite the best efforts of British diplomacy, on the one hand, and of the conservative French party, on the other. The Austrian army was led by the Hungarian general Ferencz Gyulai, while Piedmont's army was commanded by King Victor Emmanuel and supported by the Cacciatori delle Alpi (Alps Rifles), an army corps of volunteers led by General Giuseppe Garibaldi. This included members of the National Society that, as highlighted by Anna Maria Isastia, served as an intermediary between armed popular volunteers and the regular militia, allowing Piedmont's government to control popular involvement and forestall the formation of insurrectionist brigades.[9]

When news of the outbreak of hostilities reached the Neapolitan exiles, Spaventa decided in May 1859 to leave London and travel to Turin. He was finally reunited with his brother and his friends for the first time since his arrest in March 1849. A few days after his arrival, he was celebrating with other Neapolitan exiles, Giuseppe Massari and Carlo Poerio among them, the victory of the Piedmontese and French armies against the Austrians at Montebello. A sour taste still lingered, however, due to the condition of the Kingdom of Two Sicilies: 'Naples is not

---

[8] Elena Bacchin, 'Political Prisoners of the Italian Mezzogiorno: A Transnational Question of the Nineteenth Century', *European History Quarterly*, 5, no. 4, 2020: 625–649, 628.

[9] Anna Maria Isastia, *Il volontariato militare nel Risorigmento. La partecipazione alla guerra del 1859* (Rome: SME-Ufficio storico, 1990).

contributing to the making of Italy! This is the true calamity and igno-
miny.'[10] In the meantime, Britain was working to prevent the new King of
Naples, Francesco II, who had just succeeded his recently deceased father,
Ferdinando II, from entering the war against Austria. Luigi Settembrini,
who was still in London, reported to Spaventa: 'Here [in London] they are
trying to make the new king of Naples remain neutral, which, I believe,
amounts to advising him to await ruin.'[11]

Marianna Florenzi Waddington was also deeply disappointed by the
manner in which some of the British press had rallied to Austrian rule in
Lombardy. In 1859, she published a political pamphlet entitled *L'Austria in
relazione all'Italia (Austria in Its Relations with Italy)*, where she vehemently
contested the argument that the wealth and security of Lombardy compared
to that of the other Italian states was a consequence of the efficiency of the
Austrian government. Any praise for the prosperity and happiness of the
territory should be, she insisted, for the people rather than for their rulers.
About the latter she was scathing, to the extent that she drew a parallel with
the treatment of slaves in Cuba and Brazil, noting provocatively that the
provision of food and medical care for slaves was a financial investment for
their exploiters, not an act of kindness and generosity:

> Who could ever be happy in slavery? . . . Slavery and oppression are contrary
> to nature and anyone from whom a natural property has been stolen, has the
> sentiment and the consciousness of what has been stolen from them and of
> the injury received, on account of which they cannot help but entertain a
> mortal aversion to the one who dares infringe the laws of nature. It is
> beholden upon the wise to confess that material prosperity is the least of
> the goods of life, and that the true good, which none can withstand, is
> individual liberty, and it is precisely this that the Lombards lack.[12]

What the Lombards regarded as the lack of individual, civil, and political
liberty under Austrian rule was the reason why they had taken up arms,
and any settlement that accepted the continuation of Austrian rule would
not prove viable. Florenzi Waddington went on to challenge the very
notion of a happy and prosperous Kingdom of Lombardy-Venetia under
the arbitrary power of a dominator: 'Could a true Englishman call England
happy when under the government of the French? How then could
Lombardy call itself happy under the Austrian yoke?'[13] Despite the plans

---

[10] Giuseppe Massari, *Diario delle cento voci. 1858–1860* (Rome: Cappelli 1959), p. 242.
[11] A.G., XXXIX, 3368 (letter 28 May 1859).
[12] Marianna Florenzi Waddington, *L'Austria in relazione all'Italia*, 1859, p. 7.
[13] Marianna Bacinetti (Florenzi Waddington), *L'Austria in relazione all'Italia*, p. 8.

of the British government, after the Armistice of Villafranca, in August 1859, Vittorio Emanuele II and his army entered the city of Milan. Soon a referendum, in which all adult male were invited to cast a ballot, endorsed the annexation of Lombardy to the Kingdom of Sardinia. Silvio Spaventa was with Piedmont's emissaries and was impressed by the cheering of the crowd for the King, writing to Bertrando: 'The reception [granted the King] was quite wonderful; all of Milan was on the Corso, and applauded and cheered more loudly than I have ever heard for any other man.'[14] Silvio Spaventa had never considered the annexation of Lombardy to the Kingdom of Sardinia to be a territorial enlargement of the Piedmontese state, deeming it rather 'a further step in the venture of [bringing about] the Independence of Italy'.[15] After the victory in Lombardy, Silvio Spaventa moved to Florence, where he had begun to collaborate with several newspapers, including *Il Risorgimento*, *La Perseveranza*, and *La Nazione* among them. To the latter, directed by the Tuscan liberal Alessandro D'Ancona, he contributed a number of articles, written between November 1859 and March 1860, that shed light on his plans for the unification process with the South.

The unification of the Kingdom of Two Sicilies and the Kingdom of Sardinia was not a straightforward and self-evident solution. Antonino De Francesco clarifies that 'in the aftermath of 1821 nobody dared to dispute the patriotic identity of the Mezzogiorno' and that the Garibaldini were for their part still persuaded by this idea.[16] However, within the Piedmontese establishment, not all the political projects for Italian independence included the South. Moreover, the European powers, France and Austria in particular, were keen to support a confederation under the leadership of the Pope. Spaventa was himself opposed both to the temporal power of the Pope and to a confederation, bearing in mind the German case. In his article 'La Confederazione germanica e l'Italia' (The German Confederation and Italy), he thus highlights how the German Confederation still had the configuration of a 'feudal state', by which he meant a state composed of a hierarchy of dynastic states under the domination of Prussia and Austria: 'Germany is a country of liberty, and not of equality. But liberty, without the juridical limit of the essential equality of human nature, is easily transformed into servitude.'[17] Spaventa

[14] Silvio Spaventa, *Dal 1848 al 1861*, p. 257 (7 August 1859).
[15] Silvio Spaventa, 'L'Austria dopo la pace', *La Nazione*, 3 December 1859.
[16] Antonino De Francesco, *La palla al piede. Una storia del pregiudizio antimeridionale* (Milan: Feltrinelli, 2012), p. 55.
[17] Silvio Spaventa, 'La Confederazione germanica e l'Italia', *La Nazione*, 19 December 1859.

believed that Italy was in a much better state than Germany already and should now advance towards a more complete union: 'The German Confederation is a point of transition from the feudal world of nations to the new and rational organisation, to which some [nations] still aspire, while others have already reached it. Italy does not need to pass by way of this point in order to arrive at the settlement for which it is destined.'[18] Spaventa was also highly critical of the memorandum which a group of Neapolitan patriots presented to the meeting in Zurich (1859), during which the agreement of Villafranca was re-affirmed, because they seemed to be placing their trust in the reforms promised by King Francesco II and in the vouchsafed granting of a Constitution. Spaventa did not believe that the Bourbons would act any differently to the way they had in 1848, when they had granted a Constitution, only to repeal it as soon as the revolutionary crisis was over. He was convinced that there could be no Italy without the Southern provinces. So, when Garibaldi weighed anchor to reach Sicily, the Hegelian could barely contain his enthusiasm: '[Garibaldi] What a wonderful man! But the venture is difficult, and if the Kingdom remains so passive, I strongly doubt that it can triumph.'[19] The same excitement was shared by all the Neapolitan exiles, who were hastening to Naples in order to rally the revolutionary forces in the Kingdom to Garibaldi's campaign. In June, Silvio left Florence and arrived in Turin with the aim of agreeing upon policy with Cavour, who was still not completely persuaded of the urgent need to complete the unification with the Southern provinces.

Spaventa approached Luigi Carlo Farini (1812–1866), one of Cavour's main collaborators, a statesman appointed as 'Dictator' of the Duchy of Modena during the transition in July 1859. Spaventa and Farini agreed on a plan to reinforce the unitary movement in Naples while awaiting Garibaldi and to refuse any constitutional concessions that the Bourbon monarch might in due course make. In July 1860, Spaventa went back to Naples, the Piedmontese government having granted him citizenship of the Kingdom of Sardinia, so as to afford him some sort of protection. He was immediately placed under surveillance by the Bourbon police, but he was delighted to find a cultural and political ferment in favour of unification: 'The country is in a process of transformation that can barely be imagined. The government is breaking up and dissolving day by day and in a marvellous fashion. Unitary sentiment penetrates, fascinates and

[18] Spaventa, 'La Confederazione germanica e l'Italia'.
[19] Silvio Spaventa, *Dal 1848 al 1861*, p. 288 (25 May 1860).

enthrals one and all ... here the movement of opinion is very great indeed, and unanimously in favour of unification.'[20] Spaventa's main preoccupation was to ensure that the Neapolitan liberals lent their support to Garibaldi, while at the same time preventing the initiative turning into a Mazzinian operation, persuaded as he was that this would have only turned into a war and undermined unification. He was perceived as a supporter of 'a Cavourian Italy, in opposition to a Garibaldinian Italy'.[21] When, therefore, in September 1860 Garibaldi arrived in Naples, it does not come as a surprise that the General asked Spaventa to leave Naples. After a provisional government under Liborio Romano, Garibaldi accepted a new government led by Raffaele Conforti, with Francesco Crispi as General Secretary and Francesco De Sanctis as Minister of Public Education. The latter had just come back from Zurich, in exile there, as we have seen, because of his participation in the 1848 revolution.

By the end of September, Vittorio Emanuele was about to reach Naples, where the republicans Mazzini, Cattaneo, and Saffi were already trying to persuade Garibaldi to convene a National Assembly at which the manner and timescale of unification might be decided. The administration of the South was still in the hands of Bourbon officials and police corrupted by, and complicit with, the Neapolitan organised crime group, the Camorra, as indeed was the head of the first provisional government Liborio Romano. However, the Neapolitans themselves decided to seize the initiative: in early October, there was a popular manifestation in the streets of the city in favour of unification. The National Guard likewise opted for annexation by Piedmont, which was eventually confirmed by the plebiscite on the 21st of October, when a large majority of the population voted 'yes' to the annexation. With this mandate, Garibaldi met the King in Teano, completing the annexation of the Southern provinces.

Ever since December 1792, when the French fleet sailed into the Bay of Naples, the hopes of intellectuals and liberals in the Kingdom of Two Sicilies that they might overturn the absolutism of the Bourbon government had risen. The Kingdom consequently entered the European conflict and for around thirty years became a political laboratory in which revolution and war intersected: the establishment of the Neapolitan Republic in 1799 and the first restoration; the war between European coalitions and Napoleon; the opposition between liberalism and absolutism; French, British, and Austrian invasions; republican and liberal-constitutional revolutions; counter-revolutionary reactions; all these set the parameters of the

[20] Silvio Spaventa, *Dal 1848 al 1861*, p. 298 (July 1860).   [21] A.S., Cart. R, 60.2.

political conflict within the Kingdom between the counterrevolutionary forces, mainly supporters of the Bourbon dynasty, and the revolutionaries (moderate liberals and republicans alike). This political confrontation was often very violent and unfolded within an ideological elaboration that engaged with the broader European intellectual context. While in the 1820s constitutionalism represented the main line of division between the revolutionaries and the Bourbon regime, in 1848 the quest for a constitution was included in the nationalist demands. The failure of Carlo Pisacane's expedition to Sapri in 1857 confirmed the need for the national revolution to encompass regional rebellion and for strong political leadership. The year 1859 saw the outbreak of the final confrontation between these two forces, forces that had characterised the politics of the Kingdom since the 1790s.[22] Such clash culminated in the demise of what had long been the largest state by population and size in the Italian Peninsula.

Although the historical motives of the revolutionaries in this case were still focused on securing a constitutional government, as they had been in the 1820s and 1848, this time the rupture ran deeper because their aim was to overcome the local *patria* in order to affirm what they have come to celebrate as the Italian nation. This new form of the revolutionary project, which led to a change of regime, was the outcome of a seventy year–long process of integration of regional and national liberalism and the development of a connection between the Southern unitary-liberal group, the leadership of the Italian national movement, and the Savoy dynasty. The success of the Southern revolution was itself the consequence of many different elements, such as the serendipitously complementary leadership of Cavour and Garibaldi, the intersection of the Southern liberal tradition with Italian nationalism, the ability of the supporters of the project of national unity to consolidate a large social bloc, the involvement of important elements within the Neapolitan State in the change of regime, and the paralysis of the Bourbon forces. When on the evening of the 6th of September 1860, King Francesco II and his family sailed from the port of Naples, they passed through the ships of what had been their own fleet, which was already flying the Italian flag. The day after, Garibaldi reached

---

[22] For a detailed description of the early years of the unification in the South, see the recent work by Carmine Pinto, *La Guerra per il Mezzogiorno: Italiani, borbonici e briganti, 1860–1870* (Bari-Rome: Laterza, 2019). See also Marco Meriggi, 'Legitimism, Liberalism and Nationalism: The Nature of the Relationship between North and South in Italian unification', *Modern Italy*, 19, no. 1, 2014: 69–79.

Naples by train, to be acclaimed by a festive and joyous crowd. The old Kingdom had come to an end and the new State was ready to be born.

5.2   Ideas in Practice

The Southern political groups were by now becoming more integrated into the national political movements. Raffaele Conforti and Francesco De Sanctis, who oversaw the new government supported by Garibaldi after the fall of Liborio Romano, represented the moderate left group, while the Sicilian Francesco Crispi and the Calabrian Giovanni Nicotera represented the republican left inspired by Mazzini and Garibaldi. Crispi played a key role in supporting and encouraging Garibaldi's expedition, the celebrated Mille (or One Thousand), while Nicotera had himself participated in Pisacane's 1858 expedition. The moderate liberals of the Historical Right (Destra Storica) were instead an integral part of Cavourian politics. Among the main representatives of this current, were the 'Neapolitan exiles' in London, Carlo Poerio and Silvio Spaventa, as well as Giuseppe Massari, Giuseppe Pica, and Giuseppe Pisanelli. Pasquale Stanislao Mancini was likewise one of the key figures within the liberal Neapolitan movement, gaining fame thanks to his speech *On Nationality as the foundation of the law of nations* (22 January 1851), which attempted to bridge the gap between the Neapolitan Hegelian and the Piedmontese moderate visions of nationality.[23]

In the aftermath of the liberation in Naples, there was a succession of different governments: Garibaldi's 'dictatorship' (a temporary provisional government with extraordinary powers modelled on the legal institute of *dictator* in Roman Law) first, then the pro-dictatorship of Giorgio Pallavicino (1796–1878), who organised the plebiscite, and then the Lieutenancy of Farini, followed by that of Carignano-Nigra. The 'Lieutenancy' was a local government acting on behalf of the national government and charged with addressing the most urgent problems in the region. The Lieutenant was supported by a Council of Lieutenancy, an intermediate solution between a government of ministers, like the one in the capital (Turin), and a council of civil servants without political power. In March 1861, the Council was abolished and replaced with four

---

[23] On this, see Giuseppe Grieco, 'A Legal Theory of the Nation State. Pasquale Stanislao Mancini, Hegelianism and Piedmontese Liberalism after 1848', *Journal of Modern Italian Studies*, Special Issue edited by F. Gallo and A. Körner, *Hegel in Italy: Risorgimento Political Thought in Transnational Perspective*, 24, no. 2, 2019: 266–292.

Directors who were immediately answerable to the national ministers. Silvio Spaventa was first nominated to the Council of Lieutenancy and then appointed Director for Internal Affairs and Police. He was mainly responsible for the security and stability of the Southern provinces in the turbulent early years of unification. Among the many challenges he faced upon entering office were the fight against brigandage (the pro-Bourbon insurgency in many provinces of the continental south) and organised crime (the Neapolitan camorra and the Sicilian mafia), the repression of the Bourbon counterrevolutionary and autonomist forces as well as the political opposition of the republicans, and the reorganisation of the new administration and of the National Guard. It is possible to identify some of the intellectual features of his idea of the unitary state, very much influenced by his brother's writings, by looking at his action in the political sphere. Bertrando Spaventa likewise had political commitments, serving as a deputy of the Kingdom of Italy for four legislatures (1861–1865; 1867–1870; 1870–1874; 1874–1876), the common ground he shared with his brother being his support for a secular policy, in particular in matters of education. However, Bertrando's main occupation was as Professor of Theoretical Philosophy at the University of Naples. His younger brother Silvio was by contrast much more involved in unitarian politics: he sat in the Chamber of Deputies continuously from 1861 to 1889 as representative of the Historical Right (Destra storica). He was appointed Deputy Minister of Internal Affairs in the Farini and Minghetti governments (from December 1862 to September 1864), being responsible for the State's internal security policy in the febrile early years of the new State. He was also minister of public works in the second Minghetti administration (from July 1873 to March 1876).

As we saw in Chapter 1, in his early years, Spaventa's understanding of the State was influenced by Hegel's thought where its ethical ground was concerned, but Hegelian elements were at that date still intertwined with Mazzinian political thought, which had exerted a powerful influence upon young Italian Hegelians in the 1830s and 1840s. However, Spaventa's engagement with Hegel increased during his incarceration, after he had been transferred from the San Francesco prison in Naples to a penitentiary on the island of Santo Stefano, where his conditions improved. The island was situated on the archipelago of the Pontine Islands in the Tyrrhenian Sea, close to the more famous penitentiary island of Ventotene – where nearly a century later, in 1941, the antifascists Altiero Spinelli and Ernesto Rossi wrote the Manifesto *For a Free and United Europe*. Santo Stefano prison was built in 1795 during the reign of Ferdinando I and was one of the first prisons to be built following the principles of Jeremy Bentham's *Panopticon* (1791), and it was the place in which most of the revolutionaries of the old Kingdom had been incarcerated since 1799.

Close scrutiny of the correspondence between the two brothers, Bertrando in exile in Turin and Silvio in the Neapolitan prison, makes it plain that Silvio Spaventa's Hegelianism did in fact attain a more mature phase, with the State now being considered the main agency affirming the primacy of law and opposition to any form of illicit act and the arbitrary use of the law.[24] In prison, he focuses on Hegel's *Encyclopedia* and the *Phenomenology of Spirit*, of which he attempted a translation, probably in 1855, convinced as he was that a correct understanding of the Hegelian methodology was his primary duty, his aim being to 'demonstrate the perfect intelligibility and necessity for the principle of absolute knowledge'.[25] Hegel's philosophy was thus understood as a 'form of speculative knowledge worked out through a process of sceptical inquiry', as very recently highlighted by Richard Bourke.[26] In his prison notes, Spaventa defines liberty as both 'objective and subjective at the same time … it has as its content objective reason – as its form the subjectivity of the spirit … I am free if I want what is rational … .. The law is my will'.[27] Therefore, he defines liberty in its objective and subjective aspects as Hegel had done, while not clearly separating law and morality. He subscribes to Hegel's comparison of the State to 'a system of three syllogisms like the solar system': the State is 'the Universal that connects the Individual (*persona*) to Society, Law, and the Government'.[28] This means that he was also very familiar with Hegel's *Encyclopedia* (§198 in this case). He was so absorbed by Hegel's philosophy that he confessed to his brother: 'I am reduced to the following, namely, that outside of Hegel's system philosophical truth appears to me to be mistaken and inadequate to its essence; and of this system I cannot yet claim to have attained a clear understanding.'[29] After his experience in prison and his years of study, Spaventa now had the opportunity to transform the theory he had

---

[24] Regarding the correspondence between the two Spaventa brothers, see S. Spaventa, *Dal 1848 al 1861*; Bertrando Spaventa, *Epistorario (1847–1860)*, ed. Mariolina Rascaglia (Rome: Istituto Politgrafico e Zecca dello Stato, 1995); see also the very recent publication Bertrando Spaventa, *Epistolario (1847–1883)*, ed. Marco Diamanti, Marcello Mustè, and Mariolina Rascaglia (Rome: Viella, 2020).

[25] S. Spaventa, *Dal 1848 al 1861*, p. 236. The translation of Hegel's *Phenomenology of Spirit* was probably attempted in 1855 and the manuscript has ninety-two pages of a partial translation including the Preface, the Introduction, and Section A of the book. The manuscript comprises also a variety of comments and notes on Hegel's book.

[26] Richard Bourke, *Hegel's World Revolutions* (Princeton: Princeton University Press, 2023), p. xv.

[27] S. Spaventa, *Dal 1848 al 1861*, p. 192.   [28] S. Spaventa, *Dal 1848 al 1861*, p. 195.

[29] S. Spaventa, *Dal 1848 al 1861*, p. 212.

learnt into practice. In this section, we will demonstrate how his Hegelian understanding of the State served as a theoretical guide when taking political decisions to combat organised crime and brigandage in the early years after unification, to support a secular State against the demands of the Catholic Church in the 1870s, and when promoting the national railways first and then the organisation of administrative justice in the 1880s.

At the dawn of the national revolution, Spaventa, who oversaw the security of the Southern provinces on behalf of the central State, was well aware that one of the crucial issues to address was the threat posed by the Neapolitan organised crime group, the Camorra. As we have discussed in Section 5.1, under the provisional government of Liborio Romano, the *camorristi* were employed in the National Guard to help with the overall control of the territory. Romano agreed with the boss of the Camorra's families (Capintesta) Salvatore De Crescenzo and his sister Marianna De Crescenzo (whose nickname was La Sangiovannara), that he would assign to the bosses of the different families (Capisocietà) the roles of chief of police and police inspector, while the Camorra's foot soldiers (Picciotti), would serve as police officers in the National Guard. The consequence was that the organised crime group used their uniforms to commit crimes, such as smuggling or extortion, while wearing their uniforms and in the name of the unitary cause, arguing that what they demanded was 'roba d'o zi Peppe' (stuff of uncle Peppe, referring to Giuseppe Garibaldi). When Silvio Spaventa became Director of Internal Affairs and Police, he opposed this politics of collusion with organised crime groups, ordered mass arrests of the leaders, including Salvatore De Crescenzo, expelled the *camorristi* from the National Guard, sending to prison the corrupt police officers, and prohibited national guardsman to wear their uniform when off duty. He commissioned an inquiry from the journalist Vincenzo Cuciniello, a moderate liberal who thereupon wrote a 'Rapporto sulla Camorra' (Report on the Camorra) in the spring of 1861, and in April of that same year produced the first thorough investigation into the Camorra, which provided the first official information concerning its structure and activities. He warned the government how dangerous organised crime was for the stability of the newly established regime.[30] Instead of assimilating it to the

---

[30] *Memoria sulla Consorteria dei Camorristi esistente nelle Provincie Napoletane* and the *Rapporto sulla Camorra*, Archivio di Stato di Napoli (ASN), Archivio Generale. Prima serie (1860–1887), fs. 675, fasc. 1109, vol I, part I, April–May 1861. On this, see Antonio di Fiore, *Camorra e polizia nella Napoli borbonica (1840–1860)* (Naples: Federico II University Press, 2019). See also Marcella Marmo, *Il coltello e il mercato. La camorra prima e dopo l'Unità d'Italia* (Naples-Rome: L'Ancora del mediterraneo, 2011), pp. 207 segg.; F. Barbagallo, *Storia della camorra* (Rome-Bari: Laterza,

phenomenon of brigandage in the countryside, he was at pains to note that the Camorra presented itself as a parallel state, able to offer an alternative to the State's monopoly of violence and its power of punishment, therefore threatening the very core of the State's sovereignty as well as citizens' fundamental rights to security, property, and life: 'The Camorra is a criminal association with the aim of illicit profit through the use of violence and threats of the strongest men against the weakest.' This report was at the core of the best-seller *La camorra: Notizie storiche raccolte e documentate per cura di Marco Monnier* (*The Camorra: Historical Notes Collected and Documented by Marco Monnier*), written by the Italo-Swiss Marc Monnier and published in 1862. Monnier had lived for a long time in Naples, where he managed a hotel on behalf of his family and witnessed the transition from the Kingdom of Two Sicilies to the new Italian State. His book was the very first description of the political and social context of the emergence of the organised crime networks in Naples, consequently a huge success throughout Europe, and it was mainly based on the information collected by Silvio Spaventa.

Spaventa's firm opposition to the Neapolitan organised crime group made him very unpopular. The mass arrests, the restrictive policing measures, the expulsions from the National Guard, were all actions that reduced the power of the Camorra and its control over the territory. Moreover, Spaventa's report provided much information about what was supposed to be a secret organisation. It described the chain of command and line of exploitation from the top of the hierarchical structure of the Camorra (the Capintesta) to the bottom (Tamurro – the aspirant), as well as the respective spheres of influence of the different families across the twelve zones of Naples. It does not come as a surprise that in the spring of 1861 there was an attempt to kill Spaventa, probably due to either the Camorra or pro-Bourbon counterrevolutionary forces. Undeterred, after escaping the assassination attempt, Spaventa went immediately to the central café in Naples, a meeting place for fashionable society in front of the San Carlo Theatre, where the whole city would see that he was still alive and not prepared to change course. This display of defiance greatly endeared him to liberal public opinion, and he was subsequently elected to the Chamber of Deputies in Turin, later being appointed Deputy Minister of Internal Affairs.

2010); John Dickie, *Mafia Brotherhoods. Camorra, Mafia, 'Ndrangheta: the Rise of the Honoured Societies* (London: Hodder and Stoughton, 2012).

Spaventa made it clear to the central government that the reinstatement of the rule of law in the Southern provinces was of crucial importance to the establishment of the new unitary State. He was obviously worried by the activities of the organised crime group but also by the revolts spreading through Basilicata, Calabria, and the Neapolitan provinces in particular, which seemed to be the main preoccupation of the national government. The Bourbon counterrevolutionaries won the backing of both the Church and of regular criminals: the South was in flames and the central government perplexed as to how to proceed. The phenomenon of brigandage was debated at length in the national Parliament and a committee of inquiry was established. The main outcome was the understanding of brigandage as the legacy of the Bourbon regime, caused by oppression in the country-side and a willingness to keep the peasants in a condition of obscurantism, superstition, and ignorance. To the unitarians, it seemed to amount to the same political and instrumental use of the peasants as had been applied by the Bourbons since 1799: to incite the poor against the rich in order to curb revolution. The key point for the members of the Committee, led by the liberal Massari, was to highlight that the conflict with the brigands was not in fact a civil war because the enemy did not have a political vision but rather were simple criminals used by the Bourbon conspirators: 'Brigandage is a genuine war, indeed it is the worst sort of war imaginable; it is the struggle between barbarism and civilization; it is pillage and assassination that are raising the standard of rebellion against society.'[31] The Mazzinians agreed that this was a war against barbarism: as Saffi declared, 'this is a war against the legacy of barbarism to the civilisation of the nineteenth century'.[32]

A Parliamentary Commission was set up to address the large number of requests for exceptional measures of police made by Southern prefects, local political representatives, academics, members of the national guards, and local mayors. The repressive intervention of the State seemed to many the only viable solution against the brigands. This pressure culminated in the Pica Law (Legge Pica), in force from August 1863 to December 1865, which introduced the new crime of brigandage, to be punished by military tribunals, and established emergency powers in violation of the Statuto Albertino, the 1848 Piedmontese Constitution

---

[31] *Il palazzo e I briganti: Il brigantaggio nelle provincie meridionali. Relazione della Commissione d'Inchiesta Parlamentare, letta alla Camera dei Deputati da Giuseppe Massari il 3 e 4 maggio 1863* (Avigliano: Pianetalibroduemila, 2001), p. 34; on this, see also Pinto, *La guerra per il Mezzogiorno*, pp. 323–374.

[32] MCRR, CM, b.817, f. 24-2, Saffi to Massari.

which had been extended to the whole country after unification. Thanks
to the intervention of Silvio Spaventa, the crime of *camorrismo* (organised
crime) was also covered by the new law. Military tribunals were instituted
in the Southern provinces, imposing harsh punishments such as prison
terms, penal labour, or even the death penalty. Preventative measures
were introduced, meaning the application without due legal process or a
judge's authorisation of measures such as *domicilio coatto* (house arrest),
as well as the permission in certain circumstances to create volunteer
militias to round up the brigands, as well as those aiding and abetting
them. This law applied the criterion of suspicion: the different Councils
instituted by the Pica Law – composed of the Prefect (the appointed head
of elected provincial councils), the President of the Tribunal, and representatives of the King and of the Provincial Delegation – had the power
to draw up a list of suspects who could be summarily arrested, or killed,
in case of resistance, the mere fact of being on that list constituting in
itself proof of guilt. In the South, there was an effective suspension of
constitutional rights, there sometimes being overlapping civil and military
powers – as in the case of the general Alberto La Marmora, who was both
Prefect of Naples and Commander in chief of the Southern Army
between 1861 and 1863 – but mainly establishing the supremacy of
military over civil rule in the South.[33] Some scholars have argued that the
Pica Law served to legitimise a 'colonial-type' project of domination of
the Southern regions by the national government and that the lack of any
differentiation between brigands and bandits (organised crime members)
overshadowed the political connotation of brigandage.[34] This was indeed
the main purpose of the groups combatting brigandage: brigands were
not recognised as political opponents but rather as criminals who were
the product of moral corruption – the very same moral corruption that
the new State, given its ethical underpinning, was charged with overcoming. The Pica Law did not achieve its goal. The resistance of the brigands
continued until 1870. However, while bolstering the collaboration
between national and local political groups, the new law served to

[33] Salvatore Lupo, *Storia della mafia: Dalle origini ai giorni nostri* (Rome: Donzelli, 2004), p. 49.
[34] See Roberto Martucci, *Un Parlamento introvabile? Sulle tracce del sistema rappresentativo sardo-italiano in regime statutario 1848–1915*, in *Parlamento e Costituzione nei sistemi costituzionali ottocenteschi – Parlament und Verfassung in den konstitutionellen Verfassungssystemen Europas*, ed. Anna Gianna Manca, Luigi Lacchè, vol. 13 di Annali dell'Istituto storico italo-germanico in Trento – Jahrbuch des Italienisch-Deutschen Historischen Instituts in Trent, Bologna (Berlin: Il Mulino – Duncker & Humblot, 2003), p. 129; see also Giovanni De Matteo, *Brigantaggio e Risorgimento: legittimisti e briganti tra Borbone e i Savoia* (Naples: Guida, 2000), p. 23.

reinforce the perception of an unfair and violent national government throughout the Southern populations. Spaventa used the special laws, and in particular the preventative measure of house arrest, to isolate the members of the Neapolitan organised crime group and control the revolts. The differences between the South and the North were becoming ever more glaring and the 'Southern Question' firmly established in the Italian political debate.

The 'Southern Question' was a key concern also of Pasquale Villari, whose seminal studies on the matter, contained in his *Lettere Meridionali* (*Southern Letters*), were published in the journal *L'Opinione* in 1875, while he was serving as an MP during the last government of the Historical Right, led by Marco Minghetti. While Villari became a leading academic at the University of Pisa, and then of Florence, by virtue of his works on Savonarola and Machiavelli (see Chapter 3), as a politician he was particularly interested in conditions endured in Southern Italy, and in Naples in particular.

In his *Lettere Meridionali*, Villari warned that State repression was creating the preconditions for popular rebellion to coalesce into forms of criminal organisation, if not into outright revolutionary violence. His goal was to convince his readers that a solution to the 'Southern Question', criminality included, could only be found in economic reform: in short, 'the question of brigandage is an agrarian and social question' and not a criminal or anthropological one.[35] The word '*mafia*', indeed, entered the Italian cultural imaginary through a letter of March 1875: 'The Mafia is the logical, natural, necessary consequence of a particular social state, which must be modified in order to eradicate this evil.'[36]. According to Villari, the rise of organised crime in the South was due to the prevailing feudal economic structure and the 'medieval' social relationships that the Bourbons had encouraged in the South. In short, the Mafia was a *modern* institution, a response to the incomplete modernisation of the South, and the central government had a duty to address the 'Southern Question' without having recourse only to repression.

---

[35] Pasquale Villari, *Le Lettere Meridionali ed altri scritti sulla questione sociale in Italia* (Florence: Le Monnier, 1878), p 27. On the enquiry by Sidney Sonnino and Leopoldo Franchetti, see Denis Mack Smith, *The Making of Italy 1796–1866* (London: Palgrave MacMillan,1988).

[36] Villari, *Lettere Meridionali*, p 3. On this, see Roberto Dainotto, *The Mafia: A Cultural History* (Chicago: University of Chicago Press, 2015), pp. 13–53.

Together with the 'Southern Question', the other main issue faced by the new Italian government was the 'Roman Question', meaning the dispute between Church and State over the temporal power of the Catholic Church. This was given added urgency because, in the South, Bourbon counterrevolutionary drew on popular religious fanaticism, and were supported by elements within the Roman Church. The concern to curb the temporal power of the Catholic Church was indeed at the heart of Silvio Spaventa's new policy to reinforce the national State. The influence of his younger brother's thought regarding the relationship between State and Church ran deep. Bertrando's forthright criticisms of Catholicism, and of Gioberti's philosophy in particular, led to his being assaulted outside the University of Naples after giving a lecture in December 1862. He was saved by his own students, who formed a cordon around him, so as to shield him from his assailants. Since the 1850s, Bertrando Spaventa had interpreted Hegel's theory of the Ethical State, as we saw in Chapter 4, as a reappropriation on the part of the State of a divine and infinite dimension, at odds with the notion of any temporal power being vested in the Church. In his articles on *La liberta' d'insegnamento*, he distinguishes between religious sentiment and religious observance:

> The universal influence of religion in national life has its foundation in the most intimate part of the human soul, in an inviolable sphere . . . . When a man, a class and even the State [itself] attempts to invade the conscience of the individual and govern in their stead the manifestations of the religious sentiment, these latter no longer have a true value . . . . Worship is then corrupted and religion serves as a means for the passions of men, for the ambitions of the powerful, for the goals of those who govern. The history of Europe, and that of Italy in particular, demonstrate just how large a part ministers of religion themselves have had in this corruption of the religious sentiment, and how they have been the cause of infinite harm done to generation upon generation. Intolerance, fanaticism, the Inquisition, all of this they adopted in pursuit of their worldly intentions; religion was simply a pretext for suffocating every seed of liberty, civil and political, for seizing hold of governmental authority and for oppressing the peoples.[37]

And then he highlights how the freedom of people is connected to the purity of religious sentiment, which should be as far as possible from religious observance:

---

[37] B. Spaventa, *La libertà d'insegnamento*, in *Opere*, pp. 2407–2408; or see *Il Progresso*, 27 luglio 1851.

When in a country, even one that is politically free, religious sentiment is forced to manifest itself in a determinate form, and imposed externally by an authority recognized by the State, and the separation of the spiritual from the temporal does not exist, one cannot in all sincerity assert that the principle of liberty, the only reasonable basis for modern States, is fully implemented and forms the essence and substance of national life.

Freedom only exists in the State when temporal and spiritual power are separated, and the State is grounded on its ethical dimension. Where this did not happen, a servile mentality would develop, and in Italy this was the consequence of the long-enduring domination of the temporal power of the Catholic Church.

The inner damage produced by the Catholic Church in Italy was thus the cause of a moral weakness which could be fought not with weapons, Spaventa argued, but only with new ideas:

There are certain things that cannot be undone only with cannon . . . . If the Austrians are for us nothing else but armed matter, the pope, the cardinals, the priests, the friars, the Jesuits, the ignoramuses and perhaps Bourbon Ferdinand himself are half matter, and half idea; and if the arquebus is necessary for destroying the former, it does not suffice when it is a question of striking dead the latter. . . . If weapons are good for destroying and, according to some, even for maintaining States, the true unity of a nation, the liberty and greatness of a people are only obtained through great ideas. And among these I do not believe that philosophy is the last, particularly in Italy, where . . . an inner bond is necessary above all to resuscitate the ancient genius of the nation . . . . This inner bond consists principally of philosophy and of religion.[38]

The influence of the temporal power of the Catholic Church in Italy was damaging on a political level as well, weakening the function of the State. Spaventa intervened in a debate that unfolded in 1854 in the pages of the Jesuit journal *La Civilita' Cattolica* regarding the role of the State, by writing polemical articles in the Piedmontese journals *Cimento* and *Piemonte* informed by his Hegelian understanding of the State.

By the time the Italian State was to be organised, both Spaventa brothers had already developed a clear idea of the role of the State and its relationship with the Church: the modern State was – as Hegel had demonstrated – the objectification and the immanence of its divine, infinite,

---

[38] B. Spaventa, *False accuse contro l'hegelismo*, in *Opere*, p. 2392.

ethical content. This divine (or infinite) was in each and every individual
and was compatible with a plurality of faiths within the State because the
State ought not to have a specific religious observance. The State should
rather let its citizens decide which God to venerate, since it was the
'organic and living unity of all its citizens'. This means that it 'cannot
have a particular form of religious sentiment, and nonetheless it is not
atheist, it is religious. It is religious, because its citizens are religious, [and]
it is not atheist, because its citizens are not atheists.'[39]

Silvio Spaventa was well aware of his younger brother's work, and
during the political debates that characterised the end of the 1860s up to
1876, when his party, the Destra Storica, lost the majority in Parliament,
Silvio sided with the other Hegelians, such as Francesco Fiorentino and
Camillo De Meis, regarding the ethical ground of the modern State.
He believed that the new Italian State was becoming a modern State by
reappropriating its 'ethical content' from the Church and its 'psychological
content' by having it be founded upon the 'principle of nationality'.[40] The
temporal power of the Church was a threat to the moral and political
emancipation of the country. The religiosity of the State was its ethical
ground, which, in accordance with the Hegelian system, meant that the
'Infinite of Society' had of necessity to elevate the content of its form to
match up to its concept, the State. Spaventa recognised between Church
and State the Hegelian dialectical relationship of unity-distinction, as they
both had a 'religious truth':

> This need for agreement and intimate imbrication between Church and
> State establishes a necessary relation, which sometimes makes of the State
> an instrument of religion, and sometimes renders religion a servant of the
> State . . .. The truth of this relation lies in the fact that, while they remain
> distinct, they must not stop being united.[41]

This interpretation of the relationship between State and Church, based
on Hegel's philosophy, led Spaventa to disagree with the official policy of
the national party and with the strategy of separation proposed by Cavour:
the famous formula Libera Chiesa in Libero Stato (A Free Church in
A Free State) was not a viable or desirable solution according to the
Hegelian logic. For the separation to be possible, we should admit that
'both terms ought to be two finites; if one is infinite, it would overcome

[39] B. Spaventa, *La politica dei gesuiti nel secolo XVI e nel XIX*, p. 1018.
[40] For a discussion on Spaventa's understanding of the 'principle of nationality' see Chapter 1.
[41] S. Spaventa, *Frammento sulla Filosofia del Diritto di Hegel*.

the other', but the divine and infinite content is that of the State, the Ethical State. Spaventa's stance was fully articulated in his speech in the Chamber on the 20th of September 1886, *Il potere temporale e l'Italia nuova* (*Temporal Power and the New Italy*), in which he argues that, in light of the evident weakness of the Italian unitary institutions, the reconciliation of State and Church should be avoided, even though this would alienate 'the support, secure and effective, of many conservative forces, which are rooted in the religious sentiment'.[42] If the Hegelian dialectic was Spaventa's philosophical beacon, he took his cue politically from Machiavelli's preoccupation: he thus explains in the speech how Machiavelli, 'who felt the need for a great state for Italy' had already recognised that 'the greatest obstacle was the princedom of the Church'. This was important in the 1860s, where the independence of the State was particularly fragile, and where it was urgent to establish a modern State along the lines of those to be found in the rest of Europe:

> What is more truly new in European consciousness is the [realization] that the State is not something external to us, divine [in its nature] or fatal, accidental or conventional; but it is intrinsic to us, as [if it were] our own natural organism, because law, right, authority, which are its essential functions, are however human will; a will of which we feel ourselves to be capable, having as our immediate aim, not our individual good, but the common good, in which our own [good], which is covered by it, is purified and idealized. This will organized outside of us under the name of State, like a big individual distinct from the little individuals, which commands us, obliges us and forces us to [proceed towards] the common good, is our will itself. Such is the principle and the highest liberty of the modern spirit . . . . Now, Italy has re-entered, it is customary now to say, as an element of civilization in European life, because she has in common with the other peoples this principle and consciousness, and all the other peoples have recognized her right to it. It is now up to us to prove that we are worthy of it and that we will know how to carry out our duties.[43]

In the 1870s, Spaventa became more interested in theories of the *Rechtsstaat*, therefore engaging with the works of Friedrich Carl von Savigny, Johann Kaspar Bluntschli, and Rudolf von Gneist, which were circulating widely in Italy at the time. He developed a liberal defence of civil rights but not of the individualistic kind: his liberal theory was

---

[42] See S. Spaventa, *Il potere temporale e l'Italia nuova* [1886], in *La politica della Destra* (Bari: Laterza, 1910), pp. 197–198. See also S. Spaventa, *Discorsi Parlamentari*, ed. Vincenzo Ricchio (Rome: Tipografia Camera dei Deputati, 1913).

[43] S. Spaventa, *Il potere temporale e l'Italia nuova*, pp. 198 ff.

founded rather on a State governed by the rule of Law (*Rechtsstaat*), while tending towards an ethically grounded 'social' theory. This point is borne out by Silvio Spaventa's parliamentary speeches and more particularly by his approach to the problem of the nationalisation of the railways and to that of justice in the public administration.

When Spaventa became Minister of Public Works under the Minghetti government, in 1873, he oversaw the consolidation of a nationalised railway service, which was a strategic aim for those seeking infrastructural integration of the different Italian states. Between 1873 and 1875, he therefore set up the agreements with the Southern and Roman railways and those in Northern Italy, which by virtue of the Basel Convention (1876) were then separated off from the Austrian Railway. His ambition was to nationalise the whole network, but the economic interests involved were obviously very entrenched, as was a ruling class committed in the main to laissez-faire principles. In Spaventa's view, it was a matter of national interest and as such should take priority over any other claim. Broader issues were raised, however, such as State intervention in the economy and the relationship between public and private interests. Spaventa championed the role of the public sphere in managing the development of society, thus intimating, alongside the evident Hegelian legacy, a way of understanding the state as an irreplaceable instrument guaranteeing the general interest: 'Force and true authority consists today more than ever in representing ... the common interests, in directing society along its own paths, not in favour of this or that class, or of this or that man, but rather of all.'[44] By dint of their liberalism, the Neapolitan Hegelians championed a State that had obligations in terms of social justice: 'One cannot speak of a civil people where only a few know and enjoy, but a people is truly civil when the greater number know and enjoy.'[45] By contemplating this form of liberalism, we broaden our understanding of the many European strands that scholars have identified, such as those liberal traditions based on individual liberties, or on a republican tradition, as well as an 'aristocratic liberalism', based on the role of intermediary bodies.[46] For the Hegelians,

---

[44] S. Spaventa, *Discorsi parlamentari*, p. 423. Speech on the 24th of June 1876.
[45] S. Spaventa, *Discorsi parlamentari*, p. 420.
[46] On the different strands of liberalism, see G. Varouxakis, '1848 and British Political Thought on the Principle of Nationality', in *The 1848 Revolutions and European Political Thought*, ed. D. Moggach and G. Stedman Jones (Cambridge: Cambridge University Press, 2018), pp. 140–161; A. de Dijn, *French Political Thought from Montesquieu to Tocqueville. Liberty in a Levelled Society?* (Cambridge: Cambridge University Press, 2008), pp. 1–10; A. Kahan, *Aristocratic*

the State seems to be the only possible guarantor for citizens in face of the powerful economic forces operative in the country at large:

> With our social organization, with the way in which private and public wealth are constituted in Italy, and with the way in which public administrations are structured, large anonymous companies constituted on the basis of State credit, which can call upon millions in their financial statements, and may have frequent and considerable dealings with the State itself, and continuous and endless contacts across the country, are monstrous creations, against whose power and influence I do not believe that there is sufficient resistance to be found anywhere.[47]

The State appears to be that indispensable guide for a backward civil society lacking awareness. In this sense, public intervention in the economic and social sectors was presented as a form of ethical rationalisation of interests whose sum was often not sufficient to guarantee that collective interest would prevail. Therefore, once any prospect of struggle between the classes had been excluded, it became essential to integrate the working class: 'The class that has no other property but its own labour and naturally becomes ever more numerous and aspires to rise and better its own condition .... A government that today forgets these problems, can be a new temporal power, but not a modern government.'[48] The bill on the nationalisation of the railways, that Spaventa presented to Parliament on the 9th of March 1876, brought down the Minghetti administration and consequently led to the departure of the Historical Right from government. The fall of the Historical Right in 1876 prompted much reflection among the Hegelians about party politics and the role of the State. It seemed clear that the discussion about the nationalisation of the railways was turning into a discussion about the proper function of the modern State, as Fiorentino made plain in his two letters to Spaventa published in 1876 in the *Giornale napoletano di filosofia e lettere, scienze morali e politiche* with the title 'Lo Stato Moderno' (The Modern State). Fiorentino maintains there that the main contribution of Hegel to the modern idea of the State had been 'to define the State as the realisation of the ethical idea (*der Staat ist die Wirklichkeit der sittlichen Idee*), so that it is raised above the individual interest.

Liberalism (Oxford: Oxford University Press, 1992), p. 111ff.; A. Kalyvas and I. Katznelson, *Liberal Beginnings. Making a Republic for the Moderns* (Cambridge: Cambridge University Press, 2008), pp. 1–17.
[47] S. Spaventa, *Discorsi parlamentari*, p. 413.   [48] S. Spaventa, *La politica della Destra*, pp. 200f.

However, what Hegel did not, and could not, realise was the importance of nationality in determining the concrete organism of the State'.[49] He reiterated that the State is universal and necessary and that it is grounded on the consciousness of the people, a multitude that Fiorentino calls 'nation', defining the State as 'the realization of the human ideal in the individuality of a nation'.[50] To explain this bond, Fiorentino uses Manzoni's words from the poem *March 1821*, highlighting that this modern State is founded on the people:

> A people that frees every people,
> Or shall be [a] slave between the Alps and the sea;
> One in arms, in language, in faith
> In remembrance, in blood, and in heart?[51]

This ethical ground of the State serves to legitimise Silvio Spaventa's stance on the role of the State in the nationalisation of the railways. Railways, the argument runs, are works of public interest that cannot be managed by private interests unless we conceive the State to be a facilitator of private industry and insurance for private businesses. To explain the difference, Fiorentino refers to the example of British rule in India when, in 1865, a famine in Orissa was managed by the governor following the principle of *laissez faire, laissez passer*. This led, Fiorentino observes, to thousands of deaths. The modern State, Fiorentino insists, has to be a State led by public interests, one that provides public services for all its people. Fiorentino and the Spaventa brothers perceived the fall of the Right as the fall of an idea of the State that had the public interest at its heart.

When the Left rose to power, Francesco De Sanctis resigned as professor and accepted a new ministerial post, overseeing Public Education, from Benedetto Cairoli (1878–1880), the first President of the Council of Ministers under the newly elected Sinistra Storica (Historical Left). De Sanctis, like other Neapolitan Hegelians, had also had a key political role in the aftermath of unification. After 1860, he was appointed governor of the province of Avellino and for a very short period he was Director of Public Education in the Pallavicino

---

[49] F. Fiorentino, 'Lo Stato Moderno', *Giornale napoletano di filosofia e lettere, scienze morali e politiche*, 3, no. 26, 1876: 496.
[50] Fiorentino, 'Lo Stato Moderno', p. 600.
[51] A. Manzoni, *Marzo 1821*, translated in Alberto Rizzuti, 'Viganò's *Giovanna d'Arco* and Manzoni's *March 1821* in the Storm of 1821 Italy', *Music & Letters*, 86, no. 2, 2005: 186–201, 196.

government. In 1861, he was elected as deputy to the national parliament, welcoming the prospect of a liberal-democratic collaboration. He served as Minister of Public Education in the Cavour and Ricasoli governments (1861–1862), trying to oversee the difficult work of merging the school administrations of the previous Italian states. De Sanctis' main aim in this role was to reform the educational system, his aspiration being to extend the Casati Law to Southern Italy. The Casati Law had been promulgated in 1859 within the Kingdom of Sardinia: it promoted free state education for all children up to eight years old (up to ten years old in larger municipalities); it decentralised the funding and management of primary schooling at municipal level and provided national rules on the curricula and salaries of teachers. Above all, the extension of the Casati Law to the South meant offering both an alternative to Catholic education and mandatory schooling for all children.[52] As Minister, De Sanctis aimed at nationalising the Jesuit secondary schools, creating a training path for primary school teachers, and extending access to university to all students (ever since 1857, students from the provinces of the Kingdom of Two Sicilies had been forbidden to attend the University in Naples). Within this plan of reform of the university system, he created new chairs and offered professorships at the University of Naples to many intellectuals who had been exiles and prisoners under Bourbon rule, such as Bertrando Spaventa (Theoretical Philosophy), Pasquale Villari (Philosophy of History), or Pasquale Stanislao Mancini (International Law).[53] In 1862, however, he went into opposition and promoted a moderate left organisation led by Settembrini, the Unitary-Constitutional Association (founded in 1863), which had as its mouthpiece the journal *Italia*, directed by De Sanctis himself from 1863 to 1866, and promoted an opposition within the limits of the constitution. Despite his republican sympathies, nurtured during his exile in Zurich (see Chapter 3), he was always persuaded that the constitutional monarchy established in 1860–1861 was the only viable solution for the new Italian State. In this respect he disagreed from both the Mazzinian groups and the radical left.

From 1861 to 1875, De Sanctis alternates between scholarly work and political commitment, thinking of himself as a 'Janus Bifrons': 'My life has

---

[52] For a recent account surveying the reform of the Italian educational system, see Gabriele Cappelli and Michelangelo Vasta, 'A "Silent Revolution": School Reforms in Italy's Educational Gender Gap in the Liberal Age (1861–1921)', *Cliometrica*, 15, 2021: 203–229.

[53] On this, see Antonio V. Nazzaro, *F. De Sanctis riformatore dell'Università degli Studi e della Società Reale di Napoli* (Giannini, Naples: 2016), pp. 10–53.

two pages, one literary, the other political, nor do I think of tearing up either of the two: they are two duties of my history that I shall continue until the last.'[54] In 1876, with the Left prevailing, De Sanctis decided to dedicate more energies to his political commitment. Although he was in favour of popular education and the enlargement of the franchise, he believed that the leadership should be confined to the educated elite until the masses could benefit from the extension of education to the lower classes, which were otherwise more vulnerable to demagogues:

> In a country in which there are classes, the rule and political measure belong to the upper classes, which are the true forces directing society. Even if class mistrust is cancelled out, there remains as a living, irresistible force the *masses*, as the French say. And if the latter are allowed to have their way, country and government would soon be dissolved. Here is the true danger of democracy. There is no doubt that the masses are the greater number, and that, interpreting the representative system literally, Government would be up to them. And as the masses are the meaner part, not only as regards social position, but as regards instruction and morality, this strange consequence would come about, that Government would be up to the least worthy . . . . Mischief-makers, meddlers, adventurers and depraved persons have more credit with the multitudes, because by education and by manners and by language they are closer to them, and they flatter and promise without scruple. This is what is called demagogy, and it is the greatest danger that democracy must guard against.[55]

The project of a slow and progressive education of the masses by a restricted intellectual elite, which has control of the government, had already been delineated by Vincenzo Cuoco (1770–1823) in his 1809 *Progetto di decreto per l'organizzazione della pubblica istruzione*. He had there advised Gioacchino Murat, King of Naples under the Napoleonic Empire, to differentiate education according to the social classes, aiming at a gradual change. This interpretation of the role of education was clearly connected to Cuoco's theory of 'the two peoples', elaborated earlier in his *Saggio storico sulla rivoluzione di Napoli del 1799* (1801) and in his *Platone in Italia* (1806), a theory that has been used for many years now when accounting for the 'dualism' of Italian history and of the South in particular. In this celebrated essay, Cuoco investigates the reasons for the failure of the 1799 revolution, in which he had actively

[54] Letter to Carlo Lozzi, 25 June 1869, A. Marinari, G. Paoloni, and G. Talamo (eds.), *Epistolario (1863–1869)* (Turin: Einaudi, 1993), p. 741.
[55] F. De Sanctis, *I partiti e l'educazione della nuova Italia. Scritti e discorsi dal 1871 al 1883*, ed. N. Cortese (Turin: Einaudi, 1970), pp. 175–176.

participated, serving as secretary of the newly established republic in Naples. The 'two peoples' were the lower class, socially and culturally poor, such as the Neapolitan *lazzari*, and the *aristoi*, socially and intellectually rich: on one side, the 'people-nation' and, on the other side, the people in charge of the political organisation of the State. The revolution fails when the latter is unable to translate ideas into 'effective reality' (*realta' effettiva*) – a term used to refer to Machiavelli's *verita' effettuale* – creating the conditions for the first kind of people to develop and participate in political life. This shift from abstract revolutionary principles to reality seems mainly possible thanks to the gradual education of the lower classes.[56]

A similar conception was also formulated by the Hegelian Angelo Camillo De Meis, who had held republican and democratic beliefs during his youth but espoused more conservative views around 1851–1852, after the French plebiscite had led to Louis Napoleon being declared Emperor. In his 1868 *Il Sovrano. Saggio di filosofia politica con riferenza all'Italia*, he outlined his conception of a State ruled by the Savoyard King together with intellectuals and philosophers, preferably Hegelians, responsible for enlightening the masses, because 'the poor ... they don't understand anything'.[57] The role of popular education appears as a key feature of post-unification debates within liberal circles, and De Sanctis' masterpiece *Storia della letteratura italiana* (1870–1871) was indeed conceived as a book for Italian secondary schools. This also explains why De Sanctis perceived his work as professor and writer as compatible with his political commitments, his scholarly and literary endeavours being in fact in his view simply another form of political action. Echoing Bertrando Spaventa's ideas on the Ethical State, De Sanctis believed that the Italian State had a mission to actively intervene in the education of the popular classes, promoting both national culture and the ethical and social progress of citizens: 'The State had to accept as its mission that of intervening actively, of giving an impulse to all the lower strata, or organizing them,

---

[56] See Antonino De Francesco, 'Una difficile modernità italiana. Immagini e significati del *Saggio Storico* di Vincenzo Cuoco' nella cultura politica nazionale', in *Saggio Storico sulla Rivoluzione di Napoli*, ed. Vincenzo Cuoco (Bari-Rome: Laterza, 2014), pp. 7–111; Antonino De Francesco, *Vincenzo Cuoco. Una vita politica* (Rome-Bari: Laterza, 1997); Fulvio Tessitore, *Filosofia, storia e politica in Vincenzo Cuoco* (Cosenza: Lungro di Cosenza, 2002).

[57] Angelo Camillo De Meis, *Il Sovrano. Saggio di filosofia politica con riferenza all'Italia*, ed. B. Croce (Bari: Laterza, 1927), p. 58. On this, see Paolo Orvieto, *De Sanctis* (Rome: Salerno editrice, 2015), pp. 135–149.

of accelerating social movement.'[58] Although he had already distanced himself from Hegel's philosophy while in exile in Zurich – when he frankly avowed to his friend De Meis in 1857 'Hegel has done me a great good but also great harm ... I have never been Hegelian *à tout prix*'[59] – his heterodox Hegelianism led him to draw the philosopher from Stuttgart nearer to a philosophy of praxis, which we will explore at greater length in Section 5.3. More generally, De Sanctis conceived the State as having as its mission the ethical and cultural education of the people, a mission that would be the realisation of liberty inasmuch as it also represented its limit:

> Order is precisely the consistent limit within liberty, and one that realizes it ... liberty is an empty form if we do not put a content into it, namely, our national life and our ideals. And this content is the limit within liberty, what renders it not an abstract idea but a living thing.[60]

Scholars have devoted many pages to attempting to explain the different political affiliations of De Sanctis, being aligned with the Right, in the very early years after unification, and then with the Left. According to Alfonso Scirocco, De Sanctis perceived himself to be a man of the Centre-Left, with a firm belief both 'in *order* and *progress*', meaning that he respected the authority of the State but had identified the need for thoroughgoing reforms. This seemed to him first the political programme of the Right but subsequently that of the Left.[61] Alberto Asor Rosa by contrast attributed to De Sanctis the ability to present the culture of the right as if it were oriented to the Left: 'He put into practice in a Jacobin guise a culture that was fundamentally conservative in spirit and in ideals.'[62] Paolo Orvieto for his part has recently highlighted how De Sanctis' centrism led him to prefer the Right in the early years as it seemed then to be a party positioned at the centre. However, by the mid-1860s, the turn within the party to a more conservative and clerical stance drove De Sanctis leftwards. In the meantime, the Left had itself

[58] See Denis Mack Smith, *De Sanctis e I problemi politici italiani del suo tempo*, in *De Sanctis e il realismo*, pp. 1189–1216, 1196.

[59] F. De Sanctis, 'Epistolario (1856–58)', in *Opere*, ed. G. Ferretti and M. Mazzocchi Alemanni, vol. XIX (Turin: Einaudi, 1965), p. 403.

[60] F. De Sanctis, *I partiti e l'educazione della nuova Italia. Scritti e discorsi dal 1871 al 1883*, ed. N. Cortese (Turin: Einaudi, 1970), pp. 172–173.

[61] A. Scirocco, *L'impegno politico di De Sanctis nell'età della Destra e la trasformazione dei partiti*, in *Francesco De Sanctis nella storia della cultura*, ed. C. Muscetta (Rome-Bari: Laterza, 1984), vol. II, pp. 403–450, 412.

[62] A. Asor Rosa, *L'idea e la cosa: De Sanctis e l'hegelismo*, in *Storia d'Italia* (Turin: Einaudi: 1975), IV/2, pp. 850–878, 868.

taken its distance from the revolutionaries and republican ideals and changed into a moderate and progressive left respectful of constitutional limits.[63] As highlighted before, De Sanctis' Swiss experience had helped to differentiate his political and cultural understanding from that of the other Hegelians, leading then to different political choices. However, his ethical understanding of politics remained the same and he shared with his fellow Hegelians an aversion towards so-called *trasformismo*, a political practice that was becoming very common among Italian parliamentary groups and that since the fall of the Right had characterised Italian politics. Because candidacy at elections was personal and the individual parliamentarian was not tied to a specific party, majorities were usually established on the basis of a convergence of intent on limited problems rather than on long-term political programmes. The passage of a parliamentarian from one side to another was a sign of the conclusion of a negotiation in which the deputy in question had bargained for his vote in exchange for the satisfaction of certain private interests. The borders between the two political parties appeared more and more blurred instead of presenting two competing political visions and systems of ideas. De Sanctis had denounced this practice already in 1877, when he criticised the tendency to create lobbies (*consorterie*), which led to 'political atony'.[64] De Sanctis believed that by restricting political life to different groups of interests without a political vision, corruption, mendacity, and moral decadence would become inevitable, and eventually Italians would lose their liberty:

> It is not enough to decree liberty for there to be liberty. Liberty presupposes a complex of ideas, customs and habits which are not added all at once, but through the slow development of social life . . . . A people is always ripe for living freely. Liberty is learned with liberty . . . . We are not free, because politics we consider not as the duty and the right of everyone . . . and we do not invest in public affairs that same ardour and interest as we place in our own, because we do not have sufficient initiative and expect everything [to come] from government . . . . But the government is not nine ministers, it is the whole vast and stable throng of employees who constitute the immensely powerful bureaucracy.[65]

---

[63] Paolo Orvieto, *De Sanctis* (Rome: Salerno editrice, 2015), pp. 135–149.

[64] F. De Sanctis, 'L'educazione politica', *Diritto*, 11 June 1877, in *I partiti e l'educazione della nuova Italia. Scritti e discorsi dal 1871 al 1883*, ed. N. Cortese (Turin: Einaudi, 1970), p. 90.

[65] F. De Sanctis, *Il Mezzogiorno e lo Stato unitario. Scritti e discorsi politici dal 1848 al 1870*, ed. F. Ferri (Turin: Einaudi, 1960), pp. 348–350.

Here De Sanctis interprets the problem of *trasformismo* from the perspective of an ethical interpretation of the function of the State and of politics, reflecting on the problem of the relationship between government and public administration. The very problem that Silvio Spaventa was himself addressing in these same years.

During the leadership of the Left, Silvio Spaventa's contribution to the debate about the State was mainly restricted to a series of speeches in Parliament on the constitutional character of the organisation of the State. In particular, he was interested in the relationship between government and public administration, between political and administrative power, his concern being to define to what extent 'the executive power can provide of itself for its own organization'.[66] The two main voices in this debate in the 1880s were Spaventa himself and Minghetti, who, in addressing the vexed problem of *trasformismo*, offered two alternative approaches to the taming of factionalism and the securing of political freedom in modern representative governments. David Ragazzoni outlines the two different strategies: Spaventa's 'monism', which, influenced by Hegel, revolved around the primacy of the State and its unity, and Minghetti's 'pluralism', which, influenced by Tocqueville, championed self-government and multiple association in civil society.[67] The need for a constitutional guarantee to reduce the interference of political parties in public administration was at the heart of Spaventa's speech 'Giustizia nell'amministrazione' (Justice in Public Administration) on the 6th of May 1880. The main issue he highlighted there was the need to safeguard the autonomy of local administration, while at the same time guaranteeing a system of alternation of political parties in government, avoiding therefore the possibility that 'the interests of a party, of a class, of an individual ... should predominate unjustly over the interests of the others . . .. The solution lies in making a crucial distinction between government and administration'.[68] He believed that the solution consisted in providing a public law that was 'certain, clear and complete', in order to regulate the relationship between the individual and the State. When he was appointed Senator of the Kingdom in 1889, Francesco Crispi nominated him President of the IV section of the Consiglio di Stato (State Council). In this post, he organised the reform of

---

[66] S. Spaventa, *Discorsi parlamentari*, p. 476.

[67] See David Ragazzoni, 'Silvio Spaventa and Marco Minghetti on Party Government', *Journal of Modern Italian Studies*, Special Issue edited by F. Gallo and A. Körner, *Hegel in Italy: Risorgimento Political Thought in Transnational Perspective*, 24, no. 2, 2019: 293–323. On this, see also Francesco Gambino, 'La giustizia nell'amministrazione e l'idea di Stato in Silvio Spaventa', in *Il Consiglio di Stato: 180 anni di storia* (Bologna: Zanichelli, 2022), pp. 165–176.

[68] S. Spaventa, *Discorsi parlamentari*, p. 552.

justice in public administration in order to 'complete' the 1865 law on the relationship between State and citizen. By dint of this reform, administrative trials became internal to public administration and separated from ordinary justice; it defined the fundamental characteristics of the administrative trial, such as the appeal against acts or provisions for shortcomings in legitimacy (incompetence, excessive use of power, and violation of the law) to protect individual interests.[69] The main aim of Spaventa here was to establish a system to supervise the work of the administration, albeit through a system of litigation, in order to guarantee the public interest while protecting individual interests.

Silvio Spaventa's idea of the State has been interpreted in many and often contrasting ways, highlighting the coexistence in his thinking of moderate and progressive elements[70] or the development of Risorgimento liberalism in a democratic direction.[71] His contribution to the theory of the State appeared to some to betoken a decline of liberalism, since there purportedly featured in it intellectual motifs promoted later by fascism.[72] This interpretation had been fiercely contested since 1926 by Benedetto Croce and many others after him.[73] As we have seen in Chapter 4, a propensity to derive fascist intellectual motifs from nineteenth-century Hegelian political thought in Italy has long been a commonplace of scholarly debate, often revolving around the contribution of the Spaventa brothers, by the same token obscuring the real context of Risorgimento political thought and their role in it.[74] Silvio Spaventa's work in the late 1880s represented the main intervention in the direction of the development of Public Law in the modern Italian State. A reflection on the relationship between ethics, politics, and law had been at the heart of his mature work, in which the influence of Hegel was integrated with the theories of the *Rechtsstaat*, those elaborated by Rudolph Von Gneist among them, as well as with the practical needs of the new State. Politics, Spaventa insisted, had to be subordinated to the Law, the 'substance of the nation', and to Ethics, the 'intimate sentiment of morality', which gave concrete existence and moral autonomy to the nation. By elevating politics to the level of ethics, the State would become the place in which liberty would be realised and objectivised. Differently from Hegel, though, this Ethical State was not a

---

[69] See article 3, 31 March 1889, no. 5992.
[70] G. Spadolini, 'Preface' to S. Spaventa, *La giustizia amministrativa*, p. 5.
[71] C. Ghisalberti, *Stato e costituzione nel risorgimento* (Milan: A. Giuffrè, 1972), p. 249.
[72] G. De Ruggiero, *Storia del liberalismo europeo* (1925) (Rome-Bari: Laterza, 2003), p. 349.
[73] B. Croce, in the 'Preface' to S. Spaventa, *Lettere politiche* (1861–1893) (Bari: Laterza, 1926), p. 5; L. Villari, *Bella e perduta. L'Italia del Risorgimento* (Rome-Bari: Laterza, 2009), pp. 3–4.
[74] L. Villari, *Bella e perduta. L'Italia del Risorgimento* (Rome-Bari: Laterza, 2009), pp. 3–4.

reality yet, being in need of political projects and earnest endeavours 'to become ethical'.

The 1880s and the 1890s witnessed the decease of the main representatives of Hegelianism in Italy: whereas Marianna Florenzi Waddington had died earlier, in 1870, Bertrando Spaventa and Francesco De Sanctis both died in Naples in 1883, followed by Francesco Fiorentino in 1884. Angelo Camillo De Meis died in Bologna in 1891, whereas Silvio Spaventa died in Rome in 1893. In 1883, Silvio had taken into his house his seventeen-year-old nephew Benedetto Croce (1866–1952), who had in that year lost both of his parents in the earthquake that destroyed Casamicciola, a part of the island of Ischia in the bay of Naples. In the last ten years of his life, Silvio's house in Rome became an intellectual salon attended by a younger generation of southern politicians and intellectuals (Figure 5.2). In those rooms began the fruitful discussions between the young Croce and Antonio Labriola (1843–1904), respectively the future leader of the Italian liberalism and one of the main exponents of Italian Marxism. Silvio Spaventa's contribution to the building of the new Italian State by applying his Hegelian ideas to the practice of politics demonstrates the extent to which Italian political life had been influenced by Hegel's philosophy. Italian Hegelianism seemed to disappear along with the illustrious generation of scholars that had brought it to life. The generation that was educated under the Kingdom of Two Sicilies and that after exile, imprisonment, and war built the new Kingdom of Italy, had left the stage by the end of the century. However, their particular interpretation of Hegel would survive in the discussions that a younger generation of Southern Italian intellectuals and politicians, most of them educated in this same milieu, would continue, endeavoring to measure Hegel's philosophy against the new political challenges they were facing.

5.3   The Legacy

In March 1894, Antonio Labriola wrote in one of his letters to Friedrich Engels (1820–1895) that it was thanks to the Hegelian education imparted to him by his teacher Bertrando Spaventa, that he was able to understand and enjoy *The Holy Family* (1845), the first work co-written by Engels and Marx criticising the Young Hegelians.[75] It was just before the publication

---

[75] On this, see Douglas Moggach, *The Philosophy and Politics of Bruno Bauer* (Cambridge: Cambridge University Press, 2003); Douglas Moggach, *The New Hegelians: Politics and Philosophy in the Hegelian School* (Cambridge: Cambridge University Press, 2011).

Figure 5.2 'In this house Silvio Spaventa lived the last years of his life and here died on the night of the 21st of June 1893'. Commemorative plaque, Via dei Due Macelli, Rome

of Labriola's series of Marxist essays between 1895 and 1898 with the title
Saggi intorno alla concezione materialistica della storia (*Essays on the
Materialistic Conception of History*) that he decided to describe to Engels
how Hegelianism had revived in Italy first privately, between the 1840s
and the 1860s, and then publicly, taught at the University of Naples by
many scholars between the 1860s and 1870s. In this letter, he was at great
pains to emphasise how deeply the development of Italian Hegelianism
had influenced his approach to Marxism. While describing his own
intellectual path, Labriola explains to Engels the importance of the
Hegelian school in Italy:

> I have read, understood and *relished all* [of *The Holy Family*].
> Understanding it is something many will be capable of but only a few
> *now* will *relish* it as I do. In Naples, privately from 1840–60, and then
> publicly from 1860–75, there was the rebirth of Hegelianism .... Spaventa
> (the best of them all) wrote exquisitely on dialectic, discovered again Bruno
> and Campanella, delineated the useful and utilizable part of Vico, and
> found by himself (in 1864!) the connection between Hegel and Darwin.
> I was born into a milieu of this sort. At the age of 19 I wrote an invective
> against Zeller on account of his return to Kant (Heidelberg inaugural
> lecture). The whole of the Hegelian and post-Hegelian literature was
> familiar to us. Now these books are out of print, either in antiquarian
> clearance sales, or on the bookstalls. I studied Feuerbach in 1866–68, and
> then the Tübingen school: *ich habe, leider, auch Theologie studiert!*
> (Unfortunately I have studied theology too!) All that is over, because this
> country of ours is like a pit of history. Now the positivistic demi-monde is
> dominant. Perhaps – indeed, there's no perhaps about it – I became
> communist on account of my (rigorously) Hegelian education, after having
> passed through the psychology of Herbart.[76]

Of all the students who attended Bertrando Spaventa's lectures, Antonio
Labriola was indeed his dearest pupil, a young man possessed of an
uncommon passion and intelligence. Labriola enrolled to study philosophy
at the University of Naples in 1861 and attended the first courses that
Spaventa held there in the aftermath of unification.[77] The influence of his

---

[76] For the letter written on the 14th of March, see V. Gerratana, 'Per una corretta lettura di Labriola.
Precisazioni e rettifiche', *Critica marxista*, XI, 1973: 264–265. See also the letter from Labriola to
Engels on 1st July 1893 in A. Labriola, *Scritti filosofici e politici* (Turin: Einaudi, 1973), vol.
I pp. 339–343.

[77] Regarding Spaventa's influence on Labriola, see E. Garin, 'Introduzione' to A. Labriola, *La
concezione materialistica della storia* (Bari: Laterza, 1965), pp. vii–xvii; F. Sbarberi, 'Il marxismo di
Antonio Labriola', in *Scritti filosofici e politici*, ed. A. Labriola (Turin: Einaudi, 1973), pp. xi–cxiv;
L. Dal Pane, *Antonio Labriola nella politica e nella cultura italiana* (Turin: Einaudi, 1975);

teacher is manifest even in his earliest writings: as mentioned in his letter to Engels, in 1862, he wrote a response to Zeller's inaugural lecture, rejecting the very idea of a 'return to Kant'.[78] His criticism addressed Zeller's conception of logic as methodology pure and simple, an exposition of forms and rules of thought abstracted from the content. According to Labriola, this approach was problematic because it did not recognise, as Hegel had done, the dialectical synthesis between content and form of knowledge – 'real thought'. While Kant's criticism had an historical dimension because it developed a conception of knowledge as the rational production of the object, Zeller's neo-Kantianism recognised two different sources of knowledge (receptivity and spontaneity), thus simply describing a cognitive process, destined to fall into 'empirical psychologism'. Following the Vichian reading of Hegel, Labriola opposed to Zeller's view, the notion that what makes scientific knowledge possible is 'the *immanence* of the *ideal* in every *historical explication*'.[79]

The theme of the reality of knowledge is at the heart of another early essay, also unpublished, on the *Origine e natura delle passioni secondo l'etica di Spinoza* (*Origin and Nature of the Passions in Spinoza's Ethics*), written in 1866–1867. Baruch Spinoza appears to Labriola as the backbone of modern thought on account of his ability to restore a unified and coherent image of reality: the 'unconditional trust of the spirit in the objectivity of knowledge' is for Labriola the key to Spinoza's ontology.[80] This ontology based on the concept of *Substance* is an 'immense progress compared to Cartesian dualism' and 'a complete victory over any presupposition of transcendence'.[81] At a theoretical level, this unitary understanding of reality reconciles human beings with the eternal order of nature; at an ethical level, human beings are reconciled with themselves as they are in harmony with their natural passions, rather than in observance of abstract norms. This anti-subjectivistic foundation of Spinoza's *Ethics*, free from anthropocentric and teleological perspectives, is important according to Labriola because it leads to the conception of freedom in terms of

---

A. Burgio, *Antonio Labriola nella storia e nella cultura della nuova Italia* (Macerata: Quodlibet, 2005).

[78] For Labriola's early writings, see Antonio Labriola, 'Una risposta alla prolusione di Zeller' (1862), 'Della relazione della Chiesa allo Stato' (1864–1865), 'Origine e natura delle passioni secondo Spinoza' (1866–1867), now in A. Labriola, *Tutti gli scritti filosofici e di teoria dell'educazione*, ed. Luca Basile and Lorenzo Steardo (Milan: Bompiani, 2014) pp. 438–473, 475–480, 481–520.

[79] Labriola, 'Una risposta alla prolusione di Zeller', p. 473.

[80] Labriola, 'Origine e natura delle passioni secondo Spinoza' (1866–1867), p. 486.

[81] Labriola, 'Origine e natura delle passioni secondo Spinoza' (1866–1867), pp. 487–491.

consciousness, rather than as free will: Spinoza founded the moral system 'by the path of naturalism, without interruption of the constant laws of the universe'.[82]

The ethical dimension of political relationships also featured prominently in Labriola's early thought, as demonstrated by his essay on the relationship between Church and State, *Della relazione della Chiesa allo Stato*, written in 1864–1865. As anticipated in section 2.3, here he differentiates the institution of the Catholic Church from religion as a form of the spirit, an equivocation that according to him has often led to the affirmation of the superiority of the Church, infinite and supramundane, over the State, finite and mundane.

After completing his studies, economic hardship forced Labriola to look for a job outside academia, first in the prefecture and subsequently as a secondary school teacher. By the end of the 1860s and in the following decade, Labriola underwent an intellectual experience destined to profoundly affect his thought: the study of Herbart and his 'psychology of peoples', which proposed a 'scientific elaboration of the facts of historical knowledge'. Herbart's philosophy seemed to Labriola an analysis of human conduct capable of opening the way 'to a true science of genetic psychology', meeting his need for concrete historical reality. This new research perspective emerges in his first important work, published in 1871, *La Dottrina di Socrate secondo Senofonte, Platone ed Aristotele* (*The Doctrine of Socrates, according to Xenophon, Plato and Aristotle*), where his heightened attention to the 'positive', the 'detailed', the precise reconstruction of causal connections is in evidence.[83] Here, by investigating Socrates' pedagogy, the study of liberty is in connection with a genetic-evolutionary study of ethical consciousness. Likewise, in the two 1873 essays *Della Libertá morale* and *Morale e religione*, printed for the competition by virtue of which Labriola obtained the Chair of Moral Philosophy and Pedagogy at the University of Rome, psychological analysis makes a fundamental contribution to the study of ethics: human beings are free because of the 'multiplicity of their internal states' and their choices are determined by 'the sum of the inner experiences' that generate actions as well as the 'real activity of the soul'.[84] As early as the 1870s, then, Labriola was already

---

[82] Labriola, 'Origine e natura delle passioni secondo Spinoza' (1866–1867), p. 518.

[83] A. Labriola, 'La Dottrina di Socrate secondo Senofonte, Platone ed Aristotele', in *Tutti gli scritti filosofici e di teoria dell'educazione*, ed. Luca Basile and Lorenzo Steardo (Milan: Bompiani, 2014), pp. 537–662.

[84] A. Labriola, 'Della liberta' morale', in *Tutti gli scritti filosofici e di teoria dell'educazione*, ed. Luca Basile and Lorenzo Steardo (Milan: Bompiani, 2014), p. 780.

deeply interested in the development of the social sciences, the connections between 'Idea' and history and the development of social forms.

Although Labriola would later recognise that he became Marxist because of Hegel's philosophy of history and Herbart's psychology of peoples, the main question to answer would be what kind of Hegelianism trained him to look at concrete historical reality, at the 'positive'. It was indeed thanks to the critical discussion of the relationship between idealism and empiricism broached in particular by Bertrando Spaventa and Francesco De Sanctis in the 1870s and 1880s that the critical approach to Hegelianism survived beyond the group of Neapolitan Hegelians. By reflecting on developments within the field of natural and social sciences, both Bertrando Spaventa and De Sanctis recognised the important role of Darwin in identifying a 'dialectic of nature' by means of his theory of natural selection and the dialectical process that this implies.[85] When writing to Georges Sorel (1847–1922) in 1897, Labriola recognised this important philosophical overturning achieved by the Neapolitan Hegelians: nature is no longer crystallised in a system but rather forms part of the dialectical process, adopting thereby a similar approach – according to Labriola – to Engels' clarification regarding Marxist philosophy in his *Anti-Dühring* (1878). In their final years, Spaventa was particularly concerned to reflect on the active role of consciousness within experience, while De Sanctis for his part sought to elaborate a theory of form as 'plastic form', so that art could represent the reality of life. However, their understanding of the relevance of a dialectical realism was still within an idealist framework. It would be Labriola who would turn this interest in realism and the Hegelian dialectical process into the recasting of historical materialism as a 'philosophy of praxis'.[86]

The most enduring legacy of Bertrando Spaventa's philosophy as regards Labriola's Marxism was Spaventa's reform of the Hegelian dialectic and his interpretation of the practical nature of the intellect and of knowledge. This was the product of a long intellectual journey that had begun with his essay on the *Prime categorie della logica Hegeliana* (*The First*

[85] See B. Spaventa, *La legge del più forte* (1874) and *Idealismo o realismo. Nota sulla teoria della conoscenza (Kant, Herbart, Hegel)* (1874), in *Opere* (Milan: Bompiani, 2009), pp. 491–504, 505–519; F. De Sanctis, *Il darwinismo nell'arte* (Naples: Classici Italiani, 1883).

[86] For the most recent work on Italian Marxism as a philosophy of praxis, see Marcello Muste, *Marxism and Philosophy of Praxis: An Italian Perspective from Labriola to Gramsci* (London: Palgrave Macmillan, 2021). On this, see also Giuseppe Vacca, *Alternative Modernities: Antonio Gramsci's Twentieth Century* (London: Palgrave Macmillan, 2020), pp. 151–193; Domenico Losurdo, *Dai fratelli Spaventa a Gramsci: Per una storia politico-sociale della fortuna di Hegel in Italia* (Naples: La Città del Sole, 1997).

Categories of the Hegelian Logic) in 1864 – an essay written in response to a text that was then circulating in Naples, *Logische Untersuchungen* (1840) by Friedrich Adolf Trendelenburg (1802–1872) – and concluded with the book *Esperienza e Metafisica* (*Experience and Metaphysics*), published posthumously in 1888. Spaventa's reform of the Hegelian dialectic has been at the heart of many debates within Italian Idealism and was of particular relevance to Giovanni Gentile's philosophy, configuring as it did the dialectical movement as an act of thought and of subjectivity.[87] Spaventa's analysis of Hegel's *Science of Logic* is guided by his reading of the *Phenomenology of Spirit*: to understand Hegel's 'dialectic of beginning' (*die Dialektik des Anfangs*), which explores the categories of *being* (*Sein*), *nothing* (*Nichts*), and *becoming* (*Werden*), Spaventa recognises a mediator that differentiates the identification of *being* and *nothing*, which is the *Meinung*, the 'Mind'. This reference to the 'metaphysics of the mind' (*metafisica della mente*) follows Vico's interpretation of the mind as the human, therefore historical, dimension of the ideal, that here is associated with the Hegelian *Reason*: according to Spaventa, the categories of thinking are distinguished both at a theoretical level and in reality because the 'beginning' has a phenomenological (dialectical, historical) development.[88] His attention to the reality of experience, to the 'positive', had intensified by the end of the 1860s and in the course of the following decade, which saw him develop a notion of philosophy as 'science' (*scientia*) in contraposition to a 'scientific philosophy', as clarified in his 1867 work *Principi di filosofia* (*Principles of Philosophy*, republished by Giovanni Gentile in 1911 with the title *Logica e Metafisica*):

> Humanity is essentially history; and whoever says history says positivism, a posteriorism. A priori humanity is abstract, not real humanity: humanity without history. Positivism represents, then, a true element in the science of humanity. In brief, for me that is the true expression of the requirement contained in true idealism: infinite existence is activity of things and especially of humanity. This activity is the right of positivism. In this sense, I am positivist.[89]

In another essay that Spaventa wrote a few years later, *Kant e l'empirismo* (1881), the relationship between science and philosophy is further

---

[87] See Giovanni Gentile, *Le origini della filosofia contemporanea in Italia* (Messina: Principato, 1923); F. Alderisio, *Esame della riforma attualistica dell'idealismo in rapporto a Spaventa e a Hegel* (Todi: Tuderte, 1940); Vincenzo Vitiello, *Buchstabieren Hegel: Rileggendo Bertrando Spaventa interprete di Hegel*, in Bertrando Spaventa, *Opere* (Milan: Bompiani, 2008), pp. 2809–2830.

[88] B. Spaventa, *Le prime categorie della logica di Hegel*, Opere, I, p. 436.

[89] B. Spaventa, *Logica e Metafisica*, p. 7.

discussed. According to Spaventa, Kantian criticism better serves the understanding of this relationship than do the methods proposed by the natural sciences. In fact, the positive philosophies, in their attempt to derive the a priori conditions of knowledge from experience, aim to abolish metaphysics or to realise an empirical realism that would deny any possibility of a knowledge a priori. The final defence of the idealist system as a conceptual framework of reference, albeit with corrections and adjustments due to the erosion of the system, is represented by the work Spaventa drafted between 1881 and 1882 – published posthumously, in 1888, by his pupil Donato Jaja with the title *Experience and Metaphysics*. Here philosophy is both the condition of possibility of experience and its completion. However, the empirical world, reality, follows its own evolution, whose meaning is established by the knowledge of the subject. Knowledge is possible because ideas are immanent in experience: philosophy is the science of history.

This attention to realism was very clear also in Francesco De Sanctis' philosophy. As described in Chapter 1, since his first Neapolitan school in the 1840s, De Sanctis had engaged with the philosophy of Hegel, the *Aesthetics* in particular, and then translated Hegel's *Logic* while in prison after the 1848 revolution. Another great influence in those early years was of course the philosophy of Giambattista Vico and its nexus of *verum* and *factum*, universalism and particularism, thanks to which De Sanctis tended to identify the motifs of logic with the historicity of the human world. Therefore, his later attempts at rethinking Hegel's aesthetics and logic in dialectical terms portrayed them not so much as part of the system of the philosophy of the spirit but rather as a concrete expression of the unity/distinction of the human being.[90] In particular, in his work *Schopenhauer e Leopardi*, published in 1858, he opposes to the centrality of the will posited by the German philosopher, the pessimistic vision of human limits entertained by the great Italian poet. De Sanctis also clearly distinguished logic from metaphysics, thus differentiating himself from the idealist school, while however also refusing the position of the empiricist school, which separates knowledge (*scienza*) and life (*vita*). These are all anticipations of what would become De Sanctis' *realism*.[91]

With De Sanctis' work, Hegelian philosophy is oriented towards praxis. His realist understanding of philosophy is clarified in his concept of 'life'

---

[90] F. De Sanctis, 'Schopenhauer e Leopardi', *Rivista contemporanea*, XV, no. 61, 1858: 369–408.
[91] Of particular relevance to this aspect of De Sanctis' thought are his philosophical essays *La scienza e la vita* (1872) and *Il principio del realismo* (1876), as well as his 1883 *Il darwinismo nell'arte*.

(*vita*) and its connection with the Hegelian dialectic. When, in 1906, Benedetto Croce published his celebrated essay *Cio' che e' vivo e cio' che e' morto della filosofia di Hegel* (*What Is Living and What Is Dead in the Philosophy of Hegel*), he highlighted this connection when defining the purpose of the dialectic, which is 'to find a form of mind, which should be mobile as the movement of the real, which should participate in the life of things, which should feel "the pulse of reality", and should mentally reproduce the rhythm of its development, without breaking it into pieces or making it rigid and falsifying it'.[92] The abstract idea has to be in a dialectical relationship with reality, with 'life'. Indeed, when studying Hegel's *Science of Logic* in prison, De Sanctis would focus in particular on the part concerned with the *Essence* in the section on *Reality*, a reality not in a materialistic sense but rather a critical realism: 'Realism can still be regarded as a further formation of Hegel's doctrine.'[93] De Sanctis believes that there is no opposition between ideal and real:

> The real is what generates the ideal ... the ideal is a slow formation of the mind according to the factual or real conditions in which it is. As the real conditions alter, so too does the ideal alter. Hence this latter is part of organic life, indeed it is its ultimate result, its crown, the highest [result] in reality.[94]

De Sanctis maintained that the real legacy of Hegel's philosophy was realism, as it was the development of Hegel's two key principles, *being* (*Sein*) and *becoming* (*Werden*), that had made evolution (*Entwicklung*) possible:

> There are in Hegel two principles that are at the basis of all today's movement, *becoming*, [the] basis of evolution (*Entwicklung*), and *existing*, [the] basis of realism ... the new realism can be considered still as a further formation of Hegel's doctrine.[95]

According to De Sanctis, life has to enter the *logos*: his '*ragione-storia*' (Reason-History) or '*ragione vivente*' (Living Reason) establishes a relationship between the 'positive' of empirical experiences and the ideal of historical events. He suggests that knowledge (*scienza*) should be understood from the point of view of life, of society in its historical development,

---

[92] B. Croce *Cio' che è vivo e cio' che è morto della filosofia di Hegel*, in B. Croce, *Saggio sullo Hegel* (Naples: Bibliopolis, 2006), p. 144. For the English translation by Douglas Ainslie, see B. Croce, *What Is living and What Is Dead of the Philosophy of Hegel* (London: Macmillan, 1915), p. 214.

[93] F. De Sanctis, *Opere*, vol. XIV, p. 352.

[94] F. De Sanctis, *L'ideale*, in *Francesco De Sanctis*, ed. C. Muscetta (Rome: Istituto Poligrafico della Zecca, 1995), p. 1142.

[95] F. De Sanctis, *I principi del realismo*, in *L'arte, la scienza e la vita*, p. 90.

so that there is a dialectical unity of the two terms knowledge and life (*scienza e vita*).

What here seems mainly an epistemological problem has a relevant ethical-political dimension, which already emerged in our discussion of the figure of Niccolò Machiavelli (Chapter 3): 'When the ideas that constitute the life of a people die, life can continue for a little but it is already preparing for death ... the people still lives in appearance but it is already condemned to perish.'[96] Knowledge dies if it is incapable of understanding its own historical time, while it lives if it can 'intervene' and 'heal' historical reality (life).[97]

Both from De Sanctis and from Spaventa's critical understanding of Hegel, there emerges the quest for a philosophical knowledge elevated to the rank of a science of the historical world. When Labriola enhances his original understanding of Marxism as a 'philosophy of praxis', he is embarked upon the same quest: to understand Marxism as the 'philosophical method for the general understanding of life and the universe'.[98] This was in contrast with the general tendencies of European Marxism at that date, which mainly perceived philosophy as the 'implicit underpinning for all of [Marx's] political and historical understanding'.[99] The term 'philosophy of praxis' is used by Labriola for the first time in his third Marxist essay *Discorrendo di socialismo e filosofia*, published in 1898, where he reflects on Marxist philosophy as '*Lebens- und Weltanschauung* ... a general conception of life and the world' and proposes an anti-theological reading of Marx, one that would define the historical reality of ideas.[100] The 'philosophy of praxis' became then the formula used to identify the distinctive approach that a series of Italian intellectuals, from Antonio Labriola to Antonio Gramsci, assumed in their relationship with the works of Marx. This formula was at the heart of Labriola's fourth and last essay *Da un secolo all'altro* (*From One Century to the Next*), written between 1897 and 1903 and published posthumously by Benedetto Croce. Labriola's socialism, while rejecting the interpretation of Marxism as a materialist philosophy, refuted the idea that idealism was a pure speculative philosophy, which separates the ideal order from the historical develelopment. Hegel's philosophy here represents an historical conception of a reality which is the identity of thought and being. It does not come as a surprise now that Labriola's

[96] F. De Sanctis, *Saggi critici* (Bari: Laterza, 1974), p. 314.

[97] De Sanctis, *La scienza e la vita*, p. 100.   [98] Labriola, *Discorrendo di socialismo e filosofia*, p. 23.

[99] Marcello Muste, *Marxism and Philosophy of Praxis: An Italian Perspective from Labriola to Gramsci* (London: Palgrave Macmillan, 2021), p. xix.

[100] Labriola, *Discorrendo di socialismo e filosofia*, p. 667.

engagement with Marxism was recognised by the author himself as a direct consequence of the critical Hegelianism he had learned at the school of the Neapolitan Hegelians as a young student and with which he was in constant dialogue throughout his life.

De Sanctis' original interpretation of Hegelianism as realism was already highlighted by Antonio Gramsci as a 'militant criticism'.[101] More recently, scholars have gone so far as to recognise in De Sanctis the founder of modern Italian historicism. Fulvio Tessitore, for example, described his philosophy as a 'realist historicism', while Giuseppe Cacciatore wrote of a 'critical realism' and Stefania Achella of a 'critical Hegelianism'.[102] In a similar way, Bertrando Spaventa's critical engagement with the philosophy of Hegel, centred as it was on the 'positive', on the historical reality of the 'mind', has led many interpreters to highlight his relevance for the development of Italian Marxism.[103] This book does not propose a teleological reconstruction of Italian political thought, whether historicist or Marxist in emphasis. It rather uncovers and reshapes the context of Italian readings of Hegel's philosophy in the nineteenth century, exploring the creative and critical adaptation of Hegel's political thought to Italian intellectual and political milieux.

When at the turn of the century Labriola recounted 'the fate of those Hegelians who came to the fore in Italy from 1840 to 1880, especially in the South', a few of whom 'were strong thinkers' and had 'represented a revolutionary current of great importance', he bluntly concluded that 'every trace, and even the memory, of this movement [had] passed away ... after the lapse of but a few years'.[104] He believed that the rapid demise of the Hegelians was the consequence of their being detached from their own context, holding 'mental conversations with their German Comrades', writing and teaching 'as if they were living in Berlin ... instead

---

[101] A. Gramsci, *Quaderni dal carcere* (Turin: Einaudi, 1975), vol. II, p. 880.

[102] Fulvio Tessitore, 'Lo storicismo politico di Francesco De Sanctis', in *Contributi alla storia e alla teoria dello storicismo* (Rome: Edizioni di Storia e Letteratura, 1997), vol. III, pp. 77–96; Giuseppe Cacciatore, 'De Sanctis filosofo e la centralità del nesso tra la scienza e la vita', in *La scienza, la scuola, la vita: Francesco De Sanctis tra noi*, ed. Maria Teresa Imbriani (Venosa: Osanna Edizioni, 2021), pp. 39–46; Stefania Achella, 'Vita e conoscenza in Francesco De Sanctis', in *La fortuna di Hegel in Italia nell'Ottocento*, ed. Marco Diamanti (Naples: Bibliopolis, 2020), pp. 143–162.

[103] See G. Berti, 'Bertrando Spaventa, Antonio Labriola e l'hegelismo napoletano', *Società*, no. 3, 1854: 406–430; no. 4: 583–607; no. 5: 764–791; and G. Arfé, 'L'hegelismo napoletano e Bertrando Spaventa', *Società*, VII, 1952: 45–62; G. Vacca, *Politica e filosofia in Bertrando Spaventa* (Bari: Laterza, 1867). These works suggest a parallelism between the German tradition of thought Hegel-Feuerbach-Marx with an Italian tradition Spaventa-Labriola-Gramsci.

[104] Labriola, *Discorrendo di socialismo e filosofia*, p. 698.

of Naples'.[105] This portrait seems inaccurate, especially if we consider that Labriola then warns Italian Marxists to avoid a similar danger and to connect the understanding of historical materialism to Italian political and intellectual reality. The same preoccupation with the modernity of the Italian nation proposed by Spaventa in the middle of the nineteenth century is here returning in his pupil in a different form: a shift of 'the capitalist era' away from 'the Mediterranean countries', the early manifest- ation of a 'crisis in the relationship between a frail bourgeoisie and the nation', the revolts of the working class.[106] This generalised decadence called for action upon the historical course of events.

---

[105] Labriola, *Discorrendo di socialismo e filosofia*, p. 698.
[106] Labriola, *Discorrendo di socialismo e filosofia*, p. 775.

Epilogue
The Hegelian Tradition of Political Thought in Italy

The re-elaboration of the intellectual tradition of the Risorgimento in the early twentieth century was mainly due to three key protagonists of Italian political thought: Benedetto Croce (1866–1952), Giovanni Gentile (1875–1944), and Antonio Gramsci (1891–1937). They were all influenced in the development of their philosophies by the work of Antonio Labriola and the legacy of nineteenth-century Italian Hegelianism. This generation of thinkers saw in the Risorgimento a contested legacy to be reappropriated in order to address those tensions that the process of unification had left unresolved: the tension between the North and the South (the Southern Question); the tension between a catholic and a secular Italy (the Roman Question); and the tension between a 'legal Italy' and a 'real Italy', that is to say, between the set of liberal institutions resulting from the political unification and the fragmented social, economic, and cultural realities of the Peninsula. In philosophical terms, these tensions reverberated in the discussions about the relationship between the state and the nation/society, between force and consensus, and ultimately between politics and ethics. These tensions also left a wider feeling of an unfinished process that had to be realised and the need for a 'second Risorgimento' capable of completing the first.

This epilogue outlines the influence and legacy of nineteenth-century Italian Hegelianism by investigating how Croce, Gentile, and Gramsci re-elaborated this tradition in order to develop their own philosophical systems. The recasting of Hegelian political thought effected by nineteenth-century Italian Hegelians had a huge influence on the way in which these thinkers interpreted Hegel, Marx, and the relationship between politics and ethics, as well as their understanding of Italian history and of the role of intellectuals in the formation of the Italian state. This epilogue argues that these thinkers were in constant dialogue with the Italian tradition of political thought identified in this book: an intellectual history by virtue of which a specific recasting of the themes presented by Hegel's philosophy forged an understanding of history as the realm in which philosophy acquires its political relevance and ideas their practical dimension.

The reconstruction of the context of this tradition of political thought should also help in decoding that specific Italian intellectual 'jargon' that Charles Swan, an Anglican minister who was the first English translator of Alessandro Manzoni's *Promessi Sposi* (*The Betrothed Lovers*, 1828), found so hard to grasp, as his correspondence with Manzoni himself makes only too plain.[1] This shared Italian political language and the constant internal references have often proved quite difficult for scholars unfamiliar with the Italian intellectual context to identify. Richard Bellamy, for instance, rightly pointed out that Gramsci's 'ideas were constrained by the concerns and language of the Italian politics of his time'.[2] Derek Boothman highlights that Gramsci's idea of 'hegemony' as the 'combination of force and consent' and his realaboration of Marx's philosophy was influenced by Croce's 'ethico-political history' – according to which moral and civil institutions have a substansive reality.[3] These internal references to Italian political and intellectual debates would certainly entail engagement with the key themes investigated by nineteenth-century Italian interpretations of Hegel and Marx. Despite the huge differences characterising the political thought of Croce, Gentile, and Gramsci, they all shared a common ground, which was their engagement with Antonio Labriola's 'philosophy of praxis' and his interpretation of Marxism as well as with the broader tradition of Italian Hegelianism. Here we discuss their engagement first with the philosophy of Marx, then with the philosophy of Hegel, and finally their interpretations of the two crucial periods of modern Italian history: the Risorgimento and Fascism.

E.1 Rethinking the 'Philosophy of Praxis'

Benedetto Croce was a young boy when in 1883 he lost both his parents and his sister in the earthquake that destroyed Casamicciola (Ischia) while

---

[1] Alessandro Manzoni, *Tutte le lettere*, I, p. 480 (to Charles Swan, 25 January 1828). On C. Swan, see also C. Dionisotti, 'Annali manzoniani', *Manzoni e la cultura inglese*, 6, 1977: 251–265, then in *Appunti sui moderni. Foscolo, Leopardi, Manzoni e altri* (Bologna: il Mulino, 1988), pp. 299–315, 312. On this, see Rocco Rubini, '(Re-)Experiencing the Renaissance', in *The Reaissance from an Italian Perspective: An Anthology of Essays, 1860–1968* (Ravenna: Longo Editore, 2014), pp. 7–20.

[2] Richard Bellamy, 'Gramsci, Croce and the Italian Political Tradition', *History of Political Thought*, 11, no. 2, 1990: 313–337, 314. On this see also Alessandro Carlucci, *Gramsci and Languages: Unification, Diversity, Hegemony* (Leiden: Brill, 2013); Peter Ives, *Language and Hegemony in Gramsci* (London: Pluto, 2009).

[3] See Derek Boothman, 'The Sources for Gramsci's Concept of Hegemony, Rethinking Marxism', *Rethinking Marxism*, 20, no. 2, 2008: 201–215. On this, see also Peter Thomas, *The Gramscian Moment: Philosophy, Hegemony, and Marxism* (Leiden: Brill, 2009).

they were there on holidays, having then to leave Naples with his younger
brother Alfonso and move in with his uncle Silvio Spaventa. The latter was
living in Rome, was fully absorbed by the political life of the newly
established capital, and was probably unable to provide the emotional
support that the young orphan needed: Croce felt desperate and even
contemplated 'the idea of suicide'.[4] When this young boy walked through
the doors of the University of Rome, La Sapienza and, following his
uncle's recommendation, attended Antonio Labriola's lectures in moral
philosophy, he met a kind teacher, father of three, who had lost a son to
diphtheria only a few years earlier. Croce was greatly impressed by
Labriola's lectures, which made him think about the theoretical questions
surrounding history and art. Croce had found not only a teacher but also a
surrogate father figure with whom he developed a strong, albeit rather
complex, intellectual, and personal connection.[5]

Labriola was trying to encourage Croce to take on more serious commitments with his studies – indeed, Croce never graduated – while the
latter was moving away from the theory of Marx after having published in
1895 an essay entitled *Intorno al comunismo di Tommaso Campanella* (*On
the Communism of Tommaso Campanella*), clearly under the influence of
his teacher.[6] It was indeed on the interpretation of Marxism that Labriola
and Croce diverged, precisely when Labriola was publishing his essays on
Marxism, in which the latter expounded his reading of historical materialism as a 'philosophy of praxis'. We have already discussed (Section 5.3)
how the term 'philosophy of praxis' is used by Labriola for the first time in
his third Marxist essay *Discorrendo di socialismo e filosofia* (*Conversing about
Socialism and Philosophy*), published in 1898, where he proposes an anti-
theological reading of Marx, one that would define the historical reality of
ideas.[7] It is, however, in Labriola's fourth and last essay *Da un secolo
all'altro* (*From one Century to the Next*), written between 1897 and 1903
and published posthumously by Croce, that the author substituted the
term 'philosophy of praxis' for 'historical materialism'.

Labriola's socialism, as we have seen in Chapter 5, overturns the
Hegelian dialectic because the philosophy of praxis maintained that it is
only through human activity that we can gain knowledge ('conoscere

---

[4] Benedetto Croce, *Memorie della mia vita* (Naples: Istituto Italiano per gli Studi Storici, 1992), p. 17.
[5] On this relationship, see Marcello Mustè, *Marxism and Philosophy of Praxis: An Italian Perspective
from Labriola to Gramsci* (Bristol: Palgrave, 2021), pp. 47–60.
[6] Benedetto Croce, 'Intorno al comunismo di Tommaso Campanella', *Archivio storico per le province
napoletane*, 1895: 598–645.
[7] A. Labriola, *Discorrendo di socialismo e filosofia*, p. 667.

operando'), history being the progress of this knowledge acquired through human actions that therefore modify material relationships. According to Croce, conversely, Marxism had no philosophy: he dismissed the philosophy of praxis as 'a curious chapter in the history of philosophy', which seemed to him 'a condiment, and not ... a good condiment, to his [Marx's] thought'.[8] Historical materialism was also at the centre of Croce's discussions with Giovanni Gentile, with whom he had started corresponding in June 1896, when Croce had indeed returned to Naples and moved into Filomarino Palace, the same house in which Giambattista Vico had worked as a tutor more than two centuries earlier.

Gentile grew up in Sicily and in 1893 was admitted to the Scuola Normale Superiore in Pisa where his philosophy professor was Donato Jaja (1839–1914). The latter considered himself a student of Bertrando Spaventa and had built with the master a close relationship while teaching at the Liceo Antonio Genovesi in Naples (1879–1887). Their almost daily conversations carried on until Spaventa's death in 1883. Their intellectual exchanges coincided with the period in which Spaventa was working on the connections between experience and metaphysics (see Section 5.3). This influence manifested itself in Jaja's essay *Sentire e Pensare* (*Feeling and Thinking*, 1886), in which there emerge methodological questions regarding the gnoseological problem of integrating Kant's a priori so as to reform Hegel's dialectic.[9] It was indeed Jaja who took on the task of editing Spaventa's last work, *Esperienza e Metafisica* (*Experience and Metaphysics*), published posthumously in 1888. Jaja started his lectureship at the Normale in Pisa six years before Gentile was admitted. The Sicilian philosopher for his part would always acknowledge his debt towards Jaja's teaching in orienting his gnoseological interests around the possibility of knowledge of nature within the activity of Spirit.[10]

Jaja was especially important in introducing Gentile to Hegel's philosophy and Spaventa's interpretation of Hegelianism, being therefore a major influence in shaping his theory of the absolute immanence of Spirit (the theory of the Pure Act), which he would go on to formulate in his later

---

[8] B. Croce and G. Gentile, *Carteggio*, vol.1, 1896–1900, ed. C. Castellani and C. Cassani (Turin: Aragno, 2014), pp. 268, 264.

[9] Donato Jaja, *Sentire e pensare: l'idealismo nuovo e la realtà* (Naples: Tipografia Regia Università, 1886).

[10] Giovanni Gentile, 'L'esperienza pura e la realtà storica', *La Voce* (Florence, 1915), pp. 5–39. See also Giovanni Gentile, 'Donato Jaja', *Annuario della Regia Università di Pisa 1914–1915* (Pisa: Toscano, 1915), pp. 1–16. On the relationship between Jaja and Gentile, see Annalisa Passoni, 'Donato Jaja nella formazione di Giovanni Gentile: il problema del metodo tra critica gnoseologica e deduzione metafisica', *Rivista di storia della filosofia*, 55, no. 2, 2000: 205–228.

work *Atto del pensare come atto puro* (*The Act of Thinking as Pure Act*, 1912). Gentile was therefore very familiar with Hegelianism when he received Labriola's essay from Croce in February 1898 and recognised the importance of the idea that 'within historical materialism is unfolded an authentic philosophy, the philosophy of praxis'.[11] His reading of Labriola's essay led Gentile to study systematically the philosophy of Bertrando Spaventa, whose works he began to publish in 1900, starting with his *Scritti filosofici* (*Philosophical Writings*), and continuing to do so up until 1925.[12] Gentile believed that Labriola's philosophy of praxis was connected to his Hegelian education at the school of Spaventa. This course of study led to the publication of Gentile's *La filosofia di Marx* (*The Philosophy of Marx*) in 1899 and around the same time he published the intellectual biography of *Bertrando Spaventa*, then revised in 1920.[13]

Gentile agreed with Labriola and disagreed with Croce: he shared the analytical premises of Labriola – that historical materialism rests upon a philosophy of praxis – though not his conclusions. Differently from Labriola – who believed that the dialectic had to be understood from the observation of historical (objective) reality – Gentile was persuaded that the dialectic, being rational, could not be part of the phenomenic reality but rather that it was a universal and necessary determination of Spirit: each interpretation of history is not the product of history itself but rather of the thinking that determines history. Croce, on the contrary, seemed to not agree that Labriola's philosophy of praxis had resulted from the mediation of Marxism with the Hegelianism of the Southern Italian philosophers (Spaventa in particular).

Gentile was largely reading Marx through the lens of Spaventa's reform of the Hegelian dialectic and the assumption that philosophy is both the condition of possibility of experience and its completion. In this interpretation, knowledge is possible because ideas are immanent in the experience. Gentile maintained that Marxism is the 'praxis that overturns itself', meaning that individuals recognise themselves in their own social product, which they continuously overcome:

---

[11] Croce and Gentile, *Carteggio*, vol.1, p. 85.

[12] Bertrnado Spaventa's works edited by Giovanni Gentile in different journals and with different presses were then all collected and published by Italo Cubeddu in three volumes: Bertrando Spaventa, *Opere* (Florence: Sansoni, 1972). These were then republished as a single volume edited by Francesco Valagussa: Bertrando Spaventa, *Opere* (Milan: Bompiani, 2009).

[13] Giovanni Gentile, *La filosofia di Marx* (Pisa: Spoerri, 1899). Giovanni Gentile, *Bertrando Spaventa* (Naples: Morano, 1900), now in Bertrando Spaventa, *Opere* (Florence: Sansoni, 1972), pp. 3–170. For a more recent intellectual biography of Spaventa, see Fernanda Gallo, *Dalla patria allo Stato: Bertrando Spaventa, una biografia intellettuale* (Bari: Laterza, 2013).

Practice, which had the subject as starting point and the object as end point, is overturned, returning from the object (starting point) to the subject (end point). And so Marx noted that the coincidence of the changing of circumstances and human activity can be conceived as practice that overturns [itself].[14]

In this interpretation of the dialectic, Gentile proposes the synthesis as 'the subject modified by circumstances and education'.[15] There is a clear influence of the essential features of Spaventa's reform of Hegel's dialectic to engage with the interpretation of Marx's idea of praxis. This approach insists on the early Hegelian education of Marx and is central to understanding the different interpretations of Marxism offered by Croce and Gentile. While Croce and Gentile both diverged from Labriola, they also diverged from each other and went their separate ways regarding their conclusions on Marxism, and the central ideas developed through these reflections, which would form the essence of their philosophical systems soon to emerge: Croce's Absolute Historicism (or Spiritualism) and Gentile's Actualism.[16]

Croce believed it possible to identify an intrinsic rationality according to which history unfolds and therefore to establish that history is the history of the development of Spirit. From his dialogue with Labriola and Gentile on Marxism, Croce derives the key category of his philosophy of Spirit: the 'Useful' (*utile-economico*), which characterises the economic aspect of Spirit. In his 1909 *La filosofia della pratica: economica ed etica*, he maintains that practical acts, which belong to the realm of the pure concepts of 'the Useful' and 'the Good', are performed by humans for their utility and that through their historical dialectical development they will be proved to be good. This means that it is the politicians who have to evaluate economic viability while the ethical dimension lies in the judgement of history.[17] According to Gramsci, despite Croce's criticism of the philosophy of praxis, his philosophy of the absolute spirit was the speculative transcription of it: 'Croce was a philosopher of praxis without knowing it.'[18] From these same conversations, Gentile, instead, developed, as we have seen, the

---

[14] Giovanni Gentile, *La filosofia di Marx*, p. 85.   [15] Giovanni Gentile, *La filosofia di Marx*, p. 85.

[16] On this comparison see the recent work by Michele Ciliberto, *Croce e Gentile. Biografia, Filosofia* (Pisa: Edizioni della Normale, 2021).

[17] The *giudizio storico* (historical judjment) is a key concept in Croce's philosophy: on this, see Raffaello Franchini, *La teoria della storia di Benedetto Croce* (Naples: Morano, 1966); more recently Maria Giacobello, 'Una questione di Giudizio (breve nota su Benedetto Croce e Hannah Arendt)', *Diacritica*, 13, 2017: 63–74.

[18] Antonio Gramsci, *Quaderni del carcere* (Turin: Einaudi, 1975), vol. 2, p. 1298 (Q10, 20).

interpretation of Marxism as the 'overturning of praxis', an interpretation that later would deeply influence Gramsci.[19]

Antonio Gramsci grew up in Sardinia and moved from his little village to Cagliari in order to study at the Liceo there. He then moved to Turin to attend the University in 1911, when the city – once the capital of the old Kingdom of Piedmont-Sardinia – was celebrating the fiftieth anniversary of Italian unification. Given his humble origins, Gramsci had had to work since boyhood to help his family and by the same token had a hard time as a student when in Turin. After deciding not to complete his degree, in 1915, he started to work as a journalist and was then directly involved in the workers' struggles during the 'Biennio Rosso' (The Two Red Years, 1919–1920), living in one of the most industrialised cities on the Peninsula. He was one of the founders of the Italian Communist Party (PCI) in 1921 and its leader from 1924 to 1927.[20] Following his arrest on the 8th of November 1926, Gramsci was only able to begin composing his *Prison Notebooks* in February 1929, when he was finally granted permission to write in his cell.[21] This solitary work continued up to mid-1935 with over two thousand handwritten notes collected across thirty-three notebooks. For the purposes of this discussion, the most relevant parts of the notebooks are the essay on *Materialismo e Idealismo* (*Materialism and Idealism*, May 1932) and the preceding three series of *Note sulla filosofia* (*Notes on Philosophy*) which appear in Notebook 4 (§§ 1–48), written in May 1930, Notebook 7 (§§ 1–48), written between November 1930 and November 1931, and Notebook 8 (§§ 166–240), concluded in May 1932, where Gramsci regularly uses the term 'philosophy of praxis' in place of 'historical materialism.'[22]

---

[19] On the influence of Gentile on Italian Marxism, see Marcello Mustè, 'Gentile e Marx', *Giornale Critico della Filosofia Italiana*, XCIV, no. 1, 2015: 15–27; Marcello Mustè, 'Le note su Croce e la genesi del Quaderno 10', in *G. Francioni F. Giasi, Nuovo Gramsci: Biografia, temi, interpretazioni* (Rome: Viella, 2020), pp. 301–321.

[20] On Gramsci's time at university see Angelo D'Orsi, 'Lo Studente Che Non Divenne "Dottore". Gramsci all'Università di Torino', *Studi Storici*, 40, no. 1, 1999: 39–75.

[21] A first partial selection of the *Prison Notebooks* was published in 1948 by Felice Platone and Palmiro Togliatti but the first complete critical edition edited by Valentino Gerratana wass published in 1975: Antonio Gramsci, *Quaderni dal carcere* (Turin: Einaudi, 1975). A partial critical edition in English of the *Prison Notebooks* edited by Joseph Buttigieg appeared in 1992 (Vol. I) and 1996 (Vol II) published by Columbia University Press.

[22] These three series have only quite recently been dated with more accuracy thanks to a renewal of Gramscian studies. On this, see G. Vacca, *Alternative Modernities. Antonio Gramsci's Twentieth Century* (Palgrave Macmillan: Cham, 2021); G. Liguori, *Gramsci conteso. Interpretazioni, dibattiti e polemiche (1922–2012)* (Rome: Editori Riuniti University Press, 2012) – English translation: Guido Liguori, *Gramsci Contested: Interpretations, Debates, and Polemics, 1922–2012* (Leiden: Brill, 2022); G. Francioni, *Un labirinto di carta (Introduzione alla filologia gramsciana)*, pp. 7–48.

In the *Notes on Philosophy* Gramsci defines praxis as the 'relation between human will (superstructure) and the economic structure'.[23] This definition is the product of a long reflection on Labriola's Marxist essays, which he had begun in the early 1920s. His study of those essays led to an independent re-elaboration of Labriola's philosophy of praxis, which is here developed into a new approach to Marxism.[24] As important an influence as that of Croce and Gentile, Labriola's essays had shaped Gramsci's early political and theoretical education, the latter maintaining that 'it is necessary to bring Labriola back into circulation and to make his way of posing the philosophical problem predominant'.[25] Labriola presented to Gramsci a Marx who had 'a personality in which theoretical and practical activity are indissolubly intertwined'.[26] Marxism was therefore an autonomous philosophy and Labriola's interpretation had granted Italians a privileged access to Marx's philosophy.

Gramsci's engagement with Labriola focused on the essential core of the philosophy of praxis: the reform of the Hegelian dialectic and Marx's relationship with Hegel. Initially Gramsci's understanding was mediated by Croce and Gentile's interpretations: while Croce scaled down Hegel's influence on Marx, Gentile attributed the revolutionary core of the 'overturned praxis' to Hegel's dialectic. In opposition to Croce's interpretation, Gramsci believed that 'historical materialism is a reform and a development of Hegelianism'.[27] This Hegelian foundation of Marx's philosophy would be highlighted even more in the early 1930s, when Gramsci came to emphasise the Hegelian notion of civil society and the important role that 'Hegel ascribed to the intellectuals'.[28] He believed that Hegel had been the philosopher able to combine materialism and idealism and that Marx had reinstated 'this unity' after 'Hegel's successors destroyed ... [it], returning to the old materialism with Feuerbach'.[29] Gramsci insisted that a proper understanding of historical materialism entailed placing more emphasis 'on

---

[23] A. Gramsci, Quaderni del carcere, vol. 2, p. 868 (Q7§18; PN vol. 3, p. 170).

[24] Giuseppe Vacca recently noticed that the substitution of the expression 'philosophy of praxis' for 'historical materialism' 'went in parallel with a changed view of the fundamental problem underlying the "research program" of the Notebooks'. See G. Vacca, *Alternative Modernities*, p. 7.

[25] A. Gramsci, SPN, p. 388.

[26] A. Gramsci, Quaderni del carcere, vol. 1, p. 419 (Q4§1; PN vol. 2, p. 137).

[27] A. Gramsci, Quaderni del carcere, vol. 1, p. 471 (Q4§45; PN vol. 2, p. 196).

[28] A. Gramsci, Quaderni del carcere, vol. 2, p. 1054 (Q8§187; PN vol. 3, p. 343). On this, see N. Bobbio, 'Gramsci e la concezione della società civile', in *Gramsci e la cultura contemporanea*, ed. Pietro Rossi (Rome: Editori Riuniti, 1975), vol. I, pp. 75–100.

[29] A. Gramsci, Quaderni del carcere, vol. 1, p. 424 (Q4§3; PN vol. 2, p. 144).

the first word – Marx is fundamentally a "historicist"'.[30] It is indeed only after, and probably because of, the confrontation with Marx that the three Italian thinkers engaged directly with the philosophy of Hegel, and this engagement was crucial for the development of their own philosophical systems.

E.2   The Hegel-Renaissance

During the years between the nineteenth and the twentieth century, a resurgence of interest in the study of Hegel's philosophy was particularly influential in Germany, Great Britain, the United States of America, and in Italy, where this philosophical movement was defined as neo-idealism, or neo-Hegelianism, and traditionally identified with the philosophies of Croce and Gentile. Gentile himself, in a long review of a book by the Scottish scholar James B. Baillie (*The Origin and Significance of Hegel's Logic: A General Introduction to Hegel's System*, 1901), used the term *risurrezione* (resurrection) to indicate this renewed interest in Hegel's philosophy across Europe and beyond.[31] Georges Noël in France had already drawn attention to a *renaissance de l'hégélianisme* in his *La logique de Hegel* (1897) when discussing recent works published by British scholars.[32] In the same journal and the same year in which Gentile had published his review, Croce wrote a note entitled *Are We Hegelians?* (1904), in which the Neapolitan philosopher was expressing his new interest in studying Hegel's philosophy while at the same time distancing himself from the metaphysical interpretations that were at the heart of this renaissance.[33] In this pamphlet, Croce warned Italian intellectuals against engaging with Hegel's philosophy in terms of loyalty to his school, as had happened in Germany, but rather to insist on the great discovery of Hegel – the dialectic.

Indeed, the definition of Gentile and Croce as neo-Hegelians or neo-idealists loses accuracy the more we study and analyse their intellectual production, in particular with regard to Croce. Despite the scholarly consensus that this label is problematic, it seems quite clear that both

---

[30] A. Gramsci, Quaderni del carcere, vol. 1, p. 433 (Q4§11; PN vol. 2, p. 154).

[31] Giovanni Gentile, '"The Origin and Significance of Hegel's Logic" di James Black Baillie', *La Critica*, 2, 1904: 29–45.

[32] Among these British scholars, see John G. Hibben (*Hegel's Logic: An Essay in Interpretation* [New York: Scribner,1902]; it. trad. 1910), Robert Mackintosh (*Hegel and Hegelianism* [New York: Scribner, 1903]), Edward Caird (*Hegel* [Edinbrough: Blackwod, 1883]; it. trad. 1911).

[33] B. Croce, 'Siamo noi Hegeliani?', *La Critica*, 2, 1904: 261–264.

authors were grappling intellectually with the problem of the reform of the Hegelian dialectic and that they dedicated a large part of their philosophical work to Hegel's philosophy. Croce translated Hegel's *Encyclopedia* into Italian in 1905 and the year after published *What Is living and What Is Dead of the Philosophy of Hegel*, modifying the structure of his own system after close study of Hegel's philosophy.[34] The works of Croce and Gentile are part and parcel of that general movement known as the Hegel-Renaissance, which was spearheaded by the more influential German works by Wilhem Dilthey, Herman Nohl, and Wilhelm Windelband, who sought to relegate Hegel's system of logic to the margins of his philosophy.[35]

Croce's critique of Hegel's 'system' led him to oppose Hegel's 'pan-logicism', the theory of the 'Distincts' (see Section 4.3), according to which there are 'differences' among the categories of Spirit, rather than the 'oppositions' posited by Hegel. The dialectical process unfolds within each of the four categories, 'distinti' – beauty, truth, *utile* (useful), good – rather than between them, distinguishing therefore four forms of the life of Spirit in its historical reality: aesthetics, logic, economics, and ethics. The revision of Croce's philosophy of Spirit in the light of a closer engagement with Hegel is evident in his *Filosofia della pratica* (1909) and in the *Logica come scienza del concetto puro* (1909), in which he identifies the individual and historical judgement as the main theoretical act – which is the synthesis a priori of intuition and concept. This dialogue with Hegel is very central until his *Teoria e storia della storiografia* (1917), in which he maintained his theory of the contemporaneity of history and the identity of philosophy and historiography, where he therefore theorises his historicism.

Despite the influence of Hegel on Croce's system, the latter refused to be defined as neo-Hegelian and confessed how through his engagement with Hegel he had sought to present his philosophy of Spirit as a 'total subversion of Hegelianism'.[36] He criticised in particular Hegel's philosophy of nature and his philosophy of history, maintaining that only Spirit is

---

[34] On this, see Giulia Battistoni, 'Coscienza europea e modernità: Hegel e Croce, filosofi della libertà', *Archivio di filosofia*, XC, no. 1, 2022: 233–244.

[35] Wilhem Dilthey, *Die Jugendgeschichte Hegels* (Berlin: Verlag der Königlichen Akademie der Wissenschaften, 1905); Herman Nohl (ed.), *Hegels theologische Jugendschriften* (Tübingen: J. C. B. Mohr, 1907); Wilhelm Windelband, 'Die Erneuerung des Hegelianismus' (1910), in *Präludien: Aufsätze und Reden zur Philosophie und Ihrer Geschichte*, 2 vols (Tübingen: Mohr, 1915), vol. 1, pp. 273–289. On the Hegel-Renaissance, see the recent publication by Richard Bourke, *Hegel's World Revolutions* (Princeton: Princeton University Press, 2023), pp. 191–288.

[36] Benedetto Croce, *Contributo alla critica di me stesso*, in *Etica e politica*, pp. 345–389, 381.

real. However, he also had to admit that his own philosophy has in Hegel an 'ancestor' and that in studying Hegel 'I seemed to be immersing myself in myself and to be debating with my own conscience'.[37]

Gentile began his direct engagement with Hegel's philosophy around the same time as Croce, and they were then at pains to maintain a dialogue. The confrontation with Hegel's philosophy became still more important to Gentile when he was constructing his actualism with the essays on *L'atto del pensare come atto puro* (1911) and *La riforma della dialettica hegeliana* (1912). He believed that Hegel's famous formula 'the rational is actual, and the actual is rational' did not resolve the dualism between thinking and being. He suggested that the Hegelian dialectic should be conceived within the act of thinking and that there were infinite categories – not only four, as Croce believed – flowing from the originating act of thinking. Moreover, the concept of praxis developed by Hegel in the *Phenomenology of Spirit*, presupposed that 'thinking' is the creative activity of the object. Human activity should therefore move from the realm of philosophy to that of action.[38] This was work preparatory to Gentile's actualism, which he clearly theorised in his later *Teoria generale dello spirito come atto puro* (1916) and in his *Sistema di logica* (1922).[39] Gentile's actualism is indeed the product of his interpretation of Hegel. According to Hegel, the rationality of Spirit is only given by virtue of its unfolding in the dialectical process and its different moments. Gentile instead believed that Spirit is rational independently of the moments of its unfolding but within itself and its internal dialectical process, within its own act of thinking – therefore, Actualism.

Just as for Croce and Gentile, so too in Gramsci's case, his approach to Marx was influenced by his study of the Hegelian dialectic, which he believed offered the best solution to the problem of combining materialism and idealism. Gramsci placed his reflections within the broader debate between Croce and Gentile regarding the reform of the dialectic. In Notebook 10, he thus maintained that Croce proposed a 'domesticated dialectic because it "mechanically" presupposes that the antithesis should be preserved by the thesis in order not to destroy the dialectical process . . .. In real history, though, the antithesis tends to destroy the thesis'.[40] Gramsci argued that, looking at the processes in 'real history', the

[37] Benedetto Croce, *Contributo alla critica di me stesso*, in *Etica e politica*, pp. 345–389, 380, and 382.
[38] Giovanni Gentile, *La filosofia di Marx* (Pisa: Enrico Spoerri, 1899), p. 58.
[39] On this, see Alba Arcuri, 'L'esperienza hegeliana nella filosofia di Giovanni Gentile', *Idee*, 24, 1993: 111–123.
[40] A. Gramsci, *Quaderni del carcere*, vol. 1, p. 1083 (Q8§225; PN vol. 3, p. 372).

dialectical synthesis is the outcome of a real struggle, in which positive and negative compete even though having equal value and energy. Therefore, in Gramsci, the dialectic represents the concrete political struggle and he hoped, with the philosophy of praxis, to restore the revolutionary and historical dimension of the dialectic.

Croce, Gentile, and Gramsci all engaged with the Hegelian dialectic through the lens of Labriola's interpretation of Marxism as a philosophy of praxis, presenting, however, three very different philosophical interpretations. Their philosophical disagreement had never interrupted their conversations. It was instead Croce and Gentile's political disagreement about the new political force emerging, the Fascist National Party, that actually blocked their dialogue. Here we argue that their different political stances derived mainly from their differing interpretations of the Italian historical past, and in particular of the Risorgimento, and that the rise to power of Fascism led them all to rethink also their philosophical systems.

E.3   The Rise of Fascism

The rise of fascism marked a division in the interpretation of the weaknesses and strengths of the unification process and of the groups involved in its implementation. Gentile's justification of Fascism was based on the idea that it represented the 'moral force' of the 'ethical State' that would achieve consensus through its coercive actions. We have already discussed how Gentile and Croce went their separate ways, ceasing their collaboration after 1924 for both philosophical and political reasons. We have also described Croce's opposition to Fascism after this date (Section 4.3). Indeed, Croce in his 1928 *History of Italy from 1871 to 1915* and Gramsci in his *Prison Notebooks* mounted a similar challenge to Gentile's interpretation of the relationship between force and consensus, politics and ethics, highlighting instead how the rise of Fascism proved the lack of moral will among Italians and investigating the weaknesses of the liberal elite of the Risorgimento.[41] This historical understanding aimed at presenting two different political programmes, a liberal and a socialist one, that could indicate a direction for political action in their own time. Despite their differences, both Croce and Gramsci believed that the

---

[41] Benedetto Croce, *Storia d'Italia dal 1871 al 1915* (Bari: Laterza, 1928); Antonio Gramsci, *Quaderni del carcere*, ed. V. Gerratana, 4 vols. (Turin: Einaudi, 1975). For a wider discussion of the role of Gentile, Croce, and Gramsci in the development of the historiography of the Risorgimento, see Lucy Riall, *Il Risorgimento: Storia e interpretazioni* (Rome: Donzelli, 2007), pp. 33–48.

intellectual class was incapable of acting as mediators between the 'real' and the 'ideal' Italy and realising the aspirations of the Risorgimento. Gentile, on the contrary, held that the Risorgimento was the foundational event of the nation and that the process of realisation of the nation would be accomplished by the fascist state.[42]

The polemic between Croce and Gentile that developed around 1913 regarding the unity and/or distinction of Spirit was clearly related to their interpretation of Hegel's philosophy and the influence that nineteenth-century Italian Hegelianism had on their engagement with the German philosopher. This philosophical disagreement was soon exacerbated by politically more divisive tensions when World War I broke out and later with the rise of fascism. It was indeed World War I that destroyed, Croce believed, the Italian parliamentary system, facilitating therefore the rise to power of fascism. The latter is presented as an aberration resulting from World War I, whose ideals were in antithesis with liberalism.[43] Gentile instead believed that fascism represented the realisation of the nation built during the Risorgimento.

The rupture between Croce and Gentile was mainly political and it was the outcome of the opposite political choices they had made between 1922 and 1925. In 1923, Gentile joined the Fascist Party, accepting from Mussolini a membership *ad honorem*, acquiring a very important role within the regime as Chair of the Committee for the reform of the Italian Constitution, the Statuto Albertino, and as President of the National Institute of Fascist Culture (Istituto Nazionale Fascista di Cultura), being the scientific director of the Italian Encyclopedia (*Enciclopedia Italiana*). By contrast, Croce's political opposition to Fascism came to fruition between 1922 and 1924 and this realisation also affected his philosophical system.[44]

For instance, before 1924, Croce had separated politics from ethics and, as we have seen, in his 1909 *La filosofia della pratica: economica ed etica*, he claimed that the evaluation of political action in ethical terms lay with the judgement of history. In 1925, however, he rethought his theory of liberalism and then developed an ethico-political theory of history – most

---

[42] R. Dainotto, '"Tramonto" and "Risorgimento": Gentile's Dialectics and the Prophecy of Nationhood', in *Making and Remaking Italy: The Cultivation of National Identity around the Risorgimento*, ed. A. R. Ascoli and K. von Henneberg (Oxford: Oxford University Press, 2001), pp. 241–255.

[43] Federico Chabod, 'Croce storico', *Rivista Storica Italiana*, 64, 1952: 473–530.

[44] For Croce's criticism of fascism, see Benedetto Croce, *Pagine Sparse* (Bari: Laterza, 1943), vol. II, pp. 371–406. See also Richard Bellamy, 'Liberalism and Historicism: Benedetto Croce and the Political Role of Idealism in Italy', in *The Promise of History: Essays in Political Philosophy*, ed. A. Moulakis (Berlin; New York: De Gruyter, 1985), pp. 69–119.

of these writings are collected in his *Etica e politica* (1931). According to Croce, 'history is a never-ending struggle to realise human freedom through the transformation of the world and the creation of the institutions and artefacts of human society'.[45] Although ethics is distinguished from economics, they are in practice inseparable. With the revision of his liberalism, Croce in his *Storia come pensiero e come azione* (1938) attributes more importance to the ethical dimension of Spirit, which is a 'unifying force' with primacy over the other categories of Spirit: liberty and ethics become one and the same, and in Croce's absolute historicism, history becomes the history of liberty as clarified by his historical works *Storia del Regno di Napoli* (1925), *Storia d'Italia dal 1871 al 1915* (1928), *Storia dell'eta' barocca in Italia* (1929), *Storia d'Europa nel secolo decimonono* (1932).

Gramsci's fierce opposition to fascism resulted in his incarceration by the regime in 1926. At twenty years of age, he had already maintained in his journal *Ordine Nuovo* that liberal institutions were facilitating the affirmation of fascist violence.[46] A few years later, together with Togliatti, in the *Tesi di Lione* (1926), they denounced the objectives of fascism: to realise an organic unity of the different forces of the bourgeoisie under the control of a single central force that would direct the party, the government, and the State.[47] While in prison, Gramsci's understanding of fascism developed together with its transformation into a consolidated dictatorship in charge of the State and the institutions. This led to his understanding of Fascism as a 'passive revolution'.

It is interesting to note that the concept of 'passive revolution' was borrowed from Vincenzo Cuoco, who had used it in his *Saggio storico sulla rivoluzione napoletana del 1799* (1801) to describe the Neapolitan revolution of 1799 and explain its failure (see Chapter 1). Cuoco's theory of 'the two peoples' described a dichotomy between the lower class, socially and culturally poor, and the upper class, socially and intellectually rich: on one side, the 'people-nation' and, on the other side, the people in charge of the political organisation of the State. The revolution fails when the latter is unable to translate ideas into 'actual reality', thereby creating the conditions for the first kind of people to develop and participate in political life.

---

[45] Richard Bellamy 'Between Economic and Ethical Liberalism: Benedetto Croce and the Dilemmas of Liberal Politics', *History of the Human Sciences*, 4, no. 2, 1991:175–195, 185.

[46] Antonio Gramsci, *Socialisti e fascisti*, in 'L'Ordine Nuovo', 11 June 1921, now in Socialismo e fascismo, p. 186.

[47] See 'La situazione italiana e i compiti del Pci, tesi approvate al Terzo Congresso del Partito comunista italiano', in Antonio Gramsci, *La costruzione del partito comunista 1923–1926* (Turin: Einaudi, 1971), p. 495.

At first, Gramsci used this analytic category to describe the Risorgimento: the moderate liberals had created a State that responded to the needs of the Northern bourgeoise without involving the peasantry and the wider society, especially in the South, opening that chasm between the liberal State and civil society that had later facilitated the affirmation of fascism. 'Passive revolution' therefore indicates a political change that is led by the liberal bourgeoisie and that does not involve the popular classes.

While Gramsci observes the changing nature of fascism, especially in the early 1930s after the Lateran Treaty (1929) and the growing prestige enjoyed by the regime abroad, he understands that it is no longer only a repressive force but is also an agent of social and economic change in Italian society. He therefore adapts this idea of 'passive revolution' and of hegemony to the understanding of fascism, although in a different guise: it describes a political change in which power shifts from one group to another within the same hegemonic class, rather than from one hegemonic class (the nobility) to a new hegemonic class (the bourgeoisie). It identifies the novel approach of the fascist regime which places side by side repression and State intervention in the economic and social structures of the country:

> There would be a passive revolution inasmuch as by way of the legislative intervention of the State and through the corporative organization, more or less [great] modifications in the economic structure of the country would come to be introduced ... without therefore touching (or only limiting itself to regulating and controlling) the individual and group appropriation of profit.[48]

While Gramsci identified several connections between liberalism and fascism, Croce, on the contrary, defended the achievements of Italian liberalism. The representatives of the Historic Right, among them his uncles Bertrando and Silvio Spaventa, were described by Croce as gentlemen: 'A spiritual aristocracy, men of honour and fully trustworthy gentlemen.'[49] He actually attributed the failures of the liberal State to their successors as well as to the very difficult economic, social, and diplomatic conditions that Italian political leaders had had to face after unification. The rise to power of fascism therefore influenced and shaped the political thought of Croce, Gentile, and Gramsci. Although their political choices were not a consequence of their philosophical systems – strongly influenced by Hegel's philosophy as they were – they did have an impact on how they recast their political thought.

---

[48] Antonio Gramsci, *Prison Notebooks* (*Q 10, 9, 1228*).   [49] Croce, *Storia d'Italia*, p. 5.

When making their political choices, they did instead seek guidance in their interpretations of Italian history, and in particular of the Risorgimento. As we have seen, they were all very familiar with the philosophical debates that characterised the Risorgimento and reinterpreted the philosophies of Marx and Hegel through the mediation of nineteenth-century Italian Hegelians. It was Spaventa, De Sanctis, Fiorentino, Florenzi Waddington, Villari, Labriola, more than Hegel, Feuerbach, Marx, or Bauer that contributed to the development of these three major philosophical projects that have dominated twentieth-century Italian political thought and had a profound influence in Europe.

Like their predecessors, Croce, Gentile, and Gramsci engaged directly and actively in politics, acquiring leadership roles in the different parts of the political spectrum: whereas Gentile was in charge of the cultural and educational policies of the Fascist regime, Gramsci was one of the founders of the Italian Communist Party (Partito Comunista Italiano) and its leader up until his incarceration, and Croce was one of the founders of the Italian Liberal Party (Partito Liberale Italiano) and its leader from 1944 to 1947. In the same way as their nineteenth-century predecessors, they were Southern Italian philosophers wrestling with Hegel's dialectic, his logic, and his political thought, while thinking about the reconciliation of Idealism and Materialism, dedicating the same effort to reflections around the relationship between State and society, politics and ethics, history and philosophy, practice and ideas. A subversive reading of Hegel's philosophy effected at the margins of Europe shaped Italian political thought, intertwining philosophy, historiography, and politics as it had done since the 1830s.

What Italian Hegelians had established was that an intellectual amalgamation of foreign and local traditions of thought may provide a critical understanding of a body of political thought and often leads to outcomes that bear scant similarity with the original. Italian Hegelianism was shaped by a 'practical' understanding of Hegel's philosophy, where practical has a twofold meaning: it insists on the historical, ethical, and political dimension of Hegel's metaphysics and it attempts to realise Hegelian political ideas in the practice of political life. Moving beyond the classical division in Hegelian scholarship between a metaphysical or non-metaphysical understanding of Hegel, nineteenth-century Italian Hegelians reinterpreted Hegel's categories of logic in a historical and phenomenological perspective, rendering both aspects relevant to the understanding of modern historical times: not only the *Phenomenology* (1807), the *Elements of the Philosophy of Right* (1820), or the *Lectures on the Philosophy of History* (1822, 1828, 1830), but also the *Science of Logic*

(1816) and the *Encyclopedia of the Philosophical Sciences* (1817) become crucial to the understanding of Hegel's political thought. However, those ideas are valuable only insofar as they can and must turn into reality: the Italian Hegelians' direct engagement with political action is the by-product of this conviction. This critical approach will be passed on to the Italian Hegelians' most cherished pupil, the founder of Italian Marxism, Antonio Labriola, and will persist as a trait of Italian engagement with Marx's political thought in Croce, Gentile, and Gramsci. In nineteenth-century Italian political thought, philosophical knowledge acquires a "practical" dimension: if ideas are powerful because they unfold in the historical and political world and interact with it in a mutual relationship, then philosophy has a concrete dimension. Poor times shape poor ideas, great ideas shape great times.

Bibliography

Primary Sources

Balbo, Cesare, *Della storia d'Italia dalle origini fino ai nostri tempi. Sommario*, edited by Giuseppe Talamo (Milan: Giuffré, 1962).

Belgiojoso, Cristina, *Essai sur Vico* (Milan: Turati, 1844).

Burckhardt, Jacob, *Die Kultur der Renaissance in Italien* (Basel: Schweighauser, 1860).

La civiltà del Rinascimento in Italia, con aggiunte e correzioni inedite fornite dall'autore, translated by Domenico Valbusa (Florence: Sansoni, 1876).

Caird, Edward, *Hegel* (Edinbrugh: Blackwod, 1883; it. trad. 1911).

Cattaneo, Carlo, *Opere edite e inedite*, vol. V, edited by Agostino Bertani (Florence: Le Monnier, 1881).

Scritti filosofici, letterari e vari di Cattaneo, edited by Franco Alessio (Sansoni, Florence, 1963).

'Ugo Foscolo e l'Italia', in *Scritti letterari*, vol. I (Florence: Treves, 1981), p. 536.

Psychology of the Associated Minds, edited by Barbara Boneschi (Milan: EGEA, 2019).

Colecchi, Ottavio, 'Se la sola analisi sia un mezzo d'invenzione, o s'inventi con la sintesi ancora', *Progresso*, XIV, 1836: 213–228.

'Sull'analisi e sulla sintesi teorica di Vittorio Cousin. Suo esame', *Il Progresso*, XVII, 1837: 190–191.

'Della legge morale', *Il Progresso delle scienze lettere ed arti*, XXIV, no. 47, 1839: 5–27, now in O. Colecchi, *Questioni filosofiche* (Naples: Procaccini, 1980), II, p. 70.

'Sopra alcune questioni le più importanti della filosofia. Osservazioni critiche', Naples, 1843.

'Saggio sul nostro metodo di filosofare', in *Questioni filosofiche* (Naples: Procaccini, 1980), III, pp. 127–129.

Cousin, Vittorio, 'Corrispondenza inedita di Vittorio Cousin con la marchesa Florenzi Waddington', *La Rivista Europea*, I, 1870: 493–498.

Croce, Benedetto, 'Intorno al comunismo di Tommaso Campanella', in *Materialismo storico e economia marxista* (Bari: Laterza, 1968), pp. 165–201.

Estetica come scienza dell'espressione e linguistica generale (Bari: Laterza, 1902).

'Siamo noi Hegeliani?', *La Critica*, 2, 1904: 261–264.

Ciò che è vivo e ciò che è morto della filosofia di Hegel (Bari: Laterza, 1906), now in Benedetto Croce, *Saggio sullo Hegel* (Naples: Bibliopolis, 2006).

What Is living and What Is Dead of the Philosophy of Hegel, translated by Douglas Ainslie (London: Macmillan, 1915).

'Introduction', in *Teoria e storia della letteratura: Lezioni tenute in Napoli dal 1839 al 1848*, vol. I, edited by F. De Sanctis (Bari: Laterza, 1926).

Storia d'Italia dal 1871 al 1915 (Bari: Laterza, 1928).

'Contributo alla critica di me stesso', in *Etica e politica* (Bari: Laterza, 1931), pp. 345–389.

Pagine Sparse (Bari: Laterza, 1943).

'La crisi italiana del Cinquecento e il legame del Rinascimento col Risorgimento', in *Poeti e scrittori del pieno e del tardo Rinascimento* (Bari: Laterza, 1958), pp. 1–16.

Storia d'Europa nel secolo decimonono (Bari: Laterza, [1932] 1972), pp. 7–21.

Memorie della mia vita (Naples: Istituto Italiano per gli Studi Storici, 1992).

'The Italian Crisis of the 1500s and the Link between the Renaissance and the Risorgimento', in *The Reaissance from an Italian Perspective: An Anthology of Essays, 1860–1968*, edited by Rocco Rubini (Ravenna: Longo Editore, 2014), pp. 161–170.

Croce, Benedetto, and Giovanni Gentile, *Carteggio*, vol. 1, 1896–1900, edited by C. Castellani and C. Cassani (Aragno: Torino, 2014).

Cuoco, Vincenzo, *Saggio storico sulla rivoluzione di Napoli*, edited by Antonino de Francesco (Rome: Laterza, 2014).

Cusani, Stefano, 'Del metodo filosofico e d'una suo storia infino agli ultimi sistemi di filosofia che sono veduti uscir fuori in Germania ed in Francia', *Il Progresso delle scienze lettere ed arti*, XXII, 1839: 175–216.

'Del reale obietto d'ogni filosofia e del solo procedimento a poterlo raggiungere', *Il Progresso delle scienze lettere ed arti*, XXIII, 1839: 27–60.

'Della logica trascendentale', *Il Progresso delle scienze lettere ed arti*, XXVI, 1840: 161–187.

'Della Scienza fenomenologica o dello studio dei fatti di coscienza', *Il Progresso delle scienze lettere ed arti*, XXIV, no. 47, 1839: 28–83; XXV, 1840: 16–37, 187–205.

'Idea d'una storia compendiata della filosofia', *Il Progresso delle scienze lettere ed arti*, I, 1841: 113–135; II, 1842: 3–8, 97–120.

'Del modo di trattare la scienza degli esseri. Disegno di una metafisica', *Rivista napolitana*, III, no. 2, 1842: 21–22.

'Della scienza assoluta' (discorso I), *Museo di letteratura e filosofia*, IV, 1842: 110–126.

D'Azeglio, Costanza, *Lettere al figlio (1829–1862)*, vol. II, edited by Maldini Chiarito (Rome: Istituto per la Storia del Risorgimento, 1996).

De Meis, Angelo Camillo, *Il Sovrano. Saggio di filosofia politica con riferenza all'Italia*, edited by B. Croce (Bari: Laterza, 1927).

De Sanctis, Francesco, 'Machiavelli. Conferenze', in *Saggi critici*, edited by L. Russo (Bari: Laterza, 1853), vol. II.

'Schopenhauer e Leopardi', *Rivista contemporanea*, XV, no. 61, 1858: 369–408.

Saggio critico sul Petrarca (Naples: Morano, 1869).

La Storia della letteratura italiana (Naples: Morano: 1870–1872).

Il darwinismo nell'arte (Naples: Classici Italiani, 1883).

La letteratura italiana nel secolo XIX. Scuola liberale – scuola democratica, edited by Benedetto Croce and Francesco Torraca (Naples: Morano, 1902).

Lettere da Zurigo a Diomede Marvasi (1856–1860), edited by Benedetto Croce (Naples: Ricciardi, 1913).

'Le lezioni sulla storia della critica', in *Teoria e storia della letteratura: Lezioni tenute in Napoli dal 1839 al 1848*, vol. II (Bari: Laterza, 1926), pp. 61–130.

'Lezioni sulla filosofia della storia e la storia', in *Teoria e storia della letteratura: Lezioni tenute in Napoli dal 1839 al 1848*, vol. II (Bari: Laterza, 1926), pp. 131–144.

Lettere dall'esilio (1853–1860) (Bari: G. Laterza & Figli, 1938).

'Ai miei giovani. Prolusione letta all'Istituto Politecnico di Zurigo', in *Saggi Critici*, vol. II, edited by Luigi Russo (Bari: Laterza, 1960), pp. 53–64.

Il Mezzogiorno e lo Stato unitario. Scritti e discorsi politici dal 1848 al 1870, edited by F. Ferri (Turin: Einaudi, 1960).

'Epistolario (1856–1858)', in *Opere*, edited by Giovanni Ferretti and Muzio Mazzocchi Alemanni, vol. XIX (Turin: Einaudi, 1965).

'Epistolario (1859–1860)', in *Opere*, edited by Giuseppe Talamo, vol. XX (Turin: Einaudi, 1965).

'Il principio del realismo', in *L'arte, la scienza e la vita*, edited by M. T. Lanza (Turin: Einaudi, [1876] 1969), pp. 342–349.

'L'uomo di Guicciardini', in *L'arte, la scienza e la vita*, edited by M. T. Lanza (Turin: Einaudi, 1969), pp. 93–117.

I partiti e l'educazione della nuova Italia. Scritti e discorsi dal 1871 al 1883, edited by N. Cortese (Turin: Einaudi, 1970).

'Conferenze su Niccolò Machiavelli', in *L'arte, la scienza e la vita* (Torino: Einaudi, [1869] 1972), pp. 34–92.

Il Mezzogiorno e lo Stato unitario (Turin: Einaudi, 1972).

'La scienza e la vita', in *Opere. L'arte, la scienza e la vita*, vol. XIV (Turin: Einaudi, 1972), pp. 316–340.

Saggi critici (Bari: Laterza, 1974).

'La giovinezza', in *Opere*, ed. Niccolò Gallo, vol. 56 (Rome: Riccardo Ricciardi, 2004).

Dilthey, Wilhem, *Die Jugendgeschichte Hegels* (Berlin: Verlag der Königlichen Akademie der Wissenschaften, 1905).

Ferrari, Giuseppe, *La mente di Giambattista Vico* (Milan: Società tipografica dei classici italiani, 1837).

'Le révolution et les réformes en Italie', *Revue des Deux Mondes*, 16, 1844: 573–614; 17, 1845: 150–194.

Filosofia della rivoluzione (Milan: Casa Editrice Sociale: 1921).

Fiorentino, Francesco, *Prolusione al corso di Storia della Filosofia, letta nella Regia Università di Bologna il 25 Novembre 1862* (Bologna: Vitali, 1863).

La filosofia contemporanea in Italia, risposta di Francesco Fiorentino al professore Francesco Acri (Naples: Morano, 1876).

Scritti varii di letteratura, filosofia e critica per Francesco Fiorentino (Naples: Morano, 1876).

'Lo Stato Moderno', *Giornale napoletano di filosofia e lettere, scienze morali e politiche*, 3, no. 26, 1876: 485–502.

'Bertrando Spaventa', in *Ritratti storici e saggi critici*, edited by Giovanni Gentile (Florence: Sansoni, 1935), pp. 299–311.

'L'educazione politica e l'università', in *Ritratti storici e saggi critici*, edited by Giovanni Gentile (Florence: Sansoni, 1935), pp. 50–64.

'Lo Stato moderno. Due lettere a Silvio Spaventa', in *Ritratti storici e saggi critici*, edited by Giovanni Gentile (Florence: Sansoni, 1935), pp. 36-44.

Manuale di storia della filosofia ad uso dei licei, 4 vols. (Naples: La scuola di Pitagora, 2007).

Il panteismo di Giordano Bruno (Naples: La Scuola di Pitagora, 2008).

'Dedica al Cav. A. C. De Meis', in *Bernardino Telesio ossia studi storici sull'idea della natura nel Risorgimento italiano* (Naples: La Scuola di Pitagora, 2008), pp. 1–6.

Pietro Pomponazzi. Studi storici sulla scuola bolognese e padovana del secolo XVI (Naples: La Scuola di Pitagora, 2008).

Bernardino Telesio ossia studi storici sull'idea della natura nel Risorgimento italiano, 2 vols. (Naples: La Scuola di Pitagora, 2008).

Il risorgimento filosofico del Quattrocento (Naples: La Scuola di Pitagora, 2008).

Studi e ritratti della Rinascenza, edited by Luisa Fiorentino (Naples: La Scuola di Pitagora, 2008).

Foscolo, Ugo, *Della servitù d'Italia* (Florence: Le Monnier, 1852).

Galluppi, Pasquale, *Saggio filosofico sulla critica della conoscenza*, vol 4. (Naples: s. n., 1832).

Lettere filosofiche sulle vicende della filosofia relativamente ai principii delle conoscenze umane da Cartesio sino a Kant inclusivamente (Messina: Pappalardo, 1838).

Elementi di filosofia, vol I (Messina: Pappalardo, 1820–1827).

Gans, Eduard, 'Herausgegeben' to G. W. F. Hegel, *Vorlesungen über die Philosophie der Geschichte* (Berlin: Duncker & Humblot, 1837).

Gatti, Stanislao, 'Di una risposta di Vittore Cousin ad alcuni dubbi introno alla sua filosofia', *Il Progresso delle scienze lettere ed arti*, vol. XXI (Naples: Tipografia Flautina, 1838), pp. 34–52.

'Del progressive svolgimento dell'idea filosofica nella storia', *Il Museo di letteratura e filosofia*, I, 1841: 99–112; III, 1842: 3–11, 97–105.

'Introduzione', *Il Museo di letteratura e filosofia*, vol. I (Naples 1841), pp. 5–22.

'Fichte e la dottrina della scienza', *Museo di scienza e letteratura*, I, 1843: 76–94.

'La filosofia della storia', in *Scritti vari di filosofia e letteratura*, vol. I (Naples: Stamperia Nazionale, 1844), 135–165.

Genovesi, Antonio, *Elementa Metaphysicae Matematicum in Morem Adornatorum*, Editio secunda Neapolitana multo auctioret correcior (Napoli: typis Benedicti, et Ignatii Gessari, 1751–1752).

Gentile, Giovanni, *La filosofia di Marx* (Pisa: Spoerri, 1899).

Bertrando Spaventa (Morano: Naples 1900), now in Bertrando Spaventa, Opere (Sansoni: Florence, 1972).

'J. B. Baillie, *The Origin and Significance of Hegel's Logic – A General Introduction to Hegel's System*, London, Macmillian, 1901 (pp. XVIII–375)', *La Critica*, 2, 1904: 29–45.

'L'esperienza pura e la realtà storica', *La Voce* (Florence, 1915), pp. 5–39.

'Donato Jaja', *Annuario della Regia Università di Pisa 1914–1915* (Pisa: Toscano, 1915).

Teoria generale dello spirito come atto puro (1916), 269–282.

I profeti del Risorgimento (Florence: Vallecchi, 1923).

Le origini della filosofia contemporanea in Italia (Messina: Principato 1923).

Giordano Bruno e il pensiero del Rinascimento (Florence: Vellecchi, 1925).

Memorie italiana e problemi della filosofia e della vita (Florence: Sansoni, 1936).

I fondamenti della filosofia del diritto (Florence: Sansoni, 1937).

Storia della filosofia italiana. Dal Genovesi al Galluppi, vol. I (Florence: Sansoni 1942).

'Le origini della filosofia contemporanea in Italia', in *Opere* (Florence: Sansoni, 1957).

I problemi della scolastica e il pensiero italiano (Florence: Sansoni, 1963).

Studi sul Rinascimento (Florence: Sansoni, 1966).

Gino Capponi e la cultura toscana nel secolo XIX (Florence: Sansoni, 1973).

'Che cosa è il fascismo. Discorsi e polemiche', in *Politica e cultura*, vol. I (Florence: Le Lettere, 1990), p. 12.

'Bertrando Spaventa e la riforma dello hegelismo', in *Opere*, vol. XXIX (Florence: Le Lettere 2001).

Gioberti, Vincenzo, *Del primato morale e civile degli italiani* (Losanna: Bonamici, 1843).

Del rinnovamento civile d'Italia (Paris; Turin: Bocca, 1851).

Gramsci, Antonio, *Socialisti e fascisti*, *L'Ordine Nuovo*, 11 giugno 1921.

'La situazione italiana e i compiti del Pci, tesi approvate al Terzo Congresso del Partito comunista italiano', in *La costruzione del partito comunista 1923–1926* (Turin: Einaudi, 1971).

Quaderni dal carcere (Turin: Einaudi, 1975).

Prison Notebooks (New York: Columbia University Press, 2011).

Guizot, François, *Cours d'histoire moderne: histoire générale de la civilisation en Europe depuis la chute de l'empire romain jusqu'à la révolution française* (Paris: Pichon et Didier, 1828).

Hegel, Wilhelm Friedrich, 'Vorlesungen über die Philosophie der Geschichte', in *Säntliche Werke*, vol. XI (Stuttgart: Reclam, 1949).

Phenomenology of Spirit, edited by A. V. Miller (Oxford: Oxford University Press, 1979).

Jenaer Systementwürfe III: Naturphilosophie und Philosophie des Geistes, edited by Rolf-Peter Horstmann (Hamburg: Felix Meiner Verlag, 1987).

Elements of the Philosophy of Right, Allen Wood (ed.) (Cambridge: Cambridge University Press, 1991).

'The German Constitution', in *Political Writings* (Cambridge: Cambridge University Press, 1999), pp. 6–101.

Jaja, Donato, *Sentire e pensare: L'idealismo nuovo e la realtà* (Naples: Tipografia Regia Università, 1886).

Janner, Arminio, 'Jacob Burckhardt und Francesco De Sanctis', *Zeitschrift für schweizerische Geschichte* XII, no. 2, 1932: 210–233.

'Problemi del Rinascimento', *Nuova Antologia*, no. XI, 1933: 3–8.

Labriola, Antonio, 'La quistione religiosa e l'Italia. II', *Il Piccolo*, 7 October 1871.

'123 lettere inedite di Antonio Labriola a Bertrando Spaventa', edited by Giuseppe Berti, *Rinascita*, 12, 1953; 1 (1954).

'Dodici lettere inedite di Antonio Labriola a Bertrando Spaventa', edited by Giuseppe Vacca, *Studi Storici*, 7, no. 4, 1966: 757–766.

'Lettera del 1/7/1893 da Labriola a Engels', in *Scritti filosofici e politici*, vol. I (Turin: Einaudi, 1973).

Carteggio. I. (1861–1880), edited by Stefano Miccolis (Naples: Bibliopolis, 2000).

Carteggio. V. (1861–1904), edited by Stefano Miccolis (Naples: Bibliopolis, 2006).

Giordano Bruno: scritti editi e inediti, 1888–1900, edited by Stefano Miccolis and Alessandro Savorelli (Naples: Bibliopolis, 2008).

'Morale e religione (1873)', in *Tutti gli scritti filosofici e di teoria dell'educazione*, edited by Luca Basile and Lorenzo Steardo (Milan: Bompiani, 2014), pp. 785–830.

Tutti gli scritti filosofici e di teoria dell'educazione, edited by Luca Basile and Lorenzo Steardo (Milan: Bompiani, 2014).

Lerminier, J. L. E., *Introduction générale à l'histoire du droit* (Brussels: Tarlier, 1829).

Mackintosh, Robert, *Hegel and Hegelianism* (New York: Scribner, 1903).

Mamiani, Terenzio, *Confessioni di un metafisico. I: Principi di Ontologia. II: Principi di Cosmologia*, 2 vols. (Florence: Barbera, 1865).

Manzoni, Alessandro, 'Marzo 1821', translated in Alberto Rizzuti, 'Viganò's Giovanna d'Arco and Manzoni's March 1821 in the Storm of 1821 Italy', *Music & Letters*, 86, no. 2, 2005: 186–201.

Tutte le lettere, vol. I (Milan: Adelphi, 1986).

Marx, K., and F. Engels, *Collected Works*, vol. 41 (London: Lawrence and Wishart, 1985).

Massari, Giuseppe, *Diario delle cento voci. 1858–1860* (Rome: Cappelli 1959).

Il palazzo e I briganti: il brigantaggio nelle provincie meridionali. Relazione della Commissione d'Inchiesta Parlamentare, letta alla Camera dei Deputati da Giuseppe Massari il 3 e 4 maggio 1863 (Avigliano: Pianetalibroduemila, 2001).

Mazzini, Giuseppe, *Scritti editi ed inediti*, Edizione Nazionale, vol. I (Imola: Galeati, 1906).

Note autobiografiche, edited by Roberto Pertici (Milan: Rizzoli, 1986).

Michelet, Jules, *Principes de la Philosophie de l'Histoire Traduits de la Scienza Nuova de J. B. Vico, et Précédés d'un Discours sur le Système et la vie de l'Auteur* (Paris: Renouard, 1827).

Histoire de France au seizieme siecle: Renaissance (Paris: Chamerot, 1855).

Monnier, Marc, 'Le mouvement italien à Naples de 1830 à 1860 dans la literature et dans l'enseignement', *Revue des deux mondes*, LVI, 1865: 1010–1042.

Nohl, Herman (ed.), *Hegels theologische Jugendschriften* (Tübingen: J. C. B. Mohr, 1907).

Padula, Vincenzo, *Elogio dell'abbate Antonio Genovesi* (Naples: Androsio, 1869).

Pagano, Francesco Mario, *Saggi Politici: De' Principii, Progressi e Decadenza della Società* (Naples: Vivarium, 2013).

Pognisi, A., *Giordano Bruno e l'Archivio di San Giovanni Decollato. Notizia* (Turin: Paravian, 1891).

Renan, Ernest, 'M. Augustin Thierry', in *Essais de morale et de critique. Œuvres complètes*, vol. 2 (Paris: Calmann Lévy, 1910), pp. 117–118.

Romagnosi, Giandomenico, 'Alcuni pensieri sopra un'ultrametafisica filosofia della storia', in *Antologia. Giornale di Scienze, Lettere e Arti*, 46, no. 16, 1832: 23–36.

Dell'indole e dei fattori di incivilimento con esempio del suo Risorgimento in Italia (Florence: Piatti, 1834).

Schelling, Friedrich, *Bruno. Dialogo di Federico Schelling*, edited by Marianna Florenzi Waddington (Florence: Le Monnier, 1859).

Settembrini, Luigi, *Ricordanze della mia vita e scritti autobiografici* (Milan: Einaudi, 1961).

Spaventa, Bertrando, 'La Rivoluzione e l'Italia', *Progresso*, 3–15 June 1851, now in B. Spaventa, *Le Utopie, in Bertrando Spaventa pubblicista (giugno-dicembre 1851)*, pp. 48–54.

'Frammenti di studi sulla filosofia italiana del secolo XVI', *Monitore Bibliografico Italiano*, nos. 32–33, 1852: 50.

'De Anima' (M.S. 28.3, Biblioteca Nazionale di Roma – fondo Rughini-Ghezzi, 63 1862).

La filosofia di Gioberti (Naples: Morano, 1863).

Dal Carteggio inedito di Angelo Camillo de Meis, Comunicati all'Accademia Pontaniana del socio B. Croce (June 1868), edited by Benedetto Croce (Naples: Giannini, 1915).

'Una prolusione inedita di Bertrando Spaventa a un corso di diritto pubblico', in *Giornale critico della filosofia italiana*, vol. V, edited by Augusto Guzzo (1924), pp. 280–296.

'Il Socialismo e il Comunismo in Francia', *Rivista Italiana*, n.s., Turin, I, Settembre 1850: 332–333, republished in B. Spaventa, *Scritti inediti e rari (1840–1880)*, edited by G. D'Orsi (Padua: CEDAM, 1966), pp. 27–29.

Scritti inediti e rari (1840–1880), edited by G. D'Orsi (Padua: CEDAM, 1966).

'Studii sopra la filosofia di Hegel', in *Scritti inediti e rari (1840–1880)*, edited by G. D'Orsi (Padua: CEDAM, 1966).

'La politica dei gesuiti nel secolo XVI e nel XIX. Polemica con la "Civiltà Cattolica"', in *Opere*, vol. II (Florence: Sansoni, 1972), pp. 723–1020.

'Logica e Metafisica', in *Opere*, vol. 3, edited by Giovanni Gentile (Florence: Sansoni, 1972), p. 21.

Opere, 3 vols. (Sansoni: Florence, 1972).

'Paolottismo, positivismo, razionalismo', in *Opere*, vol. I (Florence: Sansoni, 1972), pp. 477–502.

Lezioni di antropologia, edited by Domenico D'Orsi (Florence-Messina: D'Anna, 1976).

Epistolario, vol. I (1847–1860), edited by M. Rascaglia (Rome: Istituto Poligrafico e Zecca dello Stato, 1995).

Lettera sulla dottrina di Bruno. Scritti inediti 1853–54, edited by Mariolina Rascaglia and Alessandro Savorelli (Naples: Bibliopolis, 2000).

Le 'lezioni' sulla storia della filosofia italiana nell'anno accademico 1861–1862, edited by Francesca Rizzo (Messina: Siciliano, 2001).

Studii sopra la filosofia di Hegel; Le prime categorie della logica di Hegel, edited by E. Colombo (Milan: CUSL, 2001).

La filosofia italiana nelle sue relazioni con la filosofia europea, edited by Alessandro Savorelli (Rome: Edizioni di Storia e Letteratura, 2003).

'Carattere e sviluppo della filosofia italiana dal secolo XVI sino al nostro tempo', in *La filosofia del Risorgimento. Le prolusioni di Bertrando Spaventa*, edited by Nicola Capone (Naples: Scuola di Pitagora, 2005), pp. 69–106.

La filosofia del Risorgimento. Le prolusioni di Bertrando Spaventa (Naples: Scuola di Pitagora, 2005).

Principi di etica (Naples: Scuola di Pitagora, 2007).

'Del principio della riforma religiosa, politica e filosofica nel secolo XVI', in *Saggi di critica filosofica, politica e religiosa* (Naples: Scuola di Pitagora, 2008), pp. 269–340.

'Principii della filosofia pratica di G. Bruno', in *Saggi di critica filosofica, politica e religiosa* (Naples: Scuola di Pitagora, 2008), pp. 139–175.

Saggi di critica filosofica, politica e religiosa, edited by Biagio De Giovanni (Naples: Scuola di Pitagora, 2008).

'Tommaso Campanella', in *Saggi di critica filosofica, politica e religiosa*, edited by Biagio De Giovanni (Naples: Scuola di Pitagora, 2008), pp. 1–136.

'False accuse contro l'hegelismo', in *Opere* (Milan: Bompiani, 2009), pp. 2422–2431.

'Idealismo o realismo. Nota sulla toeria della conoscenza (Kant, Herbart, Hegel) (1874)', in *Opere* (Milan: Bompiani, 2009), pp. 491–519.

'La legge del più forte (1874)', in *Opere* (Milan: Bompiani, 2009), pp. 544–549.

'La libertà d'insegnamento', in *Opere* (Milan: Bompiani, 2009), pp. 2407–2408.

'Le prime categorie della logica di Hegel', in *Opere*, vol. 1 (Milan: Bompiani, 2009), p. 436.

Opere, edited by Francesco Valagussa (Bompiani: Milan, 2009).

'The Character and Development of Italian Philosophy from the XVI Century Until Our Time', in *From Kant to Croce. Modern Philosophy in Italy 1800–1950*, trans. Rebecca Copenhaver and Brian P. Copenhaver (Toronto: University of Toronto, 2011), pp. 343–370.

Scritti sul Rinascimento (1852–1872), edited Giuseppe Landolfi Petrone (Rome: Fabrizio Serra, 2011).

Epistolario, edited by M. Diamanti, M. Mustè, and M. Rascaglia (Rome: Viella, 2020).

Epistolario (1847–1883), edited by Marco Diamanti, Marcello Mustè, and Mariolina Rascaglia (Rome: Viella, 2020).

'La filosofia di Kant e le sue relazioni con la filosofia italiana', in *Opere*, vol. 1, edited by Giovanni Gentile (Florence: Sansoni, 1972), pp. 173–256.

Spaventa, Silvio, 'Programma', *Il Nazionale*, 1, 1 March 1848.

'Idea del movimento italiano', *Il Nazionale*, 2, 5 March 1848.

'L'Italianità', *Il Nazionale*, 38, 18 April 1848.

'Il fine ultimo delle rivoluzioni e il fine proprio della rivoluzione italiana', *Il Nazionale*, 41, 22 April 1848.

'L'Austria dopo la pace', *La Nazione*, 3 December 1859.

'La Confederazione germanica e l'Italia', *La Nazione*, 19 December 1859.

'*Il potere temporale e l'Italia nuova*' [1886], in *La politica della Destra* (Bari: Laterza, 1910), pp. 183–202.

La politica della Destra (Bari: Laterza, 1910).

Discorsi Parlamentari, edited by Vincenzo Ricchio (Rome: Tipografia Camera dei Deputati, 1913).

Dal 1848 al 1861. Lettere, scritti, documenti (Bari: Laterza, 1923).

Sträter, Theodor, *Lettere sulla filosofia italiana* (Bomba: Troilo, 1999).

Der Gedanke. Sieben Studien zu den deutchen-italienischen Beziehungen in Philosophie und Kunst, edited by Wolfgang Kaltenbacher (Würzburg: Könighausen & Neumann, 2004).

Togliatti, Palmiro, 'Per una giusta comprensione del pensiero di A. Labriola', *Rinascita*, XI, 1954: 307–372.

Vico, Giambattista, *The New Science*, translated by Thomas G Bergin and Max H. Fisch (Ithaca, NY: Cornell University Press, 1968).

'Principi di Scienza Nuova', in *Giambattista Vico: Opere*, edited by A. Battistini (Milan: Mondadori, 1990).

Opere (Bari: Laterza, 1914).

Villari, Pasquale, *Niccolò Machiavelli e i suoi tempi*, 3 vols. (Florence: Le Monnier, 1877).

Le Lettere Meridionali ed altri scritti sulla questione sociale in Italia (Florence: Le Monnier, 1878).

I primi due secoli della storia di Firenze, 2 vols. (Florence: Le Monnier, 1893).

La storia di Girolamo Savonarola e de' suoi tempi, 2 vols. (Florence: Le Monnier, 1910).

Waddington, Marianna Bacinetti Florenzi, *L'Austria in relazione all'Italia*, 1859.

Saggio sulla filosofia dello spirito (Florence: Monnier, 1867).

Windelband, Wilhelm, 'Die Erneuerung des Hegelianismus' (1910), in *Präludien: Aufsätze und Reden zur Philosophie und Ihrer Geschichte*, 2 vols (Tübingen: Mohr, 1915), pp. 272–289.

Secondary Sources

Abulafia, David, *The Great Sea: A Human History of the Mediterranean* (Oxford: Oxford University Press, 2011).

Achella, Stefania, 'Vita e conoscenza in Francesco De Sanctis', in *La fortuna di Hegel in Italia nell'Ottocento*, edited by Marco Diamanti (Naples: Bibliopolis, 2020), pp. 143–162.

Alderisio, Felice, *Esame della riforma attualistica dell'idealismo in rapporto a Spaventa e a Hegel* (Todi: Tuderte, 1959).

Allemann, Daniel S., Anton Jäger, and Valentina Mann, *Conceptions of Space in Intellectual History* (London: Routledge, 2019).

Amorosa, Paolo, and Claire Vergerio, 'Canon-making in the History of International Legal and Political Thought', *Leiden Journal of International Law*, 35, 2022: 469–478.

Anderson, Perry, 'The Antinomies of Antonio Gramsci', *New Left Review*, 100, 1977: 15–20.

Arcuri, Alba, 'L'esperienza hegeliana nella filosofia di Giovanni Gentile', *Idee*, 24, 1993: 111–123.

Arfé, Gaetano, 'L'hegelismo napoletano e Bertrando Spaventa', *Società*, VIII, 1952: 45–62.

Argyropoulos, Roxanne, *Approaches in Modern Greek Philosophy* (Προσεγγίσεις της Νεοελληνικής Φιλοσοφίας) (Thessaloniki: Vanias 2004).

Armitage, David, 'The International Turn in Intellectual History', in *Rethinking Modern European Intellectual History*, edited by Darrin M. McMahon and Samuel Moyn (New York: Oxford University Press, 2014), pp. 232–252.

Armitage, David, and Alison Bashford, 'Introduction: The Pacific and Its Histories', in *Pacific Histories: Ocean, Land, People*, edited by David Armitage and Alison Bashford (London; New York: Palgrave Macmillan, 2014), pp. 1–28.

Asor Rosa, A. 'L'idea e la cosa: De Sanctis e l'hegelismo', in *Storia d'Italia* (Torino: Einaudi, 1975), vol. 2, pp. 1549–1581.

Scrittori e popolo (Rome: Savelli, 1979).

Astarita, Tommaso (ed.), *Companion to Early Modern Naples* (Leiden: Brill, 2013).

Bacchin, Elena, 'Political Prisoners of the Italian Mezzogiorno: A Transnational Question of the Nineteenth Century', *European History Quarterly*, 5, no. 4, 2020: 625–649.

Banti, Alberto Mario, *Risorgimento italiano* (Rome-Bari: Laterza, 2008).

Sublime madre nostra. La nazione italiana dal Risorgimento al fascismo (Bari-Rome: Laterza, 2011).

La Nazione del Risorgimento: Parentela, santita' e onore alle origini dell'Italia unita (Turin: Einaudi, 2000); English Translation: Alberto Mario Banti, *The Nation of the Risorgimento: Kinship, Sanctity, and Honour in the Origins of Unified Italy* (New York: Routledge, 2020).

Banti, Alberto Mario, and Paul Ginsborg (eds.), *Storia d'Italia. Annali 22. Il Risorgimento* (Turin: Einaudi, 2007).

et al., *Atlante culturale del Risorgimento. Lessico del linguaggio politico dal Settecento all'Unità* (Rome-Bari: Laterza, 2011).

Barbagallo, F., *Storia della camorra* (Rome-Bari: Laterza, 2010).

Battistoni, Giulia, 'Coscienza europea e modernità: Hegel e Croce, filosofi della libertà', *Archivio di filosofia*, XC, no. 1, 2022: 233–243.

Bayly, C. A., and E. Biagini, *Giuseppe Mazzini and the Globalization of Democratic Nationalism, 1830–1920* (Oxford: Oxford University Press, 2008).

Bauer, M., and Houlgate, S. (eds.), *A Companion to Hegel* (Hoboken, NJ: Wiley-Blackwell, 2011).

Bedani, G., and B., Haddock, *The Politics of Italian National Identity* (Cardiff: University of Wales Press, 2000).

Beiser, Frederick, 'Introduction: The Puzzling Hegel Renaissance', in *Hegel and Nineteenth-century Philosophy*, edited by F. Beiser (Cambridge: Cambridge University Press, 2008), pp. 1–14.

Bell, Duncan, 'International Relations and Intellectual History', *The Oxford Handbook of History and International Relations,* edited by Mlada Bukovansky, Edward Keene, Christian Reus-Smit, and Maja Spanu, (Oxford, Oxford University Press, 2003), pp. 94–110.

Bellamy, Richard, 'Liberalism and Historicism: Benedetto Croce and the Political Role of Idealism in Italy', in *The Promise of History: Essays in Political Philosophy*, edited by A. Moulakis (Berlin; New York: De Gruyter, 1985), pp. 69–119.

Modern Italian Social Theory: Ideology and Politics from Pareto to the Present (Stanford, CA: Stanford University Press, 1987).

'Gramsci, Croce and the Italian Political Tradition', *History of Political Thought*, 11, no. 2, 1990: 313–337.

'Between Economic and Ethical Liberalism: Benedetto Croce and the Dilemmas of Liberal Politics', *History of the Human Sciences*, 4, no. 2, 1991: 175–195.

Croce, Gramsci, Bobbio, and the Italian Political Tradition (Colchester: ECPR Press, 2014).

Berger, Stefan, Linas Eriksonas, and Andrew Mycock (eds.), *Narrating the Nation: Representations in History, Media, and the Arts* (New York: Berghahn, 2008).

Bernasconi, Fiorenzo, *Per un catalogo delle edizioni di Capolago* (Bellinzona: Archivio Storico Ticinese, 1984).

Berti, Giuseppe, 'Bertrando Spaventa, Antonio Labriola e l'hegelismo napole-tano', *Società*, no. 3 1854: 406–430; no. 4: 583–607; no. 5: 764–791.

'Bertrando Spaventa, Antonio Labriola e l'hegelismo napoletano', *Società*, X, 1954: 406–430; XI: 583–607; XII: 764–791.

Besomi, Ottavio, 'De Sanctis 'in partibus transalpinis' ma non "infedelium": letture zurighesi', in *Per Francesco De Sanctis*, ed. Dante Isella (Bellinzona: Casagrande, 1985), pp. 89–116.

Bhabha, Homi (ed.), *Nation and Narration* (London: Routledge, 1990).

Biagini, Enza, Paolo Orvieto, and Sandro Piazessi (eds.), 'Francesco De Sanctis, 1817–2017', special issue of *Rivista di Letteratura italiana*, 35, no. I, 2017.

Biagini, Eugenio, *Liberty, Retrenchment and Reform: Popular Liberalism in the Age of Gladstone, 1860–1880* (Cambridge, Cambridge University Press, 1992).

'Mazzini and Anticlericalism: The English Exile', in *Giuseppe Mazzini and the Globalization of Democratic Nationalism, 1830–1920*, edited by C. A. Bayly and E. Biagini (London: British Academy, 2008), pp. 145–166.

Biscione, Michele, *Neoumanesimo e Rinascimento. L'immagine del Rinascimento nella storia della cultura dell'Ottocento* (Rome: Storia e Letteratura, 1962).

'Hegel e il Rinascimento', in *Incidenza di Hegel*, edited by Fulvio Tessitore (Naples: Morano, 1970), pp. 437–451.

Bistarelli, Agostino, *Gli esuli del Risorgimento* (Bologna: Il Mulino, 2011).

Blau, Adrian, 'How (Not) to Use the History of Political Thought for Contemporary Purposes', *American Journal of Political Science*, 65, no. 2, 2020: 359–372.

Bobbio, Norberto, *Da Hobbes a Marx. Saggi di storia della filosofia* (Naples: Morano, 1965).

'Gramsci e la concezione della società civile', in *Gramsci e la cultura contemporanea*, vol I, edited by Pietro Rossi (Rome: Editori Riuniti, 1975), pp. 75–100.

Bohman, James, 'Is Hegel a Republican? Pippin, Recognition, and Domination in the Philosophy of Right', *Inquiry*, 53, no. 5, 2010: 435–449.

Bollati, Giulio, 'L'Italiano', in *Storia d'Italia. I caratteri originali*, vol. 1 (Turin: Einaudi, 1972), 951–1022.

Boothman, Derek, 'The Sources for Gramsci's Concept of Hegemony, Rethinking Marxism', *Rethinking Marxism*, 20, no. 2, 2008: 201–215.

Bouchard, Norma (ed.), *Risorgimento in Modern Italian Culture: Rethinking the Nineteenth-Century Past in History, Narrative, and Cinema* (Cranbury, NJ: Farleigh Dickinson University Press, 2005).

Bourke, Richard, *Hegel's World's Revolutions* (Princeton: Princeton University Press, 2023).

Bozzi, F., *Marianna allo specchio. Spigolature sulla vita e i pensieri della marchesa Florenzi Waddington in forma di racconto* (Perugia: Era Nuova, 1995).

Brandom, Robert, *Tales of the Mighty Dead* (Cambridge, MA: Harvard University Press, 2002).

Brett, Annabel, 'The Space of Politics and the Space of War in Hugo Grotius's De iure belli ac pacis', *Global Intellectual History*, 2016: 1–28.

Brombert, Beth Archer, *Cristina: Portraits of a Princess* (Chicago: University Chicago Press, 1977).

Bucciantini, Massimo, *Campo dei Fiori; storia di un monumento maledetto* (Turin: Einaudi, 2015).

Buchetmann, Elias, *Hegel and the Representative Constitution* (Cambridge: Cambridge University Press, 2023).

Burgio, A., *Antonio Labriola nella storia e nella cultura della nuova Italia* (Macerata: Quodlibet, 2005).

Burrow, John, *A History of Histories* (London: Penguin: 2007).

Cacciapuoti, Fabiana, 'Bruno nelle ricerche sul Rinascimento di F. Fiorentino', in *Brunus Redivivus. Momenti della fortuna di Giordano Bruno nel XIX secolo,* edited by Eugenio Canone (Pisa-Rome: Istituti editoriali e poligrafici internazionali, 1998), pp. 191–230.

'Marianna Florenzi Waddington tra panteismo e hegelismo nelle carte napoletane', in *Archivio per la storia delle donne*, vol. I, 2004, 219–226.

Cacciatore, Giuseppe, *Giordano Bruno e noi. Momenti della sua fortuna tra Settecento e Ottocento* (Salerno: Edizioni Marte, 2003).

'De Sanctis filosofo e la centralità del nesso tra la scienza e la vita', in *La scienza, la scuola, la vita: Francesco De Sanctis tra noi*, edited by Maria Teresa Imbriani (Venosa: Osanna Edizioni, 2021), pp. 39–46.

Caddeo, Rinaldo, *La tipografia Elvetica di Capolago: Uomini, vicende, tempi* (Milan: Bompiani, 1931).

Le edizioni di Capolago: Storia e critica (Milan: Bompiani, 1934).

Calaresu, Melissa, 'The Patriots and the People in Late Eighteenth-Century Naples', *History of European Ideas*, 20, nos. 1–3, 1995: 203–209.

Caligari, Guido, *L'arrivo e il soggiorno del De Sanctis a Zurigo* (Zurich: Edizioni Poligrafiche Zurigo, 1956).

Calogero, Guido, 'Spaventa, Bertrando', in *Enciclopedia italiana di scienze, lettere ed arti*, edited by Giovanni Gentile (Roma: Treccani, 1936), 313.

Canone, Eugenio, 'L'editto di proibizione delle opere di Bruno e Campanella', *Bruniana & Campanelliana*, 1, nos. 1/2, 1995:43–61.

Brunus redivivus. Momenti della fortuna di Giordano Bruno nel XIX secolo (Pisa-Rome: Istituti editoriali e poligrafici internazionali, 1998).

Cantimori, Delio, 'La periodizzazione dell'età del Rinascimento' (1955), in *Storici e storia*, edited by Delio Cantimori (Turin: Einaudi, 1971), pp. 553–557.

Eretici italiani del Cinquecento-Prospettive di storia ereticale italiana del Cinquecento, edited by Adriano Prosperi (Turin: Einaudi, 2009).

'Sulla storia del concetto di Rinascimento', *Gli Annali della R. Scuola Normale Superiore di Pisa*, 1, no. 3, 1932: 230.

'De Sanctis e il "Rinascimento"', in *Studi di storia*, edited by Delio Cantimori (Turin: Einaudi, 1959), p. 323.

Capone, Nicola (ed.), *Silvio Spaventa e i moti del Quarantotto. Articoli dal "Nazionale" e scritti dall'ergastolo di Santo Stefano* (Naples: La scuola di Pitagora, 2006).

Libertà di ricerca e organizzazione della cultura: crisi dell'Università e funzione storica delle Accademie (Naples: Scuola di Pitagora, 2013).

Cappelli, Gabriele, and Michelangelo Vasta, 'A "Silent Revolution": School Reforms in Italy's Educational Gender Gap in the Liberal Age (1861–1921)', *Cliometrica*, 15, 2021: 203–229.

Carlucci, Alessandro, *Gramsci and Languages: Unification, Diversity, Hegemony* (Leiden: Brill, 2013).

Carr, David, *Time, Narrative and History* (Bloomington: Indiana University Press, 1986).

Casati, Alessandro, and R. Foà, 'Mazzini e gli Hegeliani di Napoli', *La Critica. Rivista di Letterature, Storia e Filosofia*, 10, 1912: 73–79.

Casini, Paolo, *L'antica sapienza italica. Cronistoria di un mito* (Bologna: Il Mulino, 1998).

Cassano, Franco, 'Southern Thought', *Thesis Eleven*, 67, no. 1, 2001: 1–10.

Cazzato, Luigi Carmine, 'Fractured Mediterranean and Imperial Difference: Mediterraneanism, Meridionism, and John Ruskin', *Journal of Mediterranean Studies*, 26, no. 1, 2017: 69–78.

Cesa, Claudio, 'Introduzione', in *Dalle carte di Marianna Florenzi Waddington. Scritti inediti sul panteismo*, edited by Maria Alessandra Degl'Innocenti Venturini (Naples: Bibliopolis, 1978), pp. 16.

Chabod, Federico, 'Gli studi di storia del Rinascimento', in *Cinquant'anni di vita intellettuale italiana.' 1896–1946, Scritti in onore di Benedetto Croce per il suo ottantesimo anniversario*, edited by Carlo Antoni and Raffaele Mattioli (Naples: Edizioni Scientifiche Italiane, 1950), vol. 1, pp. 126–207.

'Croce storico', *Rivista Storica Italiana*, 64, 1952: 473–530.

L' idea di nazione (Bari-Rome: Laterza, 2008).

Chambost, A. S. 'Socialist Visions of Direct Democracy, The Mid-Century Crisis of Popular Sovereignty and the Constitutional Legacy of the Jacobins', in *The 1848 Revolutions and European Political Thought*, edited by Gareth Stedman Jones and Douglas Moggach(Cambridge: Cambridge University Press, 2018), pp. 94–119.

Chorley, Patrick *Oil, Silk and Enlightenment. Economic Problems in XVIIIth-Century Naples* (Naples: Istituto Italiano per gli Studi Storici in Napoli, 1965).

Ciccone, Anya, 'National Character in Restoration Naples: Francesco De Sanctis between Schlegel, Hegel and Bozzelli', in *Gli Hegeliani di Napoli: Il Risorgimento e la ricezione di Hegel in Italia*, edited by F. Gallo (Naples: La Scuola di Pitagora, 2020), pp. 87–118.

Ciliberto, Michele, *Croce e Gentile. Biografia, Filosofia* (Pisa: Edizioni della Normale, 2021).

Clark, Christopher, *Revolutionary Spring: Fighting for a New World 1848–49* (London: Penguin, 2023).

Collini, Stefan, 'Postscript. Disciplines, Canons, and Publics: The History of "the History of Political Thought" in Comparative Perspective', in *The History of Political Thought in National Context*, edited by D. Castiglione and I. Hampsher-Monk (Cambridge: Cambridge University Press, 2001), pp. 280–302.

Copenhaver, Rebecca, and Brian P. Copenhaver, *From Kant to Croce. Modern Philosophy in Italy 1800–1950* (Toronto: University of Toronto Press, 2012).

Corredera, Edward Jones, *The Diplomatic Enlightenment: Spain, Europe, and the Age of Speculation* (Leiden: Brill, 2021).

Cospito, G., 'Romagnosi e Cattaneo tra istanze illuministiche ed eredità vichiane', *Materiali per una storia della cultura giuridica*, 32, no. 2, 2002: 411–426.

Costa, P., *Civitas. Storia della cittadinanza in Europa*, vol. 2: *L'età delle rivoluzioni (1789–1848)* (Rome-Bari: Laterza, 2000).

Cotugno, Alessio, 'Rinascimento e Risorgimento (sec. XVIII–XIX)', *Lingua e Stile*, 2, 2012: 59–74.

Cousin, Victor, 'Préface' to the translation of the *Manuel de l'histoire de la philosophie de Tennemann*, I (Paris: Sautelet, 1829), pp. xii–xiii.

Coutelle, Louis, 'N. Lountzi's Translations for Solomos' (Zakynthian codices) ('Οι μεταφράσεις του Ν. Λούντζη για τον Σολωμό (Οι κώδικες της Ζακύνθου)', *The Gleaner, 3*, 2016: 225–248.

Cubeddu, Italo, 'Bertrando Spaventa pubblicista (giugno–dicembre 1851)', *Giornale critico di filosofia italiana*, 42, 1963: 46–93.

Cullen, Bernard, *Hegel's Social and Political Thought* (Dublin: Gill & Macmillan, 1979).

Dainotto, Roberto, '"Tramonto" and "Risorgimento": Gentile's Dialectics and the Prophecy of Nationhood', in *Making and Remaking Italy: The Cultivation of National Identity around the Risorgimento*, edited by A. R. Ascoli and K. von Henneberg (Oxford: Oxford University Press, 2001), pp. 241–256.

Europe (in Theory) (Durham NC: Duke University Press, 2007).

The Mafia: a Cultural History (Chicago: University of Chicago Press, 2015).

Dal Lago, Enrico, *The Age of Lincoln and Cavour. Comparative Perspectives on Nineteenth-Century American and Italian Nation-Building* (New York: Palgrave: 2015).

Dal Pane, L., *Antonio Labriola nella politica e nella cultura italiana* (Turin: Einaudi, 1975).

D'Andrea, Diletta, 'Great Britain and the Mediterranean Islands in the Napoleonic Wars – the "Insular Strategy" of Gould Francis Leckie', *Journal of Mediterranean Studies*, 16, 2006: 79–89.

D'Auria, Matthew, *The Shaping of French National Identity: Narrating the Nation's Past, 1715–1830* (Cambridge: Cambridge University Press, 2020).

D'Auria, Matthew, and Fernanda Gallo, 'Ideas of Europe and the (Modern) Mediterranean', in *Mediterranean Europe(s): Rethinking Europe from its Southern Shores*, edited by Fernanda Gallo and Matthew D'Auria (London: Routledge, 2022), pp. 1–19.

Davis, John, *Naples and Napoleon. Southern Italy and the European Revolutions, 1780–1860* (Oxford: Oxford University Press, 2006).

De Arcangelis, Alessandro, 'Hegelians on the Slopes of Vesuvius: A Transnational Study in the Intellectual History of Naples, 1799–1861', PhD thesis, University College London, 2018.

'*Geschichte, Histoire*, Storia: Stefano Cusani, Stanislao Gatti e la circolazione transnazionale dell'Hegelismo, 1838–48', in *Gli Hegeliani di Napoli: Il Risorgimento e la ricezione di Hegel in Italia*, F. Gallo (Naples: La Scuola di Pitagora, 2020), pp. 61–86.

De Federicis, 'Hegel in Italy (1922–1931): The Dispute on the Ethical State', in *Hegel's Thought in Europe: Currents, Crosscurrents and Undercurrents*, edited by Lisa Herzog (Basingstoke: Palgrave Macmillan, 2013), pp. 223–238.

De Francesco, Antonino, *Vincenzo Cuoco. Una vita politica* (Rome-Bari: Laterza, 1997).

La palla al piede. Una storia del pregiudizio antimeridionale (Milan: Feltrinelli, 2012).

The Antiquity of the Italian Nation: The Cultural Origins of a Political Myth in Modern Italy, 1796–1943 (Oxford: Oxford University Press, 2013).

'Una difficile modernità italiana. Immagini e significati del *Saggio Storico* di Vincenzo Cuoco' nella cultura politica nazionale', in *Saggio Storico sulla Rivoluzione di Napoli*, edited by Vincenzo Cuoco (Bari-Rome: Laterza, 2014), pp. vii–cxxiii.

De Laurentiis, A., and L. J. Edwards (eds.), *The Bloomsbury Companion to Hegel* (London: Bloomsbury, 2012).

De Matteo, Giovanni, *Brigantaggio e Risorgimento: legittimisti e briganti tra Borbone e i Savoia* (Naples: Guida, 2000).

De Meis, Angelo Camillo, *Il Sovrano. Saggio di filosofia politica con riferenza all'Italia*, edited by B. Croce (Bari: Laterza, 1927).

Degli Oddi, Ippolita, *Marianna Florenzi Waddington: Dalla vita di una donna alla storia di un paese; Manoscritti e inediti* (Perugia: Edizioni Guerra, 2001).

De Ruggiero, G., *Storia del liberalismo europeo* (1925) (Rome-Bari: Laterza, 2003).

De Sanctis, Francesco, *La Giovinezza: Frammento autobiografico* (Naples: Morano, 1889).

Diamanti, Marco (ed.), *La fortuna di Hegel in Italia nell'Ottocento* (Naples: Bibliopolis, 2020).

Dickie, John, *Darkest Italy: The Nation and Stereotype of the Mezzogiorno, 1860–1900* (London: Macmillan, 1999).

Mafia Brotherhoods. Camorra, Mafia, 'Ndrangheta: the Rise of the Honoured Societies (London: Hodder and Stoughton, 2012).

Di Fiore, Antonio, *Camorra e polizia nella Napoli borbonica (1840–1860)* (Naples: Federico II University Press, 2019).

Dijn de, Annelien, *French Political Thought from Montesquieu to Tocqueville. Liberty in a Levelled Society?* (Cambridge: Cambridge University Press, 2008).

Dionisotti, Carlo, 'Manzoni e la cultura inglese', *Annali manzoniani*, 6, 1977: 251–265.

Appunti sui moderni. Foscolo, Leopardi, Manzoni e altri (il Mulino, Bologna 1988).

'Rinascimento e Risorgimento: la questione morale', in *Il Rinascimento nell'Ottocento in Italia e Germania/ Die Renaissance im 19. Jahrhundert in Italien und Deutschland*, edited by Auguat Buck and Cesare Vasoli (Bologna; Mulino; Berlin: Duncker & Humblot, 1989), pp. 235–246.

'Renaissance and Risorgimento: the Moral Question', in *The Reaissance from an Italian Perspective: an Anthology of Essays, 1860–1968*, edited by Rocco Rubini (Ravenna: Longo Editore, 2014), pp. 541–571.

Donati, Benvenuto, 'L'insegnamento della filosofia del diritto e l'attività didattica di Bertrando Spaventa all'Università di Modena nel 1859–60', *Rivista internazionale di filosofia del diritto*, XVIII, 1938: n.p.

D'Orsi, Angelo, 'Lo Studente Che Non Divenne "Dottore". Gramsci all'Università di Torino', *Studi Storici*, 40, no. 1, 1999: 39–75.

'One Hundred Years of the History of Political Thought in Italy', in *The History of Political Thought in National Context*, edited by D. Castiglione and I. Hampsher-Monk (Cambridge: Cambridge University Press, 2001), pp. 80–106.

D'Orsi, Domenico, 'Prefazione', in B. Spaventa, *Scritti inediti e rari (1840–1880)*, edited by G. D'Orsi (Padua: CEDAM, 1966), pp. 5–15.

'Bertrando Spaventa: Lezioni inedite di storia della filosofia greca', *Sophia*, XXXVIII, nos. I–II, 1970: 80–92.

Duranti, F., 'La Marchesa Florenzi, Terenzio Mamiani e una traduzione italiana dello Schelling', *Rassegna storica del Risorgimento*, no. XXIX, 1942: 421–426.

Esposito, Roberto, *Pensiero vivente. Origine e attualità della filosofia italiana* (Turin: Einaudi, 2012); English translation Roberto Esposito, *Living Thought. The Origins and Actuality of Italian Philosophy*, trans. Zakiya Hanafi (Stanford: Stanford University Press, 2012).

Febvre, Lucien, 'Comment Jules Michelet inventa la Renaissance', *Le Genre Humain*, 1, no. 27, 1993 : 77–87.

Ferguson, Wallace K., *The Renaissance in Historical Thought. Five Centuries of Interpretation* (Cambridge, MA: Riverside Press Cambridge, 1948).

Ferretti, Giovanni, *Esuli del Risorgimento in Svizzera* (Bologna: Zanichelli, 1948).

Firpo, Luigi, *Il processo di Giordano Bruno* (Rome: Salerno, 1993 [1949]).

Fitzmaurice, Andrew, *King Leopold's Ghostwriter: The Creation of Persons and States in the Nineteenth Century* (Princeton, Princeton University Press, 2021).

Fogu, Claudio, *The Fishing Net and the Spider Web: Mediterranean Imaginaries and the Making of Italians* (London: Palgrave, 2020).

Fonnesu, Luca, and Barbara Henry (eds.), *Diritto Naturale e filosofia classica tedesca* (Pisa: Pisa Editore, 2003).

Foot, M. R. D., and Matthew, H. C. G. (eds.), *The Gladstone Diaries*, vol. IV, 1848–1854 (Oxford: The Clarendon Press, 1974).

Forlenza, Rosario, and Bjørn Thomassen, *Italian Modernities: Competing Narratives of Nationhood* (Basingstoke: Palgrave Macmillan, 2016).

Formigoni, Guido, *L'Italia dei cattolici. Dal Risorgimento ad oggi* (Bologna: Il Mulino, 2010).

Franchini, Raffaello, *La teoria della storia di Benedetto Croce* (Naples: Morano, 1966).

Francioni, Gianni, 'Un labirinto di carta (Introduzione alla filologia gramsciana)', *International Gramsci Journal*, 2, no. 1, 2016: 7–48.

Franco, Paul, *Hegel's Philosophy of Freedom* (New Haven, CT: Yale University Press, 1999).

Frasner, A. Elisabeth, *The Mobility of People and Things in the Early Modern Mediterranean: The Art of Travel* (New York: Routledge, 2020).

Franzese, Rosa, and Emma Giammattei (eds.), *Studi su Vittorio Imbriani* (Naples: Guida, 1990).

Fruci, G. 'Democracy in Italy: From Egalitarian Republicanism to Plebiscitary Monarchy', in *Re-imagining Democracy in the Mediterranean 1750–1860*, edited by J. Innes and M. Philp (Oxford: Oxford University Press, 2018), pp. 25–50.

Fubini, Riccardo, 'Considerazioni su Burckhardt. Il libro sul Rinascimento in Italia; De Sanctis e Burckhardt', *Archivio Storico Italiano*, 158, no. 58, 2000: 85–118.

Gallo, Fernanda, 'Il manoscritto "De Anima" di Bertrando Spaventa', *Logos*, no. 6, 2011: pp. 323–336.

Dalla patria allo Stato: Bertrando Spaventa, una biografia intellettuale (Laterza: Bari, 2013).

'The Shaping of European Modernities: The Renaissance and the Neapolitan Hegelianism, 1848–1862', *History*, 103, no. 356, 2018: 25–50.

(ed.), *Gli Hegeliani di Napoli: il risorgimento e la ricezione di Hegel in Italia* (Naples: Scuola di Pitagora, 2020).

'The United States of Europe and the "East(s)": Giusppe Mazzini, Carlo Cattaneo, and Cristina Trivulzio di Belgiojoso', in *Europe and the East: Historical Ideas of Eastern and Southeast Europe, 1789–1989*, edited by Mark Hewitson and Jan Vermeiren (London: Routledge, 2023), pp. 133–162.

Gallo, F., and A. Körner, 'Challenging Intellectual Hierarchies. Hegel in Risorgimento Political Thought: An Introduction', *Journal of Modern Italian Studies*, 24, no. 2, 2019: 209–225.

Gallo, F., and M. D'Auria (eds.), *Mediterranean Europe(s): Rethinking Europe from its Southern Shores* (London: Routledge, 2022).

Gambino, Francesco, 'La giustizia nell'amministrazione e l'idea di Stato in Silvio Spaventa' in *Il Consiglio di Stato: 180 anni di storia* (Bologna: Zanichelli, 2022), pp. 165–176.

Garin, Eugenio, *Un secolo di cultura a Firenze. Da Pasquale Villari a Piero Calamandrei* (Florence: La Nuova Italia, 1960).

'Introduzione', to A. Labriola, *La concezione materialistica della storia* (Bari: Laterza, 1965), pp. vii–xvii.

Storia della filosofia italiana, III vols. (Turin: Einaudi, 1967).

'La "fortuna" nella filosofia italiana', in *L'opera e l'eredità di Hegel*, edited by G. Calabrò (Bari: Laterza, 1972), pp. 123–138.

Filosofia e politica in Bertrando Spaventa (Naples: Bibliopolis, 2007).

Gentile, Luigi, *Coscienza nazionale e pensiero europeo in Bertrando Spaventa* (Chieti: Noubs, 2000).

Gerratana, Valentino, 'Per una corretta lettura di Labriola. Precisazioni e rettifiche', *Critica marxista*, XI, 1973: 264–265.

Ghisalberti, Alberto M, 'Esuli italiani in Svizzera nel Risorgimento', *Il Veltro*, XI, nos. 3–4, 1967: 387–394.

Ghisalberti, C. *Stato e costituzione nel risorgimento* (Milan: A. Giuffrè, 1972).

Giacobello, Maria, 'Una questione di Giudizio (breve nota su Benedetto Croce e Hannah Arendt)', *Diacritica*, 13, 2017: 63–74.

Giammattei, Emma, 'Idea e figura del Rinascimento fra De Sanctis e Carducci', *Intersezioni*, XXXV, no. 1, 2015: 35–61.

Giarrizzo, Giuseppe, *Vico, la politica e la storia* (Naples: Guida, 1981).

Ginsborg, Paul, *Salviamo l'Italia* (Turin: Einaudi, 2010).

Ginzburg, Leone, *La tradizione del Risorgimento* (Rome: Castelvecchi, 2014).

Gossman, Lionel, *Basel in the Age of Burckhrdt* (Chicago: University of Chicago Press, 2000).

Gramsci, Antonio, *Quaderni dal carcere* (Turin: Einaudi, 1975).

Grieco, Giuseppe, 'British Imperialism and Southern Liberalism: Re-Shaping the Mediterranean Space, c. 1817–1823', *Global Intellectual History*, 3, 2018: 202–230. 'A Legal Theory for the Nation State. Pasquale Stanislao Mancini, Hegelianism and Piedmontese Liberalism after 1848', *Journal of Modern Italian Studies*, 24, no. 2, 2019: 266–292.

Griffin, Ben, 'From Histories of Intellectual Women to Women's Intellectual History', *Journal of Victorian Culture*, 24, no. 1, 2019: 130–133.

Grimaldi, Angelo, 'La Costituzione Siciliana del 1812', *Revista de Derecho*, 48 (2017): 208–233.

Haddock, Bruce, 'State, Nation and Risorgimento', in *The Politics of Italian National Identity*, ed. G. Bedani and B. Haddock (Cardiff: University of Wales Press, 2000), pp. 11–49.

Haddock, Bruce, and James Wakefield (eds.), *Thought Thinking: The Philosophy of Giovanni Gentile* (Cardiff: Imprint Academic, 2015).

Hardimon, Michael, *Hegel's Social Philosophy* (Cambridge: Cambridge University Press, 1994).

Hartmann, Klaus, 'Hegel: A Non-Metaphysical View', in *Hegel*, edited by A. MacIntyre (New York: Doubleday, 1972), pp. 101–124.

Hassanzadeh, Navid, 'The Canon and Comparative Political Thought', *Journal of International Political Theory*, 11, no. 2, 2015: 184–202.

Hauswedell, T., A. Körner, and U. Tiedau (eds.), *Remapping Centre and Periphery: Asymmetrical Encounters in European and Global Context* (London: UCL Press, 2019).

Herzog, Lisa (ed.), *Hegel's Thought in Europe: Currents, Crosscurrents and Undercurrents* (Basingstoke: Palgrave Macmillan, 2013).

Henrich, Dieter, *Konstellationen: Probleme und Debatten am Ursprung der idealistischen Philosophie (1789–1795)* (Stuttgart: Klett-Cotta, 1991).

Hibben, John G., *Hegel's Logic: An Essay in Interpretation* (New York: Scribner, 1902).

Hill, Peter, *Utopia and Civilization in the Arab Nahda* (Cambridge: Cambridge University Press, 2020). New York: Scribner, 1902

Horden, Peregrine, and Nicholas Purcell, *The Corrupting Sea: A Study of Mediterranean History* (Oxford: Blackwell, 2000). 'The Mediterranean and "The New Thalassology"', *American Historical Review*, 111 (2006): 722–740.

Horden, Peregrine, and Sharon Kinoshita (eds.), *A Companion to Mediterranean History* (Chichester: John Wiley & Sons, 2014).

Hutchings, K., and P. Owens, 'Women Thinkers and the Canon of International Thought: Recovery, Rejection, and Reconstitution', *American Political Science Review*, 115, no. 2, 2021: 347–359.

Iannelli, F., F. Vercellone, K. Vieweg, *Hegel und Italien, Italien und Hegel: Geistige Synergien von Gestern und Heute* (Milan: Mimesis, 2019).

Iermano, Toni, 'Francesco De Sanctis, La storia della letteratura italiana', *Studi Rinascimentali*, 8, 2010: 15–35.

"'Era il popolo men serio del mondo e meno disciplinato": Risorgimento e Rinascimento nella "Storia della letteratura italiana"', in *La prudenza e l'audacia. Letteratura e impegno politico in Francesco De Sanctis* (Naples: L'ancora del Mediterraneo, 2012), pp. 75–104.

Incisa, Ludovico, and Alberica Trivulzio, *Cristina di Belgiojoso. La principessa romantica* (Milan: Rusconi, 1984).

Innes, Joanna, and Mark Philp (eds.), *Re-Imagining Democracy in the Mediterranean, 1780–1860* (Oxford: Oxford University Press, 2018).

Isabella, Maurizio, *Risorgimento in Exile: Italian Émigrés and the Liberal International in the Post-Napoleonic Era* (Oxford: Oxford University Press, 2009).

Southern Europe in the Age of Revolutions (Princeton: Princeton University Press, 2023).

Isabella, Maurizio, and Konstantina Zanou, *Mediterranean Diasporas. Politics and Ideas in the Long Nineteenth Century* (London: Bloomsbury, 2015).

Isastia, Anna Maria, *Il volontariato militare nel Risorigmento. La partecipazione alla guerra del 1859* (Rome: SME-Ufficio storico,1990).

Isella, Dante, *Per Francesco De Sanctis, nel centenario della morte: Atti del convegno di studi, 2 dicembre 1983, Politecnico di Zurigo* (Bellinzona: Casagrande, 1985).

Ives, Peter, *Language and Hegemony in Gramsci* (London: Pluto, 2009).

Janz, Oliver, and Lucy Riall (eds.), 'The Italian Risorgimento: Transnational Perspectives', *Modern Italy*, 19, no. 1, 2014: 1–4.

Jaume, Lucien, *Le Religieux et le politique dans la Révolution française. L'idée de régénération* (Paris: PUF, 2015).

'Réformer, Régénérer, Renaître: un imaginaire de l'Occident? La clef Révolution française', *Transversalités*, 137, 2016: 25–35.

Kahan, A., *Aristocratic Liberalism* (Oxford: Oxford University Press, 1992).

Kalyvas, A., and I. Katznelson, *Liberal Beginnings. Making a Republic for the Moderns* (Cambridge: Cambridge University Press, 2008).

Kapila, Shruti, *Violent Fraternity: Indian Political Thought in the Global Age* (Princeton: Princeton University Press, 2021).

Kelley, Donald R., 'Eclecticism and the History of Ideas', *Journal of the History of Ideas*, 62, 2001: 577–592.

Körner, Axel, *Politics of Culture in Liberal Italy: From Unification to Fascism* (London: Routledge, 2009).

America in Italy: The United States in the Political Thought and Imagination of the Risorgimento, 1763–1865 (Princeton: Princeton University Press, 2017).

'Transnational History: Identities, Structures, States', in *International History in Theory and Praxis*, edited by B. Haider-Wilson, W. D. Godsey, and W. Mueller (Vienna: Verlag der Österreichischen Akademie der Wissenschaften, 2017), pp. 265–290.

'National Movements against Nation States. Bohemia and Lombardy between the Habsburg Empire, the German Confederation and Piedmont', in *The 1848 Revolutions and European Political Thought*, edited by D. Moggach and

G. Stedman Jones (Cambridge: Cambridge University Press, 2018), pp. 345–382.

Laicata C., and F. Sabetti, 'Carlo Cattaneo and Varieties of Liberalism', in *Civilization and Democracy*, edited by C. G. Lacaita and F. Sabetti (Toronto: University of Toronto Press, 2006), pp. 3–52.

Lacaita, Carlo G., and Filippo Sabetti (eds.), *Civilization and Democracy: The Salvemini Anthology of Cattaneo's Writings* (Toronto: Toronto University Press, 2006).

Landucci, Sergio, 'Il giovane Spaventa fra hegelismo e socialismo', *Annali dell'Istituto Giangiacomo Feltrinelli*, VI, 1963: 647–707.

'L'hegelismo in Italia nell'età del Risorgimento', *Studi Storici* 4, 1965: 597–628.

Leerssen, Joep, 'Setting the Scene for National History', in *Nationalizing the Past: Historians as Nation Builders in Modern Europe*, edited by Stefan Berger and Chris Lorenz (Basingstoke: Palgrave Macmillan, 2010), pp. 71–85.

Leso, Erasmo, *Lingua e rivoluzione: Ricerche sul vocabolario politico italiano nel triennio rivoluzionario 1796–1799* (Venice: Istituto Veneto di Scienze lettere e arti, 1991).

Liguori, G., *Gramsci conteso. Interpretazioni, dibattiti e polemiche (1922–2012)* (Rome: Editori Riuniti University Press, 2012).

Llobera, *Josep R.*, *The God of Modernity: The Development of Nationalism in Western Europe* (London: Bloomsbury, 1996).

Losurdo, Domenico, *Dai fratelli Spaventa a Gramsci. Per una storia politico-sociale della fortuna di Hegel in Italia* (Naples: Città del Sole, 1997).

Lovett, Clara Maria, *Carlo Cattaneo and the Politics of the Risorgimento, 1820–1860* (The Hague: Mārtiṇus Nijhoff, 1972).

Lupo, Salvatore, *Storia della mafia: dalle origini ai giorni nostri* (Rome: Donzelli, 2004).

Mack Smith, Denis, *Cavour e Garibaldi nel 1860* (Turin: Einaudi, 1962).

The Making of Italy 1796–1866 (London: Palgrave MacMillan, 1988).

Modern Italy: A Political History (New Haven; London: Yale University Press, 1997).

'De Sanctis e I problemi politici italiani del suo tempo', in *De Sanctis e il realismo* (Naples: Giannini, 1978), pp. 1189–1216.

Mackinnon, Emma Stone, 'Toward a Democratic Canon', *Contemporary Political Theory*, 2022: 1–13.

Maissen, Thomas, *Die Geburt Der Republic*, Auflage: 2 (Göttingen: Vandenhoeck & Ruprecht, 2006).

Mali, Joseph, *The Legacy of Vico in Modern Cultural History: From Jules Michelet to Isaiah Berlin* (Cambridge, Cambridge University Press 2012).

Mander, W. J., *British Idealism. A History* (Oxford: Oxford University Press, 2011).

Manieri, Santina, *Il 'ritorno a Kant' e lo studio del Rinascimento in Francesco Fiorentino e Felice Tocco* (Cosenza: Pellegrini, 2006).

Manzoni, Romeo, *Gli esuli italiani nella Svizzera* (Lugano-Milan: Libreria Arnold, 1922).

Marmo, Marcella, *Il coltello e il mercato. La camorra prima e dopo l'Unità d'Italia* (Naples; Rome: L'Ancora del mediterraneo: 2011).

Martinaro, M., *Giuseppe Ferrari editore e interprete di Vico* (Naples: Guida, 2001).
'Giambattista Vico a Milano: le interpretazioni di Francesco Predari e Giuseppe Ferrari', *Il Pensiero Italiano. Rivista di Studi Filosofici*, 2, nos. 1–2, 2018: 19–42.

Martucci, Roberto, 'Un Parlamento introvabile? Sulle tracce del sistema rappresentativo sardo-italiano in regime statutario 1848–1915', in *Parlamento e Costituzione nei sistemi costituzionali ottocenteschi - Parlament und Verfassung in den konstitutionellen Verfassungssystemen Europas*, edited by Anna Gianna Manca, Luigi Lacchè, vol. 13 di Annali dell'Istituto storico italo-germanico in Trento – Jahrbuch des Italienisch-Deutschen Historischen Instituts in Trent (Bologna; Berlin: Il Mulino - Duncker & Humblot, 2003), pp. 127–174.

Marx, Anthony W., *Faith in Nation: Exclusionary Origins of Nationalism* (Oxford: Oxford University Press, 2003).

Mellone, Viviana, 'La rivoluzione napoletana del 1848. Fonti e metodi per lo studio della partecipazione politica', *Meridiana*, no. 78, 2013: 31–51.

Mercati, Angelo, *Il sommario del processo di Giordani Bruno: con un'appendice di documenti sull'eresia e l'Inquisizione a Modena nel secolo XVI* (Città del Vaticano: Biblioteca Apostolica Vaticana, 1942).

Meriggi, Marco, 'Legitimism, Liberalism and Nationalism: The Nature of the Relationship between North and South in Italian Unification', *Modern Italy*, 19, no. 1, 2014: 69–79.

Moe, Nelson, *The View from Vesuvius: Italian Culture and the Southern Question* (Berkeley: University of California Press, 2002).

Moggach, Douglas, *The Philosophy and Politics of Bruno Bauer* (Cambridge: Cambridge University Press, 2003).
The New Hegelians: Politics and Philosophy in the Hegelian School (Cambridge: Cambridge University Press, 2006).
Politics, Religion and Art: Hegelian Debates (Evanston, IL: Northwestern University Press, 2011).
'Hegelianism, Republicanism and Modernity', in *The New Hegelians. Politics and Philosophy in the Hegelian School* (Cambridge: Cambridge University Press, 2011), pp. 1–23.

Moos, Carlo, *L' 'altro' Risorgimento: L'ultimo Cattaneo tra Italia e Svizzera* (Milan: FrancoAngeli, 1992).

Moore, Lisa L., Joanna Brooks, and Caroline Wigginton (eds.), *Transatlantic Feminisms in the Age of Revolutions* (Oxford: Oxford University Press, 2012).

Motta, Emilio, *Le tipografie del Canton Ticino dal 1800 al 1859* (Lugano: Topi, 1964).
Centocinquanta anni di attività grafico-editoriale, 1830–1980: Dalla Tipografia Elvetica di Capolago alla Stampa commerciale e alla Arche tipografia di Milano (Milan: Cavallotti Editori-Libritalia, 1981).

Moyar, D. (ed.), *The Oxford Handbook of Hegel* (Oxford: Oxford University Press, 2017).

Müller, Jahn-Werner, 'On Conceptual History', in *Rethinking Modern European Intellectual History*, edited by D. M. McMahon and S. Moyn (Oxford: Oxford University Press, 2014), pp. 74–93.

Munslow, Alun, *Narrative and History* (Basingstoke: Palgrave, 2007).

Mustè, Marcello, 'Gentile e Marx', *Giornale Critico della Filosofia Italiana*, XCIV, 1, 2015: 15–27.

'Le note su Croce e la genesi del Quaderno 10', in *G. Francioni F. Giasi Nuovo Gramsci: Biografia, temi, interpretazioni* (Rome: Viella, 2020), pp. 301–321.

Mustè, Marcello, Stefano Trinchese, and Giuseppe Vacca, *Bertrando Spaventa. Tra coscienza nazionale e filosofia europea* (Rome: Viella, 2018).

Marxism and Philosophy of Praxis: An Italian Perspective from Labriola to Gramsci (London: Palgrave Macmillan, 2021).

Nazzaro, Antonio V., *F. De Sanctis riformatore dell'Università degli Studi e della Società Reale di Napoli* (Naples: Giannini, 2016).

Nussbaum, Martha, *Political Emotions. Why Love Matters for Justice* (Cambridge, MA: Harvard University Press, 2013).

Nuzzo, Angelica, 'An Outline of Italian Hegelianism (1832–1998)', *The Owl of Minerva*, 29, no. 2, 1998: 165–205.

O'Brian, G. D., *Hegel on Reason and History* (Chicago: University of Chicago Press, 1975).

Oldrini, Guido, *La cultura filosofica napoletana dell'Ottocento* (Bari: Laterza: 1973).

Gli Hegeliani di Napoli: Augusto Vera e la corrente ortodossa (Milan: Feltrinelli, 1964).

Omodeo, Adolfo, *Studi sull'età della restaurazione* (Turin: Einaudi, 1970).

Orvieto, Paolo, *De Sanctis* (Rome: Salerno editrice, 2015).

Ossola, Carlo, 'E Aby scoprì Bruno', *Il Sole* 24 ore, 9 July 2008.

Ozouf, Mona, *L'homme régénéré: Essais sur la Révolution française* (Paris: Gallimard, 1989).

Owens, P., and K. Rietzler (eds.), *Women's International Thought: A New History* (Cambridge: Cambridge University Press, 2021).

Palermo, Antonio, 'Il 'Rinascimento' e l'invenzione della "Storia della letteratura italiana"', *Studi Rinascimentali*, 1, 2003: 161–167.

Panzera, Fabrizio, 'Gli esuli italiani nelle città svizzere tra Otto e Novecento', in *Città e pensiero politico italiano dal Risorgimento alla Repubblica*, edited by Robertino Ghiringhelli (Milan: Vita e Pensiero, 2006), pp. 321–323.

Papenheim, Martin, 'Roma o Morte: Culture Wars in Italy', in *Culture Wars: Secular-Catholic Conflict in Ninetenth-Century Europe*, edited by Christopher Clark and Wolfram Kaiser (Cambridge: Cambridge University Press, 2003), pp. 202–226.

Papini, Giovanni, 'Rinascimento e Risorgimento', in *Politica e civiltà* (Milan: Mondadori, [1943] 1965), p. 654.

Passoni, Annalisa, 'Donato Jaja nella formazione di Giovanni Gentile: Il problema del metodo tra critica gnoseologica e deduzione metafisica', *Rivista di storia della filosofia*, 55, no. 2, 2000: 205–228.

Patriarca, Silvana, 'Indolence and Regeneration: Tropes and Tensions of Risorgimento Patriotism', *The American Historical Review*, 110, no. 2, April 2005: 340–408.

Italian Vices: Nation and Character from the Risorgimento to the Republic (Cambridge; New York: Cambridge University Press, 2010).

Patriarca, Silvana - Lucy Riall (eds.), *The Risorgimento Revisited. Nationalism and Culture in Nineteenth-Century Italy* (New York: Palgrave Macmillan, 2014).

Patten, Alan, *Hegel's Idea of Freedom* (Oxford; New York: Oxford University Press, 2002).

Payne, Alina (ed.), *Dalmatia and the Mediterranean: Portable Archaeology and the Poetics of Influence* (Leiden: Brill, 2013).

Pécout, Gilles, *Il lungo Risorgimento: La nascita dell'Italia contemporanea (1770–1922)* (Milan: Mondadori, 2011).

Petrusewicz, Marta, *Come il Meridione divenne una Questione. Rappresentazione del Sud prima e dopo il Quarantotto* (Soveria Mannelli: Rubbettino, 1998).

'Rethinking Centre and Periphery in Historical Analysis: Land-based Modernization as an Alternative Model from the Peripheries', in *Remapping Centre and Periphery: Asymmetrical Encounters in European and Global Context*, edited by T. Hauswedell, A. Körner, and U. Tiedau (London: UCL Press, 2019), pp. 17–26.

Pettit, Philip, *Republicanism: A Theory of Freedom and Government* (Oxford: Oxford University Press, 1997).

Pieretti, A., and C. Vinti, 'La riflessione filosofica di Marianna Florenzi Waddington: dimensioni storiche e teoretiche', Introduction to M. Florenzi Waddington, *Saggio sulla natura* (Perugia: Fabrizio Fabbri Editore, 2000), vii–liv.

Pinkard, Terry, *Hegel: A Biography* (Cambridge: Cambridge University Press, 2001).

Pinto, Carmine, '1820–21. Revolución y Restauración en Nápoles. Una Interpretación Histórica', *Barceo. Revista Riojana de Ciencias Sociales y Humanidades*, 179, 2020: 56–66.

La Guerra per il Mezzogiorno: Italiani, borbonici e briganti, 1860–1870 (Bari-Rome: Laterza, 2019).

Piovani, Piero, *Indagini di storia della filosofia* (Naples: Liguori, 2006).

Piperno, Marina, *Rebuilding Post-revolutionary Italy: Leopardi and Vico's 'New Science'* (Oxford: Voltaire Foundation, 2018).

Pippin, Robert, *Hegel's Idealism: The Satisfactions of Self-Consciousness* (Cambridge: Cambridge University Press, 1989).

Hegel's Practical Philosophy: Rational Agency as Ethical Life (Cambridge: Cambridge University Press, 2008).

Pippin, Robert B., and Otfried Hoffe (eds.), *Hegel on Ethics and Politics* (Cambridge: Cambridge University Press, 2004).

Pitillo, Federica, 'Una rivoluzione silenziosa: Storia e diritto nelle edizioni pre-unitarie di Hegel (1840–1848)', in *La fortuna di Hegel in Italia nell'Ottocento*, edited by Marco Diamanti (Naples: Bibliopolis, 2020), pp. 17–37.

Pocock, J. G. A., 'Introduction: The State of the Art', in *Virtue, Commerce and History: Essays on Political Thought and History, Chiefly in the Eighteenth Century* (Cambridge: Cambridge University Press, 1985), pp. 1–34.

Virtue, Commerce, and History (Cambridge: Cambridge University Press, 1985).

The Machiavellian Moment: Florentine Political Thought and the Atlantic Republican Tradition (Princeton: Princeton University Press, 2003).

Political Thought and History. Essays on Theory and Method (Cambridge: Cambridge University Press, 2009).

'On the Unglobality of Contexts: Cambridge Methods and the History of Political Thought', *Global Intellectual History*, 4, no. 1, 2019: 1–14.

Poli, Alessandro, 'Idealismo platonico e filosofia della natura nel pensiero di Marianna Florenzi Waddington. Note sull'edizione della *Monadologia* di Leibniz', in *Voci dell'Ottocento*, edited by I. Pozzoni (Villasanta: Limina Mentis, 2010), pp. 15–56.

Provvidera, Tiziana, 'Note su Gioberti, Bruno e il panteismo', in *Brunus redivivus. Momenti della fortuna di Giordano Bruno nel XIX secolo*, edited by Eugenio Canone (Pisa-Rome: Istituti editoriali e poligrafici internazionali, 1998), pp. 279–287.

Racinaro, Roberto, 'Rivoluzione e Stato in alcuni momenti della riflessione di Bertrando Spaventa e Francesco de Sanctis', in *Gli hegeliani di Napoli e la costruzione dello Stato unitario* (Rome: Istituto poligrafico e Zecca dello Stato, 1989), pp. 179–200.

Ragazzoni, David, 'Giuseppe Mazzini's Democratic Theory of Nations', in *Nazione e nazionalismi. Teorie, interpretazioni, sfide attuali*, edited by A. Campi, S. De Luca, and F. Tuccari (Rome: Historica, 2018), pp. 279–305.

'Silvio Spaventa and Marco Minghetti on Party Government', *Journal of Modern Italian Studies*, 24, no. 2, 2019: 293–323.

Rawls, John, *Lectures on the History of Moral Philosophy* (Cambridge, MA: Harvard University Press, 2000).

Recchia, Sandro, and Nadia Urbinati (eds.), *A Cosmopolitanism of Nations: Giuseppe Mazzini's Writings on Democracy, Nation Building, and International Relations* (Princeton: Princeton University Press, 2009).

Reill, Dominique Kirchner, *Nationalists Who Feared the Nation. Adriatic Multi-Nationalism in Habsburg Dalmatia, Trieste, and Venice* (Stanford, CA: Stanford University Press, 2012).

Riall, Lucy, 'Which Italy? Italian Culture and the Problem of Politics', *Journal of Contemporary History*, 39, no. 3, 2004: 437–446.

Il Risorgimento. Storia e interpretazioni (Rome: Donzelli, 2007).

'The Politics of Italian Romanticism: Mazzini and the Making of a Nationalist Culture', in *Giuseppe Mazzini and the Globalisation of Democratic Nationalism 1830–1920*, edited by C. A. Bayly and E. F. Biagini (Oxford: Oxford University Press, 2008), pp. 167–186.

et al., 'Alberto Banti's Interpretation of Risorgimento Nationalism: A Debate', *Nations and Nationalisms* 15, no. 3, 2009: 446–454.

Ricci, Saverio, *Dal 'Brunus redivivus' al Bruno degli italiani* (Rome: Edizioni di Storia e Letteratura, 2009).

Ricci, Saverio, and Cesare Scarano (eds.), *Silvio Spaventa politico e statista dell'Italia unita nei documenti della Biblioteca Civica 'A. Mai' di Bergamo* (Bergamo, Comune di Bergamo, 1990).

Ricœur, Paul, *La mémoire, l'histoire, l'oubli* (Paris: Seuil, 2000).

Roberts, David, *Historicism and Fascism in Modern Italy* (Toronto: University of Toronto Press, 2007).

Robertson, John, *The Case for the Enlightenment. Scotland and Naples, 1680–1760* (Cambridge: Cambridge University Press, 2005).

Rockmore, T., *Hegel, Idealism, and Analytic Philosophy* (New Haven, CT: Yale University Press, 2005).

Roedel, Reto, 'I rapporti fra Italia e Svizzera nel Risorgimento', *Archivio Storico Ticinese*, no. 7, 1961: 347–358.

Rogers, Melvin L., and Jack Turner (eds.), *African American Political Thought: A Collected History* (Chicago: University of Chicago Press, 2021).

Romani, Roberto, *National Character and Public Spirit in Britain and France, 1750–1914* (Cambridge: Cambridge University Press, 2002).

'Reluctant Revolutionaries: Moderate Liberalism in the Kingdom of Sardinia, 1849–1859', *The Historical Journal*, 55, no. 1, 2012: 45–73.

Romano, Paolo, *Silvio Spaventa. Biografia politica* (Bari: Laterza, 1942).

Rörig, Karoline, *Cristina Trivulzio di Belgiojoso (Milano 1808 – Milano 1871): storiografia e politica nel Risorgimento* (Milan: Scalpendi, 2021).

Rota, Giovanni, 'La "circolazione del pensiero" secondo Bertrando Spaventa', *Rivista di storia della filosofia*, LX, no. 4, 2005: 655–686.

Rubini, Rocco, *The Other Renaissance: Italian Humanism between Hegel and Heidegger* (Chicago: Chicago University Press, 2014).

'(Re-)Experiencing the Renaissance', in *The Renaissance from an Italian Perspective: An Anthology of Essays, 1860–1968* (Ravenna: Longo Editore, 2014), pp. 7–20.

'The Vichian "Renaissance" between Giuseppe Ferrari and Jules Michelet', *Intellectual History Review*, 26, no. 1, 2016: 9–15.

Posterity: Inventing Tradition from Petrarch to Gramsci (Chicago: University of Chicago Press, 2022).

Ruehl, Martin A., *The Italian Renaissance in the German Historical Imagination, 1860–1930* (Cambridge: Cambridge University Press, 2015).

Ruffini, Francesco, *La vita religiosa di Alessandro Manzoni* (Bari: Laterza, 1931).

Russo, Luigi, *Francesco De Sanctis e la cultura napoletana* (Rome: Editori Riuniti, 1983).

Sabbatino, Pasquale, "Letteratura e «risurrezione della coscienza nazionale». Le occorrenze di Risorgimento e Rinascimento nella Storia di Francesco De Sanctis e il Rinnovamento dei tempi moderni', in *La nuova scienza come rinascita dell'identità nazionale: la Storia della letteratura italiana di Francesco De Sanctis (1870–2010)*, edited by Toni Iermano and Pasquale Sabbatino (Naples: Edizioni Scientifiche Italiane, 2012), pp. 53–88.

'Rinascimento, Risorgimento e Alto Evo Moderno nella storiografia letteraria tra Otto e Novecento', *Studi Rinascimentali*, 8, 2010: 37–55.

Sabetti, Filippo, *Civilization and Self-Government. The Political Thought of Carlo Cattaneo* (Lanham, MD: Lexington Books, 2010).

Sasso, Gennaro, *Le due Italie di Giovanni Gentile* (Bologna: Mulino, 1998).

Savorelli, Alessandro, *Le Carte Spaventa della Biblioteca Nazionale di Napoli* (Naples: Bibliopolis, 1980).

L'aurea catena. Saggio sulla storiografia filosofica dell'idealismo italiano (Florence: Le Lettere, 2003).

'Manoscritti spaventiani nella Biblioteca Nazionale di Roma', *Giornale critico della filosofia italiana*, II, no. 7 (2006).

'Biblioteche di hegeliani e positivisti (maestri, convertiti, apostati)', in *Biblioteche filosofiche private in età moderna e contemporanea*, edited by F. M. Crasta (Florence: Le Lettere, 2010), pp. 237–249.

Sbarberi, F., 'Il marxismo di Antonio Labriola', in *Scritti filosofici e politici*, edited by A. Labriola (Turin: Einaudi, 1973), pp. xi–cxiv.

Scazzola, Andrea, *Giovanni Gentile e il Rinascimento* (Naples: Vivarium, 2002).

Schneider, Jane (ed.), *Italy's 'Southern Question': Orientalism in One Countr* (London: Bloomsbury, 1998).

Scirocco, A., 'L'impegno politico di De Sanctis nell'età della Destra e la trasformazione dei partiti', in *Francesco De Sanctis nella storia della cultura*, edited by C. Muscetta (Rome-Bari: Laterza: 1984), pp. 403–450.

Severgnini, Luigi, *La principessa di Belgiojoso. Vita e opere* (Milan: Edizioni Virgilio, 1972).

Siep, Ludwig, *Aktualität und Grenzen der praktischen Philosophie Hegels* (Leiden: Brill, 2010).

'Hegel's Liberal, Social, and "Ethical" State', in *The Oxford Handbook of Hegel*, edited by D. Moyar (Oxford: Oxford University Press, 2017), pp. 515–534.

Skazkin, S. D., *Russia and Italy: From the History of Russian-Italian Cultural and Societal Relations Nauka* (Moscow: Nauka, 1968).

Skinner, Quentin, *Liberty before Liberalism* (Cambridge: Cambridge University Press, 1998).

'Motives, Intention, and Interpretation' in *Visions of Politics. Vol. 1: Regarding Method* (Cambridge: Cambridge University Press, 2002).

Visions of Politics, Regarding Method (Cambridge: Cambridge University Press, 2002). Vol. 1:

Siegelberg, Mira, *Statelessness: A Modern History* (Boston: Harvard University Press, 2020).

Sismondi, Jean-Charles-Léonard Simonde de, *Histoire des républiques italiennes du moyen âge* (Paris: Furne et ce, 1840).

Sotiropoulos, Michalis, *Liberalism after the Revolution: The Intellectual Foundations of the Greek State, c. 1830–1880* (Cambridge: Cambridge University Press, 2023).

Smith, Hilda L., 'Women's History as Intellectual History: A Perspective on the Journal of Women's History', *Journal of Women's History*, 20, no. 1, 2008: 26–32.

Smith, Steven, *Hegel's Critique of Liberalism* (Chicago: University of Chicago Press, 1989).

Spini, Giorgio, *Risorgimento e protestanti* (Turin: Il Saggiatore, 1989).

Stedman Jones, Gareth, *Karl Marx: Greatness and Illusion* (Cambridge, MA: Harvard University Press, 2016).

Stedman Jones, Gareth, and Gregory Claeys (eds.), *The Cambridge History of Nineteenth Century Political Thought History of Ideas and Intellectual History* (Cambridge: Cambridge University Press, 2011).

Stuurman, Siep, 'The Canon of the History of Political Thought: Its Critique and a Proposed Alternative', *History and Theory*, 39, no. 2, 2000: 147–166.

Talamo, Giuseppe, *De sanctis politico e altri saggi* (Rome: E. De Santis, 1969).

Tallgren, I. (ed.), *Portraits of Women in International Law: New Names and Forgotten Faces* (Oxford: Oxford University Press, 2023).

Taylor, Charles, *Hegel* (Cambridge: Cambridge University Press, 1975).

Hegel and Modern Society (Cambridge: Cambridge University Press, 1979).

Tessitore, Fulvio, 'La cultura filosofica tra due rivoluzioni (1799–1860)', in *Storia di Napoli* (Naples: ESI, 1972), vol. IX.

Comprensione storica e cultura: revisioni storicistiche (Guida: Naples, 1979).

'Lo storicismo politico di Francesco De Sanctis', in *Contributi alla storia e alla teoria dello storicismo* (Rome: Edizioni di Storia e Letteratura, 1997), pp. 77–96.

Filosofia, storia e politica in Vincenzo Cuoco (Cosenza: Lungro di Cosenza, 2002).

Thom, Martin, *Republics, Nations and Tribes* (London: Verso, 1995).

'City, Region and Nation: Carlo Cattaneo and the Making of Italy', *Citizenship Studies*, 3, no. 2, 1999: 187–201.

Thomas, Peter, *The Gramscian Moment: Philosophy, Hegemony, and Marxism* (Leiden: Brill, 2009).

Thomson, Ann, *Bodies of Thought: Science, Religion, and the Soul in Early Enlightenment* (Oxford: Oxford University Press, 2008).

Todorova, Maria, *Imagining the Balkans* (Oxford: Oxford University Press, 1997).

Tognon, Giuseppe, 'Bertrando Spaventa e la "filosofia del diritto" di Hegel', in *Filosofia e coscienza nazionale in Bertrando Spaventa*, edited by Guido Oldrini (Urbino: Quattro Venti, 1988), pp. 61–71.

Traniello, Francesco, *Religione cattolica e Stato nazionale. Dal Risorgimento al secondo dopoguerra* (Bologna: Il Mulino, 2007).

Tunick, Mark, *Hegel's Political Phiosophy* (Princeton: Princeton University Press, 1992).

Urbinati, Nadia, *Le civili libertà: Positivismo e liberalismo nell'Italia unita* (Venice: Marsilio, 1990).

Vacca, Giuseppe, *Politica e filosofia in Bertrando Spaventa* (Bari: Laterza, 1967).

Alternative Modernities: Antonio Gramsci's Twentieth Century (London: Palgrave Macmillan, 2020).

Varouxakis, Georgios, 'The Discreet Charm of "Southernness"', *Journal of Modern Italian Studies*, 17, no. 5, 2012: 547–550.

'1848 and British Political Thought on the Principle of Nationality', in *The 1848 Revolutions and European Political Thought*, edited by D. Moggach and G. Stedman Jones (Cambridge: Cambridge University Press, 2018), pp. 140–161.

Veloudis, Giorgos, *Dionysios Solomos, Romantic Poetry and Poetics. The German Sources (Διονύσιος Σολωμός. Ρομαντική ποίηση και ποιητική. Οι γερμανικές πηγές)* (Athens: Gnosi, 1989).

'The Ionian Hegelianism', in *Odd and Even. Ten Modern Greek Studies* ('Ο επτανησιακός εγελιανισμός', στο Μονά ζυγά. Δέκα νεοελληνικά μελετήματα (Athens: Gnosi, 1992).

Venturi, Franco, *Riformatori napoletani* (Milan; Naples: Ricciardi, 1962).

Venturini, Maria Alessandra Degl'innocenti, 'Marianna Florenzi Waddington; una traduttrice di Schelling', *Archivio di Filosofia*, 1, 1976: 173–175.

'Marianna Florenzi Waddington: Lo Svolgimento del suo pensiero filosofico', *Annali dell'istituto di filosofia*, 2, 1980: 311–350.

'Marianna Florenzi Waddington e il Risorgimento Italiano', *Rassegna storica del Risorgimento*, 68, 1981: 273–302.

Villari, Lucio, *Bella e perduta. L'Italia del Risorgimento* (Rome-Bari: Laterza, 2009).

Viroli, Maurizio, *Niccolo's Smile: A Biography of Machiavelli* (Princeton: Princeton University Press, 1999).

Republicanism (New York: Farrar Straus and Giroux, 2002).

As If God Existed: Religion and Liberty in the History of Italy (Princeton NJ: Princeton University Press, 2012).

Machiavelli's God (Princeton NJ: Princeton University Press, 2012).

For Love of Country: An Essay on Patriotism and Nationalism (Oxford: Oxford University Press, 1995).

'Preface' to Leone Ginzburg, *La tradizione del Risorgimento* (Rome: Castelvecchi, 2014), pp. 1–7.

Vitiello, Vincenzo, 'Buchstabieren Hegel: rileggendo Bertrando Spaventa interprete di Hegel', in *Opere*, edited by Bertrando Spaventa (Milan: Bompiani, 2008), pp. 2809–2830.

Waldmann, Felix, 'Natural Law and the Chair of Ethics in the Univeristy of Naples, 1703–1769', *Modern Intellectual History*, 19, 2022: 54–80.

Weiss, Penny A., *Canon Fodder: Historical Women Political Thinkers* (University Park: Penn State University Press, 2009).

Werner, Kaegi, *Jacob Burckhardt: Eine Biographie*, VII vols. (Basel; Stuttgart: Schwabe, 1949), vol III, pp. 598–600.

White, Hayden, *The Content of the Form: Narrative Discourse and Historical Representation* (Baltimore: Johns Hopkins University Press, 1990).

Wood, Allen, *Hegel's Ethical Thought* (Cambridge: Cambridge University Press, 1990).

Wood, Sharon, 'Cristina di Belgiojoso: Scholar in Exile', *The Italianist*, 33, no. 1, 2013: 49–73.

Zanou, Konstantina, *Transnational Patriotism in the Mediterranean, 1800–1850: Stammering the Nation* (Oxford: Oxford University Press, 2018).

Zoppi, Giuseppe, *Francesco de Sanctis a Zurigo: Prolusione letta nel Politecnico federale il 16 gennaio 1932* (Sauerländer: Aarau, 1932).

Manuscripts and Collections

Archivio di Stato di Napoli (ASN), fondo Pironti-Poerio, b. 13, n. 40; Cart. R, 60.2.

Archivio Generale, XXXIX, 3368 (letter 28 May 1859).

Biblioteca Nazionale di Napoli (BNN) – Ms. XXXI – Lettera (D.1. Carta 21, Società di storia patria, 8 December1861); and MCRR, CM, b.817, f. 24-2.

Biblioteca Nazionale di Roma – Fondo Rughini-Ghezzi.

Collezione delle leggi, de' decreti e di altri atti riguardati la pubblica istruzione, Naples 1861–1863, II, pp. 4–6 (decreto 2 Giugno).

List of Members of the Imperial Academy of Science, 1725–1907 (Saint Petersburg: The Imperial Academy of Sciences, 1908).

Memoria sulla Consorteria dei Camorristi esistente nelle Provincie Napoletane and the *Rapporto sulla Camorra*, Archivio di Stato di Napoli (ASN), Archivio Generale. Prima serie (1860–1887), fs. 675, fasc. 1109, vol I, part I, April–May 1861.

The National Archive, Home Office, 45/6872, letter from George Sandes Gravet to the Inspector General, 6 March 1859.

Società di storia patria, Napoli, Ms XXXI. D.1.

Index